I0818481

GREAT DIVING SPOTS

WORLD

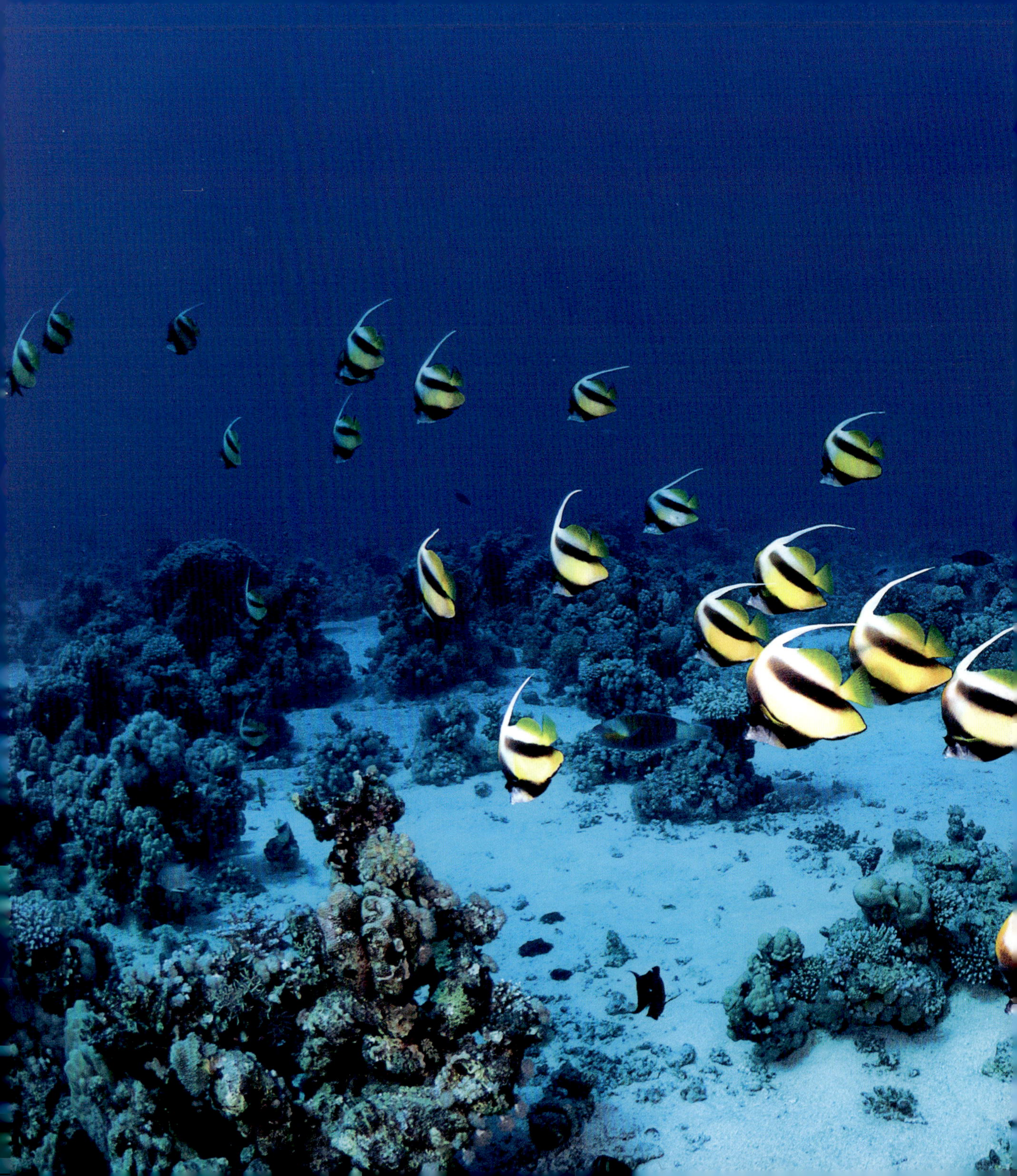

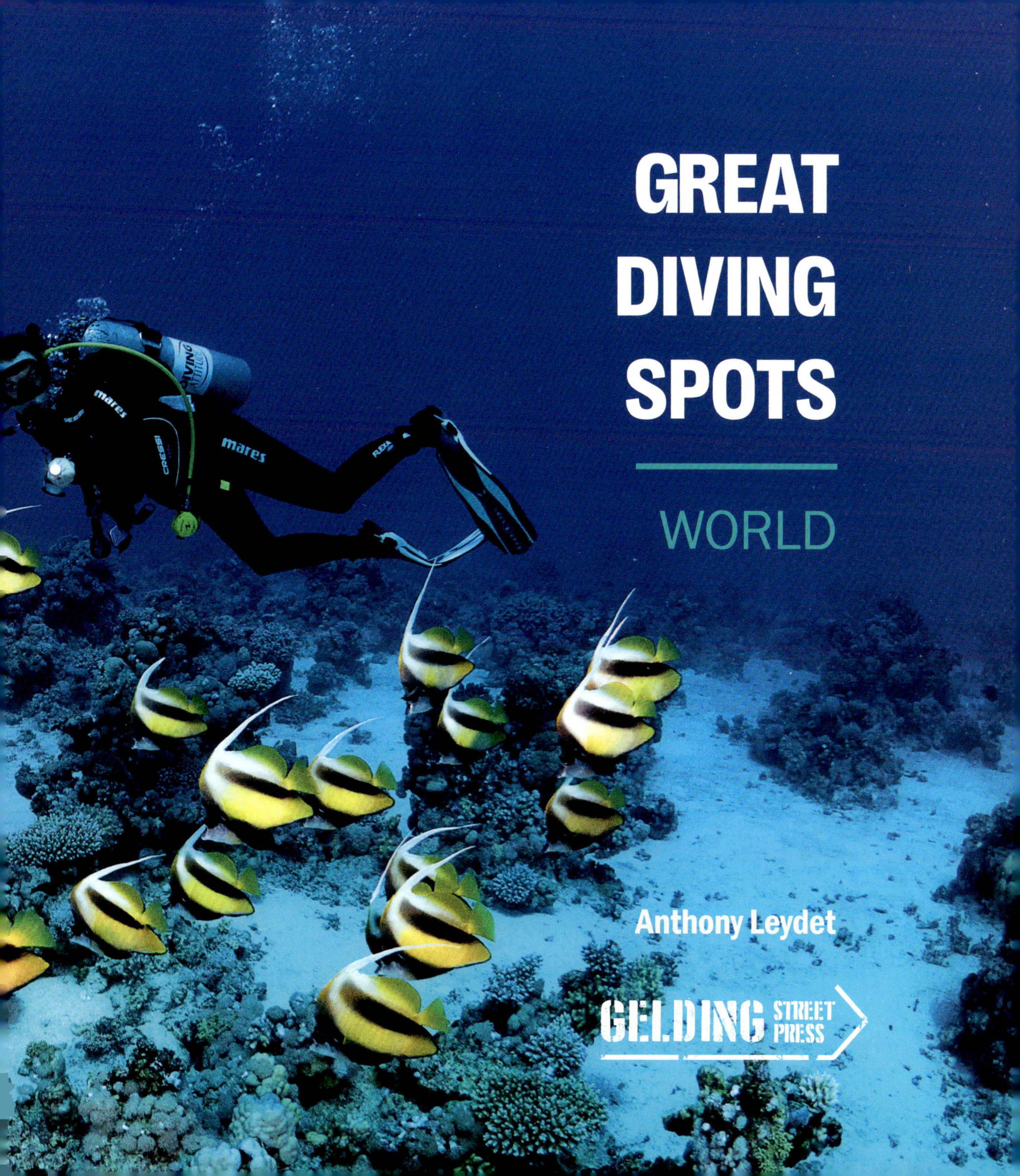
GREAT
DIVING
SPOTS
WORLD
Anthony Leydet
GELDING STREET PRESS

A Gelding Street Press book
An imprint of Rockpool Publishing
PO Box 252
Summer Hill
NSW 2130
Australia

geldingstreetpress.com
Follow us! geldingstreet_press
Tag your images with #geldingstreetpress

Originally published in French by Larousse as *100 Spots De Plongée A Couper Le Souffle*
under ISBN: 9782036054776, copyright © Larousse 2023

This edition published in 2026 by Rockpool Publishing
ISBN: 9781922662309

Design and typesetting by Sara Lindberg, Rockpool Publishing
Translated by Nicola Thayil
Translation edited by Brooke Halliwell

Note: All information correct at the time of writing.

Printed and bound in China
10 9 8 7 6 5 4 3 2 1

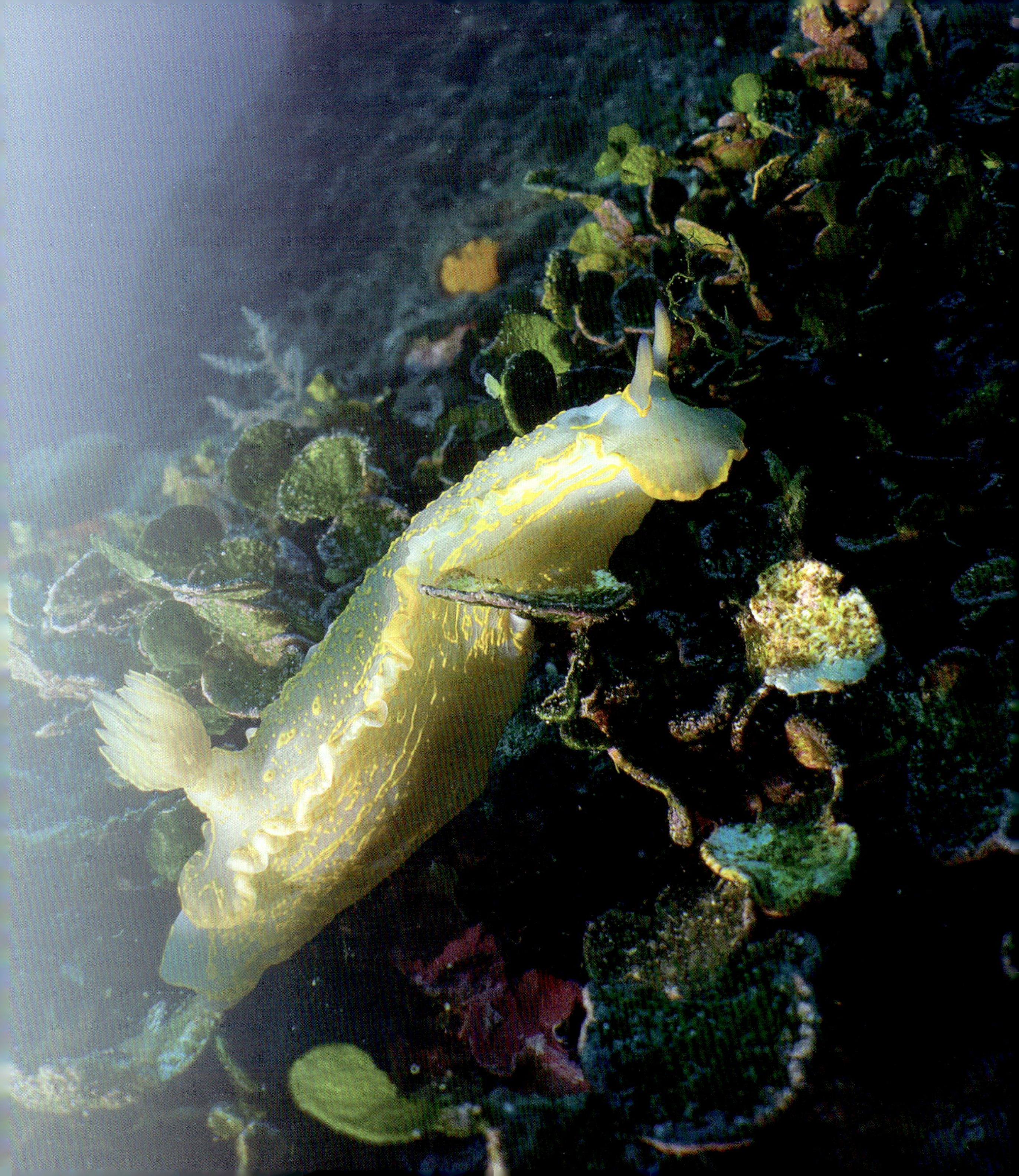

CONTENTS

CONTENTS

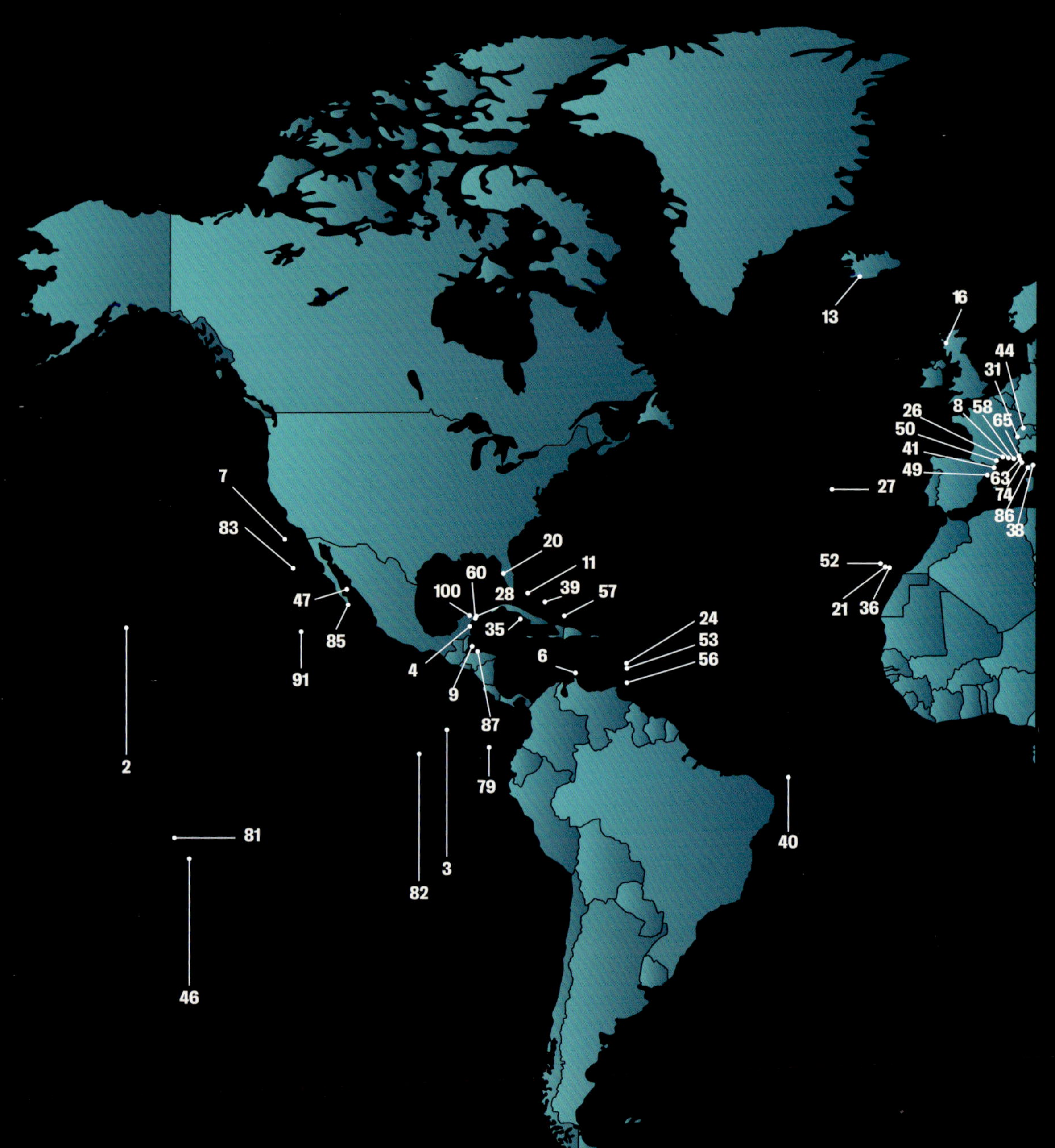

16
13
44
31
8
58
26
65
50
41
49
63
27
74
86
38
7
83
20
60
11
100
28
39
57
47
35
85
24
53
56
91
4
6
9
87
2
79
81
82
3
40
46
52
21
36

DIVE LOCATIONS

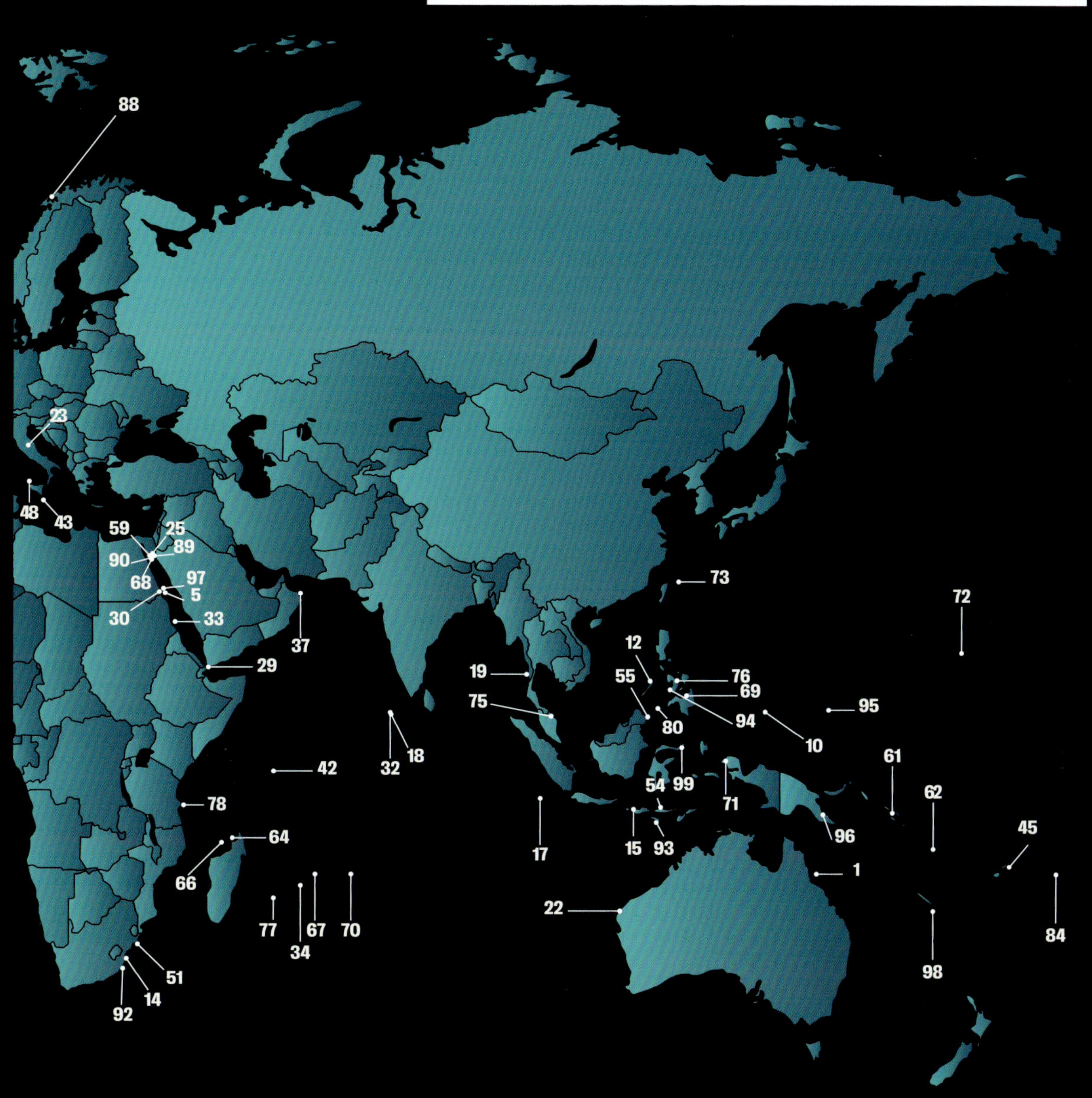

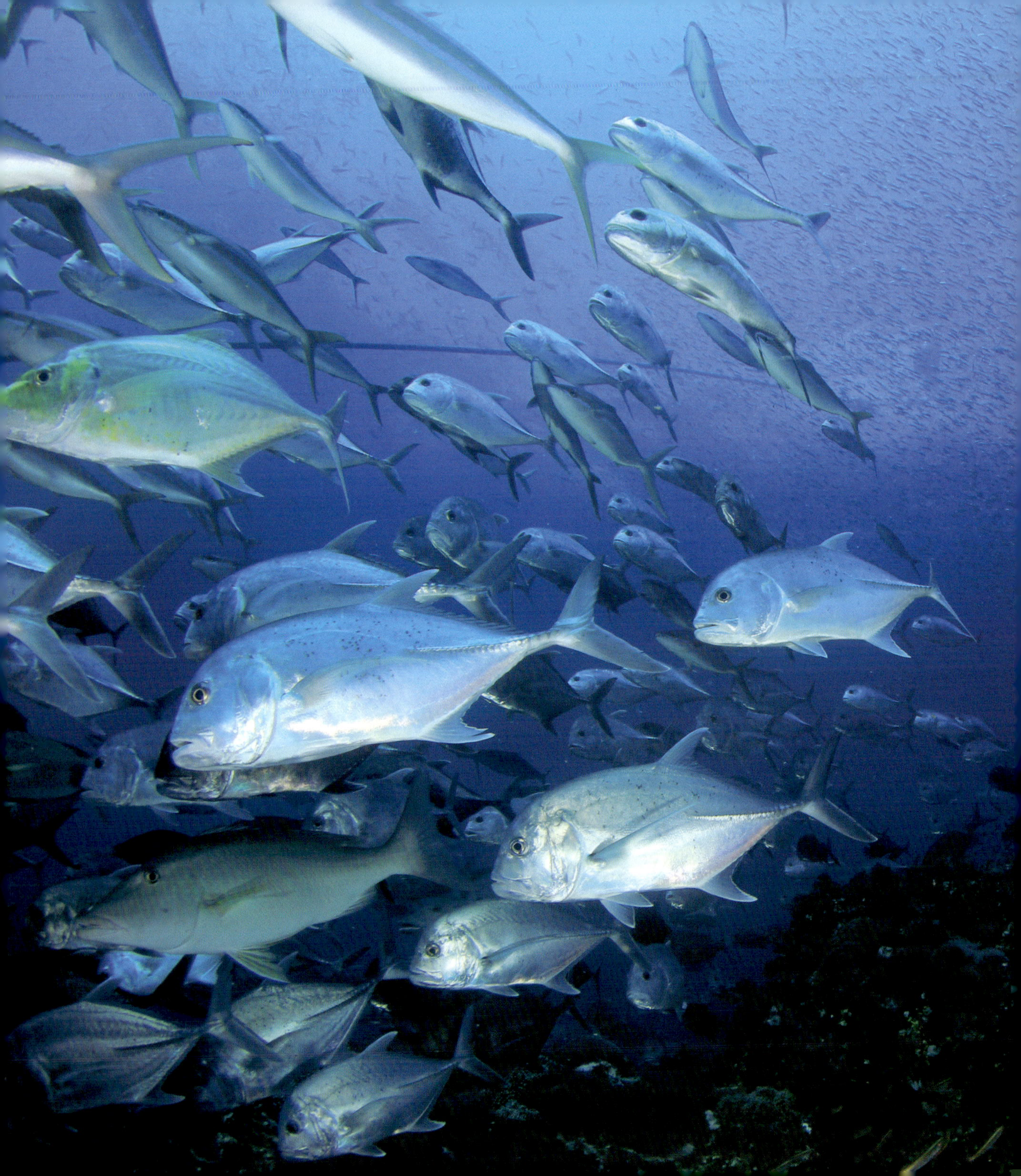

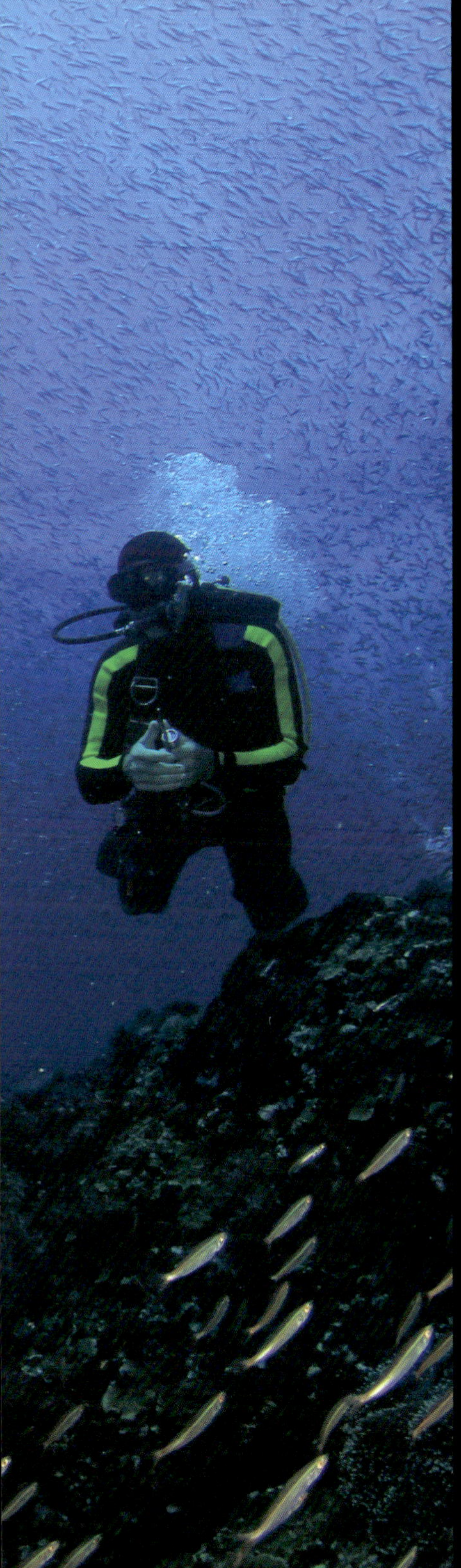

Introduction

Diving is like entering another world, a kingdom of silence and light where time seems suspended. Each immersion is an encounter: with the unexpected, with raw beauty, with oneself.

From the vibrant, flourishing coral reefs that teem with colourful marine life to the haunting remnants of shipwrecks that whisper tales of adventure and history, the underwater world offers an array of experiences. Imagine descending into mysterious depths where sunlight fades into a soothing twilight or gliding through crystal-clear lagoons that shimmer invitingly under the sun.

This book is an invitation to embark on a journey through 100 carefully curated diving locations, each chosen for its magic, uniqueness and ability to take your breath away – literally and figuratively. Some of these sites are legendary, while others remain hidden gems known only to a few, but all have in common an emotion that only the ocean can offer. Each site tells a story of fascinating and fragile nature, a world where humanity is only a guest.

Whether you are a seasoned diver eager for your next adrenaline rush or simply an ocean enthusiast captivated by the allure of the sea, the hope is that these pages ignite a spark in you – a desire not just to explore, but also to protect and cherish our oceans. Below the waves lies a vibrant world rich with secrets waiting to be unveiled, inviting those who approach with curiosity and reverence to uncover its treasures.

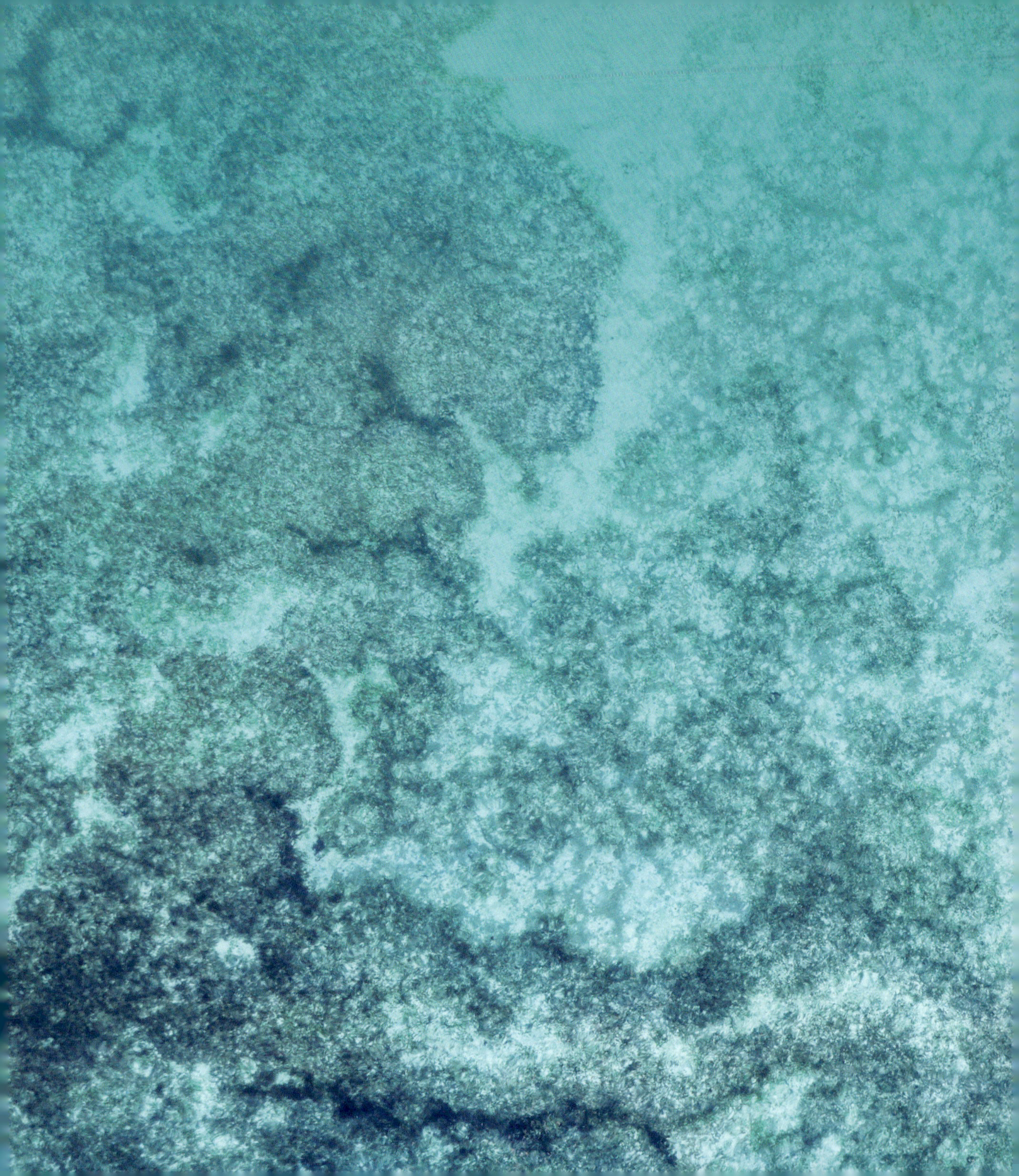

DIFFERENT TYPES OF DIVING

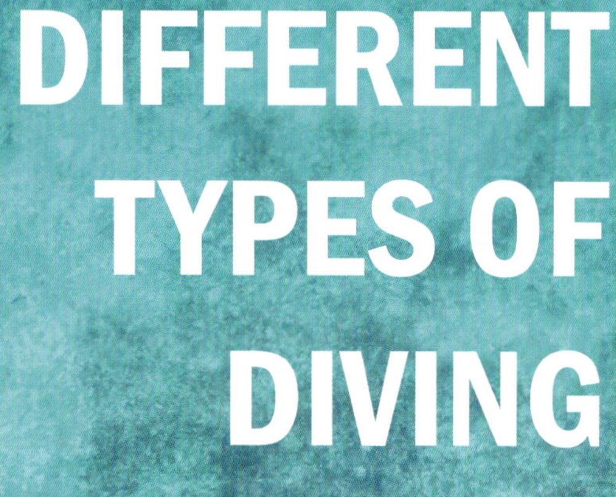

Different diving experiences are available to suit all skill levels and expectations. Here are some examples.

Traditional diving

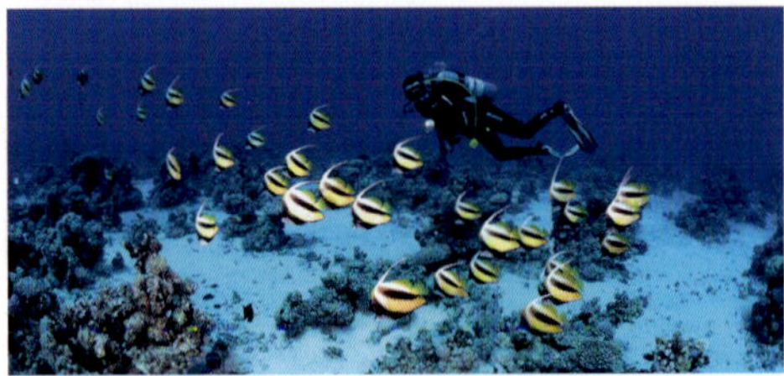

This is the most common type of diving around the world. Explore vibrant coral gardens, drop-offs or rocky areas – there's so much to discover. The main goal is to have fun and make the most of the experience, with no pressure or limitations – except to ensure you keep yourself and the environment safe.

Drift diving

When currents intensify, stay alert to avoid drifting away from the dive site. Allowing yourself to be gently swept across a breathtaking underwater landscape without even needing to kick is an indescribable feeling. Drift dives are not complicated, but they still require good buoyancy control.

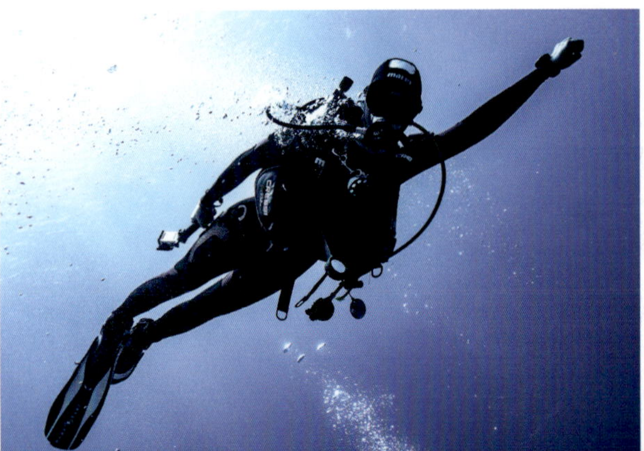

Night diving

Night diving offers unique sensations that set it apart from traditional diving: the senses become heightened as you quickly recognise the lively sounds made by nocturnal herbivores that emerge at night to graze on algae found on rocks and corals. You also get to discover a multitude of species never seen during the day.

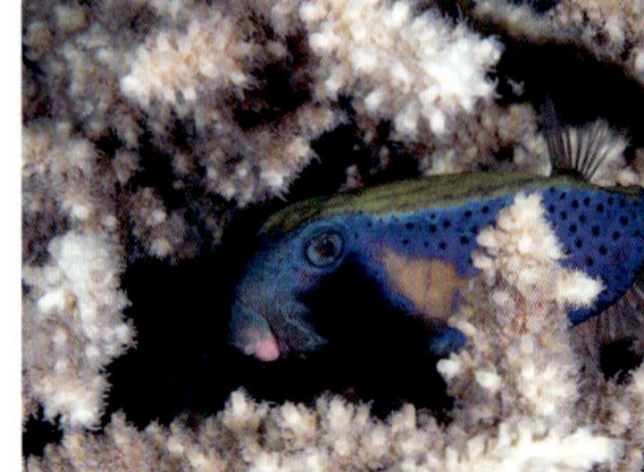

Wreck diving

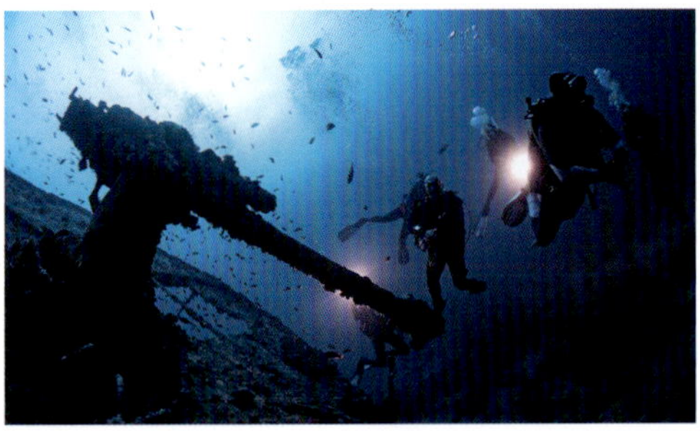

Some divers are captivated by wrecks, while others may not find them particularly intriguing. However, these underwater relics often spark the imagination and ignite curiosity. Even if they aren't remnants of the infamous pirate era, wreck diving remains incredibly popular. There's something for everyone: the adrenaline rush from exploring a wreck's hidden corridors and rooms, to those where you can discover small marine life taking refuge, and others that provide a fascinating glimpse into the past.

Muck diving

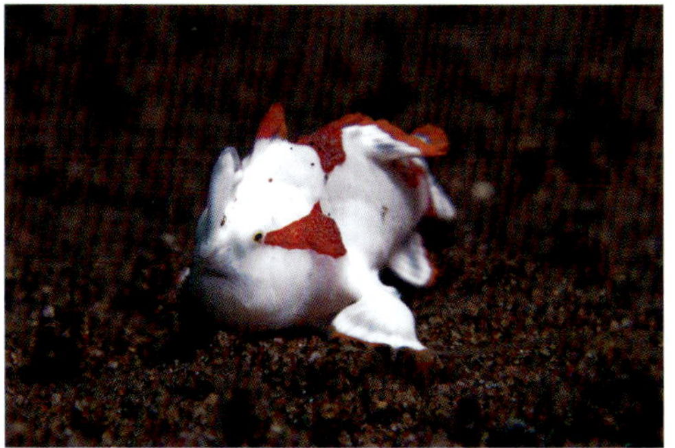

This lesser-known type of diving is practised in select locations around the world, typically over sandy or muddy bottoms, often of volcanic origin. These dives offer the chance to observe a diverse array of species that have perfectly adapted to this unique environment. While it may seem unexpected, you'll quickly get the hang of it and start searching for a multitude of incredible creatures.

Bio diving

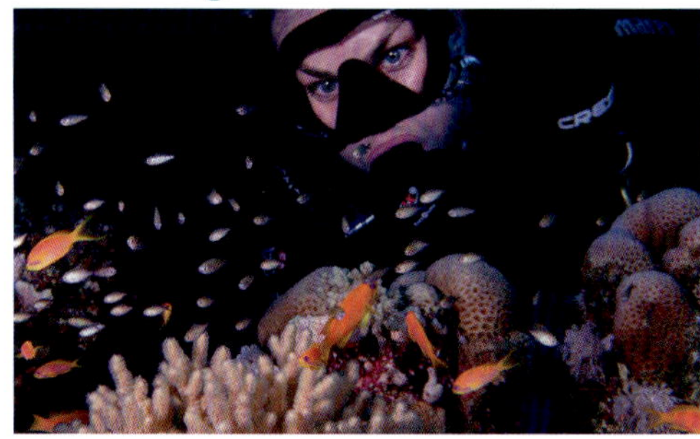

For nature and biodiversity enthusiasts, these dives allow you to spend your time digging around to uncover rare or remarkable animal and plant species. This activity complements the art of underwater photography perfectly.

Deep blue diving

Certain dive sites are renowned for their pelagic species, including sharks. To boost your chances of an unforgettable encounter, consider drifting away from the drop-off and into the deep blue.

Snorkelling and freediving

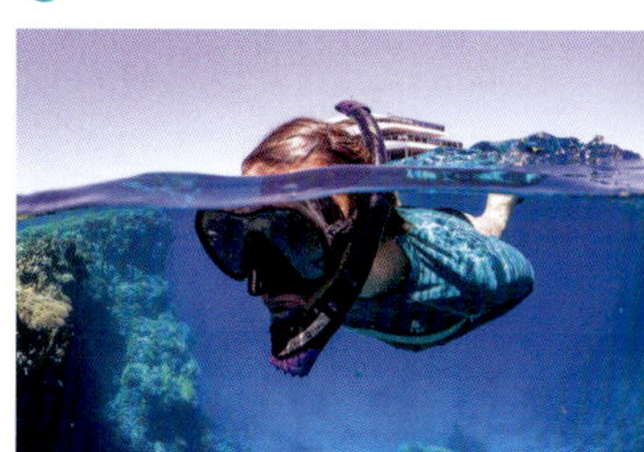

Leave the cumbersome scuba diving gear behind for a truly refreshing experience. With just a mask, snorkel and fins, this activity is accessible to everyone, as long as safety guidelines are followed.

Technical diving (tech or tec)

More experienced divers seeking to explore greater depths or to dive for longer have the option of using gas mixtures like nitrox or trimix, as well as machines that recycle air (recyclers), allowing for extended underwater time. This enables them to reach depths that are typically off-limits to recreational dives and tackle more advanced diving experiences.

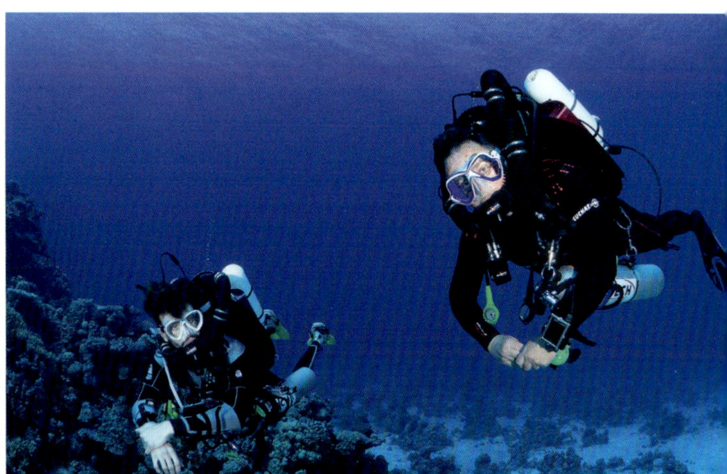

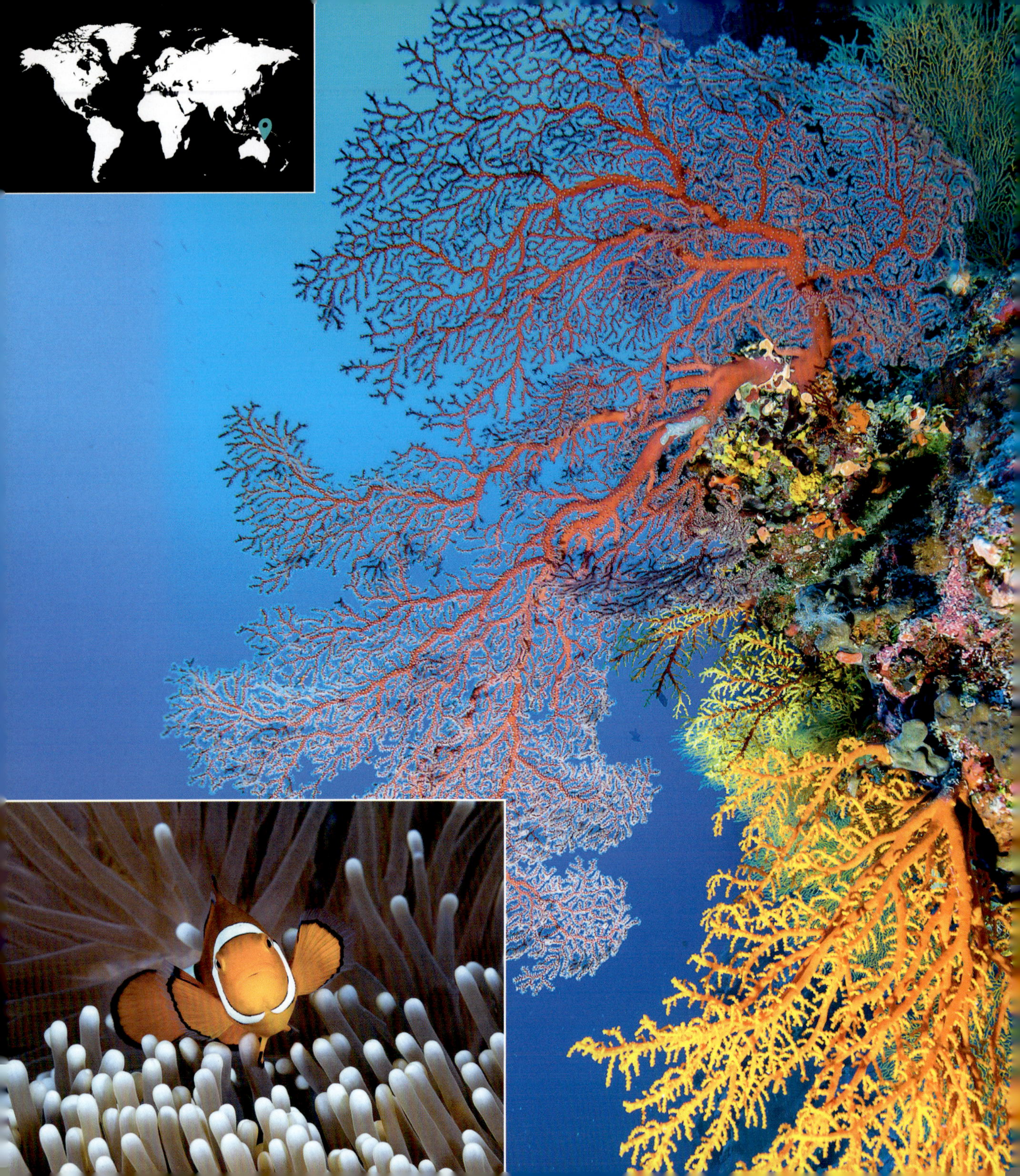

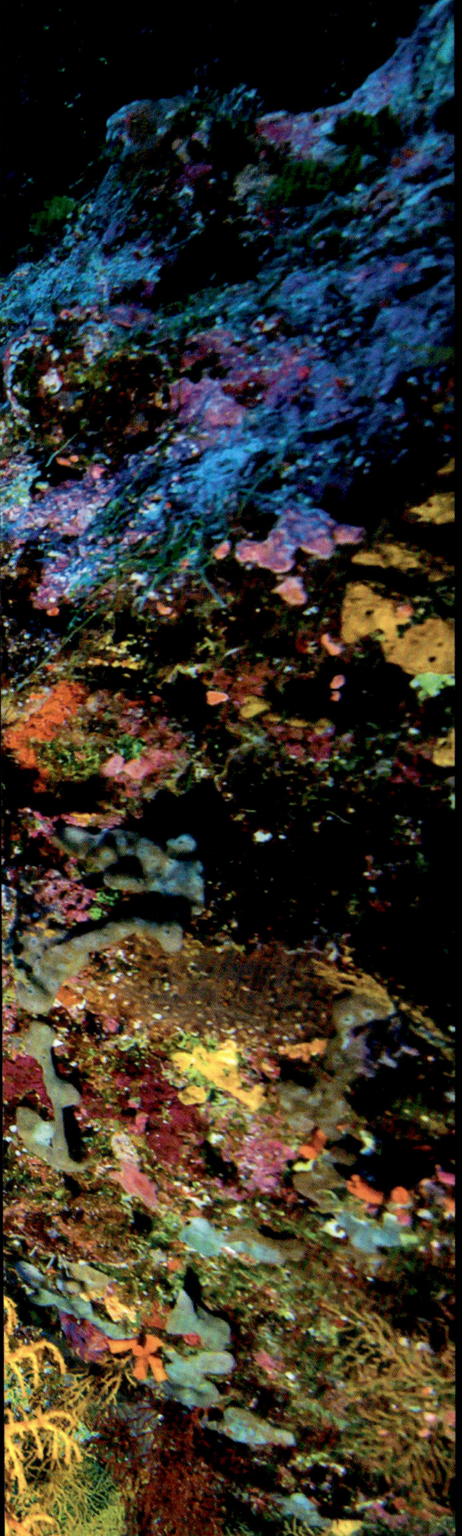

1 Ribbon Reef

Australia

What better place to experience marine life than the Great Barrier Reef on the coast of Queensland, Australia. Stretching 2,300 kilometres (1,429 miles), the Great Barrier Reef is the world's largest coral reef and the only living structure visible from space. It has been a UNESCO World Heritage Site since 1981. It is home to an astounding diversity of marine life, including over 1,500 species of fish, 400 species of coral and 4,000 species of molluscs.

Among its many wonders, Ribbon Reef comprises 10 well-preserved reefs, renowned as one of Australia's most beautiful dive sites.

The marine life here is incredibly abundant, with opportunities to see both small and large species. Whether you are a fan of nudibranchs, shrimp or massive schools of fish, the reef offers something for every diver. Expect to encounter moray eels, yellow banded sweetlips, clownfish (see inset photo), Napoleon wrasse, cuttlefish, sea snakes, turtles, rays, sharks and more. One of the most popular dive sites is Cod Hole, located north of Ribbon Reef, famous for its impressive potato grouper. For those lucky enough to dive in June and July, minke whales often join the underwater spectacle.

Essential info

Due to its popularity, some areas can become crowded. It's essential to choose a certified advanced ecotourism operator (ECO) that is committed to minimising its ecological footprint.

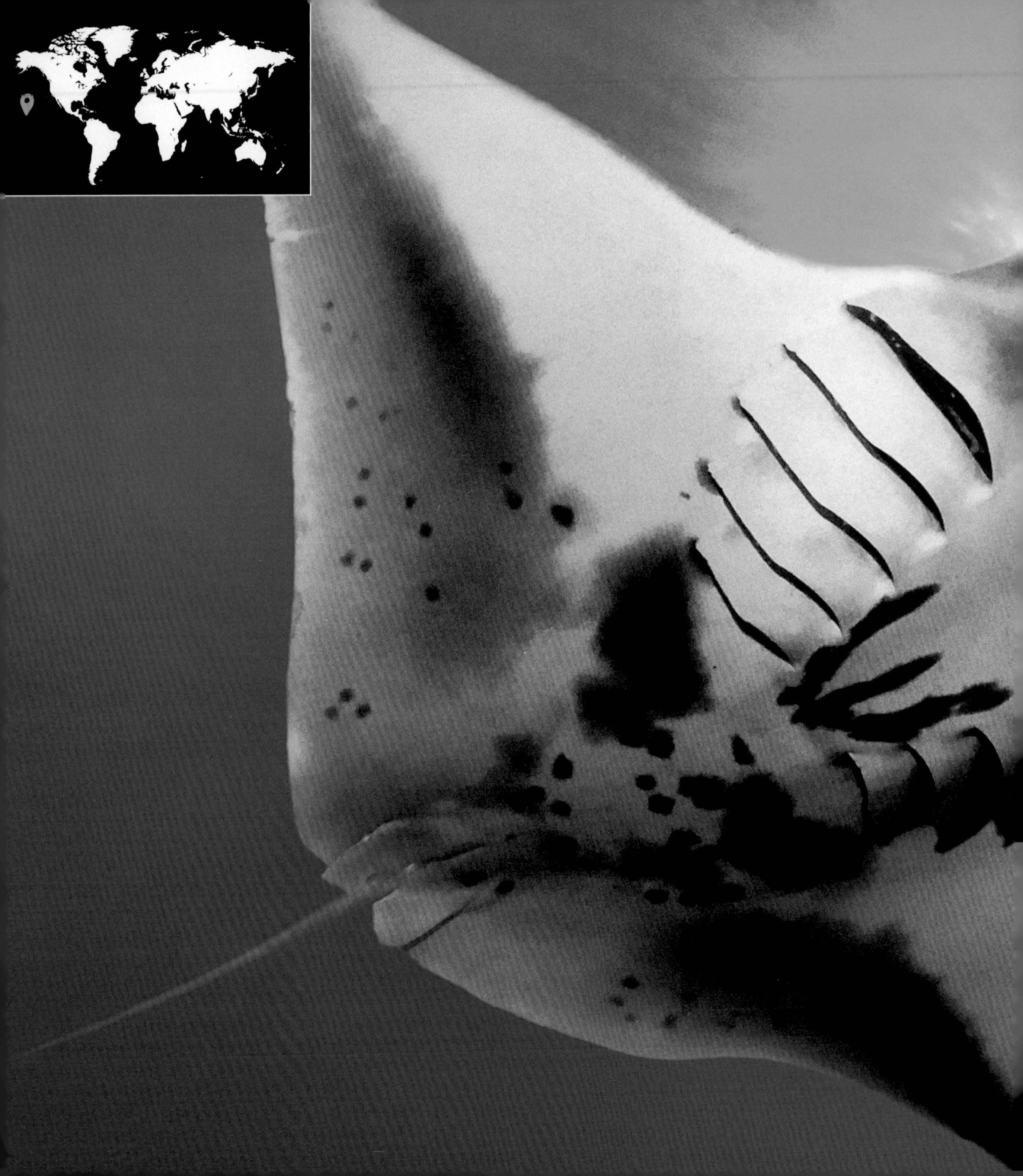

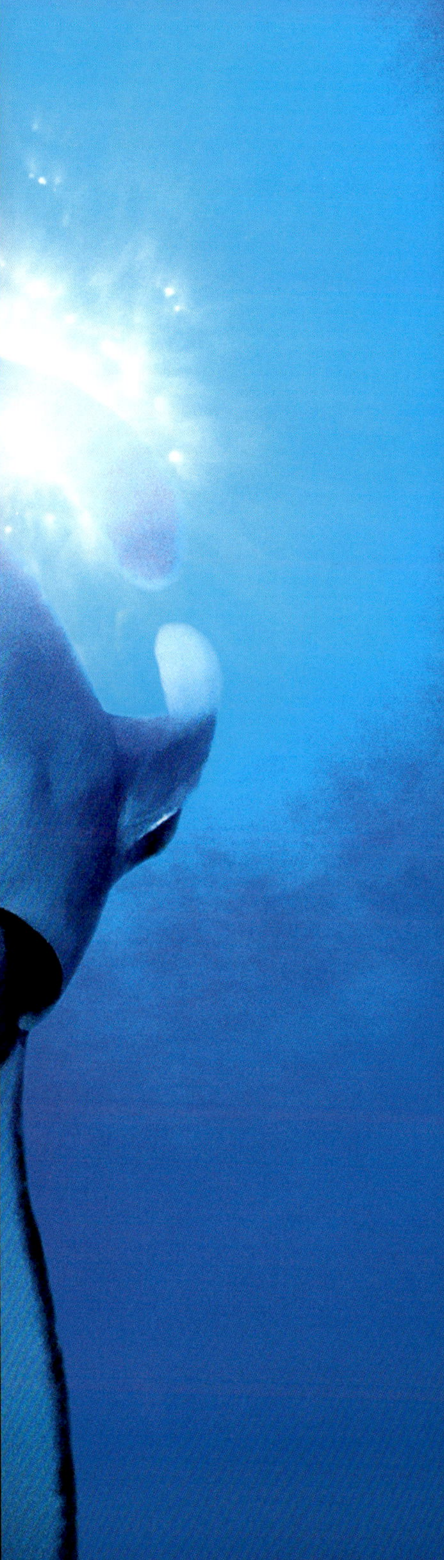

2 Big Island manta rays

Hawaii, USA

As the 50th state of the United States, the Hawaiian archipelago is a dream destination for sea lovers, located in the heart of the North Pacific. Renowned as a surfing paradise, Hawaii also offers breathtaking underwater landscapes that attract divers from around the globe. Hawaii Island, often referred to as the Big Island, is the largest but least populated of the islands, providing a tranquil escape.

With its extensive coastline compared to the other islands in the archipelago, the Kona region in particular serves as an ideal diving location. The active lava flows have created a stunning underwater topography featuring tunnels, arches and caves, many of which are now adorned with vibrant corals and teeming with marine life. Here, you'll find an abundance of green sea turtles and a spectacular variety of tropical fish. One of the most unforgettable experiences in Hawaii is night diving with manta rays. Each evening, currents in Keahole Bay bring an influx of plankton, which attracts dozens of manta rays eager to feed. Divers are treated to a mesmerising display, enhanced by underwater blue lights that illuminate the scene, creating a breathtaking spectacle.

Essential info

The beautiful underwater ballet of the manta rays can be experienced by snorkelling as well as diving. Rules are strict, and touching the rays is prohibited.

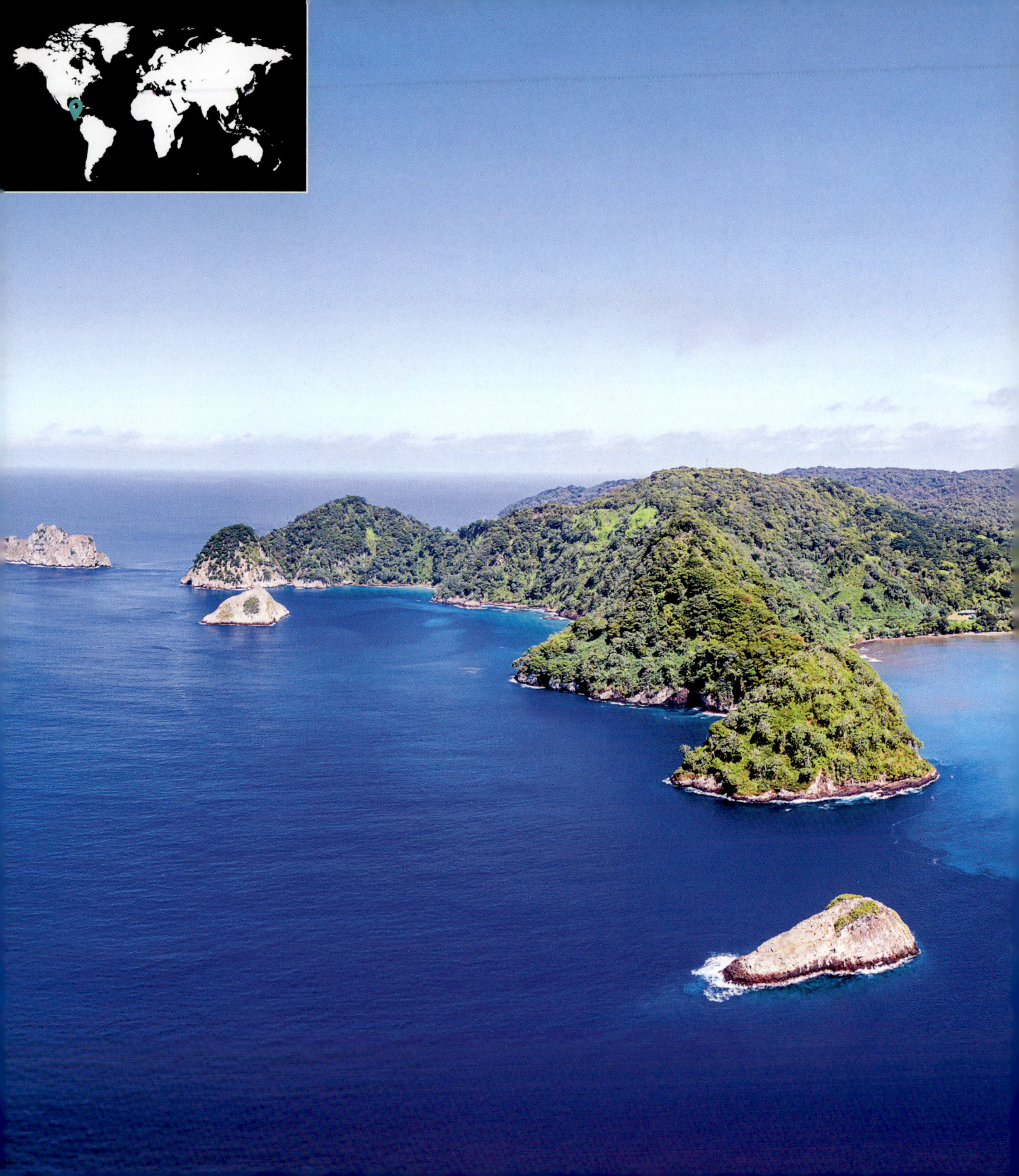

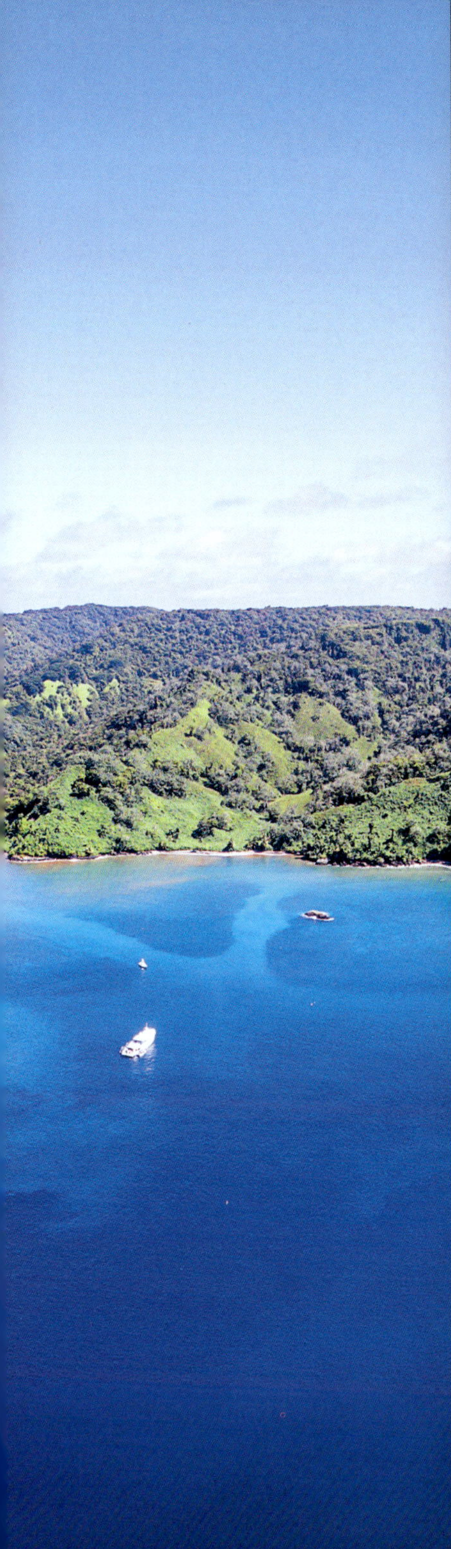

3 Cocos Island

Costa Rica

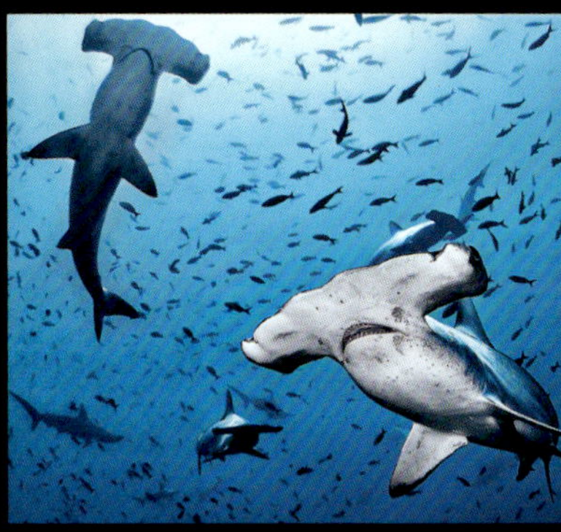

Cocos Island, a remote paradise over 500 kilometres (310 miles) from the coast of Costa Rica, is blanketed by lush forests. The journey to reach this natural wonder takes approximately 36 hours by boat, yet this does not deter divers eager to experience its incredible underwater spectacle. Although it inspired Robert Louis Stevenson's *Treasure Island*, the author likely had no idea of the underwater treasures hidden beneath its waves.

World-renowned for its massive schools of hammerhead sharks, Cocos Island is one of the most impressive scuba diving destinations on the planet.

The Bajo Alcyone dive site, featuring an underwater mountain rising to 25 metres (82 feet) below the surface, is known for attracting one of the largest concentrations of hammerhead sharks globally (see inset photo). Sit in the shelter at the top of the mountain and simply observe. Divers at Cocos can also encounter manta rays, whale sharks, tiger sharks and various other large pelagic species. This remarkable biodiversity led to the island being designated a UNESCO World Heritage Site in 1997.

Essential info

Diving at Cocos Island, known for its strong currents and diverse shark population, requires significant experience – at least 50 logged dives are recommended.

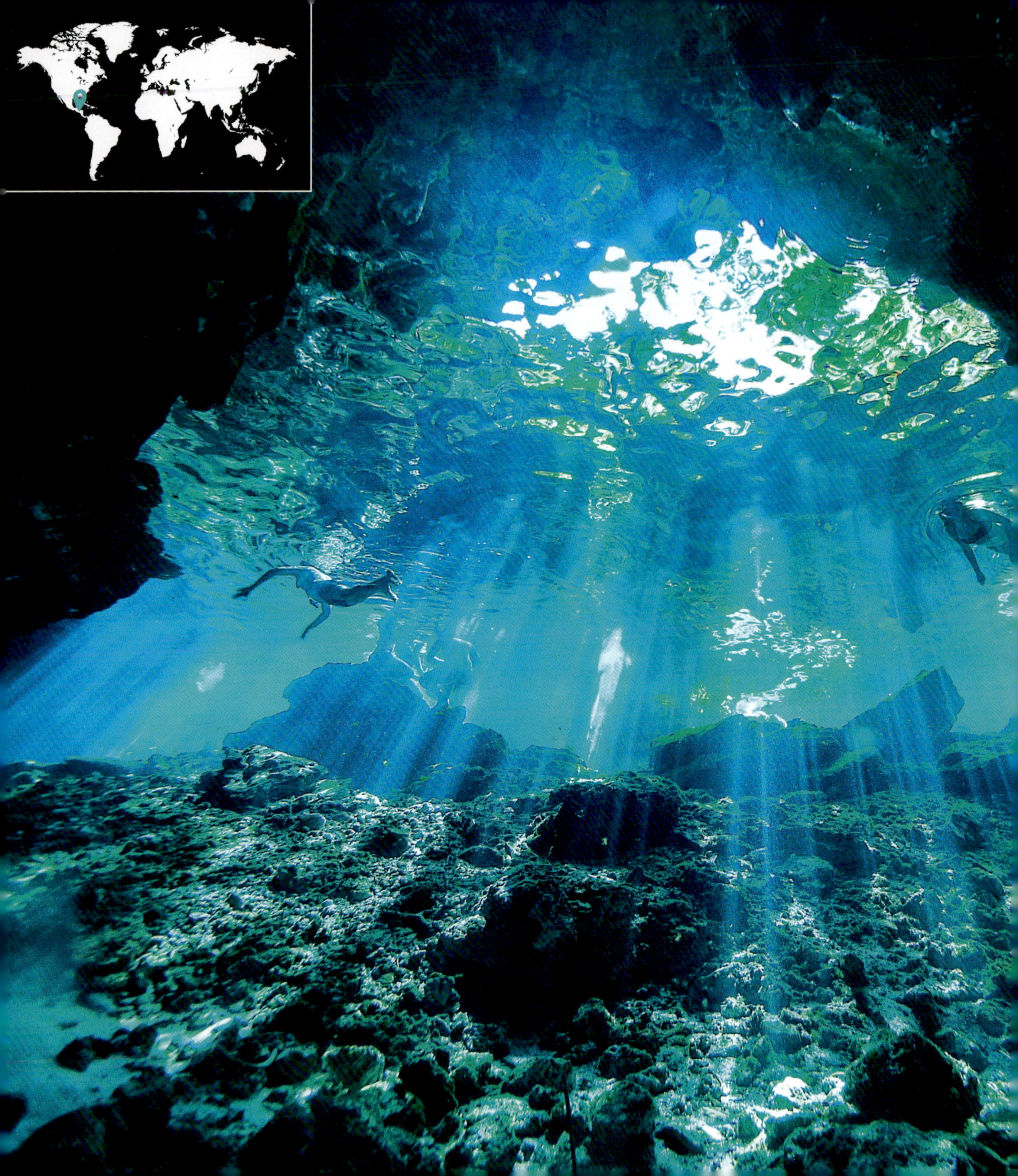

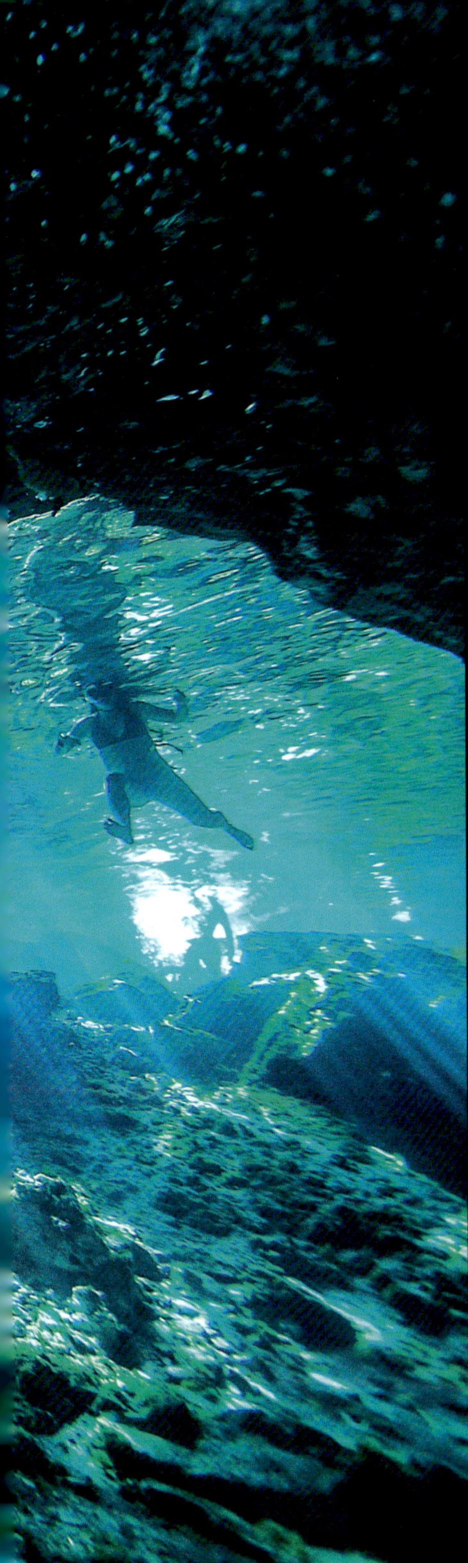

4 Cenotes

Mexico

For divers seeking adventure in Mexico, names like Angelita, Chak Mool, Carwash and Dos Ojos evoke a sense of wonder and excitement. Renowned for their breathtaking reefs and stunning landscapes, these dive sites also feature a truly unique natural wonder: the cenotes of the Yucatán Peninsula. This region boasts an intricate network of underground rivers, with cenotes – derived from the Mayan term *tzonot* – large sinkholes often hidden within forests.

Historically, these freshwater reservoirs were vital for local communities and held sacred significance, believed to be gateways to the underworld of Xibalba. They were often the sites of ceremonial rituals and offerings. Today, explorers from around the globe flock to these mystical underwater passages, where light filters through skylights, casting ethereal reflections and creating almost 'divine' atmospheres, as seen in Tajma-Ha. During your dives, you may even encounter ancient bones, adding an intriguing layer of mystery to these extraordinary experiences.

Essential info

Since the water around the cenotes is mostly shallow, diving and snorkelling are accessible at all levels. However, some areas are a little more difficult to access and require more experience. The water temperature is about 24°C (75°F).

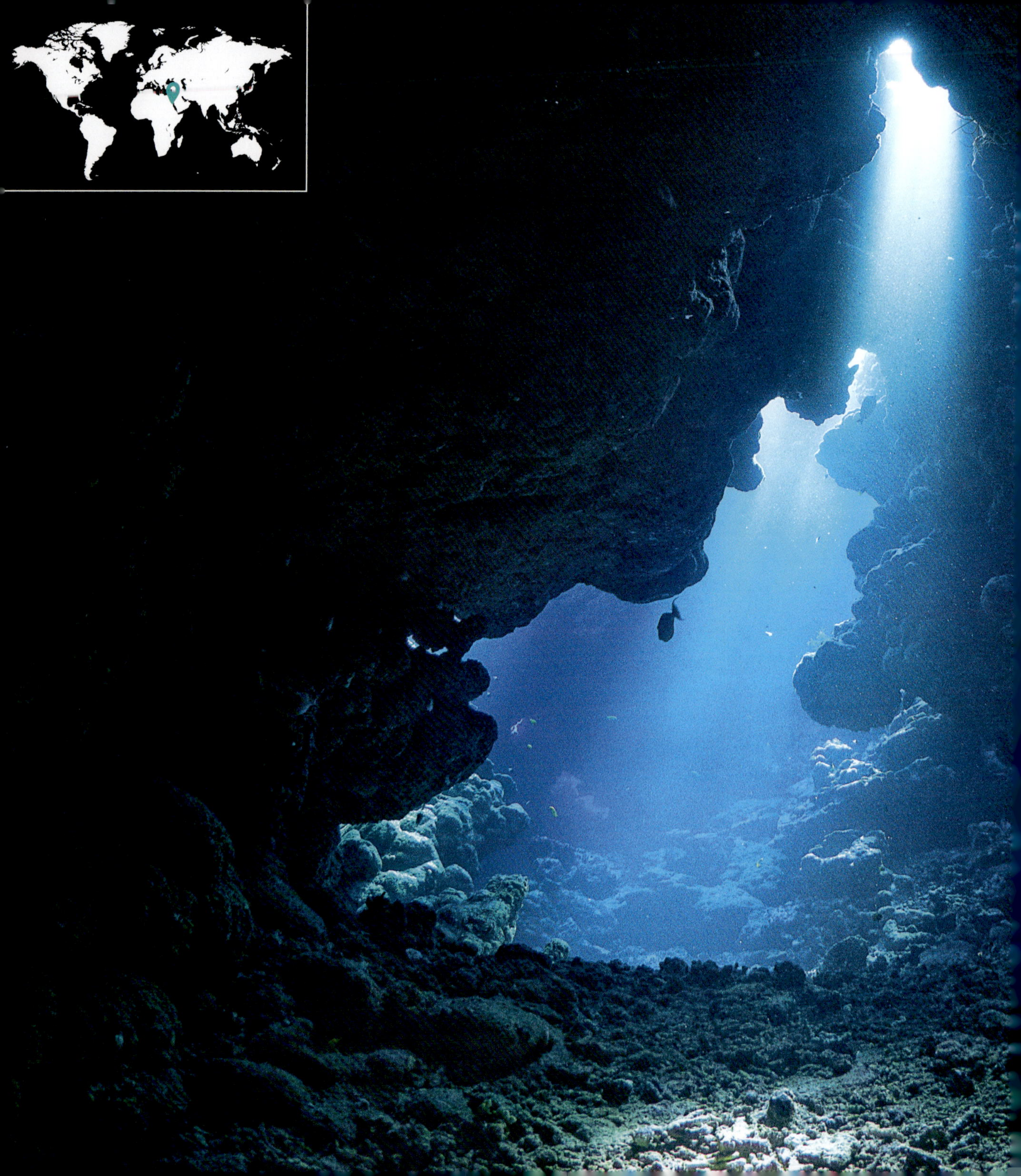

5 Sha'ab Claudio

Egypt

Beyond their ecological significance as hotspots of biodiversity and biomass, coral reefs also draw tourists from around the globe. The Red Sea is a premier diving destination, and in southern Egypt the reefs are untouched and teeming with life.

Did you know you can actually swim inside a coral reef? One such location is Sha'ab Claudio Reef, situated in the Fury Shoals area, north of Berenice Point. This small reef features several openings that provide access to its interior, allowing for easy exploration. Just a few centimetres (one inch) below the surface, the upper part of the reef is dotted with numerous holes that let sunlight filter through. The effect is truly magical, especially during the middle of the day when the sun is high in the sky, allowing soft beams of light to dance gently across the dark water.

Essential info

Sha'ab Claudio is a dive suitable for everyone, with depths reaching just 10 metres (33 feet), and exits always within easy reach. However, it's essential to use careful finning techniques to avoid disturbing the sediments.

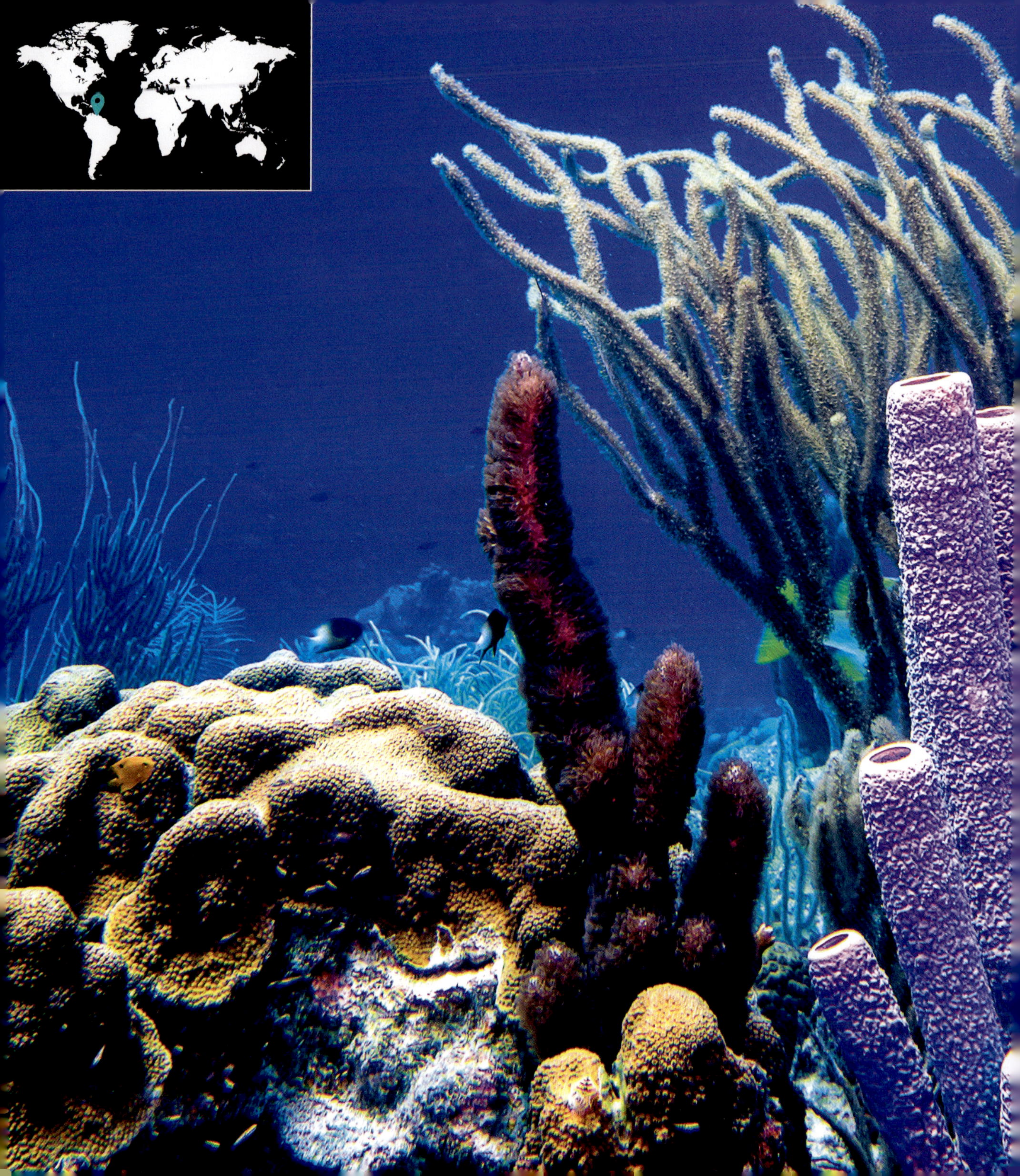

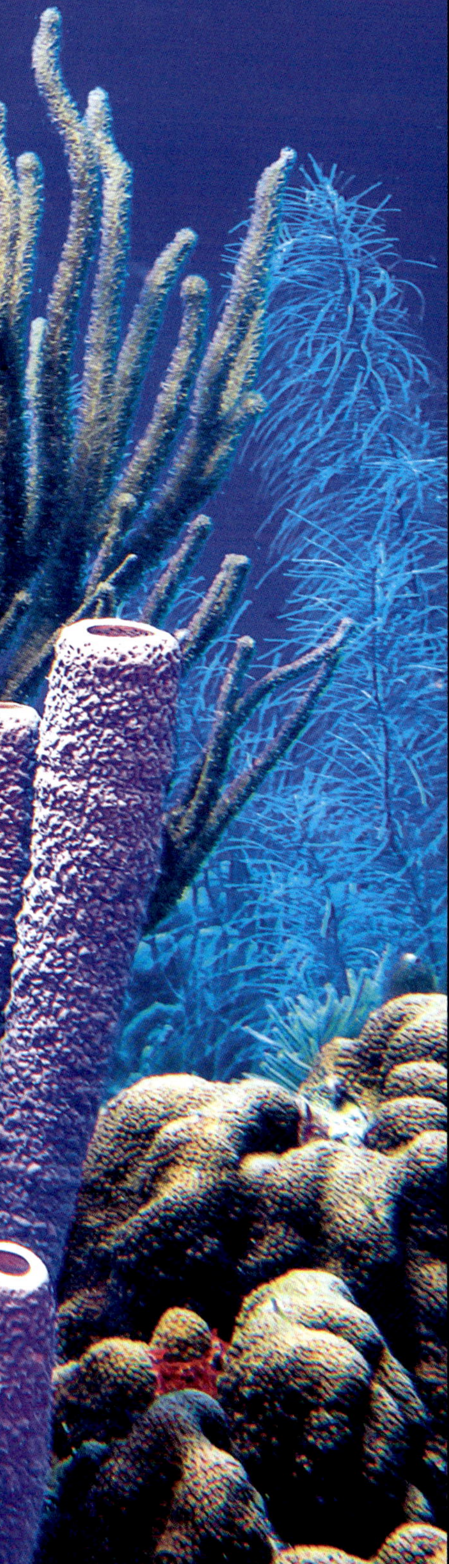

6 Bonaire

Caribbean

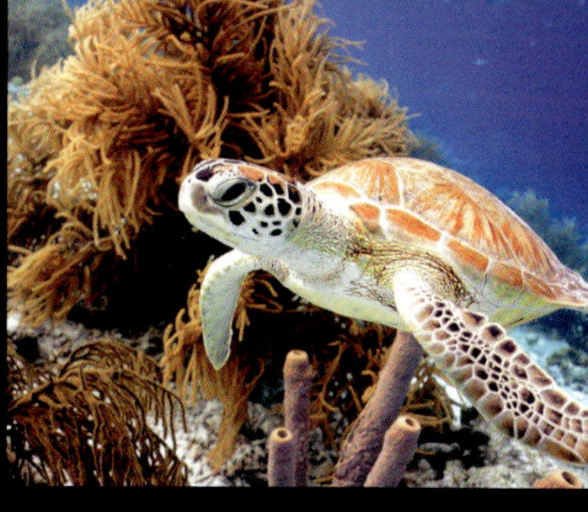

Some places are more surprising than others, with unique ways of doing things. In the middle of the Caribbean Sea, north of Venezuela, the small island of Bonaire is one of these places. Renowned for its exceptional scuba diving, Bonaire offers an experience unlike any other in the world. Diving enthusiasts head out from the dive centre equipped with oxygen tanks, diving gear and even a ute. As they embark on their adventure, they explore the island's numerous dive sites, each marked with a numbered sign along the roadside that can be located using the map provided.

Since its protection in 1979, the seabed has flourished, and the coral reefs remain nearly pristine. A vibrant array of Caribbean marine life gathers here in abundance, offering something for everyone – whether you're captivated by schools of colourful fish or interested in macro photography. Bonaire truly stands alone as the world capital of shore diving.

Essential info

Well-protected, Bonaire is an ideal diving destination year-round, with water temperatures consistently ranging between 26°C and 29°C (about 79°F and 84°F), making diving here accessible for all skill levels.

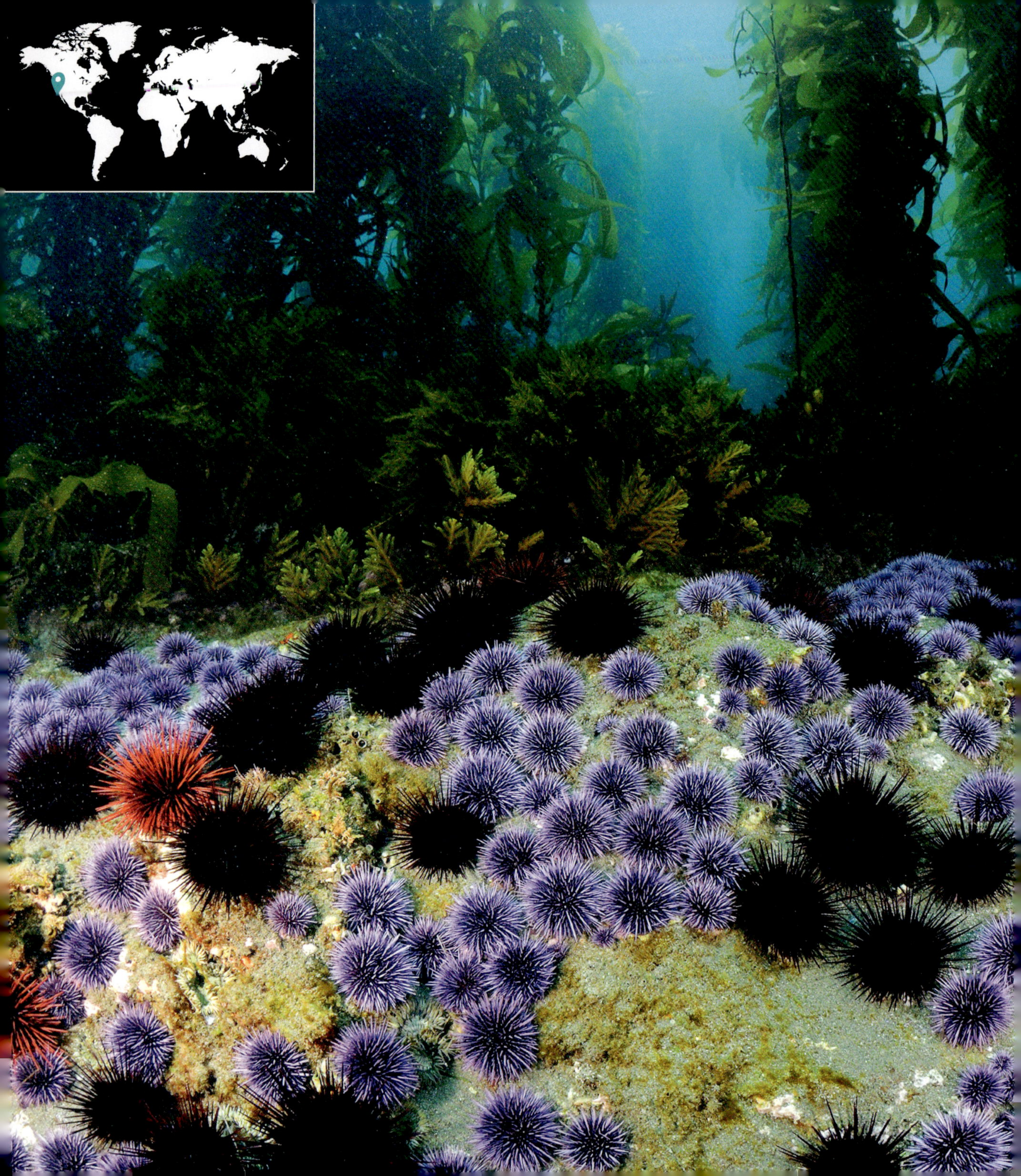

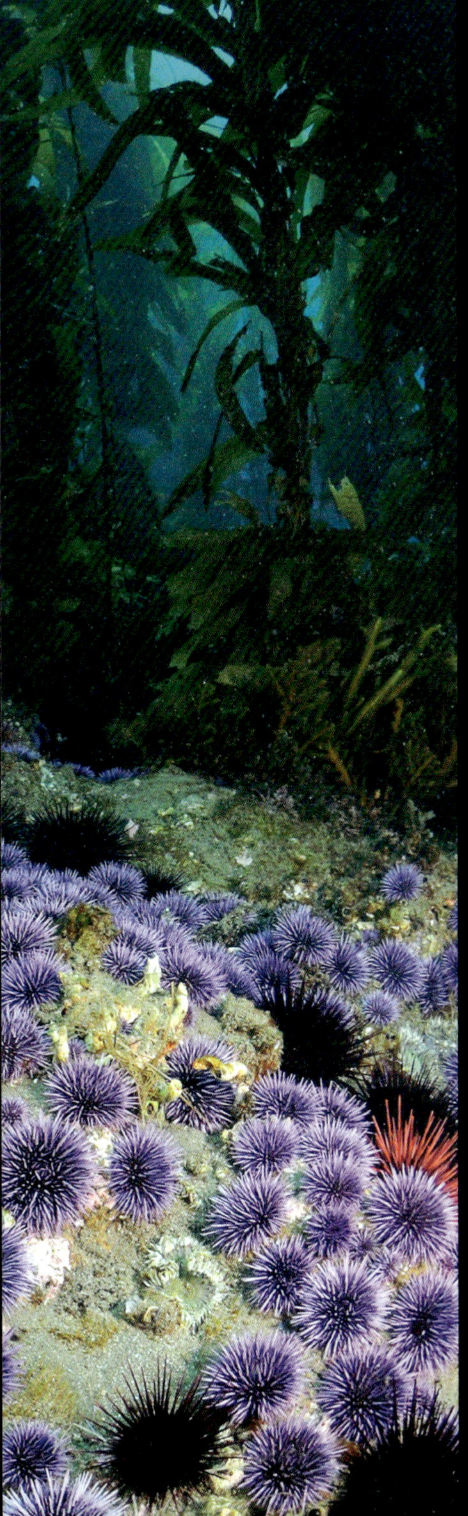

7 Channel Islands

California, USA

The famed west coast of the United States, particularly California, is known worldwide for its endless beaches and surf-friendly waves.

Just off Los Angeles, the Channel Islands archipelago, made up of eight islands, offers breathtaking diving experiences. The northern islands – Santa Cruz, Anacapa, Santa Rosa, Santa Barbara and San Miguel – are protected within Channel Islands National Park and boast some of the richest and most vibrant marine landscapes. The southern islands, on the other hand, are home to magnificent kelp forests, with algae stretching several metres (10 feet) long, creating unexpected underwater scenery (see photo).

Marine life here is just as impressive, with sightings of giant octopuses, eels, lobsters, large sea bass and an array of other fish. Sea lions are known to dart around divers before vanishing into the kelp. Macro photographers will find plenty of captivating subjects, from a multitude of nudibranchs to photogenic blennies and vibrantly coloured invertebrates. With some luck, divers may even spot dolphins or whales passing by.

Essential info

The waters are quite cool in the Channel Islands, usually between 10°C and 18°C (50°F and 64°F). It is possible to do day dives or take a two- or three-day cruise.

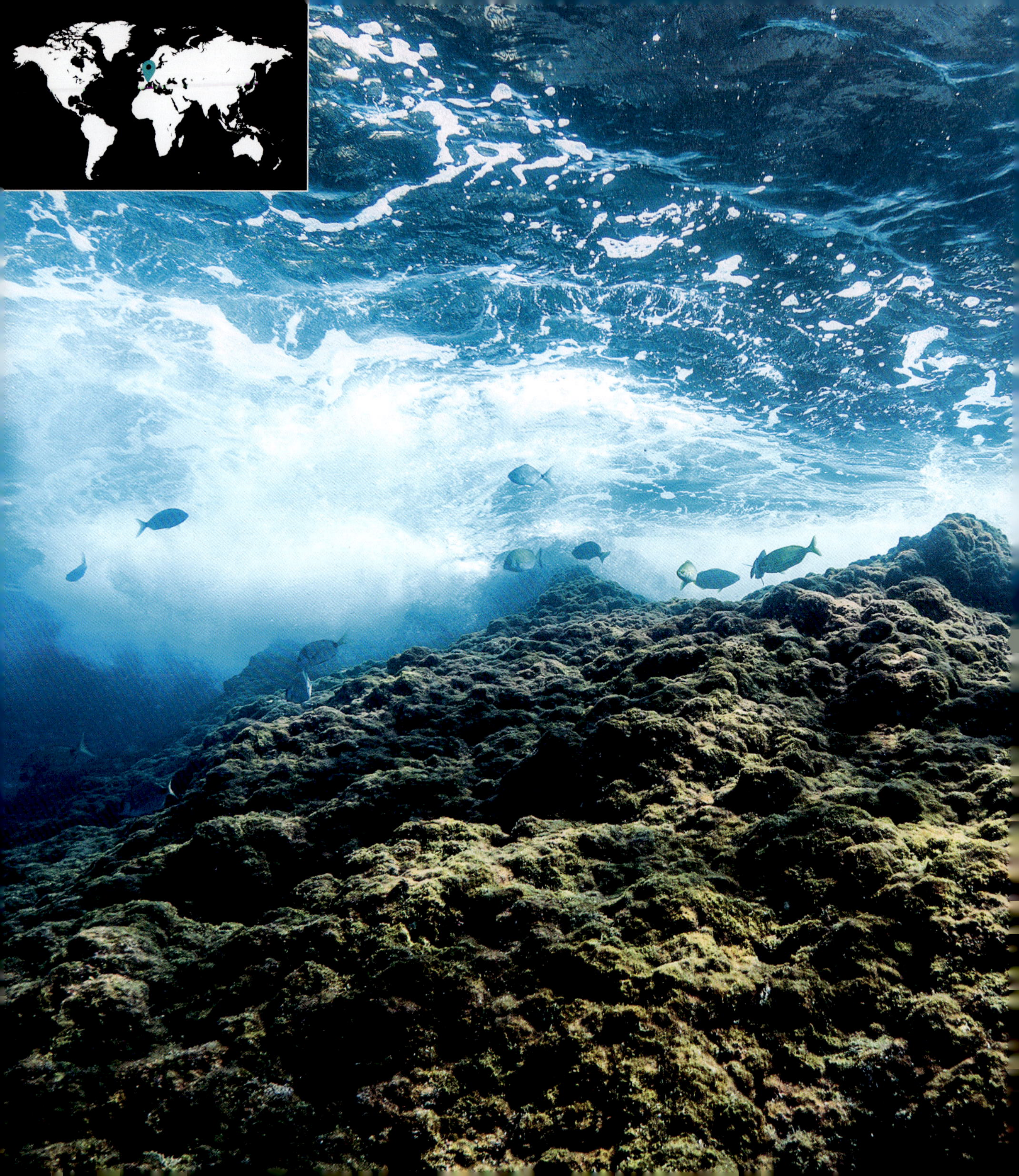

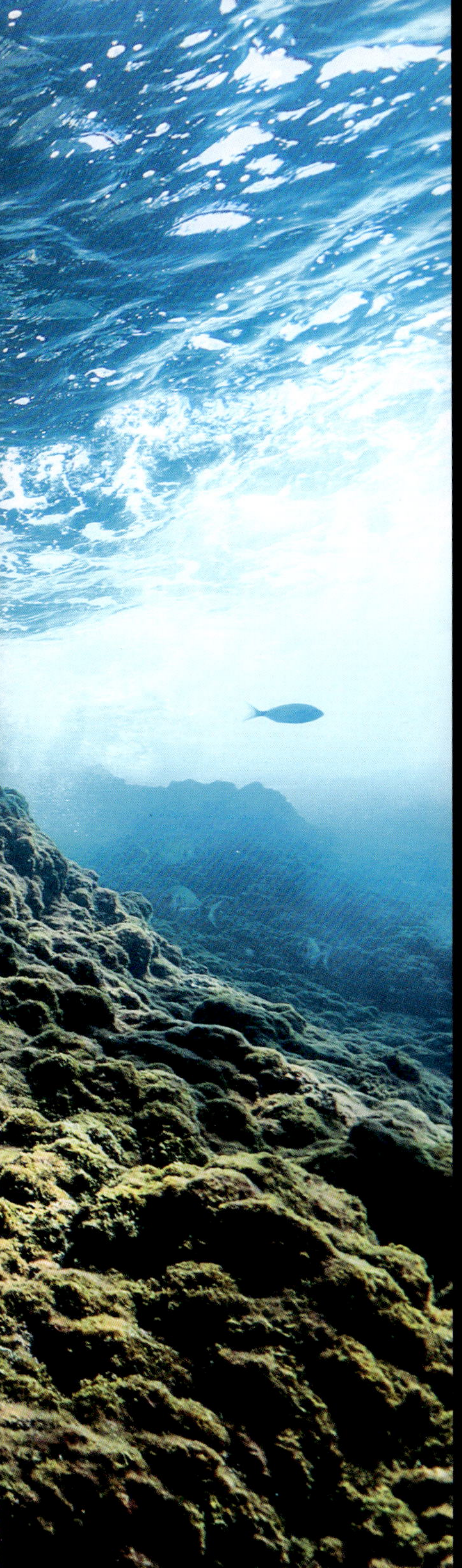

8 The Calanques of Marseille

Bouches-du-Rhône, France

After years of damage from pollution and overfishing, the Calanques National Park (established in 2012) has breathed new life into this once-ailing gem. Now a premier diving destination in both France and the Mediterranean, Marseille's underwater world offers endless discoveries for divers of all levels, from beginners to experts. Caves, shipwrecks, towering drop-offs, crevices and seagrass meadows await exploration. Vibrant walls of yellow anemones and red coral light up this underwater wonderland that is home to a wealth of hidden marine life. Schools of barracuda, saupe, and sars weave in and out under the watchful eyes of the impressive dusky groupers that have returned in healthy numbers.

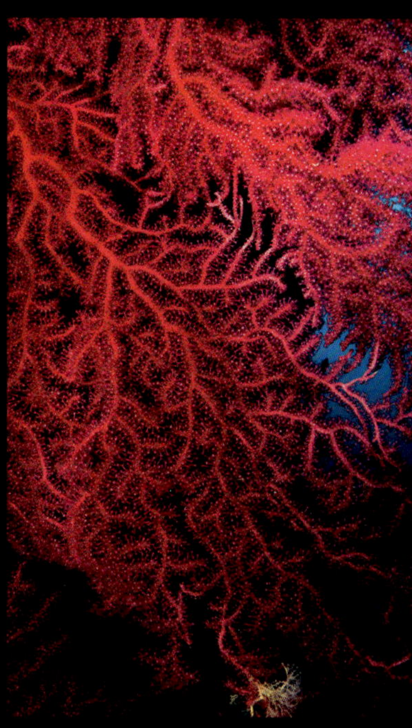

Essential info

Marseille boasts dozens of dive sites suited to all levels of experience. The best time to enjoy warmer water is from August to October. Keep in mind that when the mistral wind sweeps in, water temperatures can drop sharply, but quickly warm up again.

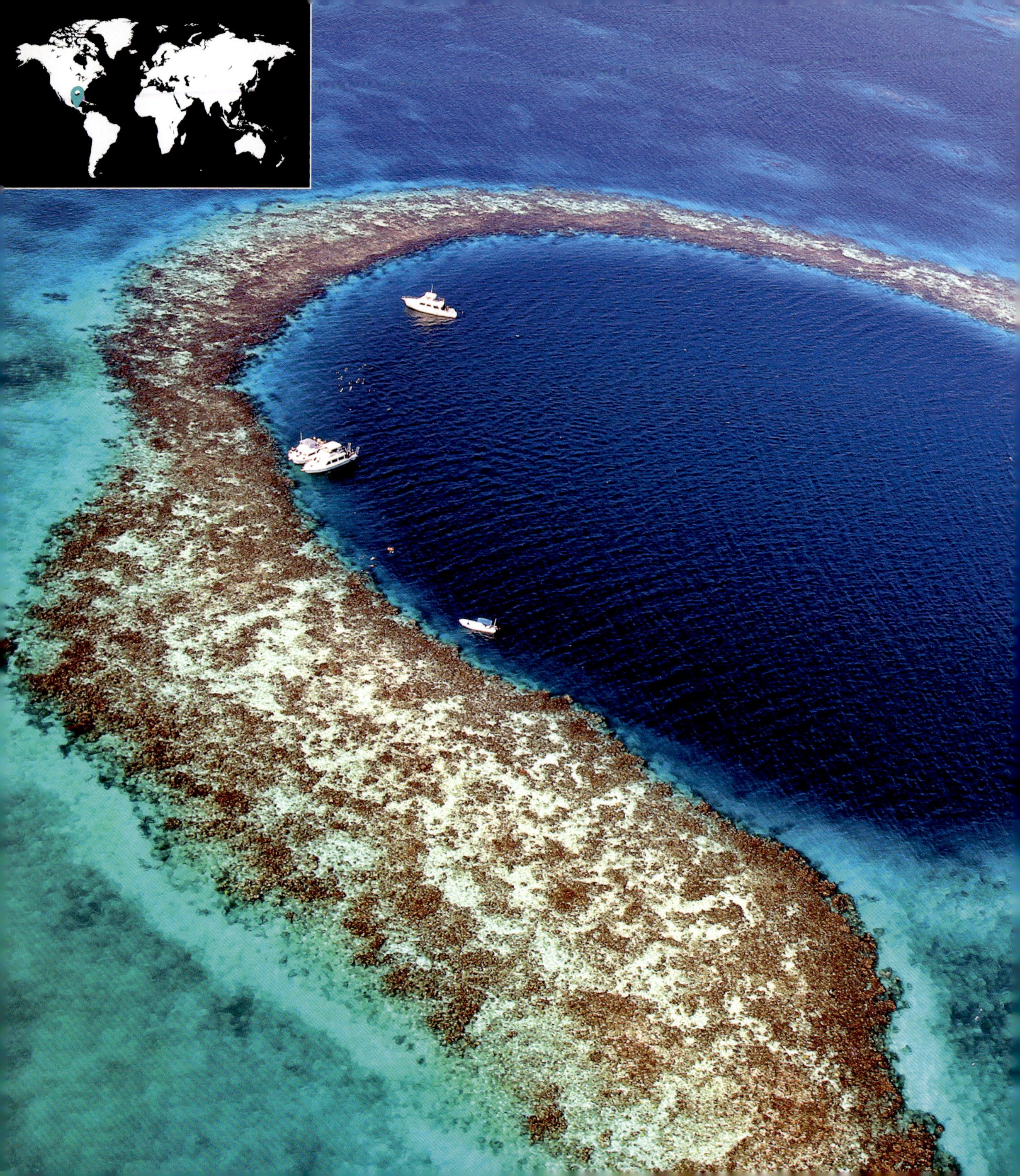

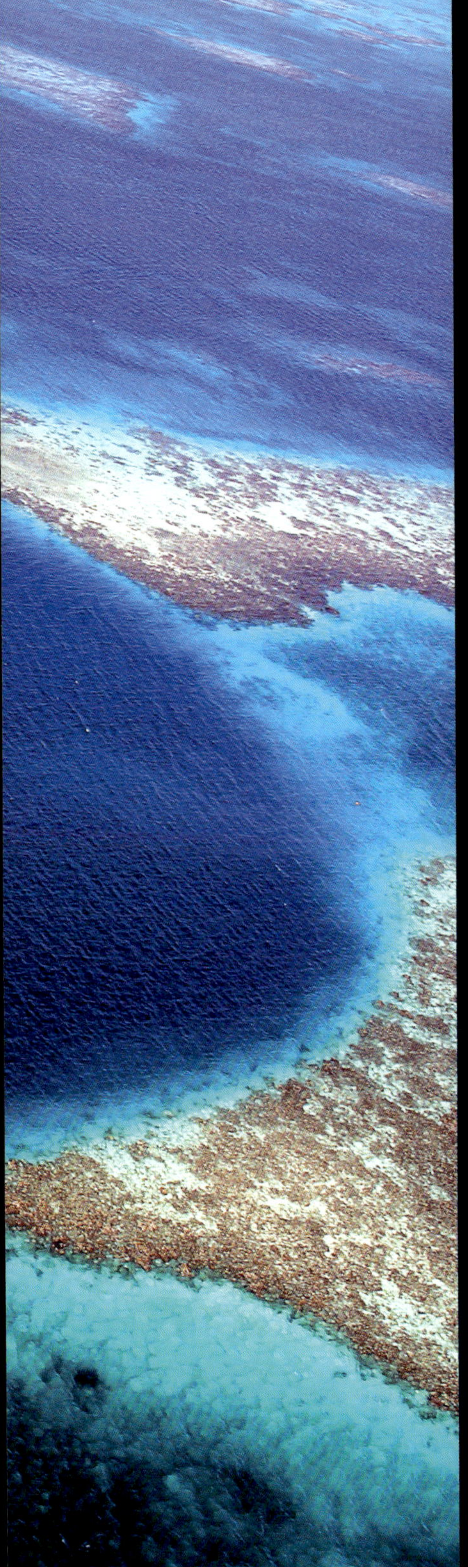

9 Great Blue Hole

Belize

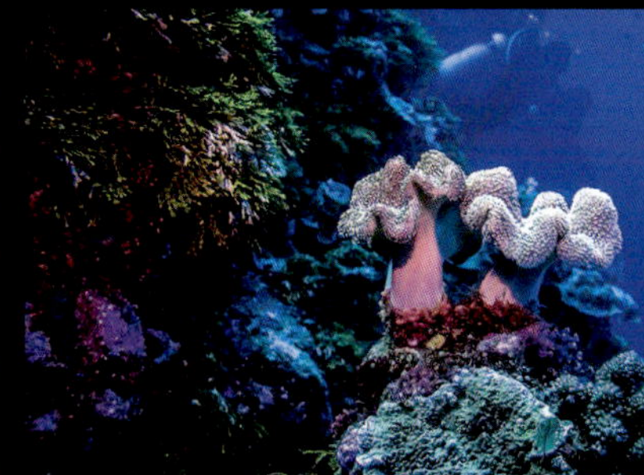

Wedged between Mexico, Guatemala and the Caribbean Sea, Belize is a tiny country with the largest coral reef in the northern hemisphere. It has 300 kilometres (186 miles) of coastline with atolls and coral islets, nestled in turquoise waters renowned for having some of the best visibility in the world.

Numerous extraordinary sites and drop-offs await divers, but perhaps the most impressive is the Great Blue Hole, located on Lighthouse Reef Atoll. Discovered in 1971 by Commander Cousteau, this ancient limestone cave, formed when its ceiling collapsed, became submerged at the end of the last ice age around 15,000 years ago. Today, divers from around the globe come to experience this thrilling dive, plunging into the vast 300-metre (985 feet)-diameter hole that descends over 100 metres (328 feet) deep.

Stalactites adorn the walls, while various sharks – hammerheads, bull sharks, nurse sharks – along with barracudas and sea turtles, patrol the waters. The largest blue hole on the planet, the Great Blue Hole is listed as a UNESCO World Heritage Site.

Essential info

The Great Blue Hole is accessible to divers of all levels, but an advanced level will allow you to enjoy it more fully.

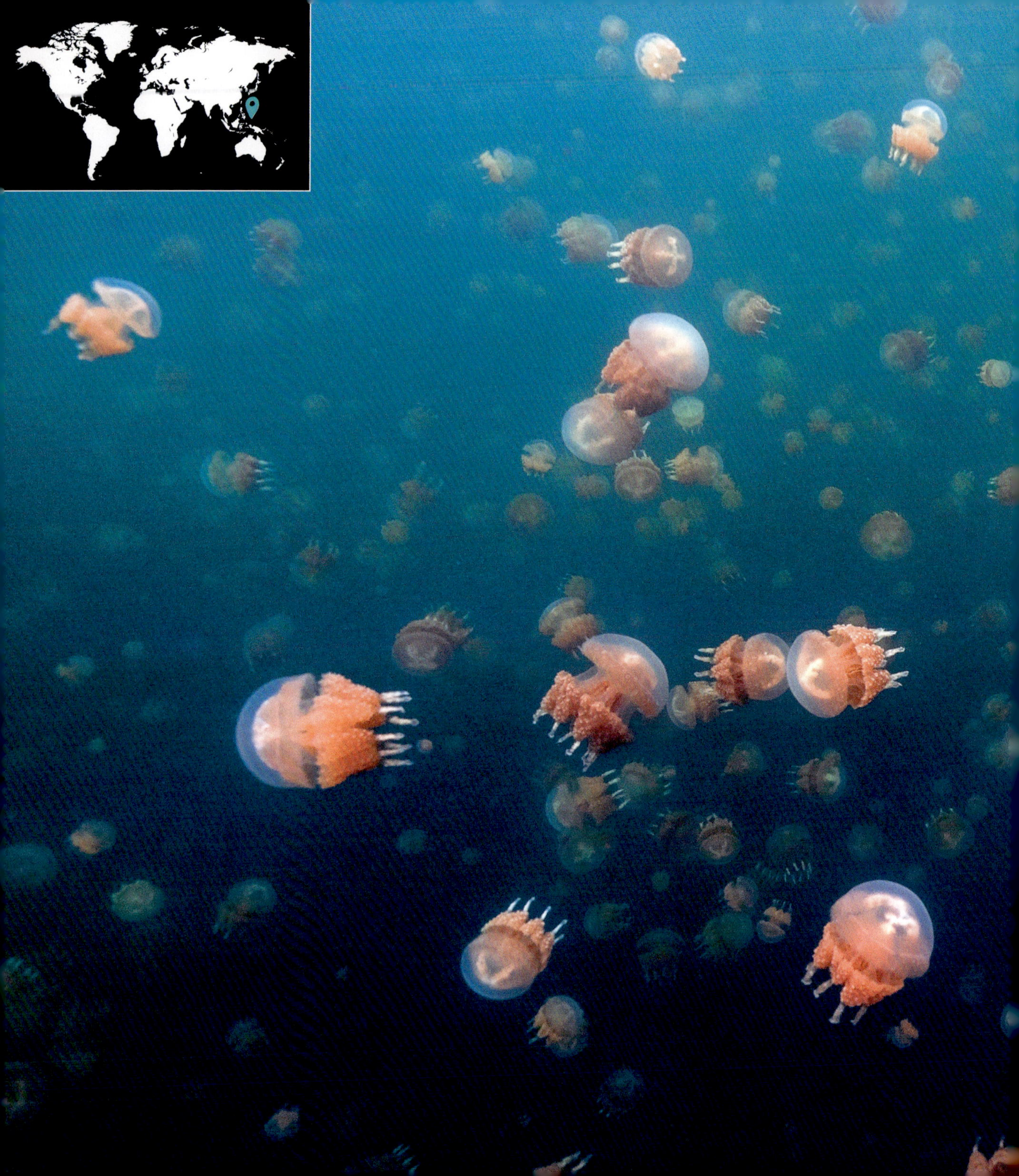

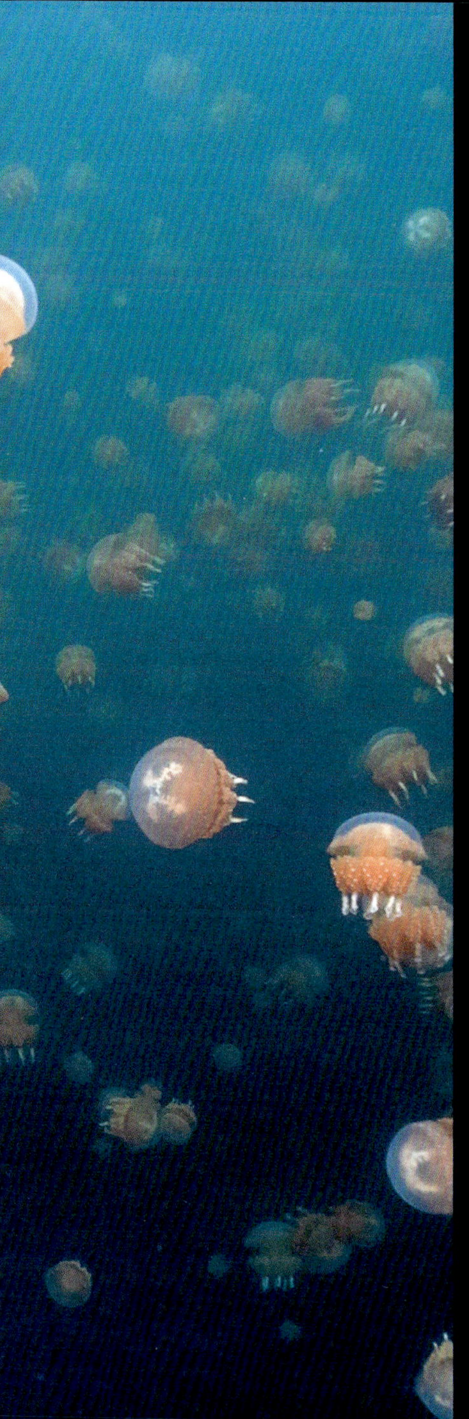

10 Jellyfish Lake

Palau, Micronesia

Every summer, jellyfish stings are a common concern for swimmers. Yet these creatures, which have inhabited the seas for over 600 million years, play a crucial role in maintaining balanced marine ecosystems. While some species produce some of the animal kingdom's most potent venoms, others are completely harmless.

In Micronesia, some Mastigias papua jellyfish were cut off from the ocean 12,000 years ago. They adapted to life within a brackish lake, called Ongeim'l Tketau, in Palau. With no natural predators, they've lost their stinging abilities and developed a symbiotic relationship with photosynthetic algae that supply the nutrients they need to survive. Drifting peacefully among thousands of jellyfish in this secluded lake, both protected and open to visitors, offers one of the most remarkable experiences in the aquatic world. Once the initial hesitation fades, it's pure exhilaration.

Essential info

Only accessible by freediving. The permit costs about a hundred dollars. Only reef safe sunscreens are allowed.

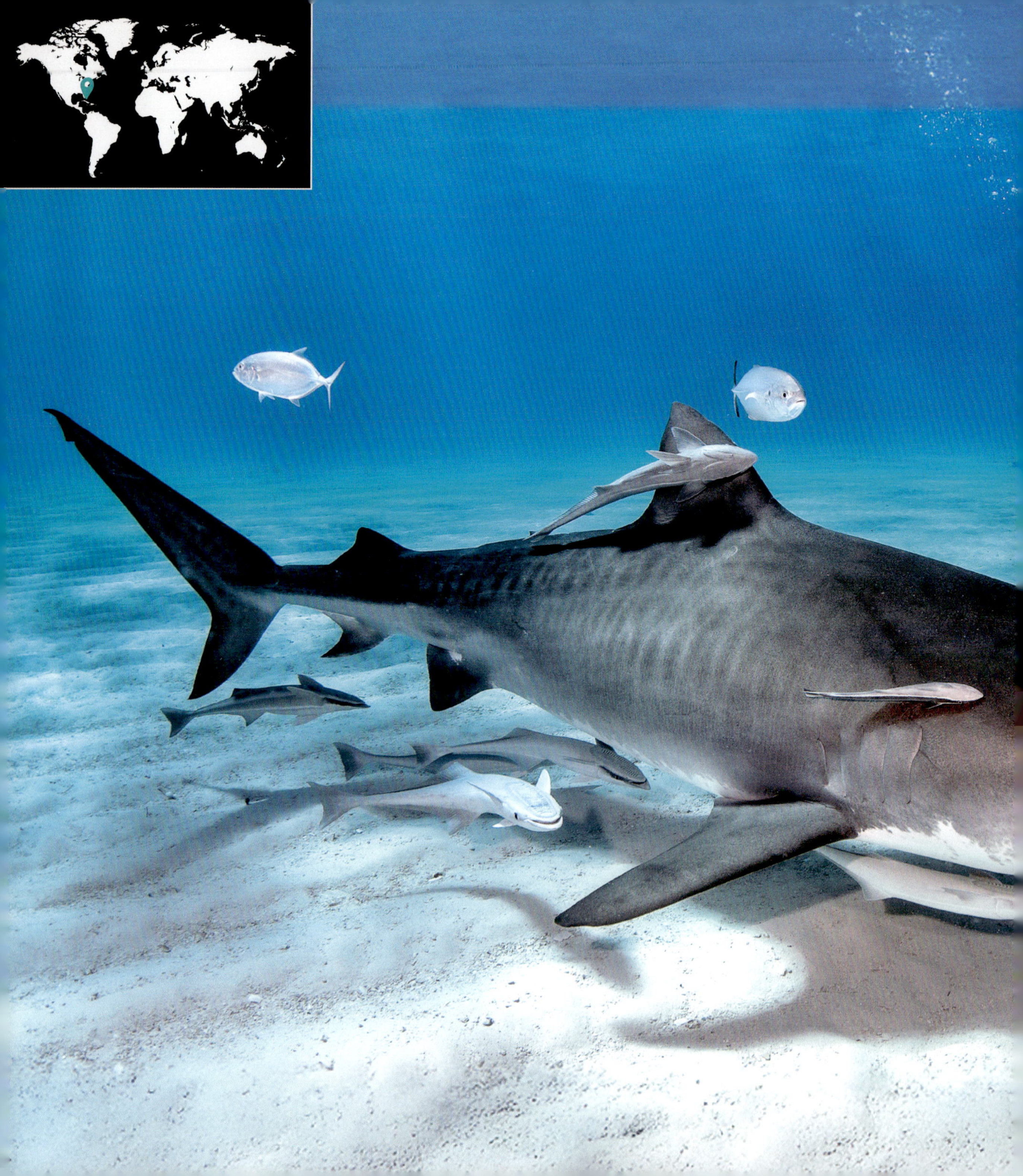

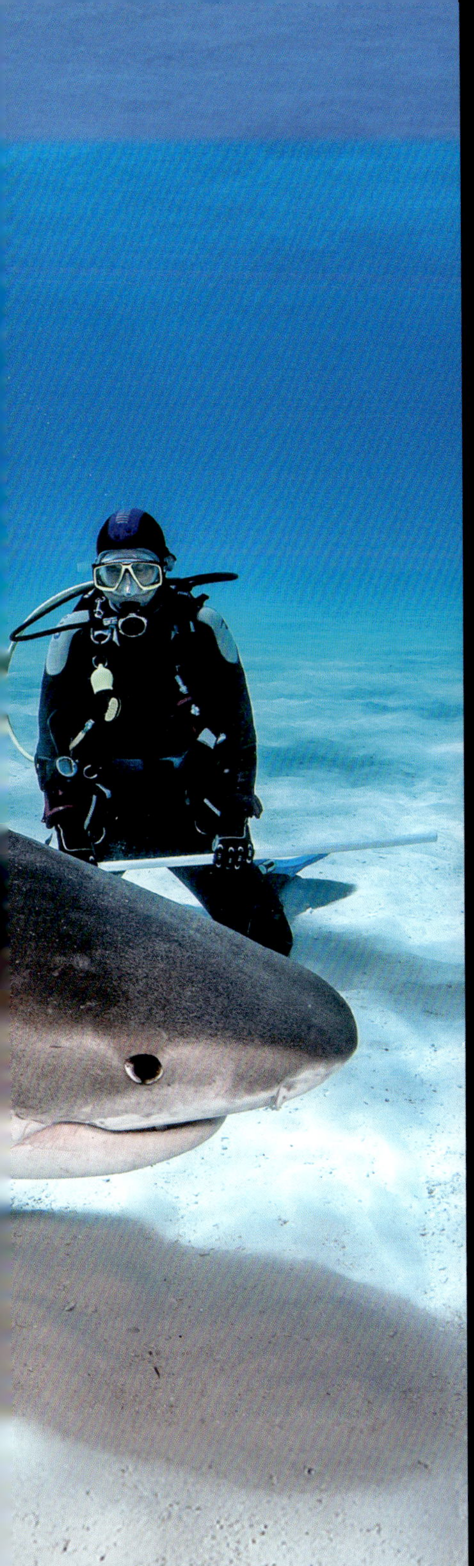

11 Tiger Beach

Bahamas

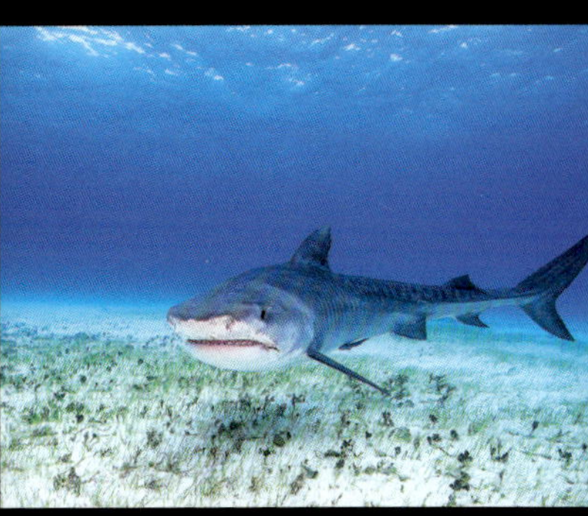

The Bahamas archipelago, with over 700 islands and coral islets just off the coast of Florida, boasts breathtaking scenery. Imagine pristine beaches and sandbanks encircled by turquoise lagoons featuring crystal-clear waters, perfect for enjoying a conch salad, the local specialty.

The Bahamas' seabed also offers a rare opportunity to encounter unique wild marine animals. On Grand Bahama, about 50 kilometres (31 miles) from the western tip, lies a shallow sandbank called Tiger Beach – a popular spot for divers eager to see tiger sharks up close. The calm, warm waters here are ideal for female sharks, especially those in gestation. Even non-pregnant females seem to enjoy this area, likely appreciating the reduced presence of males and less harassment. Just a few metres (10 feet) beneath the surface, divers can simply rest on the sandy bottom and watch these majestic sharks glide by, sometimes coming incredibly close to their masks.

Essential info

In the Bahamas, thrilling shark dives are often conducted using bait to draw the animals in. However, sharks are fully protected here, as the archipelago has become a sanctuary for some 40 shark species.

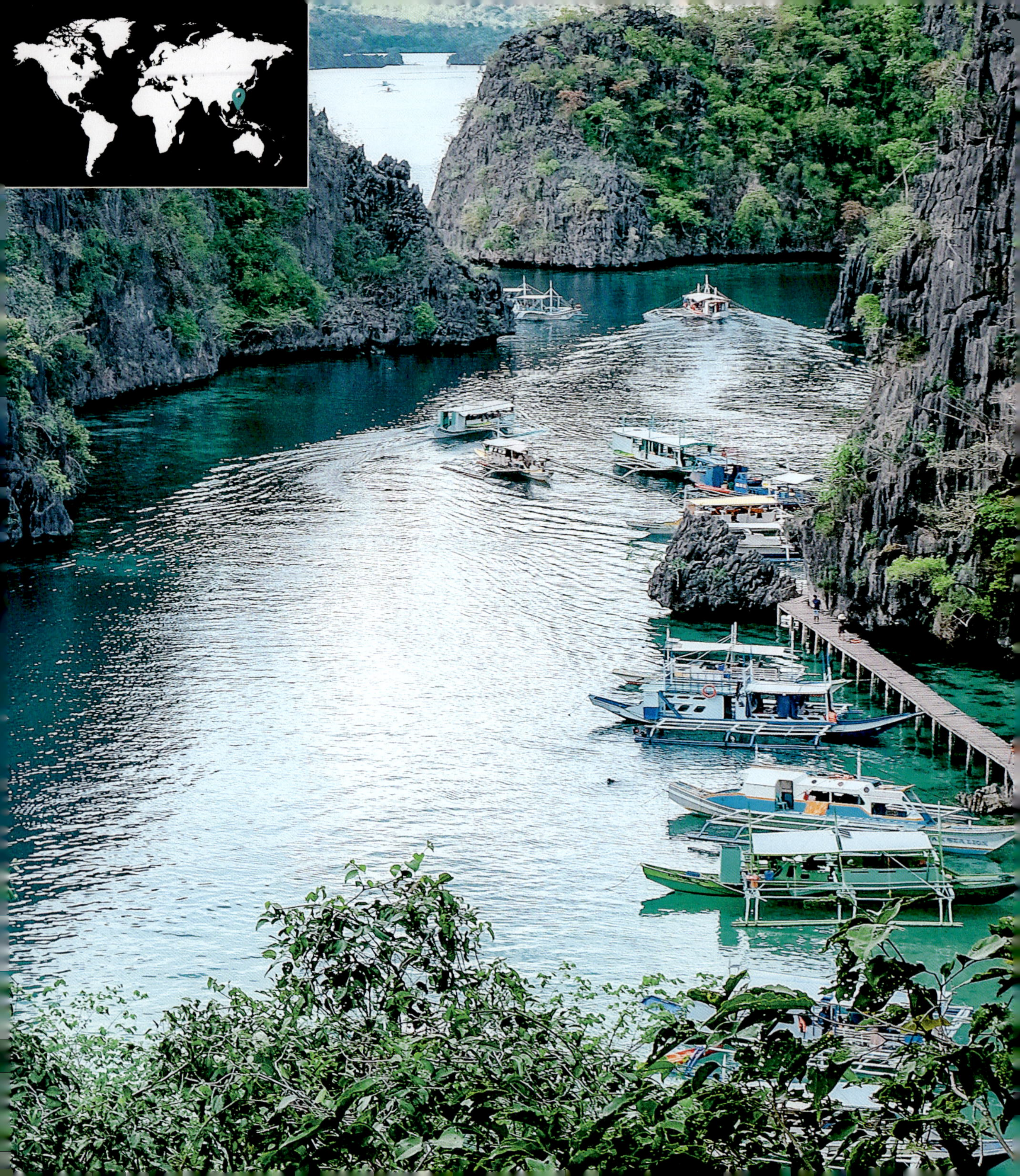

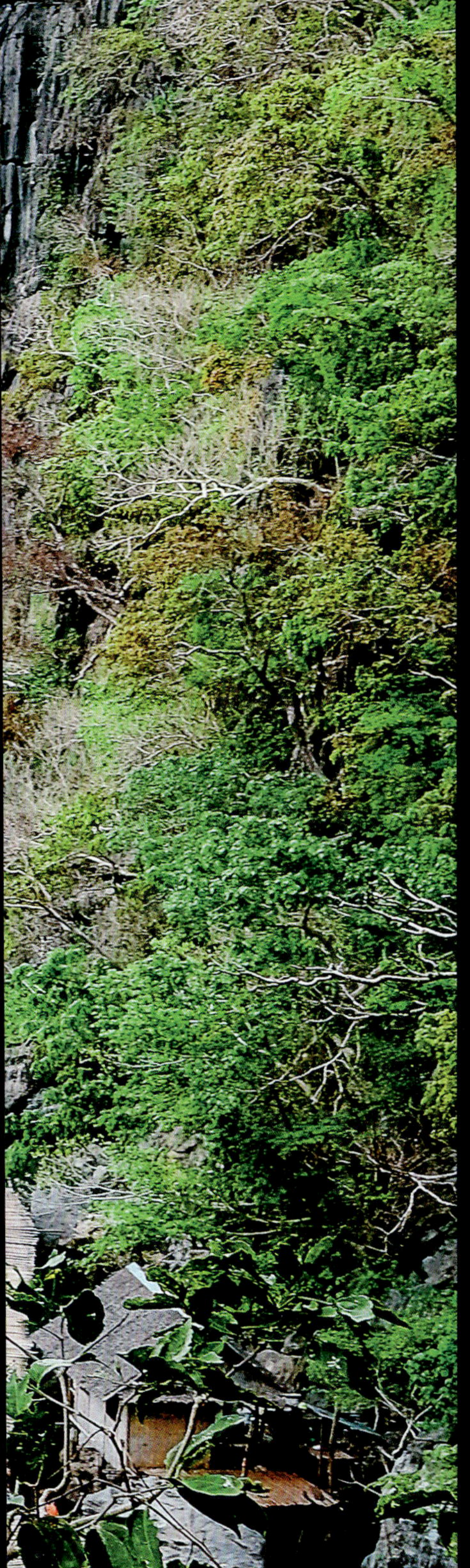

12 Coron Bay

Palawan, Philippines

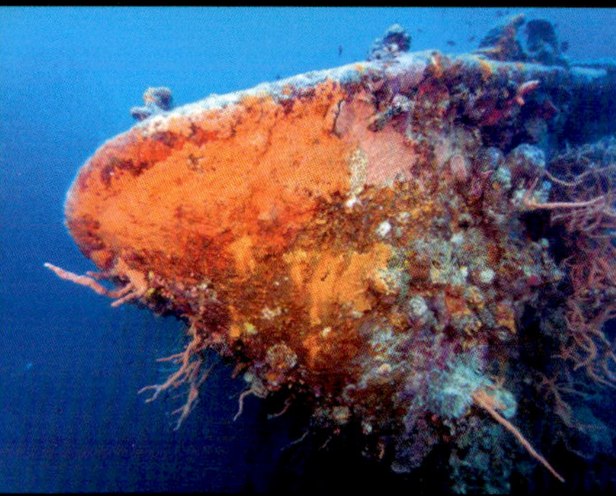

On 24 September 1944 in Coron Bay, during a fierce period of fighting between the Americans and the Japanese during the Pacific War, 150 American planes flying in formation delivered a final blow in just 40 minutes, sinking dozens of Japanese warships anchored in the bay.

Today, the waters are home to one of the highest concentrations of wrecks worldwide, with a dozen or so easily accessible, with depths up to 40 metres (130 feet).

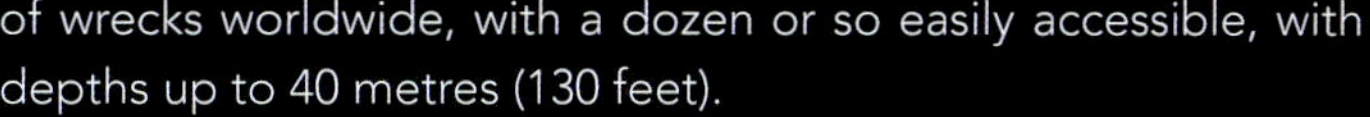

Even though the waters are sometimes murky, they are teeming with life, creating an otherworldly diving experience. It's a ghostly yet lively underwater world where schools of fish, like snappers and barracudas, swirl around the steel giants, while large groupers drift through open sections, and sea turtles nestle quietly among them. The soft and hard corals have taken hold across the metal structures, interspersed with splashes of colour from various nudibranchs.

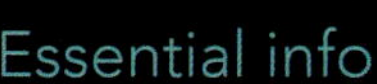

Essential info

Some of the wrecks are shallow and accessible to level 1 divers, but to make the most of exploring the wrecks, level 2 is necessary.

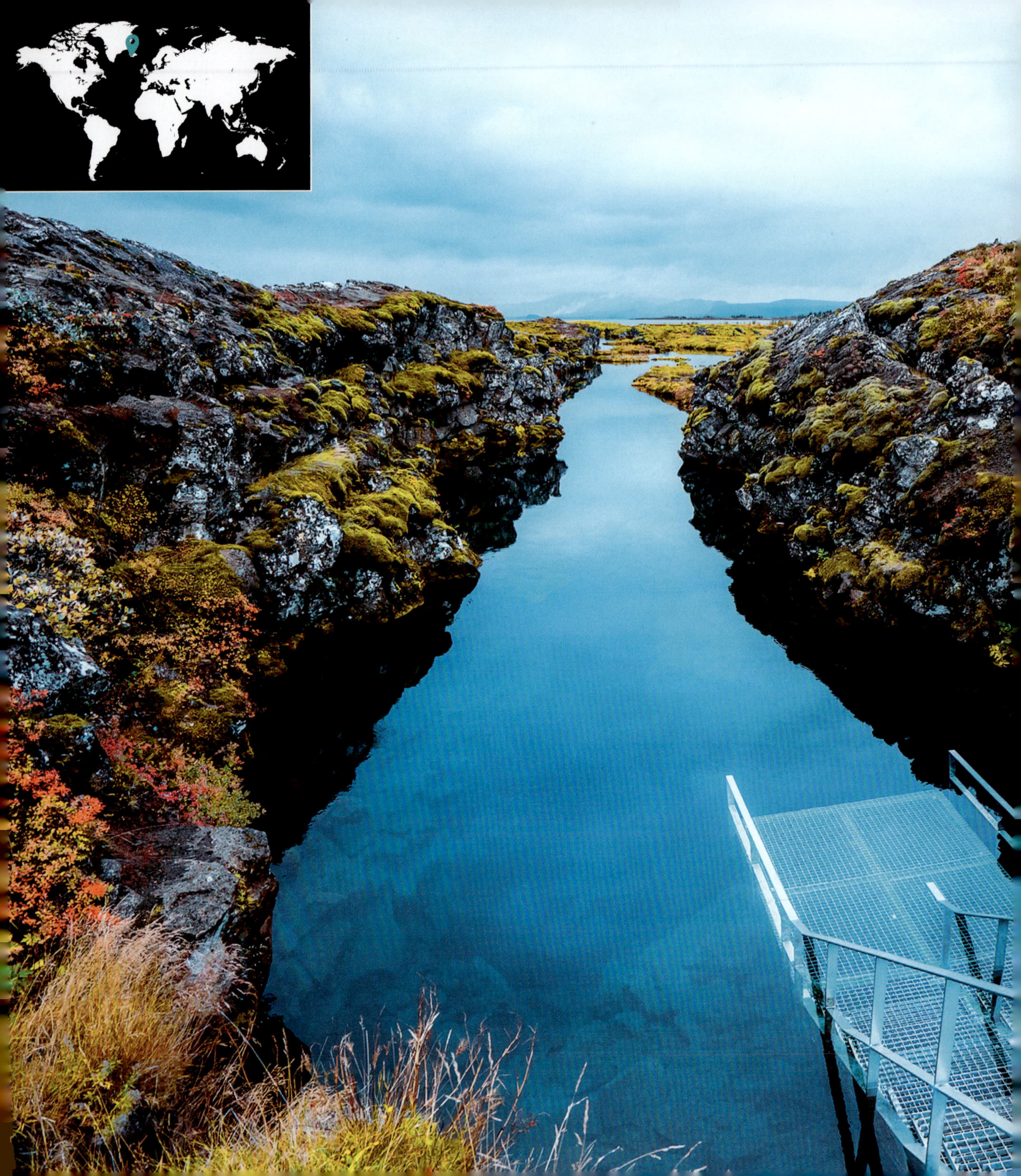

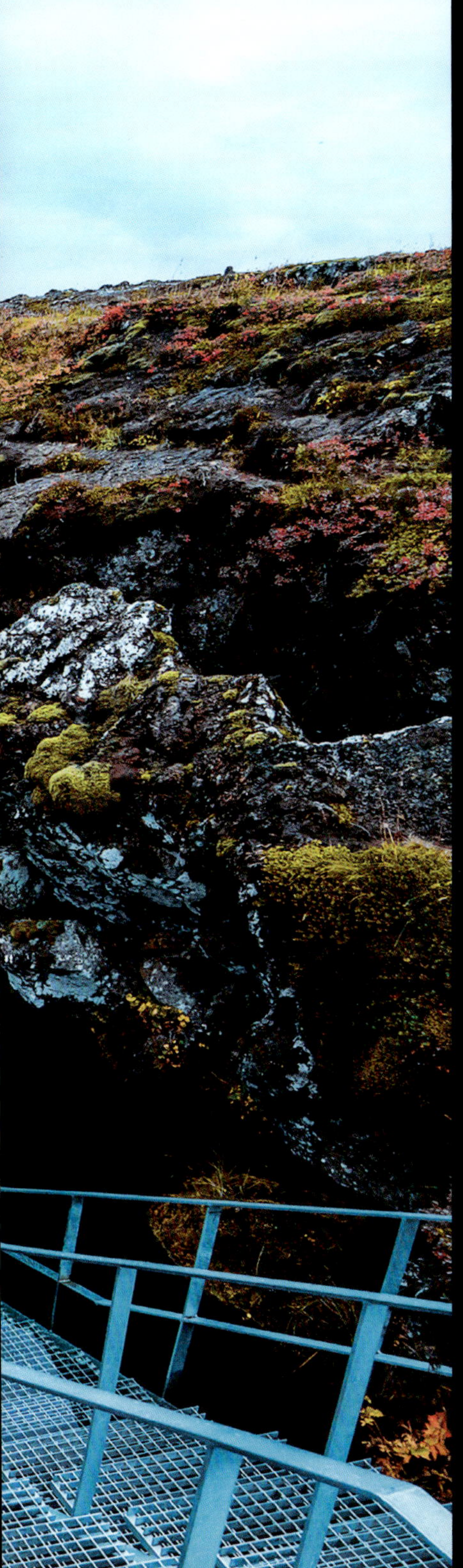

13 Silfra Fissure

Iceland

While scuba diving is often associated with warm water and corals, there are a few famous exceptions to this rule. This is precisely the experience offered by Iceland's Silfra Fissure, where water temperatures hover around a chilly 2°C (35°F) all year round.

Located at the meeting point of the Eurasian and North American tectonic plates, which drift apart by two centimetres (one inch) annually, this fissure near Reykjavik is hailed as one of the world's most stunning cold-water dive sites. With crystal-clear waters and visibility reaching up to 100 metres (328 feet), Silfra invites divers and snorkellers to glide between its two majestic mineral walls, creating an otherworldly experience – a truly unique diving adventure, even though marine life is scarce. This is the only location on Earth where you can dive between two tectonic plates and actually touch them with both hands at the same time.

Essential info

This experience is accessible to everyone, whether from the surface for non-divers or by scuba diving. Wetsuits and diving equipment are available on-site, but it's essential to remember to dress warmly underneath the wetsuit.

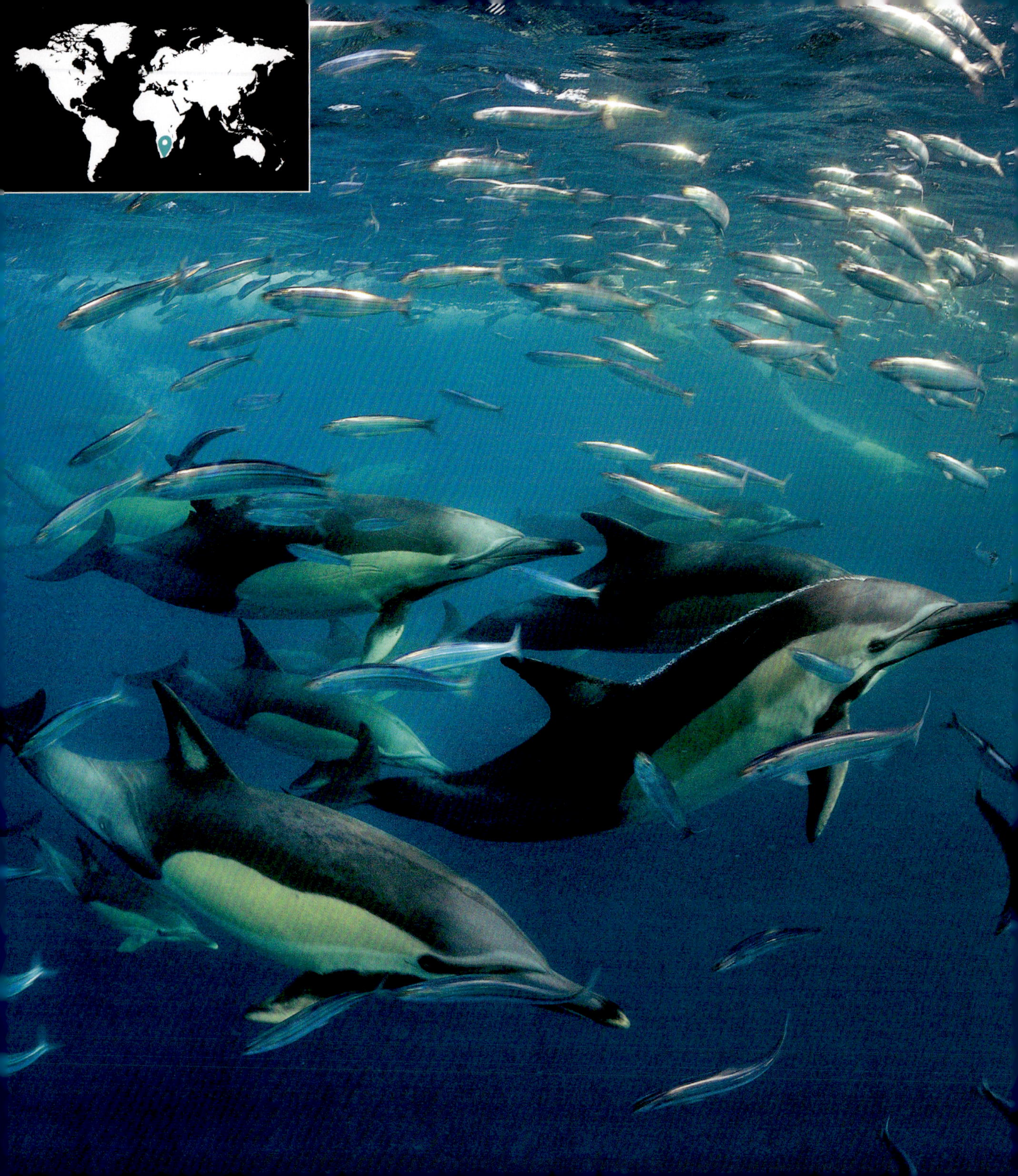

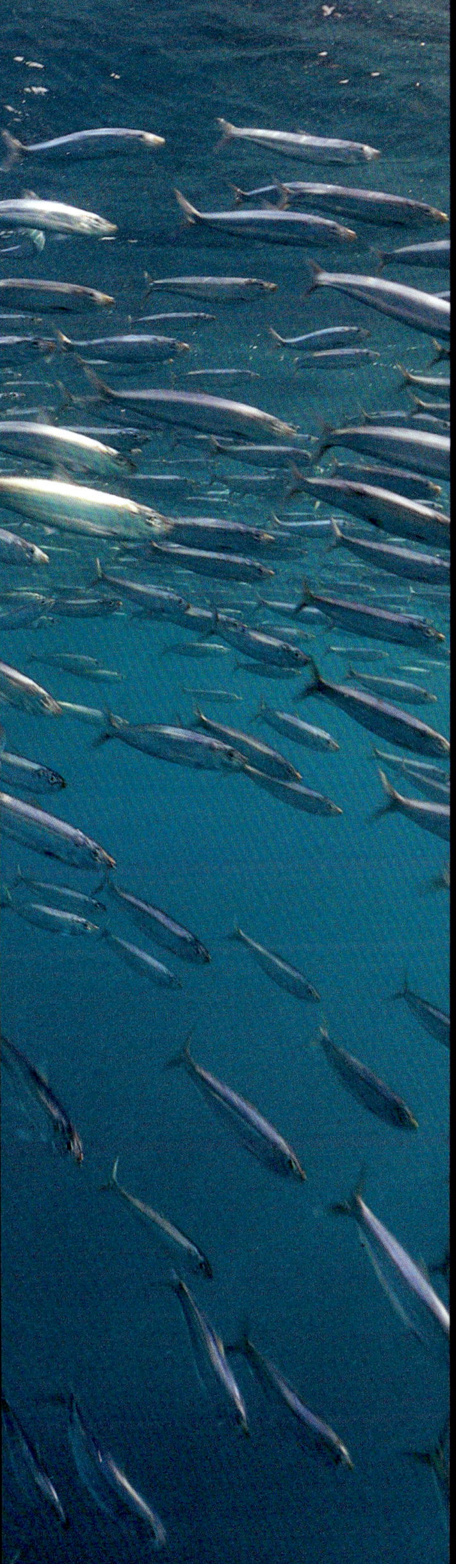

14 Sardine Run

South Africa

Considered one of the best countries for watching sharks in their natural environment, South Africa has many other wonderful surprises to offer its visitors. Every year along South Africa's east coast, millions of sardines converge, following the Agulhas Current southward – a phenomenon known as the Sardine Run, which offers an unexpected feeding opportunity. This event attracts a host of predators, all gathering for an epic feast in what is considered the largest animal gathering on the planet. The scene is extraordinary with sharks, dolphins, tuna, baleen whales, orcas, sea lions and even penguins swarming together from all sides.

From above, cape gannets dive into the water at lightning speed to join the feeding frenzy, making this June and July event a spectacle for all who witness it – something to be experienced at least once in a lifetime.

Essential info

There is no need to be a certified diver to access Sardine Run, as it can easily be enjoyed by snorkelling. However, it is necessary to be a strong swimmer. Divers can scuba dive down deeper to appreciate the vibrant underwater spectacle.

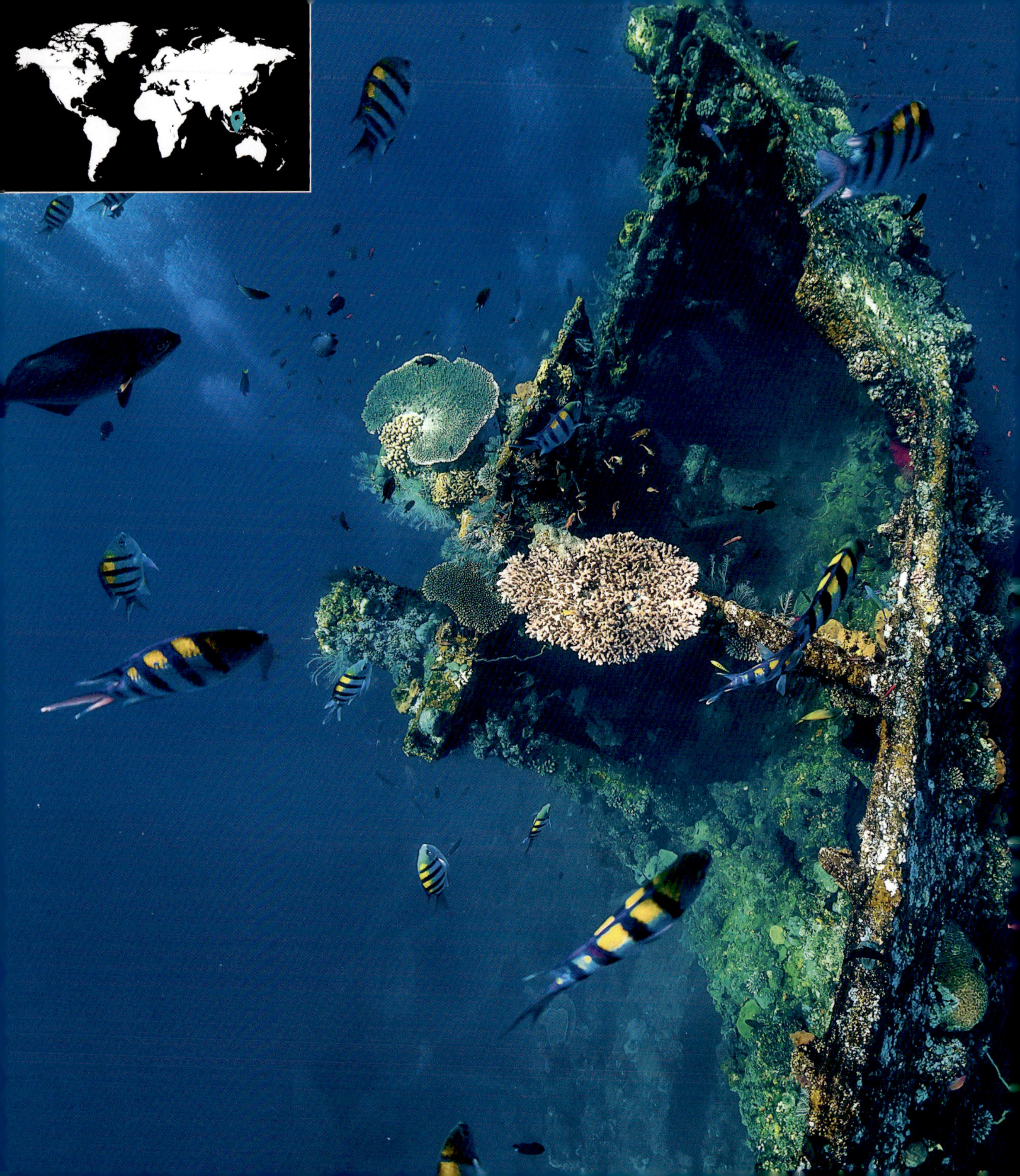

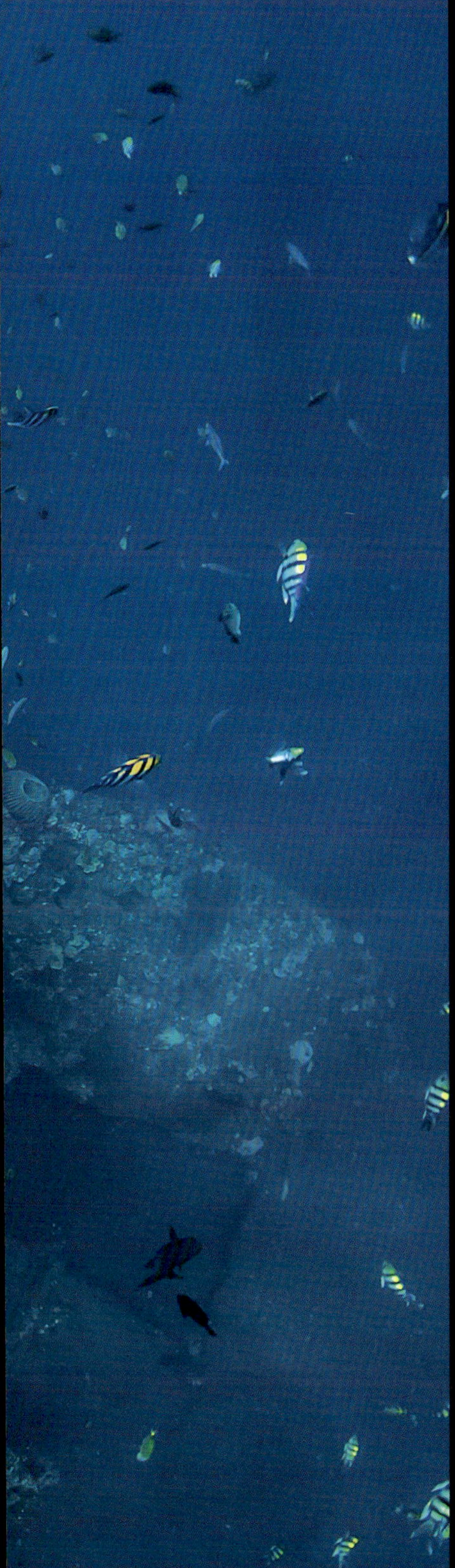

15 *USS Liberty* wreck

Bali, Indonesia

In the northeast of Bali Island, Indonesia, Tulamben Beach is home to one of the most famous shipwrecks for divers. Only a few dozen metres (39 feet) from the shore, the *USS Liberty* rests at a depth of between five and 30 metres (16 and 98 feet). This American military ship was torpedoed by the Japanese on 11 January 1942 in the Lombok Strait as it tried in vain to reach Singaraja, north of Bali. It ran aground on this beach and remained dry until 1963, when a lava flow moved it offshore, causing it to sink beneath the surface. The *USS Liberty* wreck is easily accessible to all levels and has become Bali's most famous dive site.

Now largely colonised, the wreck resembles a vibrant aquarium teeming with marine life. Corals and sponges blanket much of its surface, while fish inhabit every nook and cranny. For a stunning experience, dive early in the morning to witness a school of large humphead parrotfish, which typically seek refuge there overnight – a truly captivating sight.

Essential info

Just 30 metres (98 feet) from the shore, this exceptional site is accessible to divers of all levels, as well as those interested in snorkelling and free diving.

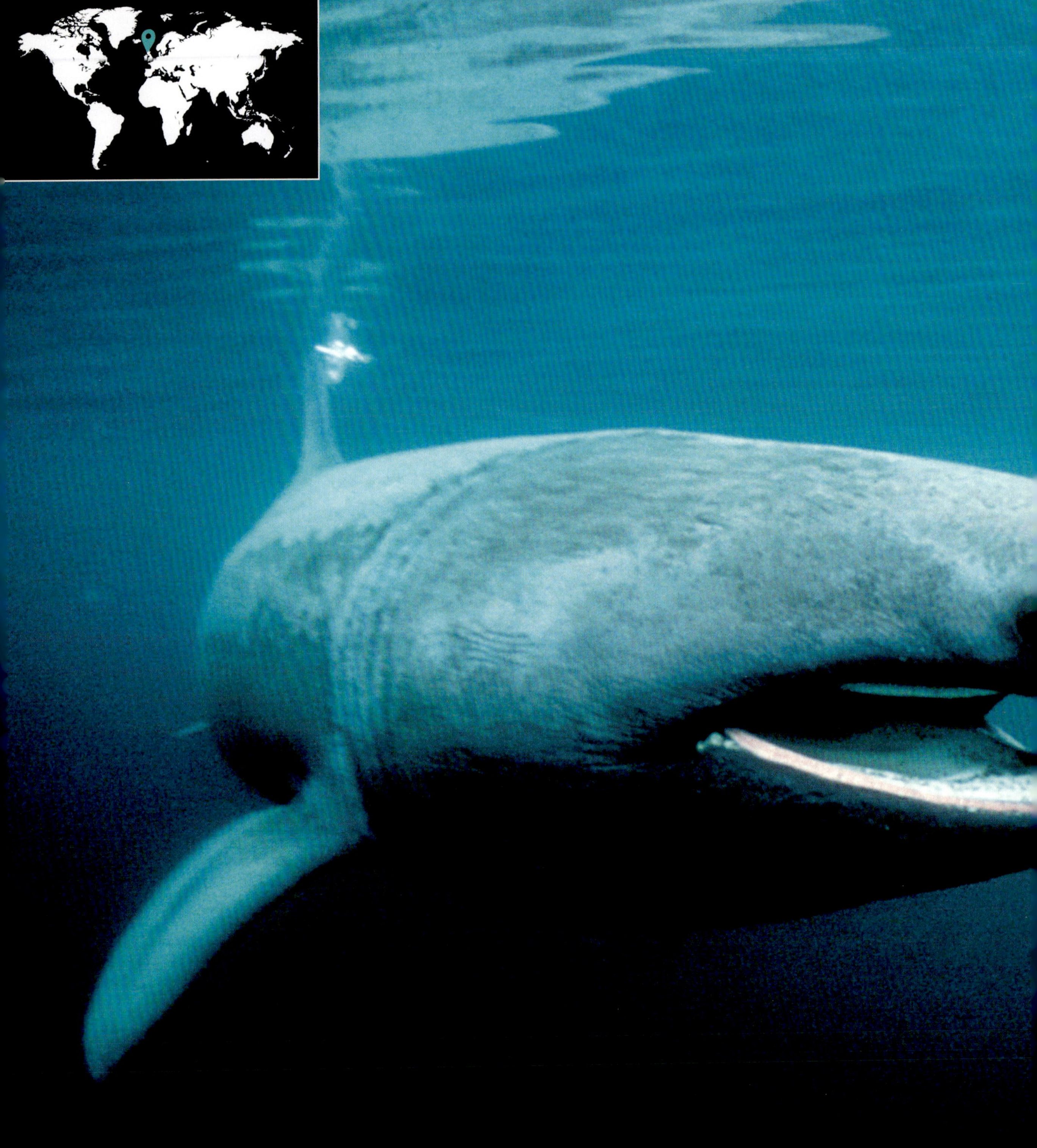

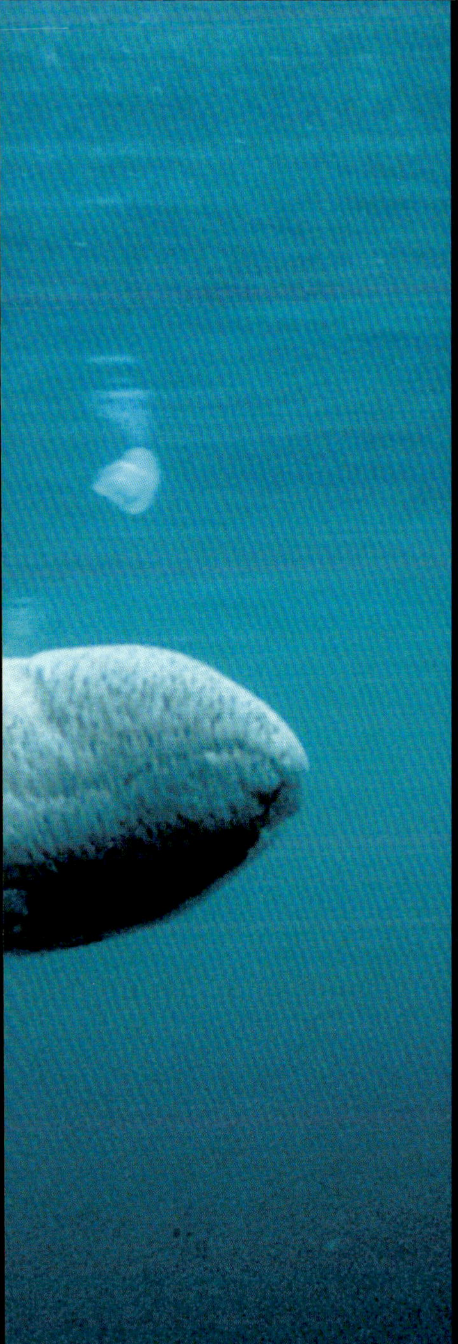

16 Sound of Mull basking sharks

Scotland

Some dive destinations are clearly specialised in diving to meet sharks: South Africa, Polynesia, Maldives, or Cocos or Guadalupe Islands, for example. Hammerhead, white, tiger, whale or blue sharks all provide unique experiences. In northern Europe, Scottish waters are also a gathering place for large sharks during the warmer months, when the waters are loaded with plankton.

In the Sound of Mull, in western Scotland, just below the surface, dark masses with gaping mouths pierce the green water. Fond of nourishing plankton, the completely harmless basking shark is nevertheless one of the most impressive, even if it is not as graceful as others. As the second-largest fish in the world, this giant remains relatively elusive. The Sound of Mull is one of the few places where you can easily observe the basking shark in its natural habitat and swim just a few metres (10 feet) away from it.

Essential info

August is considered to be the month with the greatest chance of meeting basking sharks in Scottish waters. Simply contact a centre that offers these encounters and get yourself a wetsuit, mask, snorkel and fins ready to dive. Suitable for all levels.

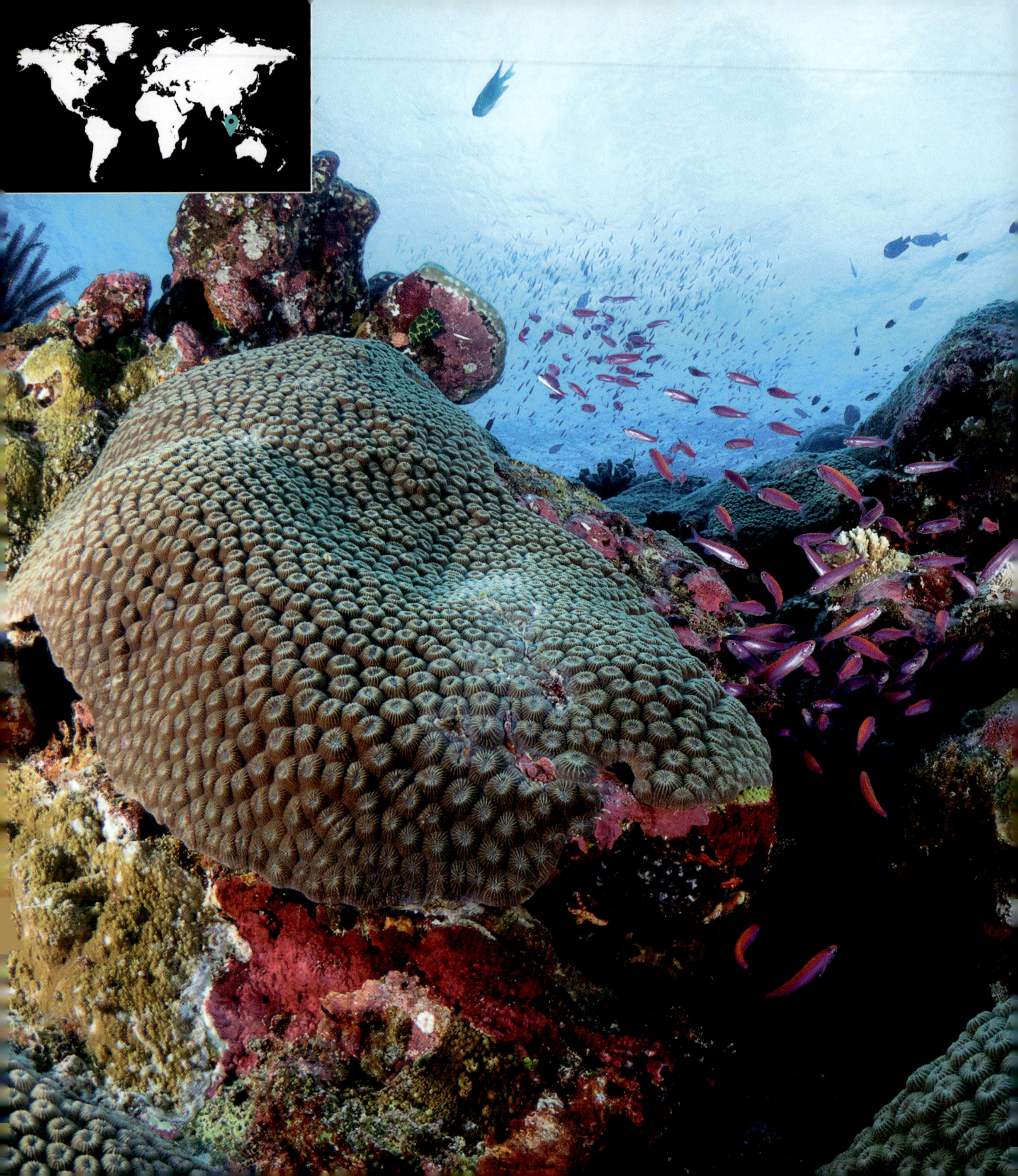

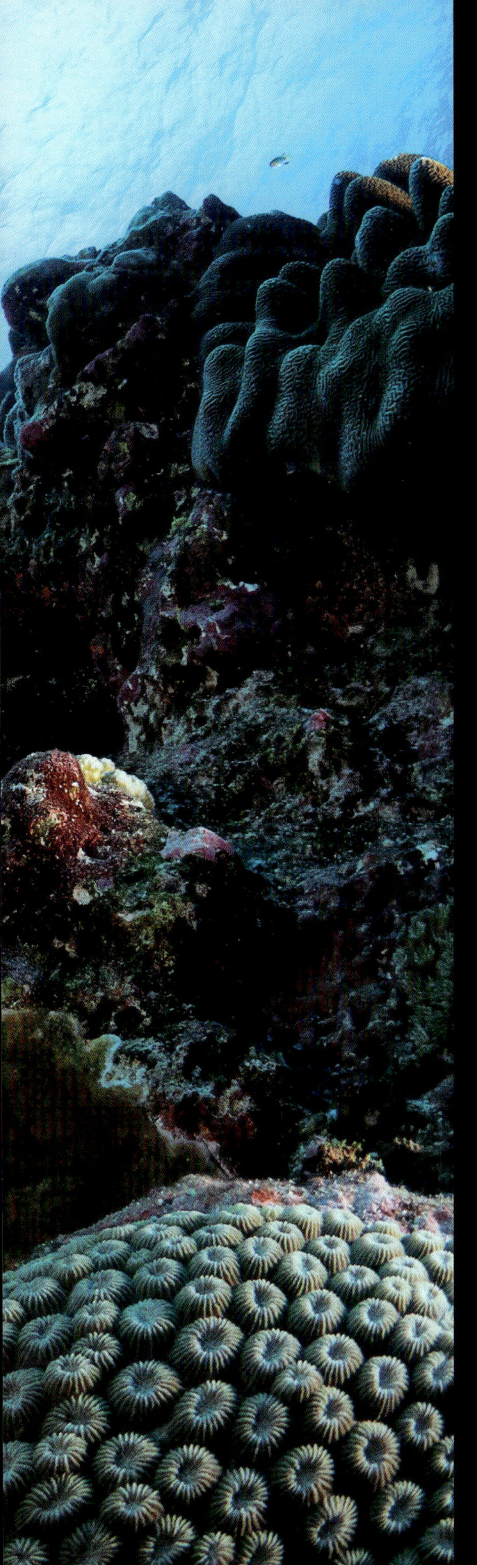

17 Christmas Island

Australia

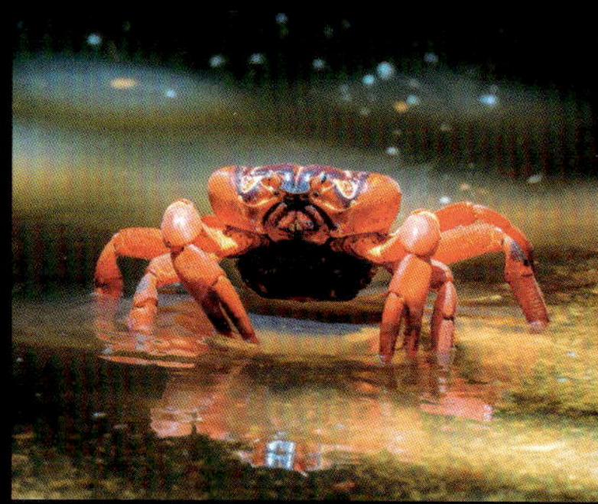

Located a few hundred kilometres (186 miles) southwest of Java, Christmas Island – also known as the 'Galápagos of the Indian Ocean' – is an Australian territory that offers a wealth of surprises, yet remains largely unknown to Europeans. Surrounded by a narrow fringing reef, which is around 20 metres (65 feet) from the shore, the island boasts stunning underwater landscapes. Divers can explore over 60 dive sites featuring steep drop-offs, vast gorgonians and impressive caves in warm, clear waters where divers enjoy breathtaking encounters with marine life.

In addition to the myriad small creatures found in the reefs, such as nudibranchs, mantis shrimp or harlequins, Christmas Island is also an excellent location for observing pelagic species. Divers can see manta rays, hunting sharks and sea turtles. Between October and April, whale sharks visit these nutrient-rich waters to feed on abundant plankton, delighting divers with their presence.

Essential info

Two-thirds of the island is designated as a national park, providing a habitat for the famous red crabs (see inset photo), known for their remarkable migration from the forest to the shore to breed. During this event, millions of crabs flood the coastline, creating an extraordinary spectacle.

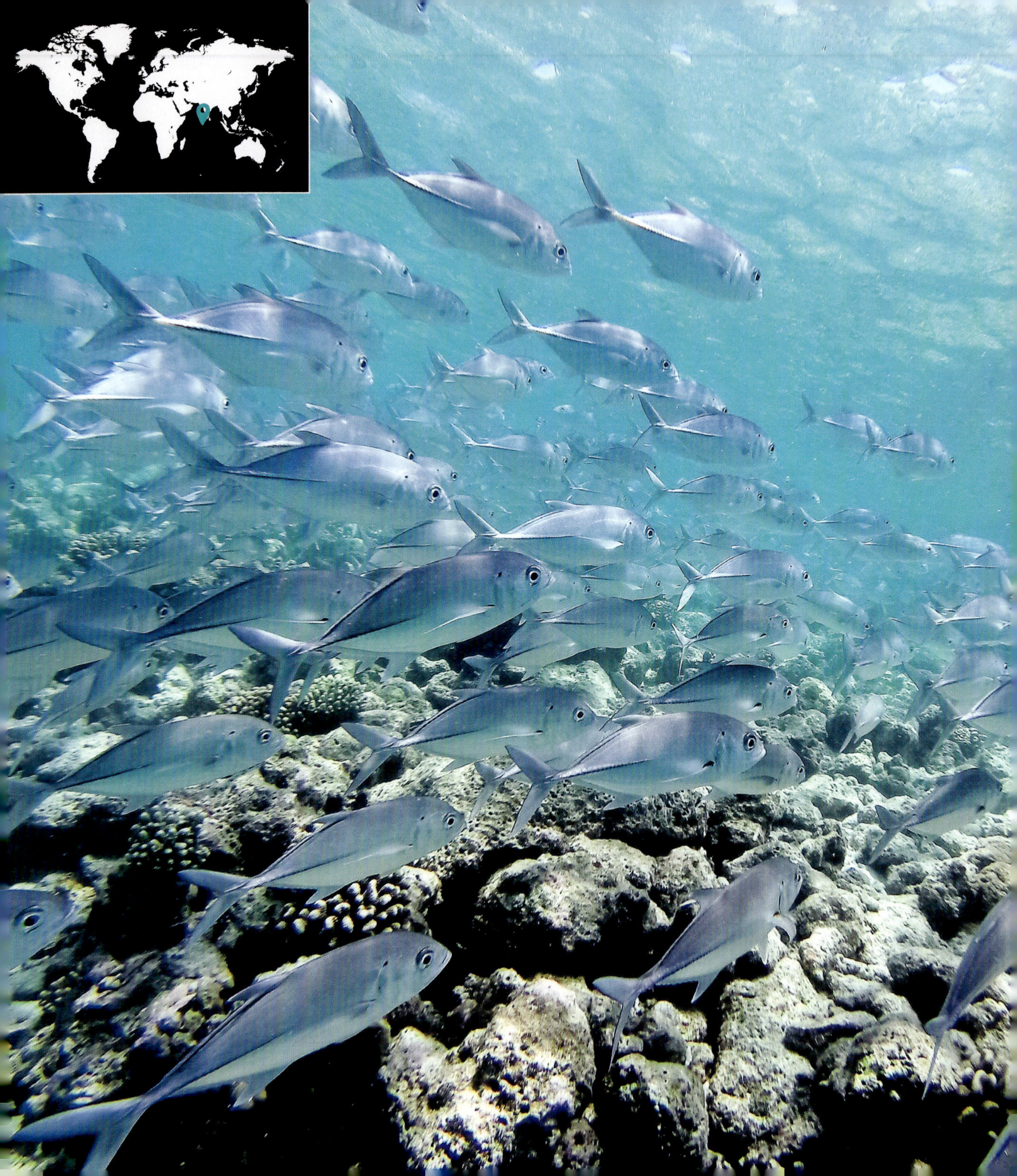

18 Alimathaa

Maldives

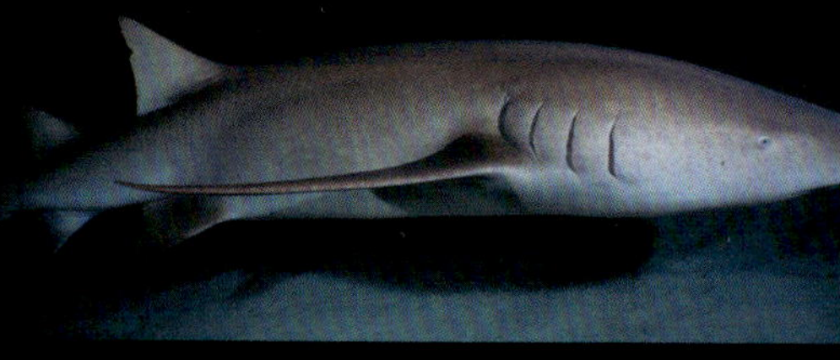

This is one of the most unusual dives in the Maldives archipelago. The islet of Alimathaa is renowned for its population of nurse sharks, which are drawn to the water by food scraps discarded by the hotel on the island. The area is well known, and divers benefit from protection throughout the year.

It's once night falls that you plunge into the darkness. Large shadows loom in the lighthouse's beam as you descend into the depths. The spectacle begins almost immediately, with nurse sharks making their entrance, closely followed by numerous sizeable stingrays and occasionally a dense school of smaller fish becomes the target for the giant trevally, and the scene unfolds in a flash, creating a brief underwater commotion.

Essential info

This night dive is relatively shallow but can be exhilarating due to the presence of these large, harmless sharks. However, do not dive without informing specialised centres and being adequately prepared.

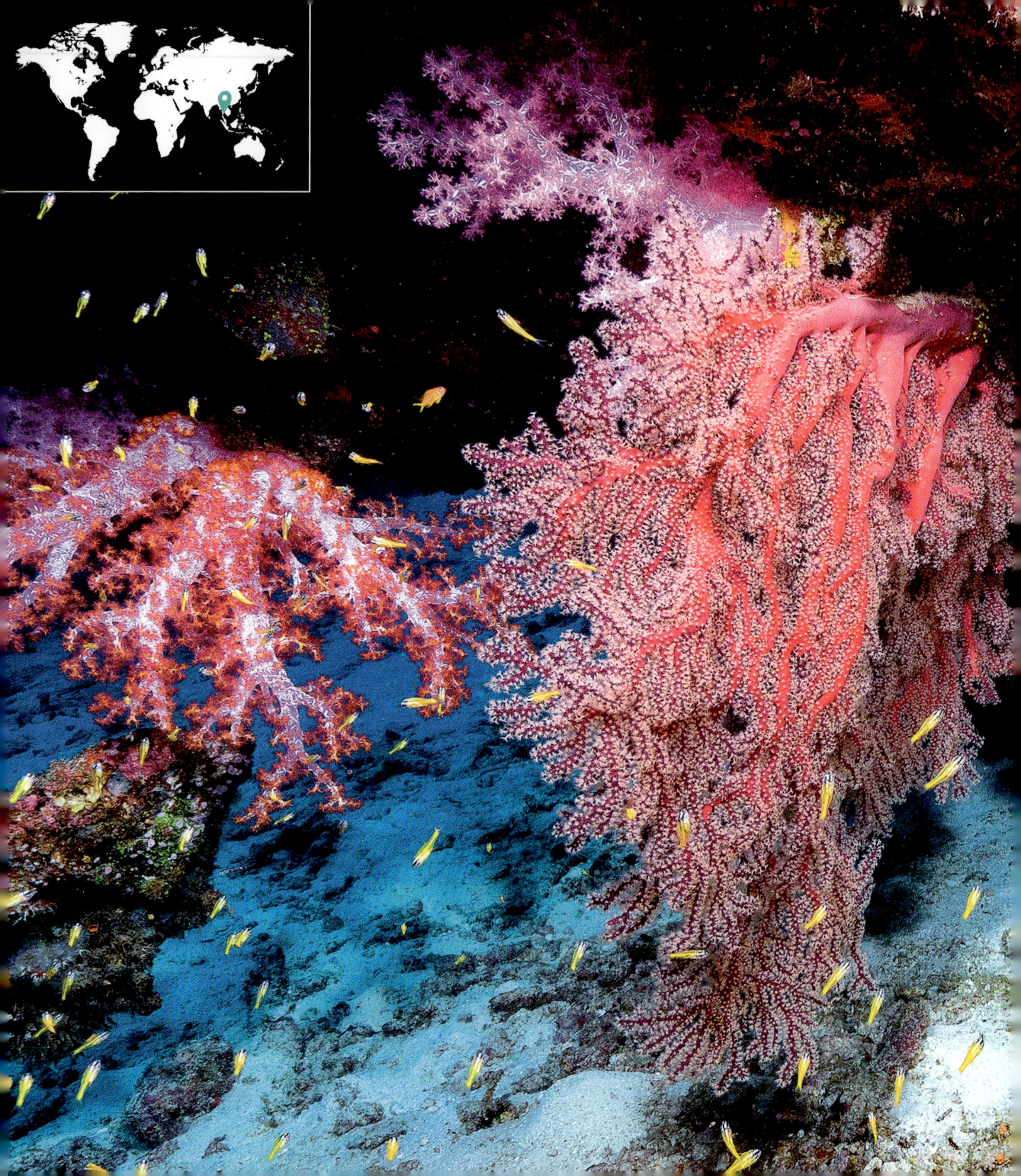

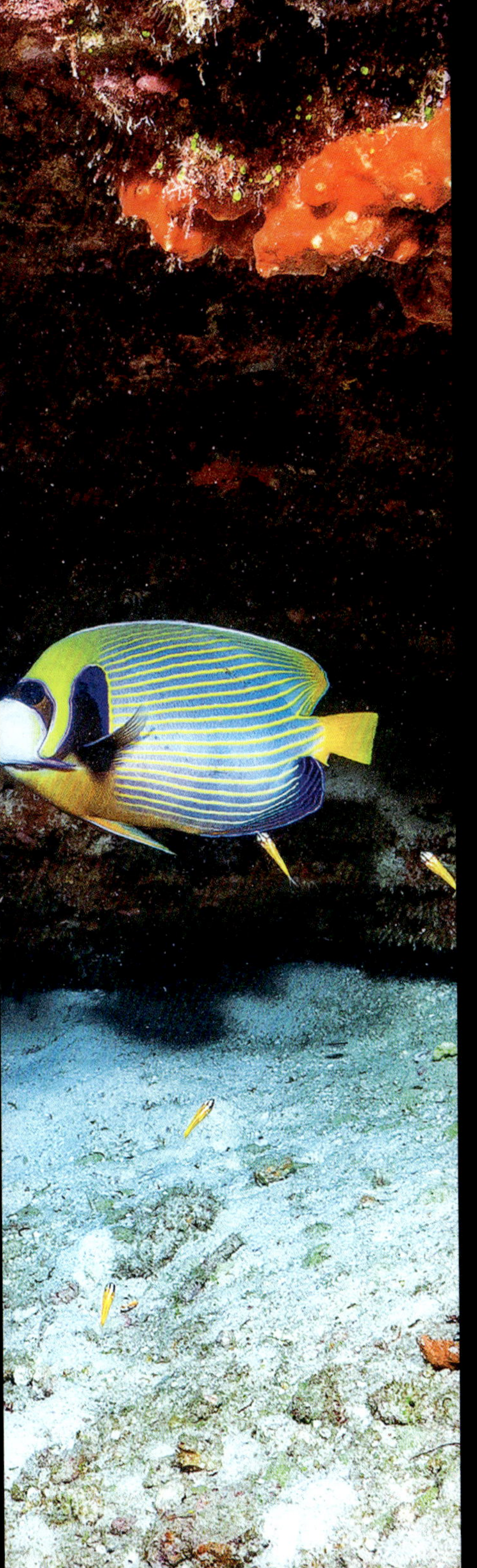

19 Similan Islands

Thailand

Located 70 kilometres (43 miles) off the coast of Phang-Nga province, the Similan Islands, a national park spanning over 140 square kilometres (87 square miles) in Thailand's Andaman Sea, are known to divers all over the world. This is where coral is most stunning, and marine life abounds, far from tourist groups.

Koh Tachai Island is renowned for the Dome, a dive site that promises to fulfil nearly every diver's wish. A true whale shark magnet, this exceptional dive site is home to a spectacular underwater reef covered with soft corals flowing alongside gorgonians and other anemones. Fine sand carpets the reef's base, and despite occasionally strong currents, divers are frequently treated to sightings of barracuda schools, manta rays twirling in breathtaking loops, curious leopard sharks and turtles gliding gracefully through the water. With an immaculate marine ecosystem and unparalleled natural beauty, the Similan Islands have rightfully earned their place as one of the world's premier diving destinations.

Essential info

The best time to dive is between November and May. February's peak current intensity draws a higher concentration of pelagic species, including whale sharks and manta rays.

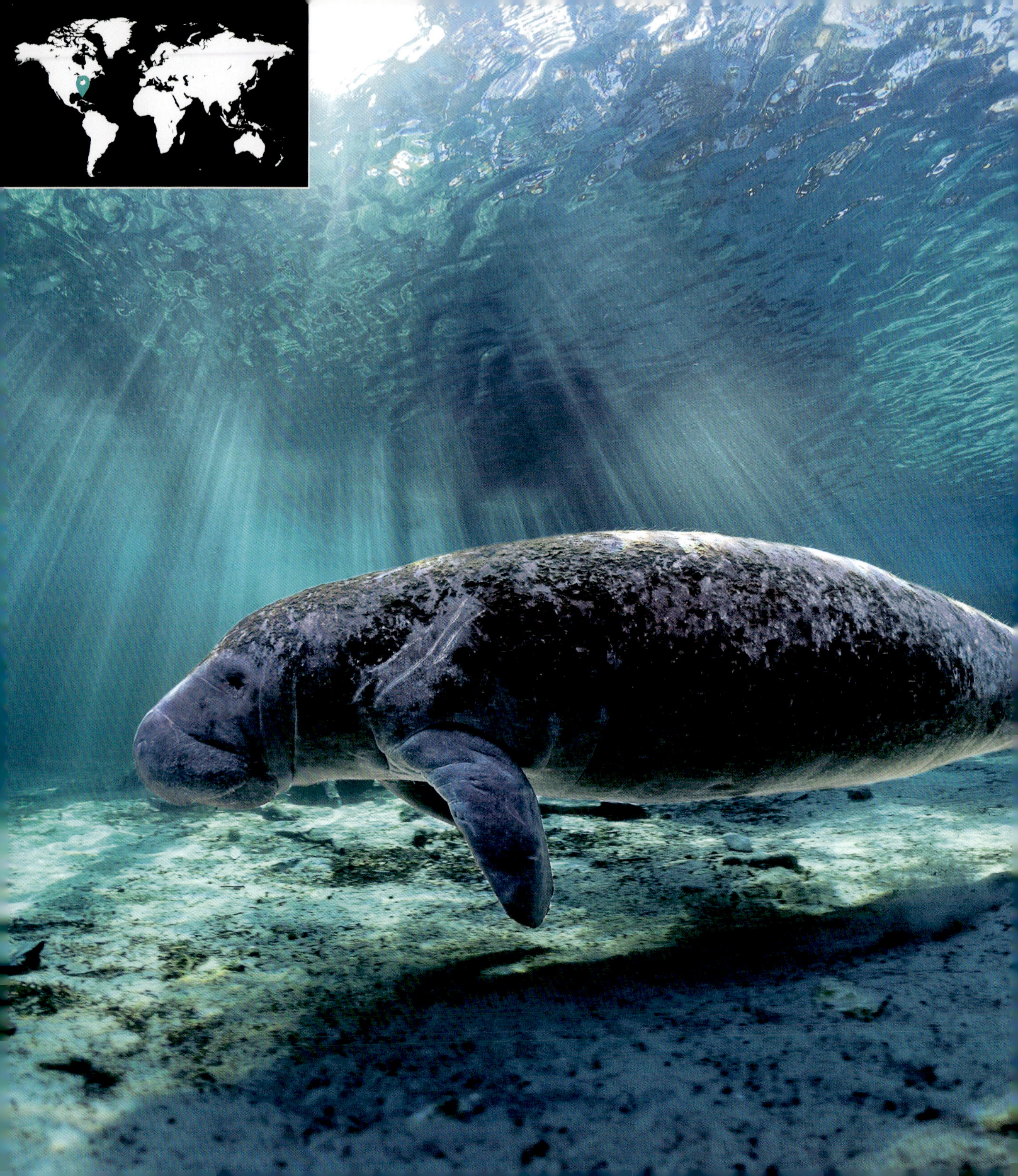

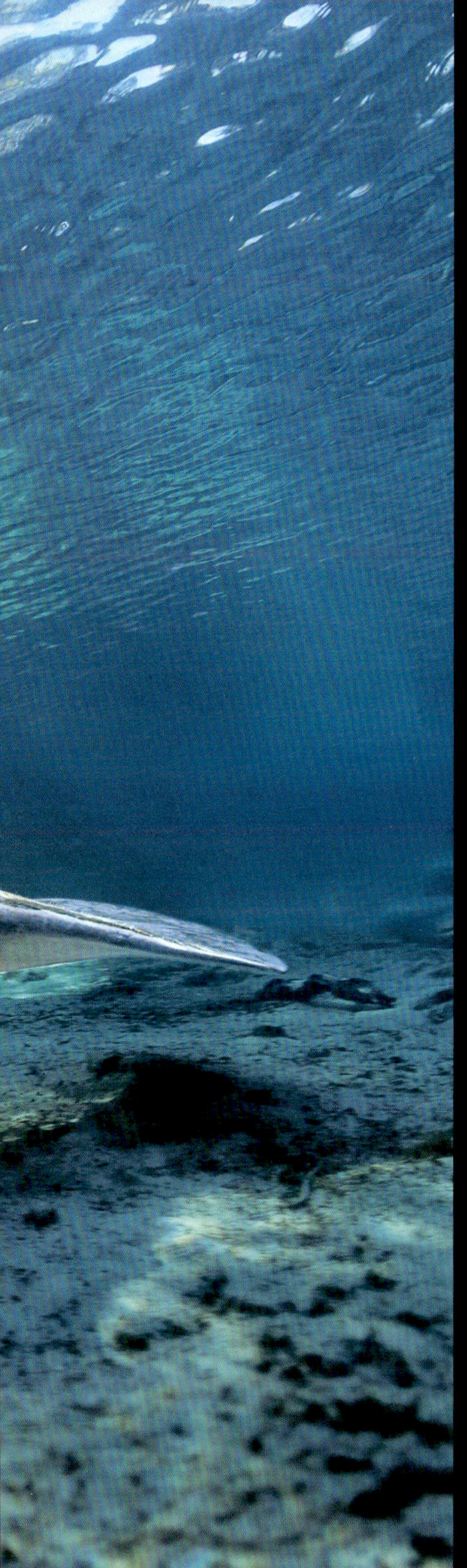

20 Crystal River

Florida, USA

Marine animals, especially mammals, have long fuelled human imagination, inspiring fables and legends. In Florida, a unique spot offers the chance to swim with creatures that inspired the myth of mermaids – the gentle manatees.

According to legend, these placid manatees are what sailors, after months at sea, mistook for half-woman, half-fish beings rising from the water. Along with dugongs, they are the only two species within the Sirenia order.

Equipped with snorkelling gear, visitors can swim in Crystal River, where large numbers of manatees gather to enjoy the warm, clear waters. By following strict guidelines to protect these highly endangered animals, swimmers can move among these 'sea cows' as they peacefully graze on seagrass. Diving here is a surreal encounter, somewhere between dream and reality.

Essential info

The best season to observe manatees in their natural environment is from mid-November to the end of March.

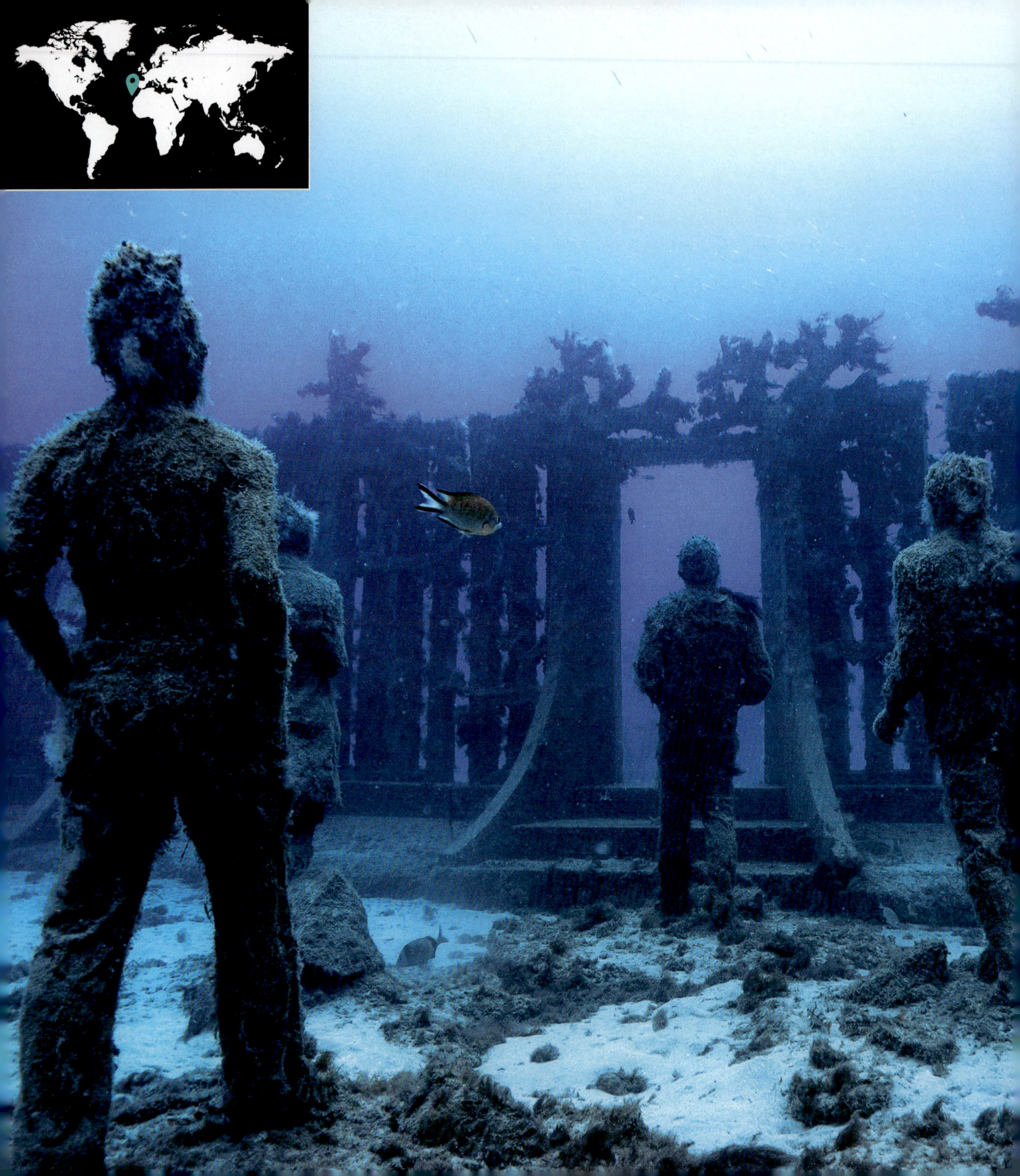

21 Museo Atlántico

Lanzarote, Canary Islands

The Canary Islands can be considered the southernmost point of Europe. This archipelago, surrounded by the waters of the Atlantic, serves as a gateway to tropical waters, where you can encounter both Mediterranean and temperate marine life. Here, parrotfish swim alongside sars and trumpet fish.

Located south of Lanzarote, known as the 'island of eternal spring', the Museo Atlántico was established in 2016 and is one of the first underwater museums in the world.

Featuring over 300 life-size cement sculptures (made with neutral pH to ensure no negative impact on the ecosystem), the statues are arranged in six groups that invite visitors to reflect on pressing issues such as climate change, the refugee crisis and our place in nature. This profound immersion offers a moving experience, allowing visitors to appreciate the intricately sculpted faces of the figures created by the artist based on real people.

Essential info

Located only a dozen or so metres (40 feet) from the shore, the museum is accessible to swimmers. At a depth of 12 metres (40 feet), it is also popular with diving centres. Accessible to all levels.

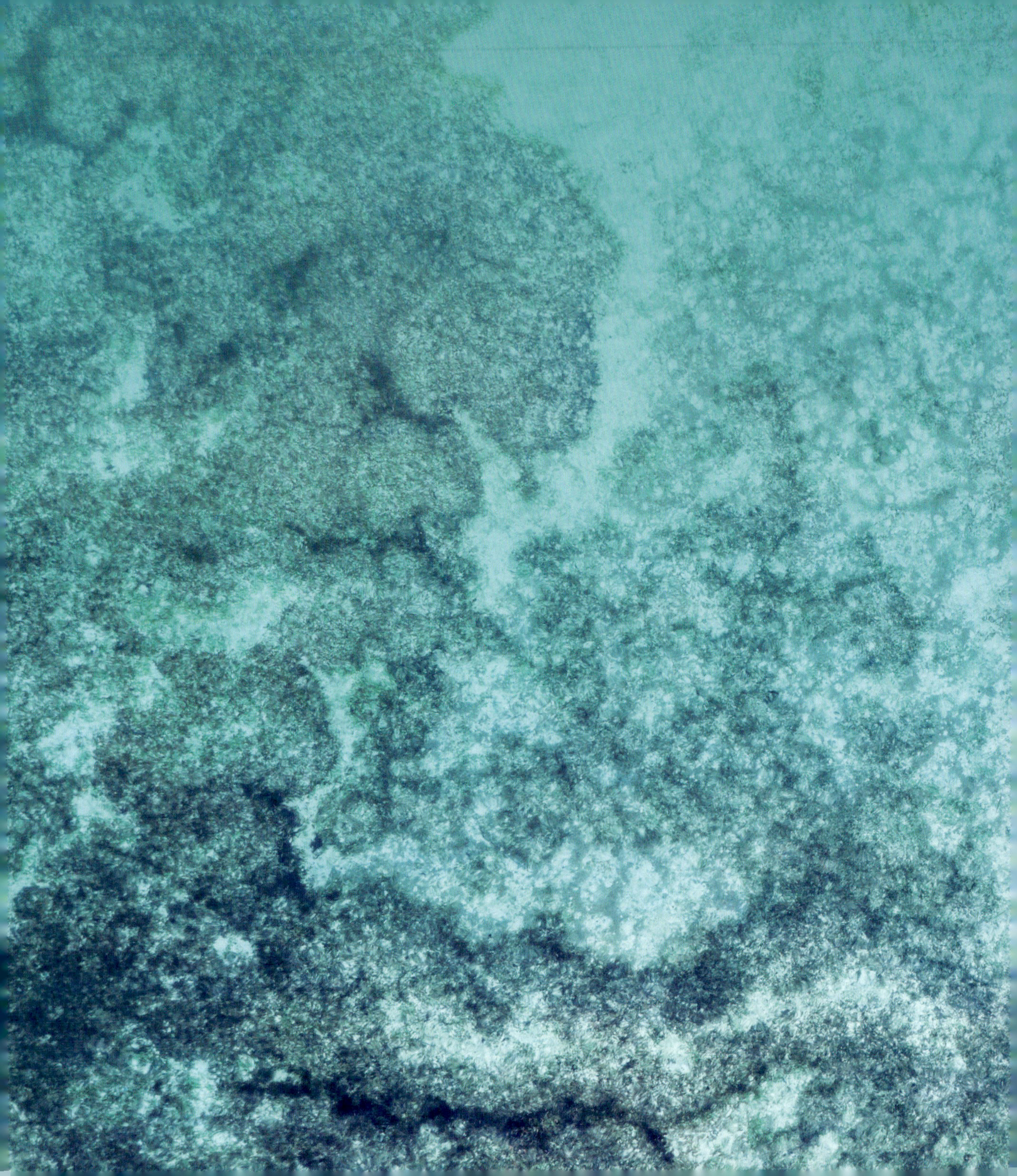

EELS: misunderstood creatures of the deep

The diversity of life and the ingenuity of nature are truly captivating. Some species evoke different feelings among divers; for instance, we admire dolphins for their apparent 'smile', even though they don't actually have one. Conversely, moray eels can instil fear in many with their long, sharp teeth and intense gaze, leading some to view them as rather menacing. But are they really that dangerous?

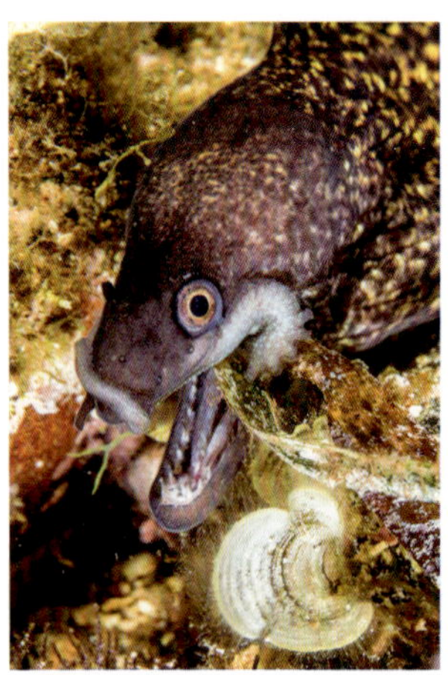
Common moray eating an octopus.

Moray eels, belonging to the family *Muraenidae* within the *Anguilliformes* order, are widespread, bony fish that primarily inhabit rocky bottoms and coral reefs filled with numerous crevices and hiding spots. They tend to spend a significant part of the day hiding from potential predators. With around 200 species worldwide, they are predominantly found in marine environments, while only a few species live in freshwater.

Two pairs of jaws

Cinema is sometimes inspired by nature. *Alien,* Ridley Scott's famous film (1979), presents a horrible creature with two pairs of jaws. Is this purely fictional? It's actually not, because this system exists in moray eels. They form 15 genera, of which the most represented, with 125 species, is *Gymnothorax*.

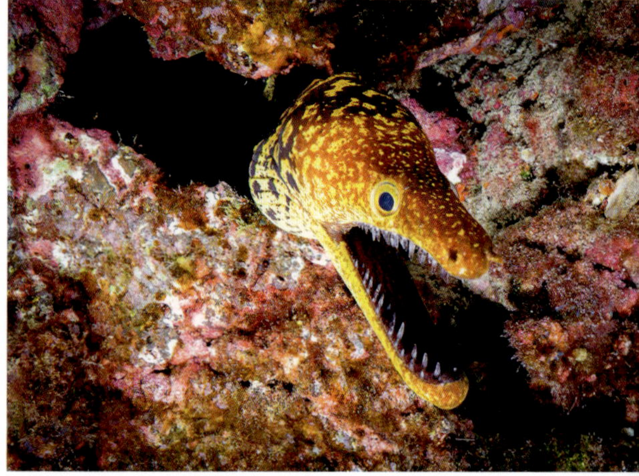
Tiger moray eel.

The primary jaws are used to securely catch their prey, the second pair, known as pharyngeal jaws, extend from the pharynx within the mouth to grip the prey and pull it back, enabling the eel to swallow it. Ingenious as they are, eels are not aggressive towards humans at all with their diet primarily consisting of fish.

Not all fish are covered with scales. This is the case for the blenny, but also for eels, which have smooth skin. This is advantageous for an animal that navigates in and out of tight spaces in search of food. As it sometimes needs to back out, scales would hinder its ability to reverse out of a hole.

Unlike other fish, they have small gills that are tucked in, requiring them to create their own current to draw in the oxygen they need while remaining motionless in their hiding spots. This is why they open and close their mouths continuously.

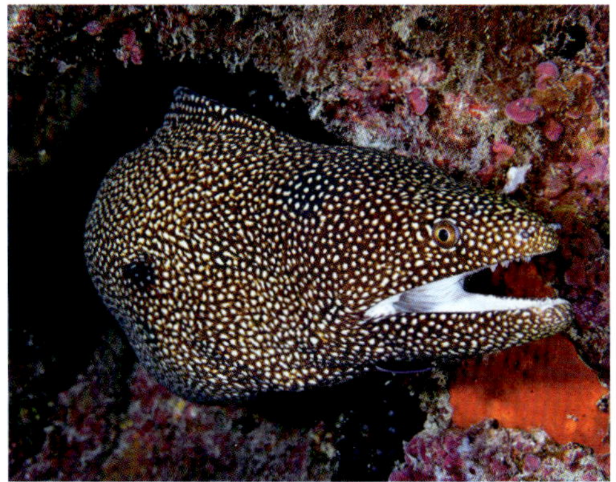

Spotted moray eel.

The sociable moray eel

It's common to see moray eels interacting with other species. For instance, they often rely on symbiotic shrimp to remove parasites, which not only provides excellent protection but also helps clean their teeth, skin and the inside of their mouths. Additionally, short-term partnerships can occur during hunting, such as with groupers. Together, these fish can hunt more efficiently in coral reefs, significantly increasing their chances of catching prey.

While morays tend to be discreet during the day, they become more active at night when they hunt. As a result, encounters with eels are more likely during night dives, as they glide along the ocean floor in search of food.

The giant moray (*Gymnothorax javanicus*) can exceed 2.5 metres (8 feet) long and weigh over 30 kilograms (66 pounds). It lives in the Red Sea, the Indian Ocean and the Indo-Pacific. It's not the longest, but is by far the most impressive species.

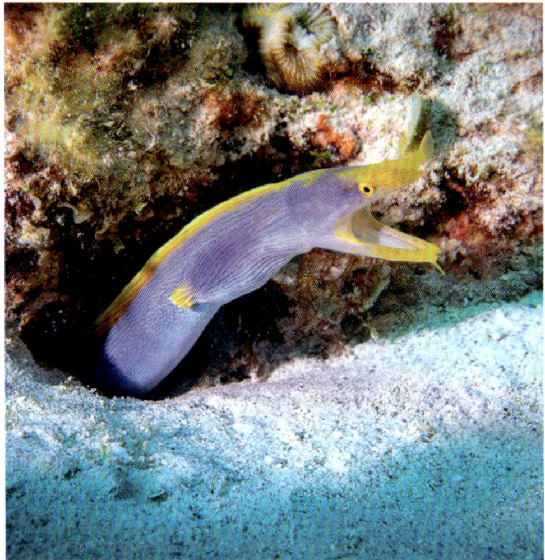

Ribbon moray eel.

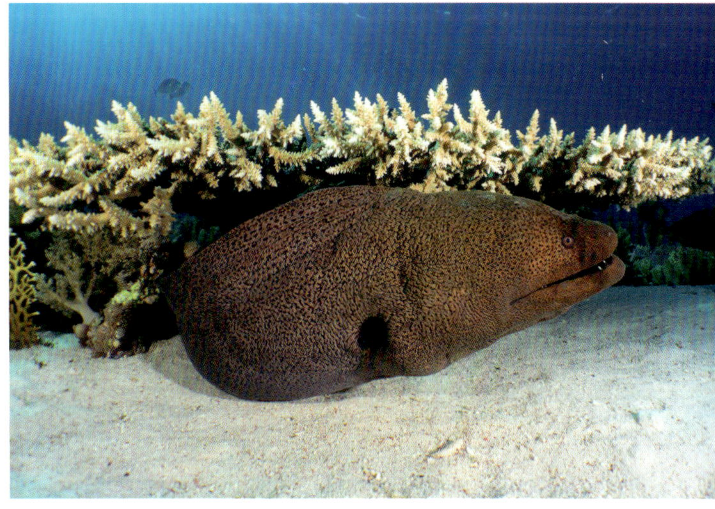

A giant moray eel in the Red Sea.

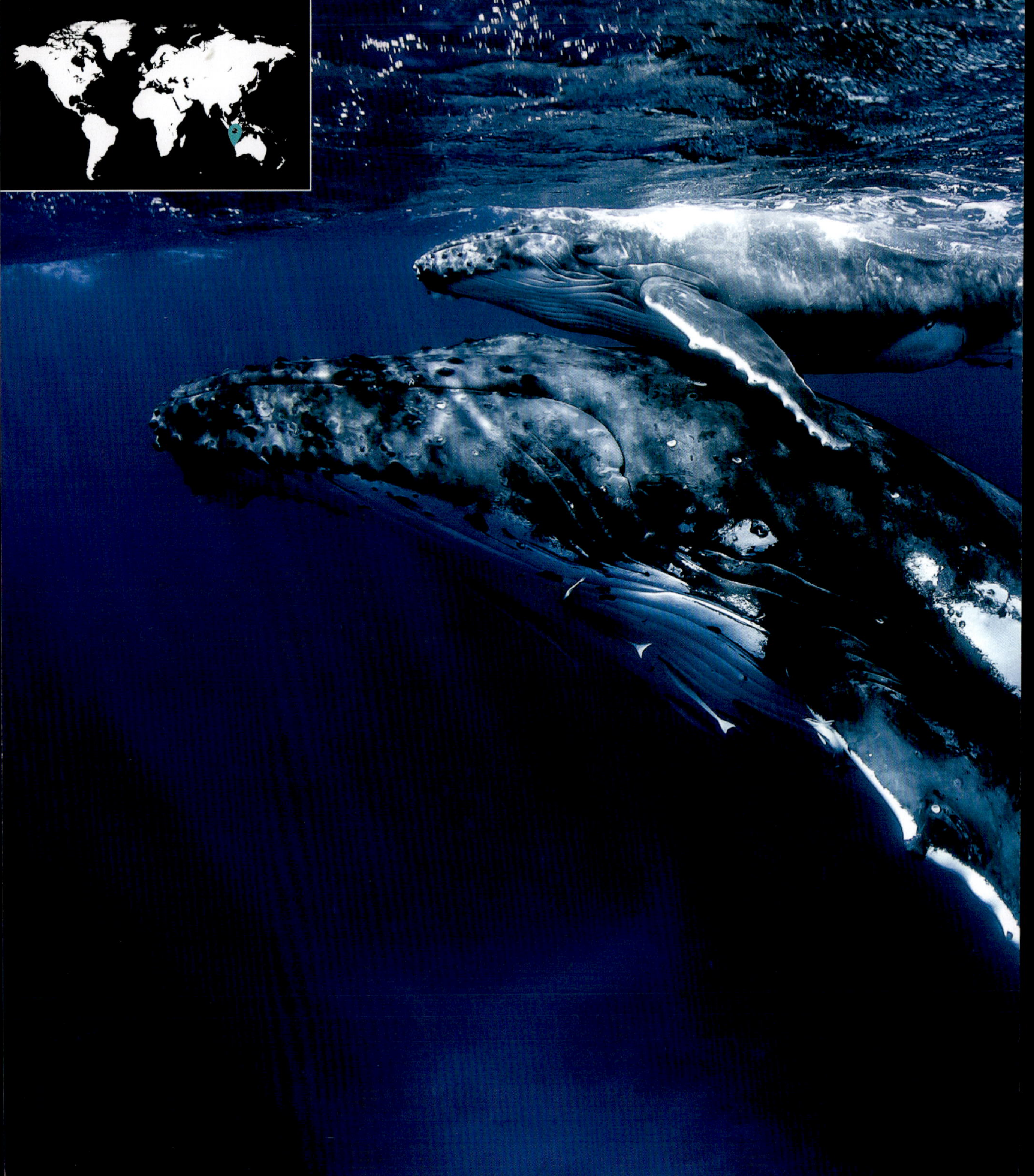

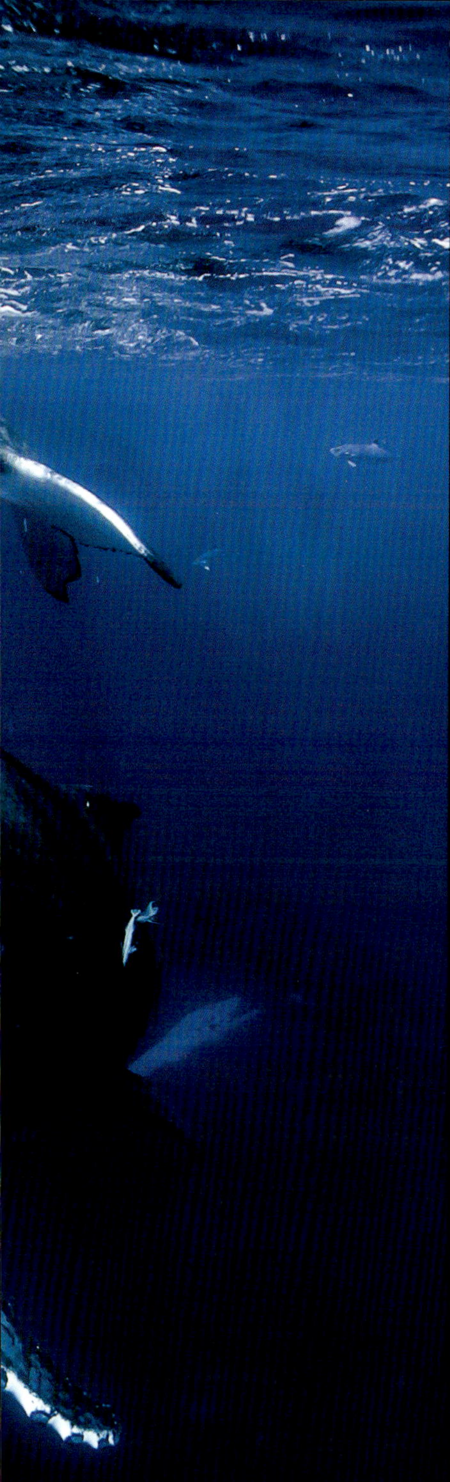

22 Ningaloo Reef

Australia

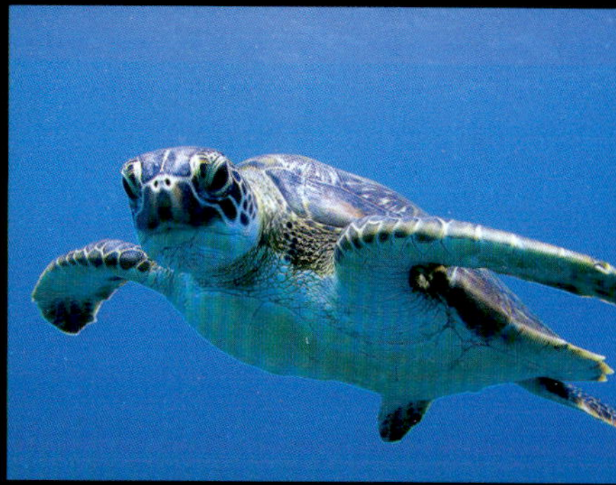

Far from the bustling Great Barrier Reef and its often-overcrowded coastlines, Australia's west coast is wilder and more remote, offering a chance to connect with nature in peaceful surroundings.

Approximately 1,200 kilometres (745 miles) north of Perth, the Ningaloo Reef is a vast fringing reef nearly 300 kilometres (186 miles) long. The quality of diving and snorkelling, along with the incredible marine encounters, has earned this location a world-renowned reputation. It has been a UNESCO World Heritage Site since 2011. The waters are home to an impressive diversity of life, with over 250 species of corals, 700 species of fish and 14 species of marine mammals, including dolphins, turtles, dugongs, orcas and various whales, along with an abundance of vibrantly coloured tropical fish. From March to July, whale sharks gather along Ningaloo Reef, while the annual migration of humpback whales occurs from July to October (see photo). Manta rays are present throughout the year.

Essential info

Ningaloo Reef is accessible to divers of all skill levels, allowing snorkellers or experienced divers to enjoy this location to the fullest.

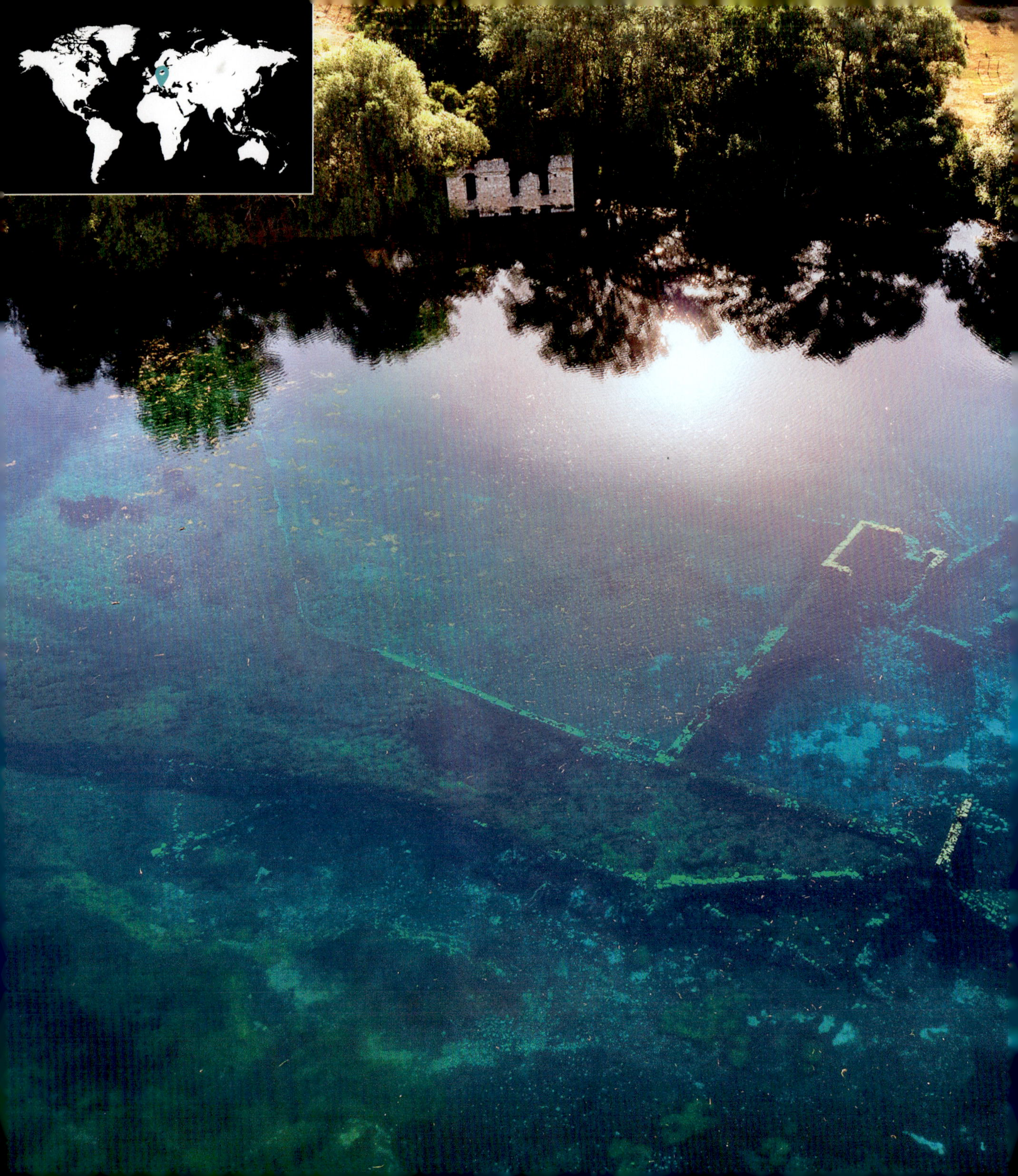

23 Lake Capodacqua

Italy

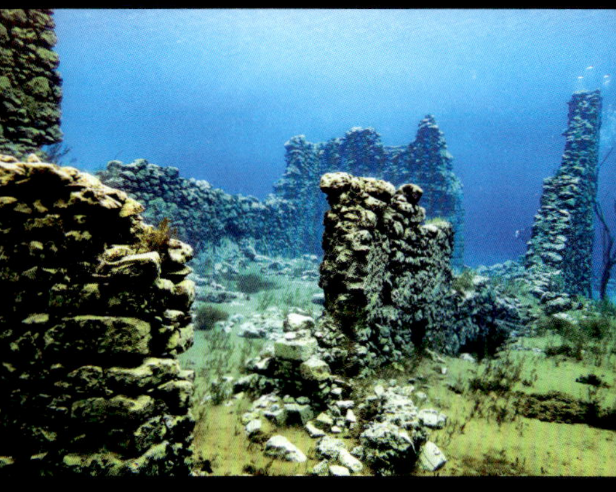

Some of Earth's bodies of water hide unexpected landscapes that are the result of ancient human activity. For divers, this usually means exploring imposing wrecks, often the remnants of tragic shipwrecks. However, in the central region of Italy, a small lake within the Gran Sasso e Monti della Laga National Park is home to medieval structures. During this period, two mills and a paint factory were constructed near alpine springs.

In the 1950s, to facilitate irrigation for the surrounding agricultural land, the valley was artificially flooded, submerging these medieval remains.

While the factory remained above water, the two mills now lie approximately nine metres (29 feet) below the surface. Today, divers are attracted by the lake's crystal-clear waters that provide incredible visibility, and a memorable journey through time.

Essential info

The remains are shallow enough to be visible from the surface and are therefore accessible by swimmers as well.

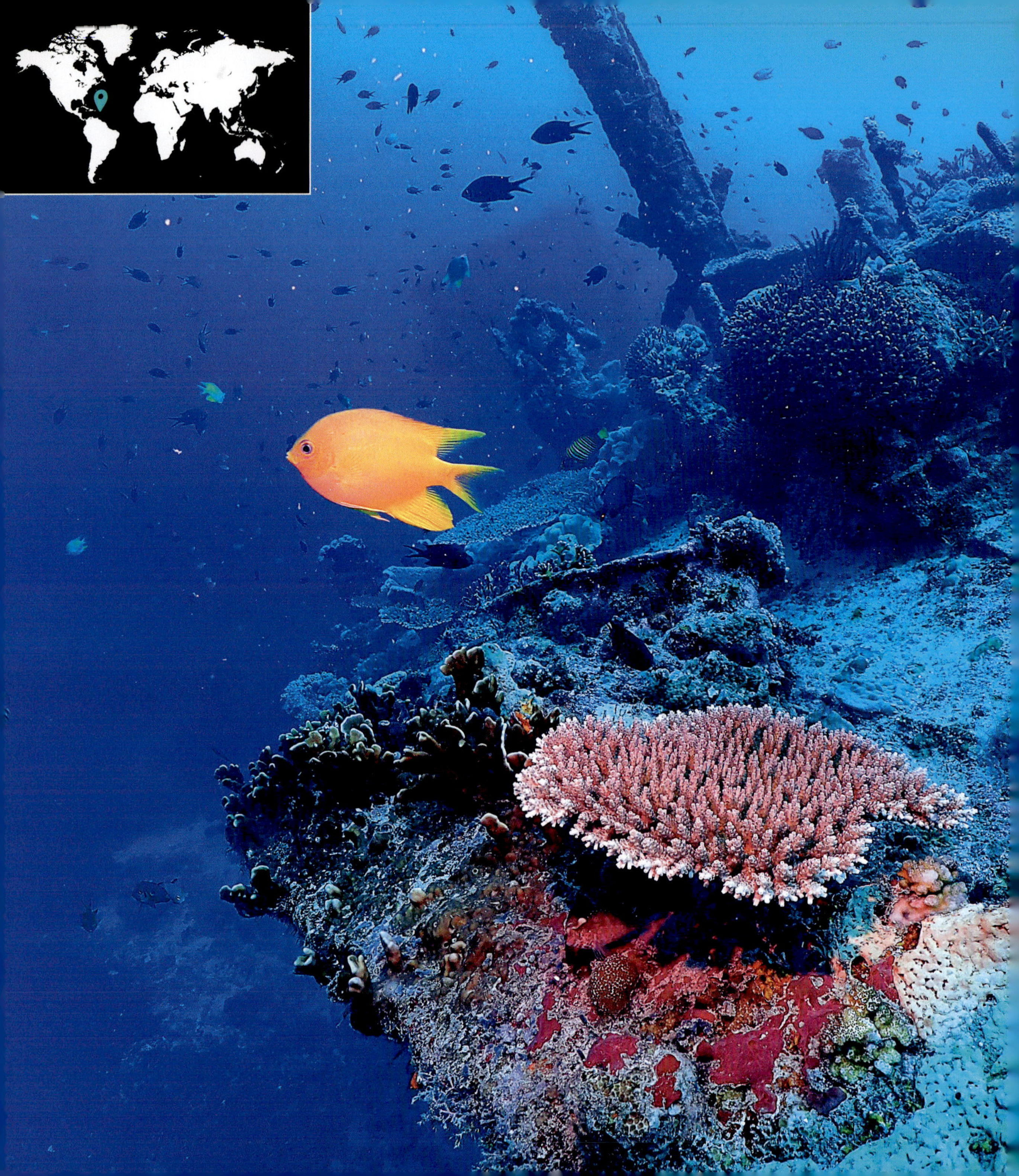

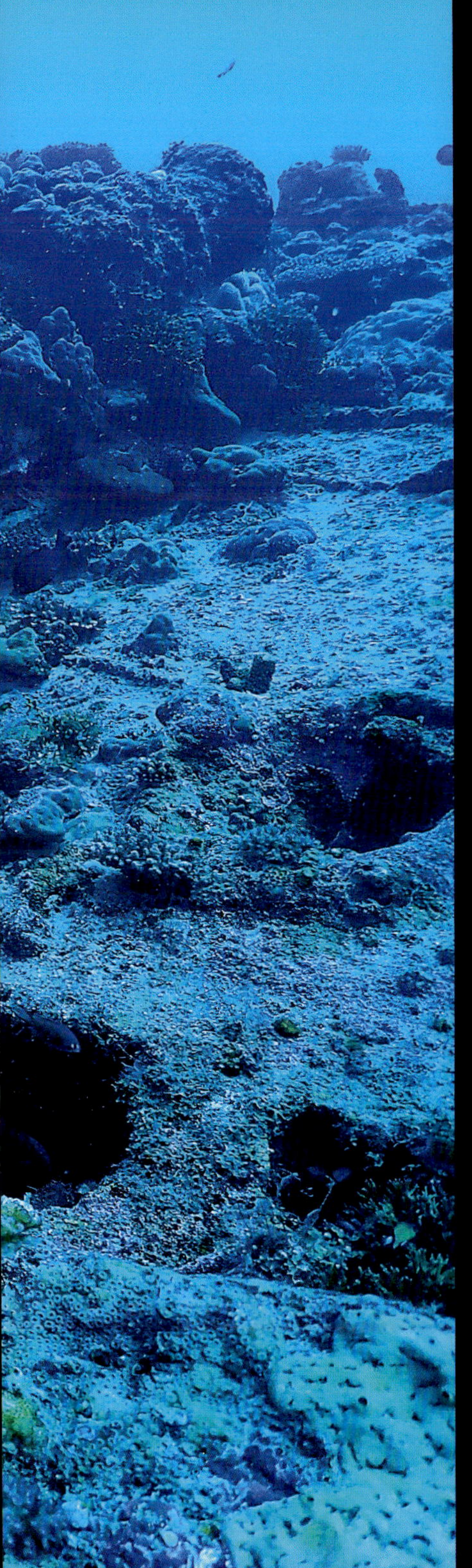

24 Cousteau Reserve

Guadeloupe, French Antilles

Nestled in the heart of the Caribbean arc, which separates the Caribbean Sea from the Atlantic Ocean, the archipelago of Guadeloupe resembles a butterfly and boasts seabeds that attract divers and snorkellers eager to encounter magnificent green turtles.

It was along the west coast, near Malendure, that Commander Cousteau explored the underwater wonders of these French islands in the 1970s. Enchanted by the breathtaking beauty, he advocated for the preservation of these waters, leading to the establishment of the Cousteau Reserve. Within this protected area, you'll discover some of the island's most stunning dive sites, offering something for everyone. From vibrant reefs and coral gardens adorned with massive sponges typical of the Caribbean, to intriguing shipwrecks, each dive is a colourful adventure. Experience the thrill of encountering a rich array of marine life, including tropical fish like angelfish and butterflyfish, along with barracudas, striking lobsters, majestic eels and turtles.

Essential info

Pigeon Island in the Cousteau Reserve is ideal for snorkelling. Knowing how to swim is the only prerequisite.

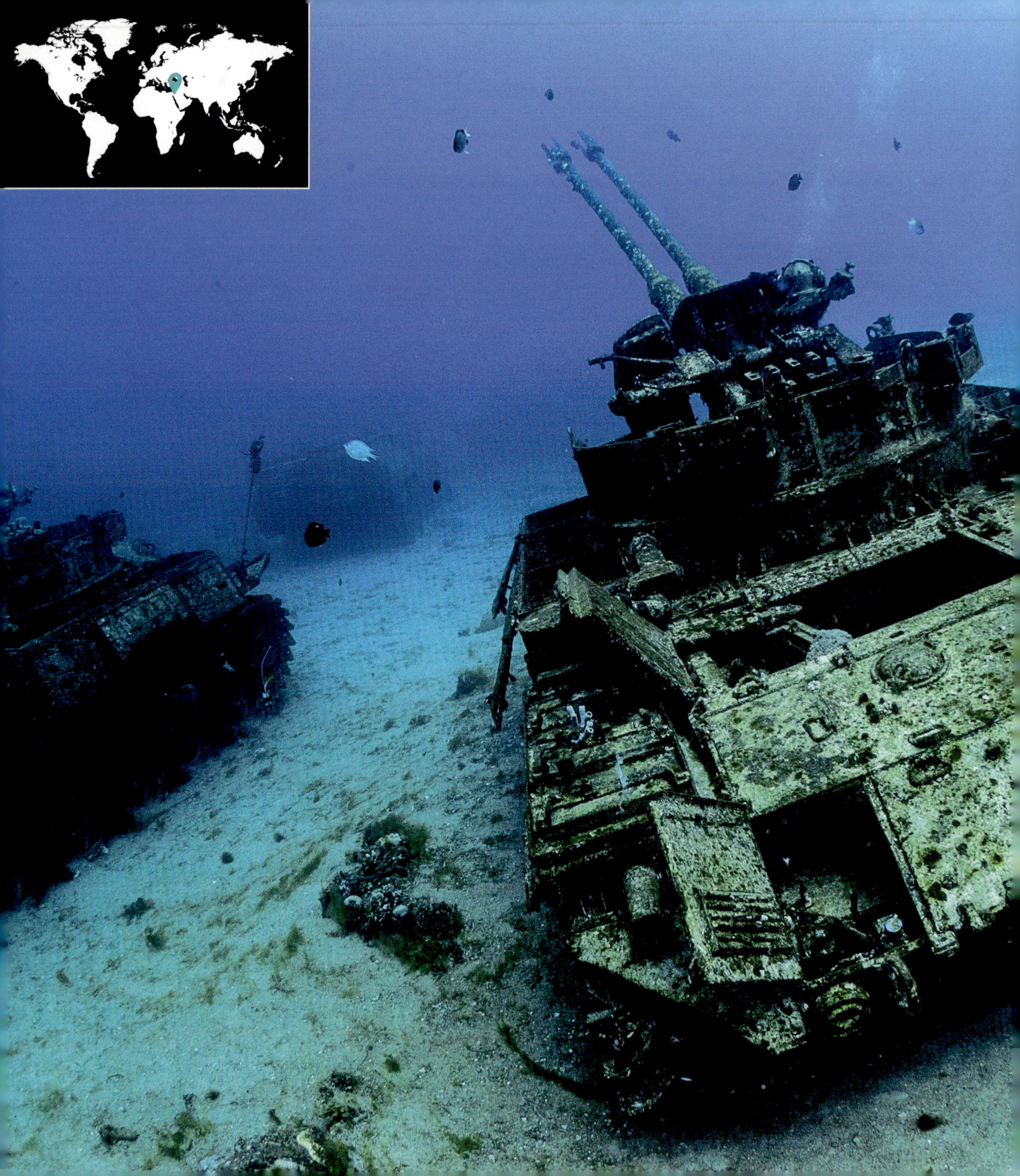

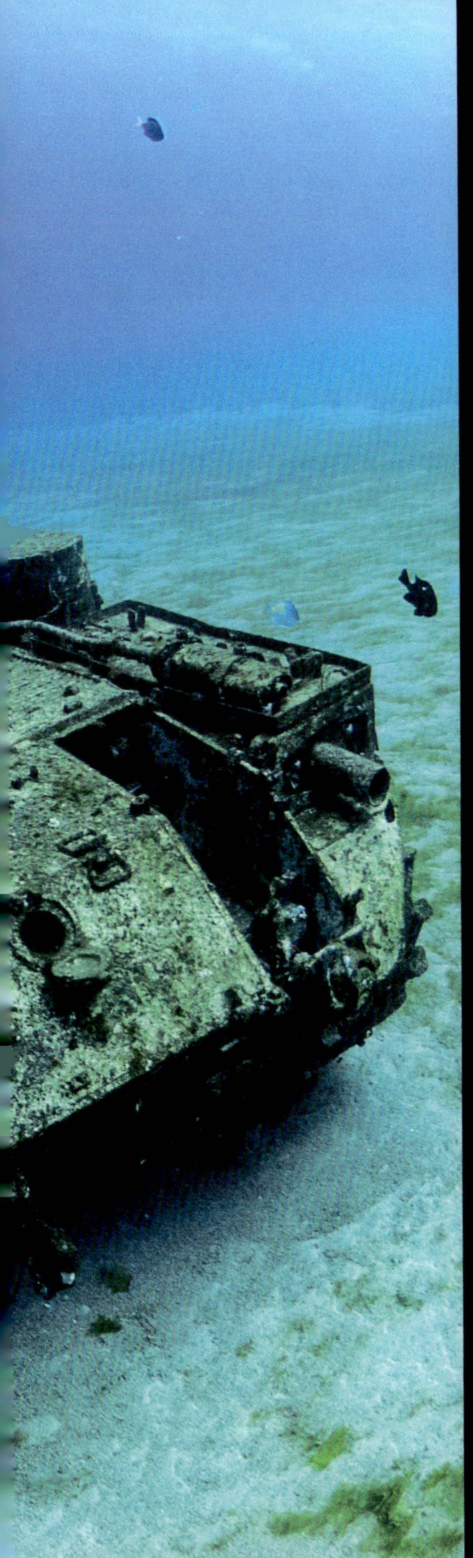

25 Underwater military museum

Aqaba, Jordan

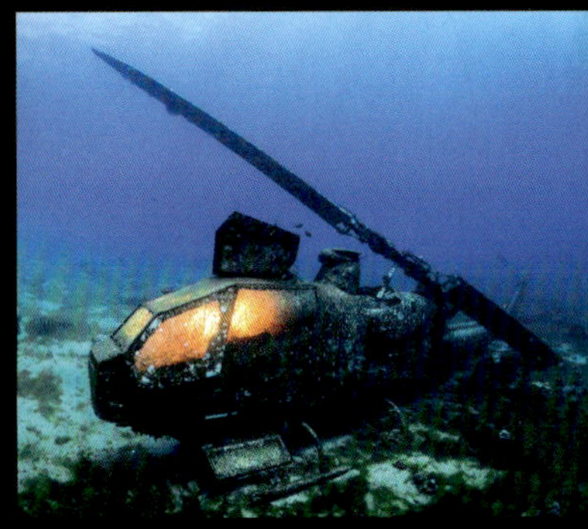

Jordan truly maximises its 27 kilometres (17 miles) of stunning coastline along the Red Sea and the Gulf of Aqaba. Under the leadership of King Abdullah II, a passionate scuba diver, the country has channelled substantial resources into attracting divers from around the globe.

The creation of the Aqaba Underwater Military Museum in 2019 – one of a kind in the world – reflects this commitment. This extraordinary site features no fewer than 19 military aircraft arranged in tactical formation, along with two jeeps positioned just metres from the beach. Here, combat helicopters, tanks, anti-aircraft guns, ambulances and troop carriers create a surreal underwater landscape. For a moment, you might even imagine these relics coming to life beneath the surface.

Essential info

With a maximum depth of 27 metres (88 feet), this dive site is accessible to all divers and even snorkellers will enjoy the shallower areas – the jeeps are just five metres (16 feet) from the surface.

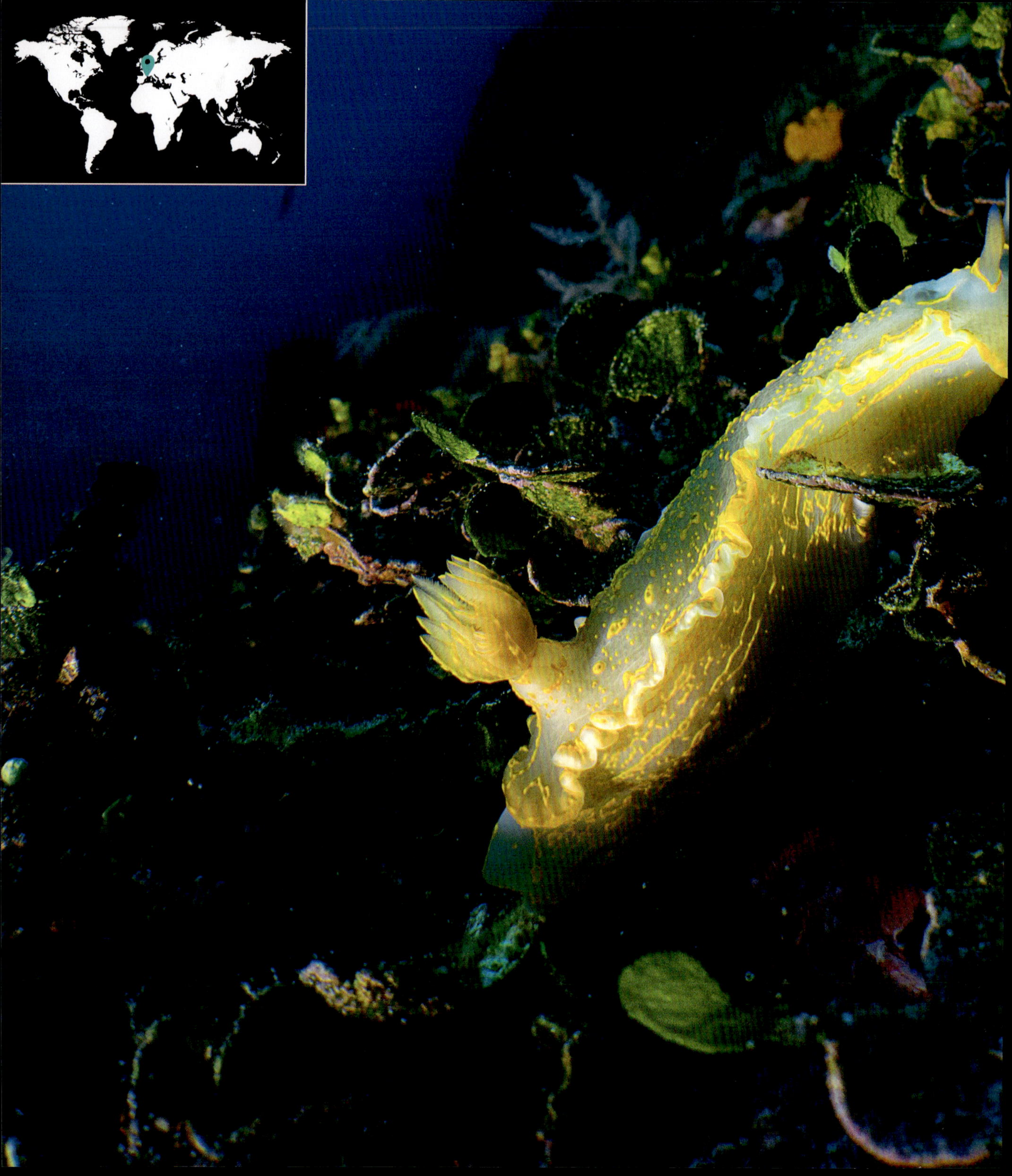

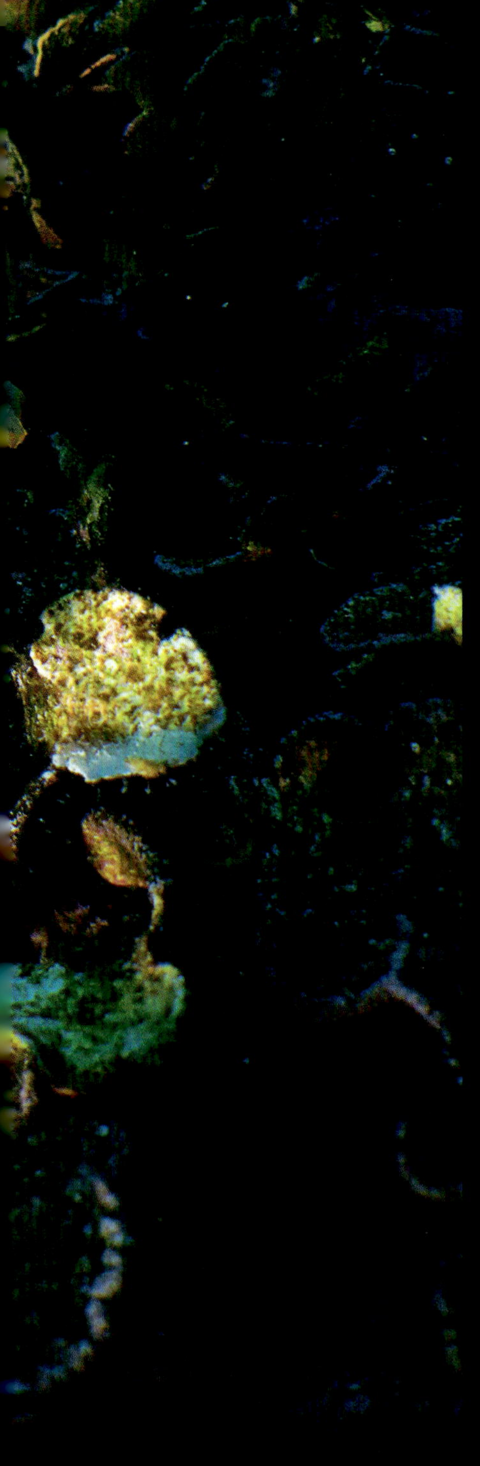

26 The Calanque of Figuerolles

La Ciotat, Bouches-du-Rhône, France

The French Mediterranean coasts are home to some truly amazing sites, and for those willing to put in the effort to seek them out, it's well worth it. This is the ideal spot for a relaxed, independent dive with friends.

Just east of Marseille, in the charming seaside town of La Ciotat, the Calanque of Figuerolles is a hidden gem that walkers enjoy visiting year-round. After descending 87 steps to reach the small pebble beach, dive gear in hand, you're rewarded with the pleasure of taking in the breathtaking beauty of this unique setting. Framed by towering cliffs, this sheltered natural pool is a paradise for enthusiasts of Mediterranean marine life. Heading out of the cove to the right, you'll discover a striking crevice teeming with a diverse array of species – from bright red coral and delicate nudibranchs to other transparent shrimp.

Essential info

Suitable for divers of all levels, the inside of the cove is easy to manage and only reaches a depth of 18 metres (59 feet). Beyond this, depths range from 25 to 28 metres (82 to 91 feet). However, diving independently here is not to be taken lightly. It's best to stick to familiar sites, dive in favourable weather, maintain a reasonable depth, and, most importantly, know your limits to avoid unnecessary risks.

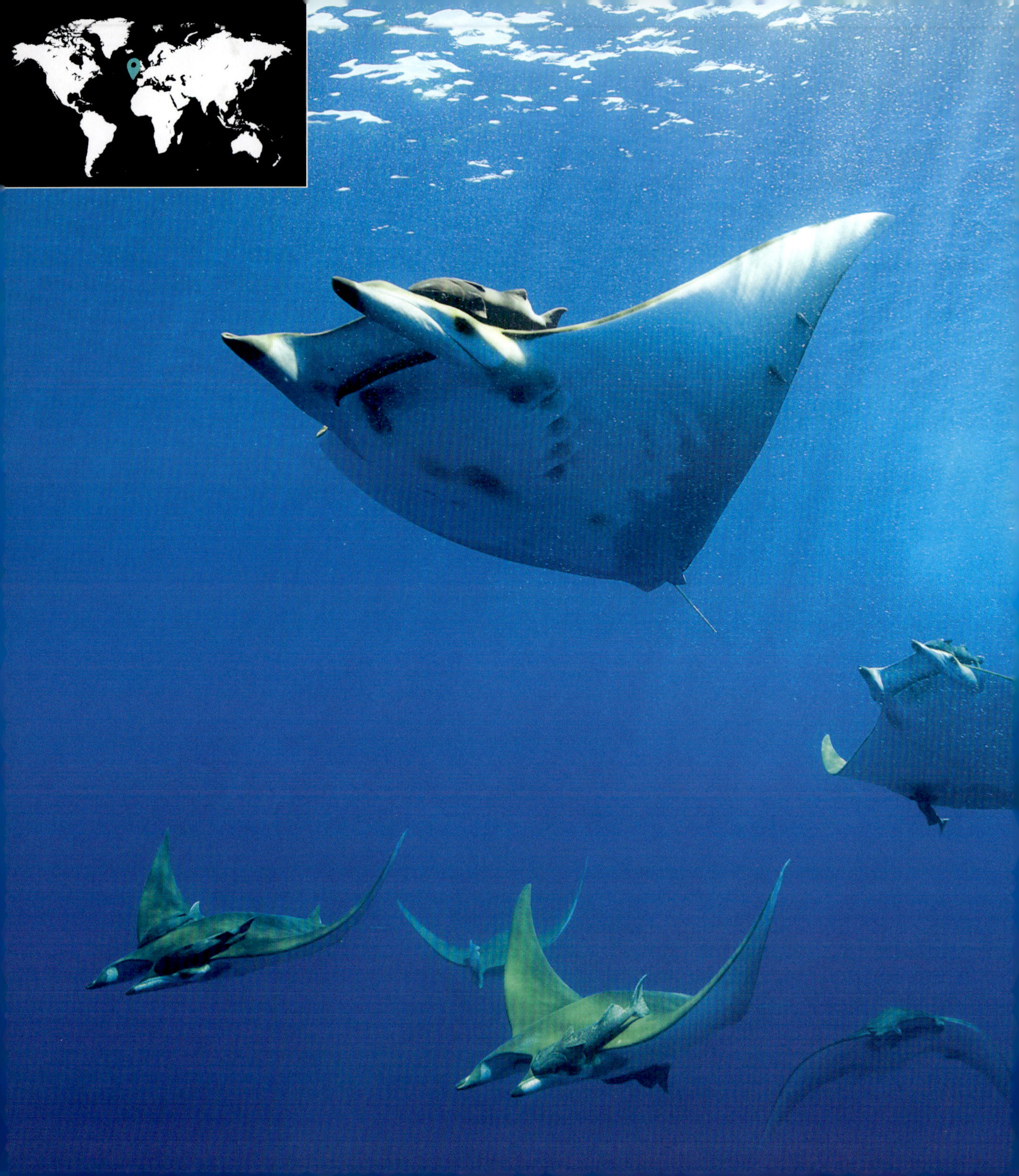

27 Princess Alice Bank

Azores, Portugal

Located 1,300 kilometres (807 miles) off the coast of Portugal, nearly in the heart of the Atlantic Ocean, the Azores archipelago and its nine volcanic islands rise from the vast sea, resembling Noah's Ark both above and below the surface – an oasis in the midst of the ocean's expanse. The favourable climate of these lush green islands nurtures a bountiful nature, making them an ideal destination for those looking to fully recharge their batteries.

Between the Pico and Faial islands lies Princess Alice Bank, a seamount that extends to a depth of around 35 metres (114 feet). It is one of the most stunning and impressive dive sites in the Atlantic.

Only experienced divers can access this remarkable location, where the summit of this geological formation presents a spectacular show featuring a variety of pelagic species. Ocean manta rays, mobula rays, tunas, greater amberjacks and Galápagos sharks are regular visitors to this underwater mountain, which was first studied in 1896 during the oceanographic expedition of Prince Albert of Monaco aboard his ship – aptly named *Princess Alice*.

Essential info

Deep-sea enthusiasts can dive to encounter blue sharks at Mount Condor, accessible from Faial and Pico.

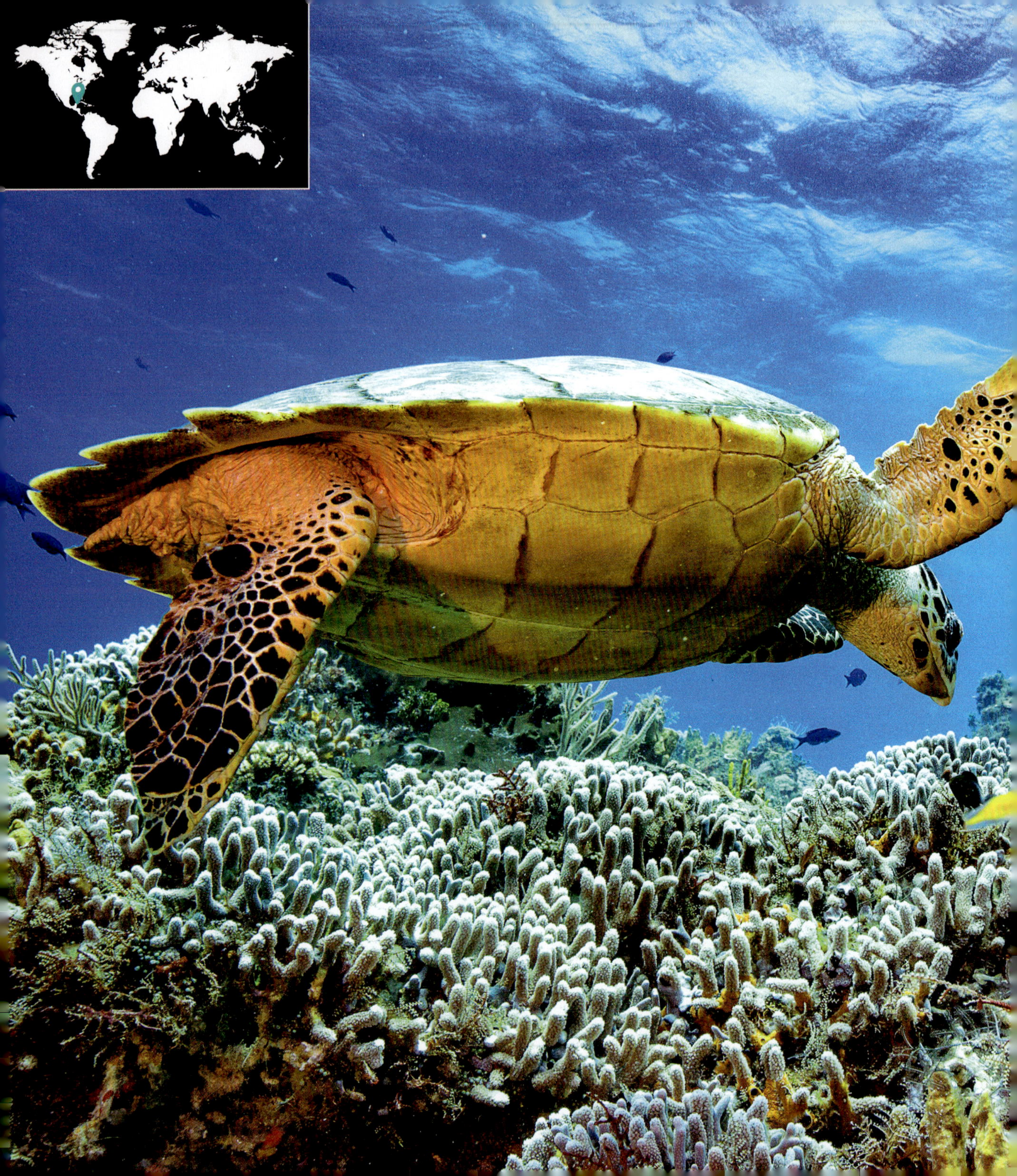

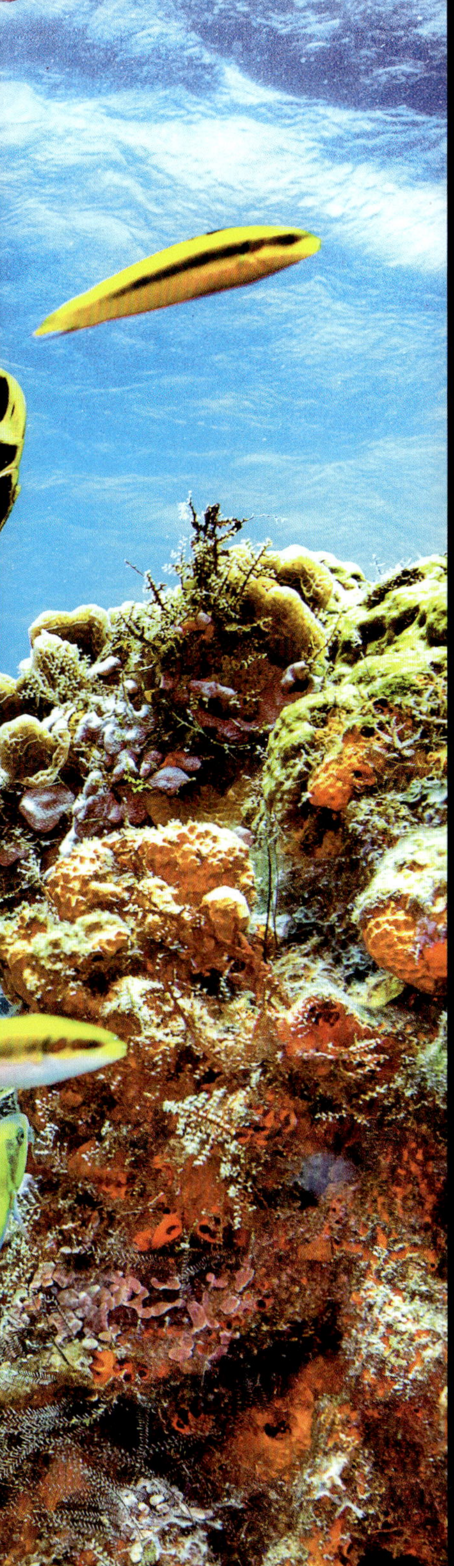

28 Cozumel

Mexico

For many years now, Mexico has positioned itself as a top destination for scuba diving enthusiasts. The Yucatán region is one of the most interesting in the world. It offers a stunning array of underwater encounters and types of dives, as well as rich cultural experiences like exploring ancient Mayan temples.

Off the vibrant shores of Playa del Carmen, Cozumel Island was described by Jacques Cousteau as one of the finest diving locations worldwide. Most dives here are drift dives, allowing divers to glide over drop-offs and reef flats. The crystal-clear waters of these breathtaking reefs are dotted with massive, colourful sponges and teeming with an array of Caribbean marine life. Divers can expect to encounter turtles, schools of red snapper, eagle rays, angelfish, groupers and eels. The seabed is particularly photogenic, making it a paradise for underwater photographers. Look out for the discreet reef toadfish (*Sanopus splendidus*), an endemic species that thrives in these waters.

Essential info

Cozumel offers numerous drift diving opportunities, often accompanied by strong currents. It's essential for divers to master stabilisation techniques to fully enjoy the experience.

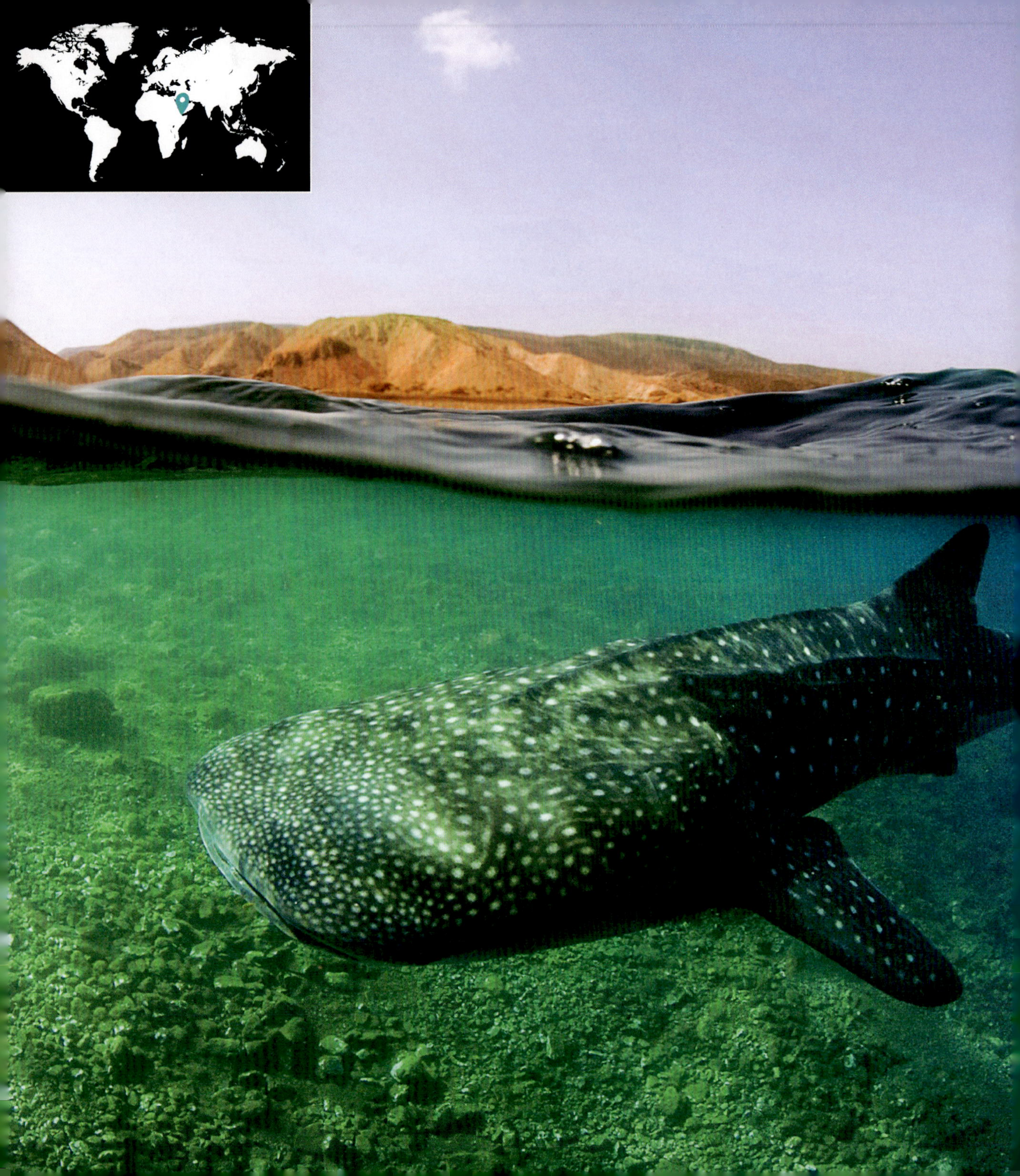

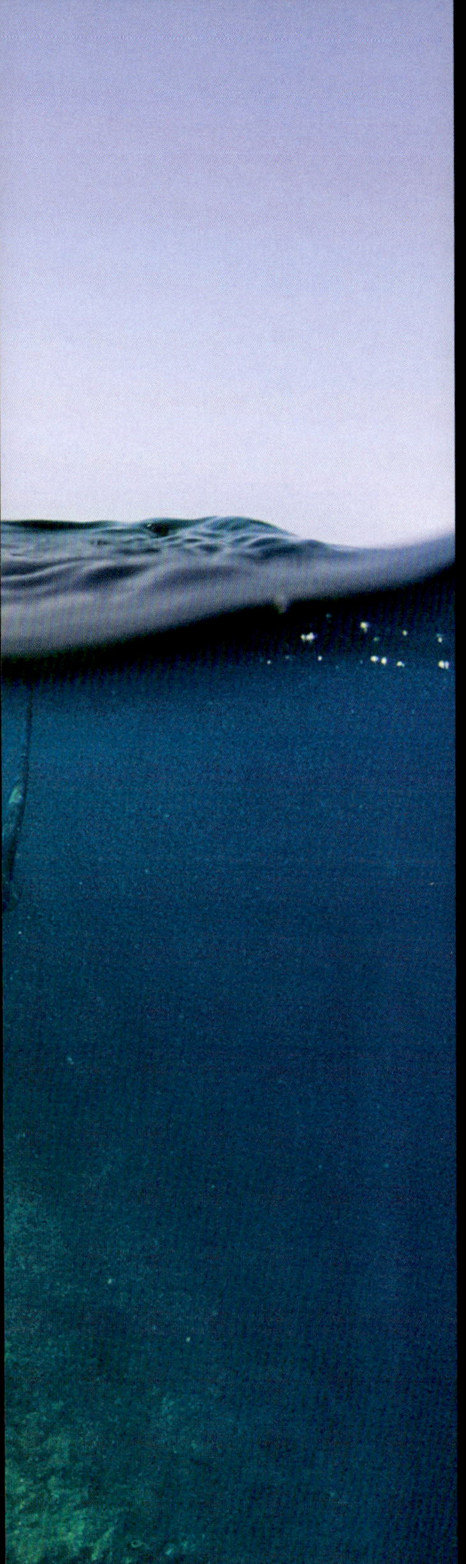

29 Gulf of Tadjourah whale sharks

Djibouti

For several years, adventurer, writer and arms merchant Henry de Monfreid frequented the stunning landscapes of Djibouti, passionately detailing his experiences in *Secrets of the Red Sea*. This unique location serves as a gateway between the clear waters of the Red Sea and those of the more vibrant and nutrient-rich Gulf of Aden. The Gulf of Tadjourah extends deep into the heart of the country, and from October to February each year, it welcomes a remarkable influx of whale sharks that gather in its tranquil, plankton-rich waters.

These gentle giants, mostly young specimens measuring between four and six metres (13 and 20 feet) long, may be joined by larger individuals. Snorkelling is the primary way to encounter these (small) giants, requiring minimal effort to observe them in their natural habitat. You might find yourself amidst a bustling highway of whale sharks, needing to navigate around these magnificent creatures, so get ready for an unforgettable adrenaline rush.

Essential info

This dive must be supervised by professionals and remains reserved for experienced divers. Scuba divers can continue with their stay in the Seven Brothers Islands, an archipelago world-renowned for the quality of its dives. On land, a visit to Lake Assal is a must-do.

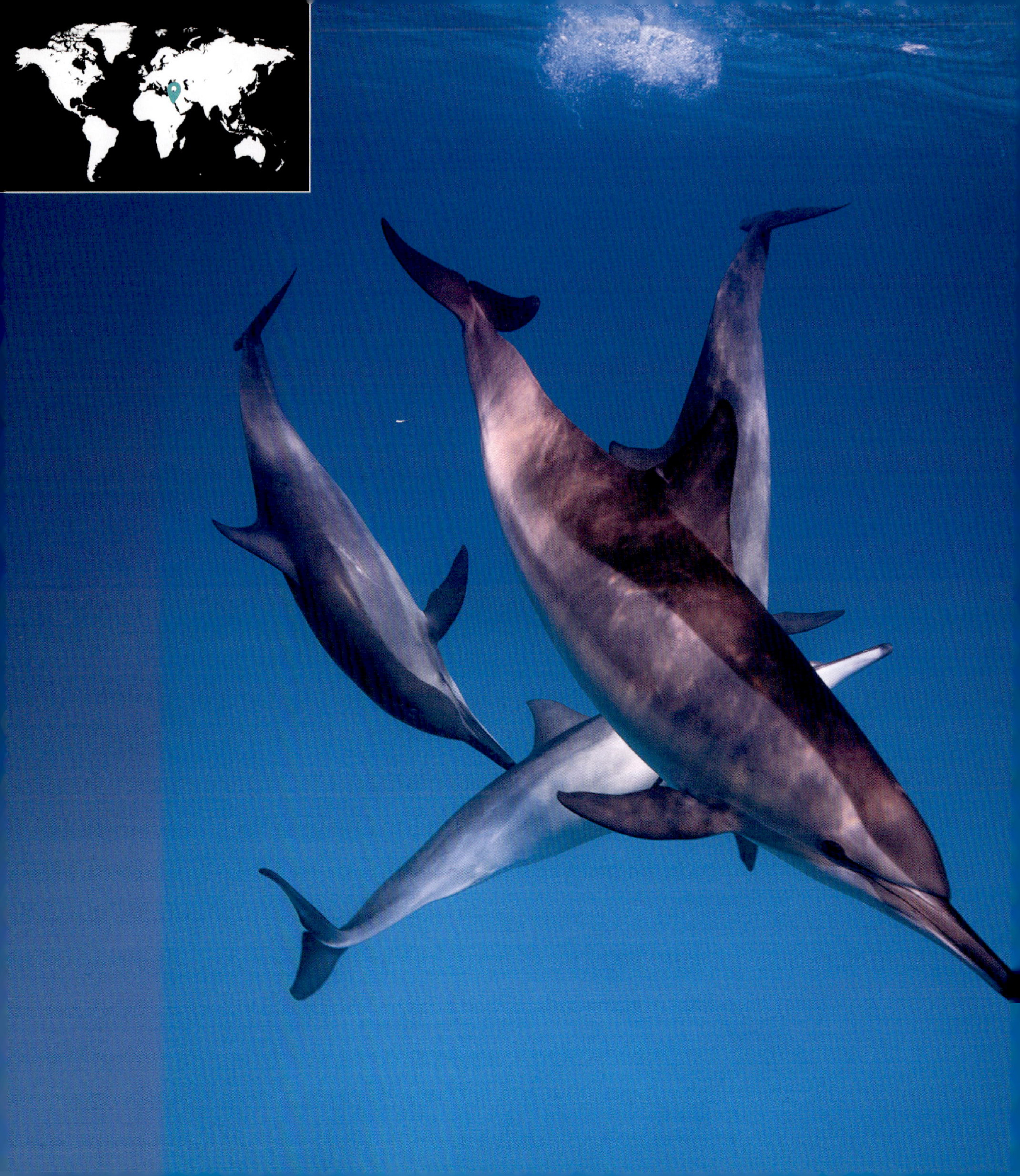

Fury Shoals, Egypt

Sometimes it's quite enjoyable to leave the bulky scuba gear behind and instead explore the seabed with greater freedom by snorkelling – certain locations are particularly suited to this activity.

In southern Egypt, the Fury Shoals region is home to the large Sataya coral reef, which hosts an incredible colony of over a hundred long-beaked dolphins, renowned for their social nature. Witnessing them in their natural habitat is a truly rare experience. Whether resting, playing, teaching or courting, these dolphins often come close to swimmers. It's essential to follow guidelines to avoid disturbing them and make the encounter as special as possible. In the summer months, you might even spot young calves, sometimes just a few days old, swimming alongside their mothers.

Essential info

This experience is accessible to everyone, even non-divers, as long as you can swim. The lagoon is calm and sheltered, but be sure to wear protective clothing, as the sun can be damaging to the skin.

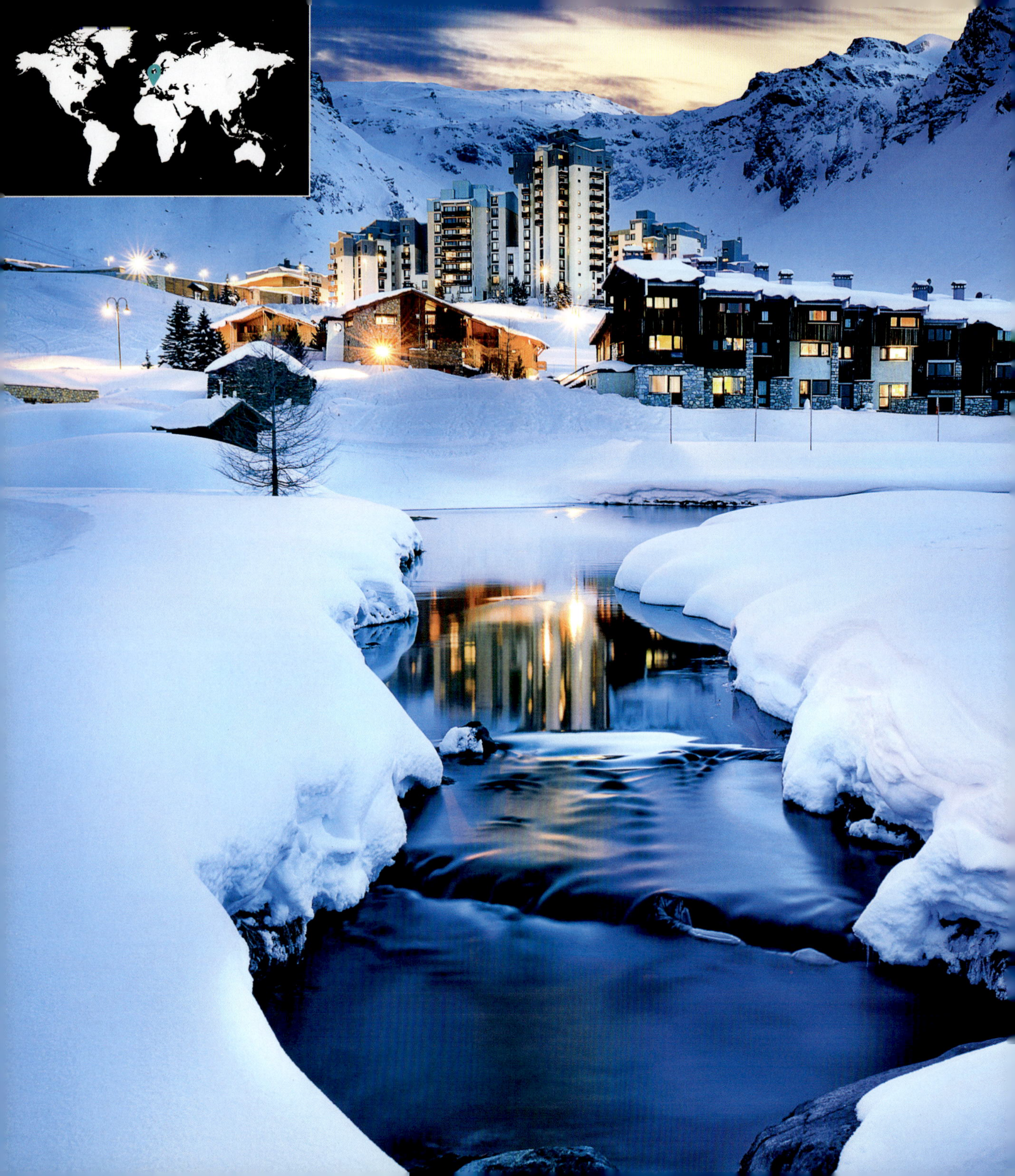

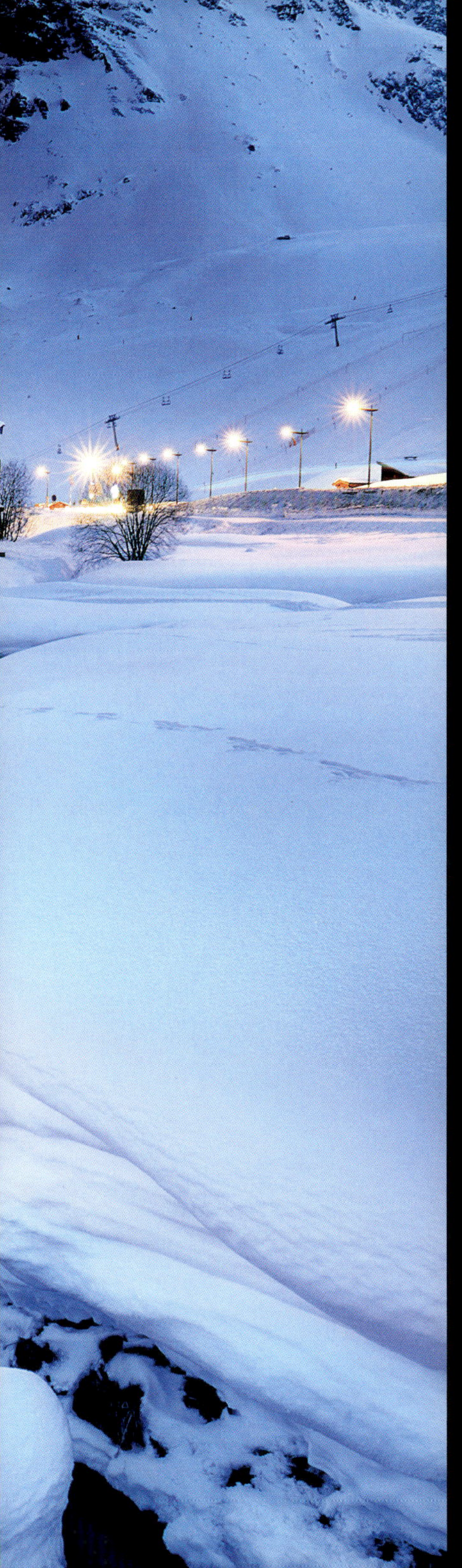

31 Ice diving in Tignes

Savoie, France

Diving in icy waters is far from a standard dive. It's a truly unique experience that's sure to thrill adventurous divers. Every winter, the lake in Tignes, Savoie, freezes over and is covered in a soft white blanket, creating the perfect setting for an extraordinary dive. After layering a thick wetsuit over warm clothing and an important safety briefing, it's time for the big moment.

Divers head to the lake, where a specially cut opening in the ice awaits. As you slip through the narrow entrance, you're transported to a mesmerising parallel world.

In the crystal-clear, dark two-degree-Celsius water, divers glide freely, tethered to a safety line, while bubbles dance and break against the frozen barriers overhead, creating a surreal, otherworldly spectacle.

Essential info

Both certified divers and beginners can experience this dive, under the guidance of experienced instructors. Access to this activity is generally between December and April.

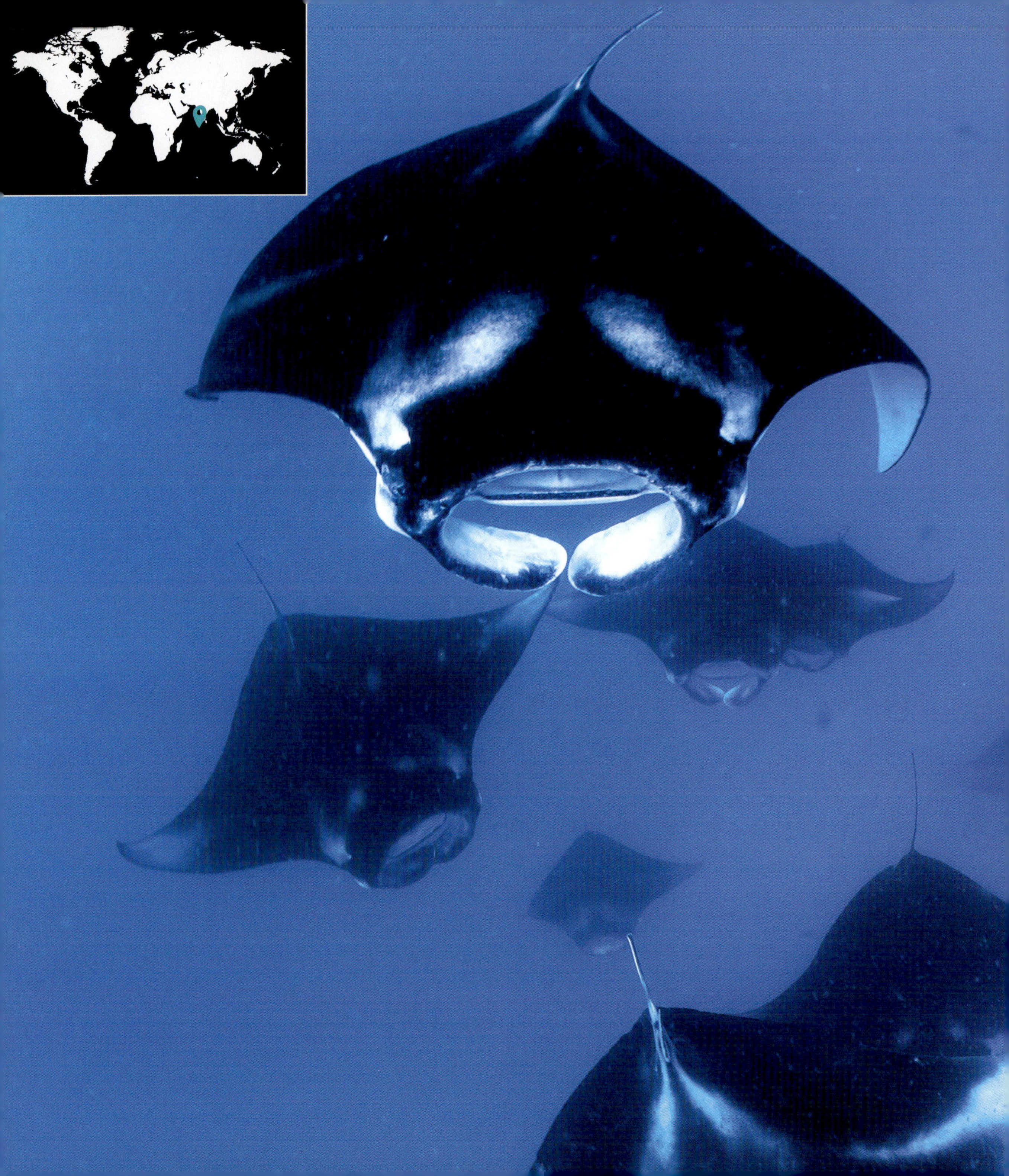

32 Hanifaru Bay

Baa Atoll, Maldives

In 2011, Baa Atoll, in the Maldives archipelago, was designated a Biosphere Reserve by UNESCO. Every year, in Hanifaru Bay, between May and October, the largest gathering of manta rays in the world makes it an exceptional place to observe one of this region's iconic animals.

During this season, the sea currents bring astonishing amounts of plankton into the bay, creating a vast food reservoir that attracts large pelagic species for an unexpected feast. Dozens of manta rays – sometimes numbering up to 200 – gracefully perform an endless ballet, their mouths wide open to consume the nutritious plankton. These elegant cousins of sharks are often accompanied by even larger giants: whale sharks. As the biggest fish in the world, they join the feast, providing an even more impressive spectacle.

Essential info

Snorkelling is the only way to witness this gathering of manta rays in Hanifaru Bay. Strict guidelines are enforced to protect both the animals and their habitat.

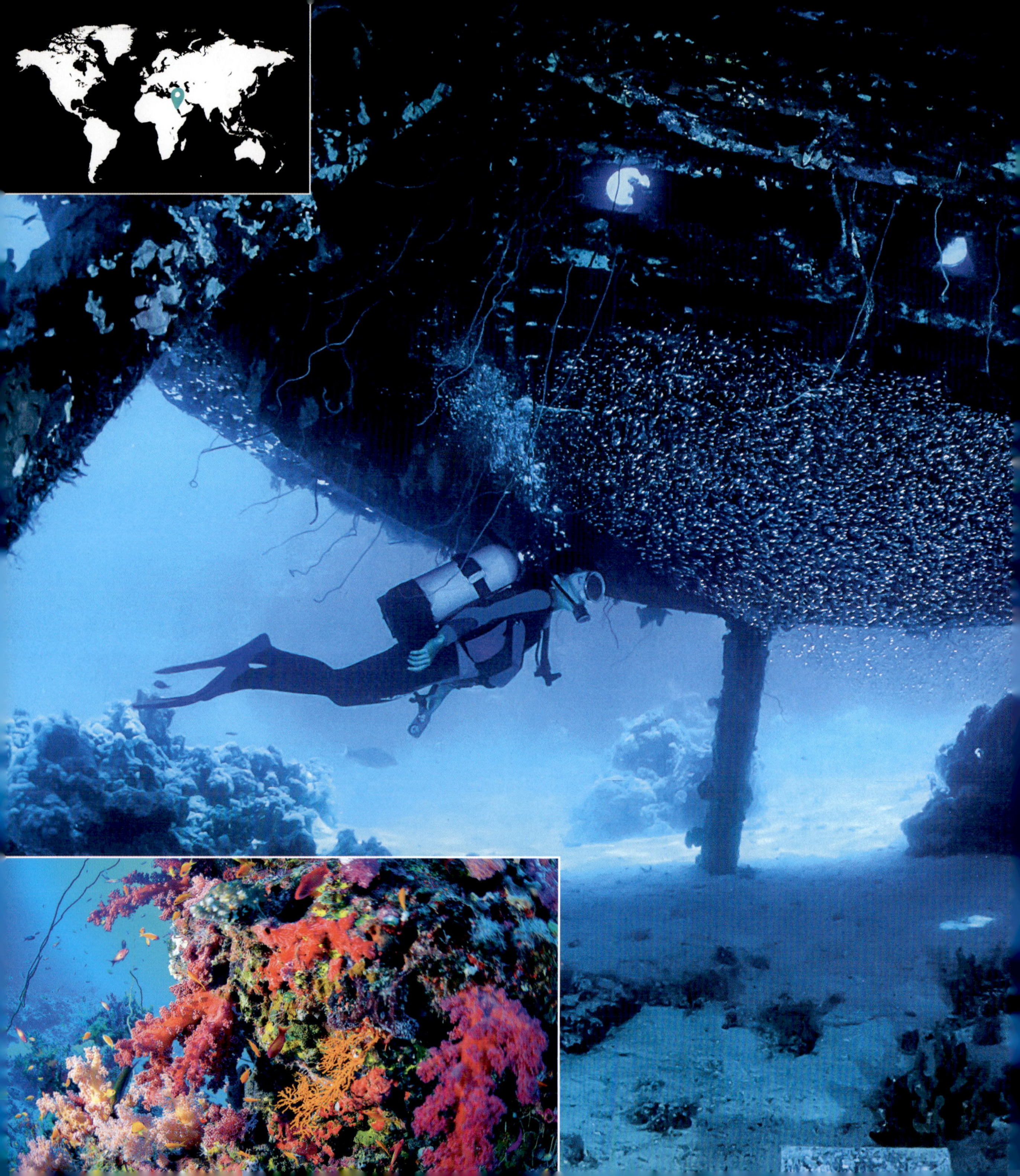

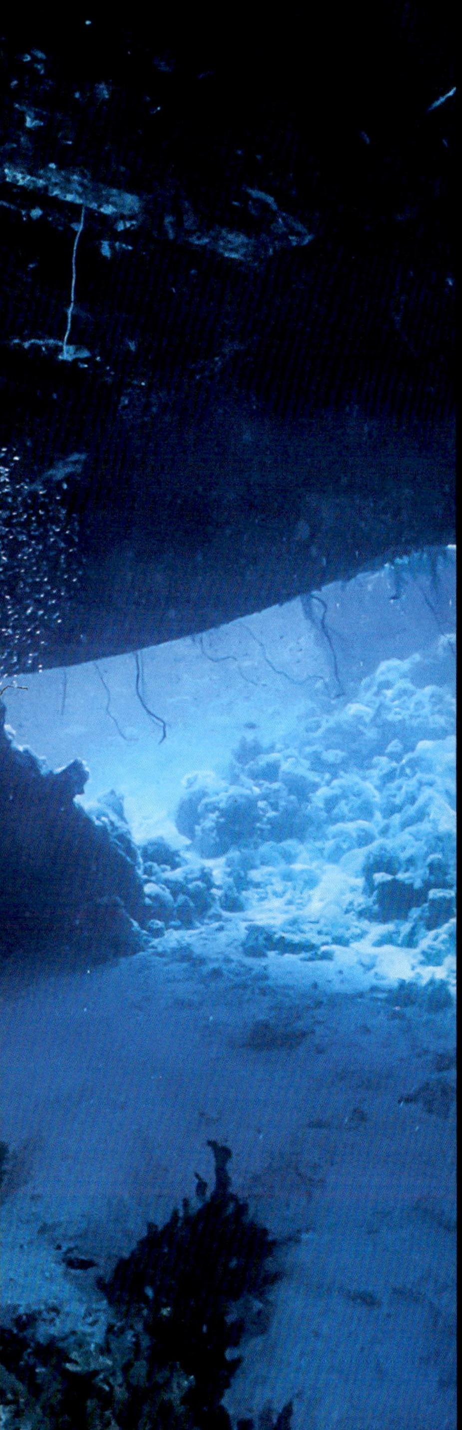

33

Précontinent II

Sha'ab Rumi, Sudan

In the Red Sea, Sudan boasts some of the most stunning coral reefs and crystal-clear waters. Despite the country's instability, many adventure-seekers are eager to dive into its depths, attracted by its schools of hammerhead sharks, which often form impressive walls, as well as its beautiful, secluded reefs. Divers are also drawn to the breathtaking wreck of the *Umbria*, a nearly intact vessel that was scuttled in 1940 off the coast of Port Sudan. One of the highlights is the Sha'ab Rumi reef, featuring an exquisite inner lagoon. This site gained fame over 60 years ago when Commander Cousteau made it the location for the Précontinent II submarine base. For a month, oceanauts lived in this remarkable habitat, which included residences at 10 metres (33 feet) deep and at 25 metres (82 feet), a dome-shaped garage for a diving saucer and a shed for scooters.

Today, only the garage, shed and shark cages remain, transformed into a unique underwater landmark. Nature has reclaimed the site, with vibrant corals covering part of the metal structures, and schools of fish and sharks accompany divers as they explore.

Essential info

Although this dive is straightforward, the majority of dives in Sudan require a good level of experience due to the currents and the presence of many sharks.

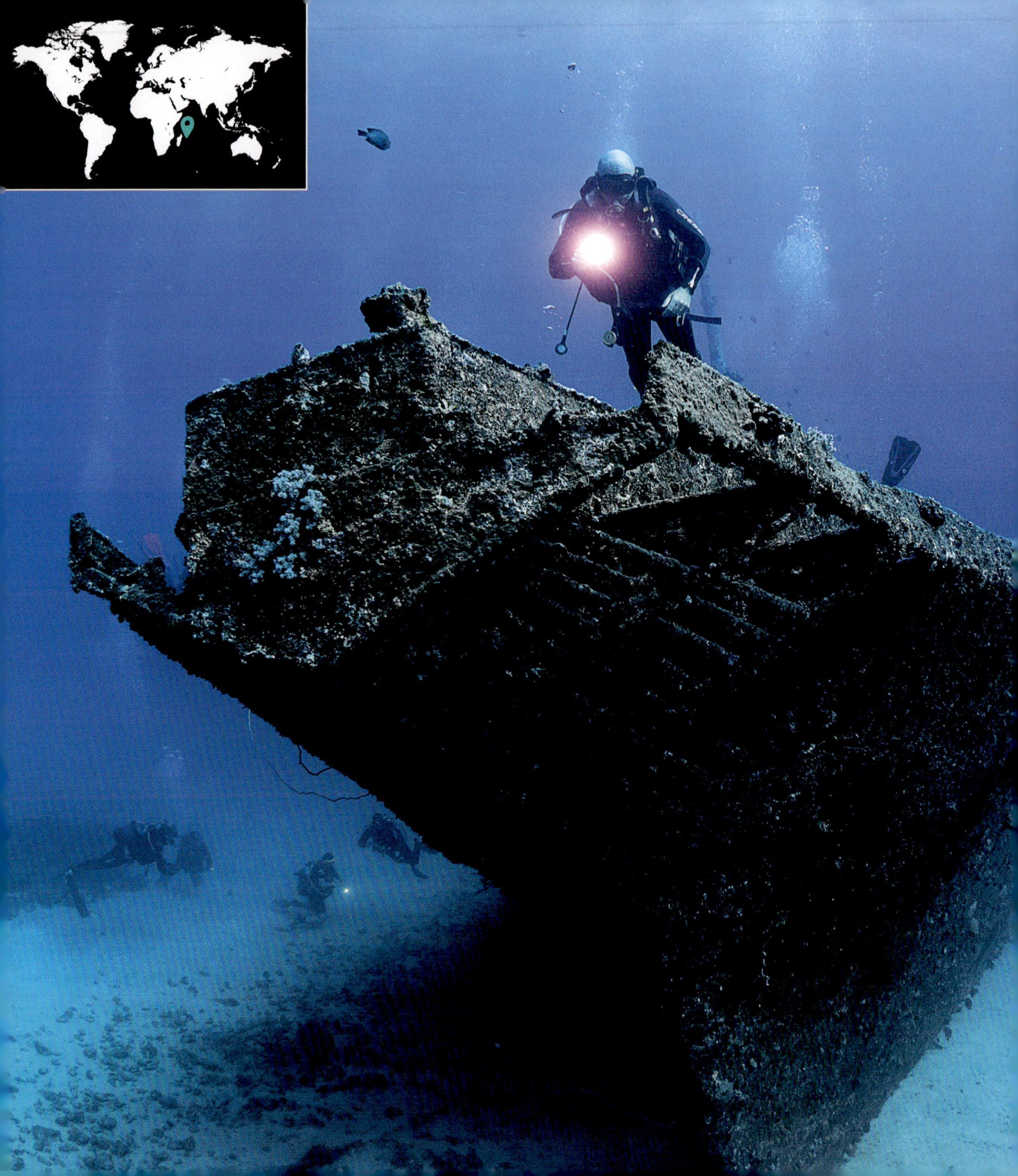

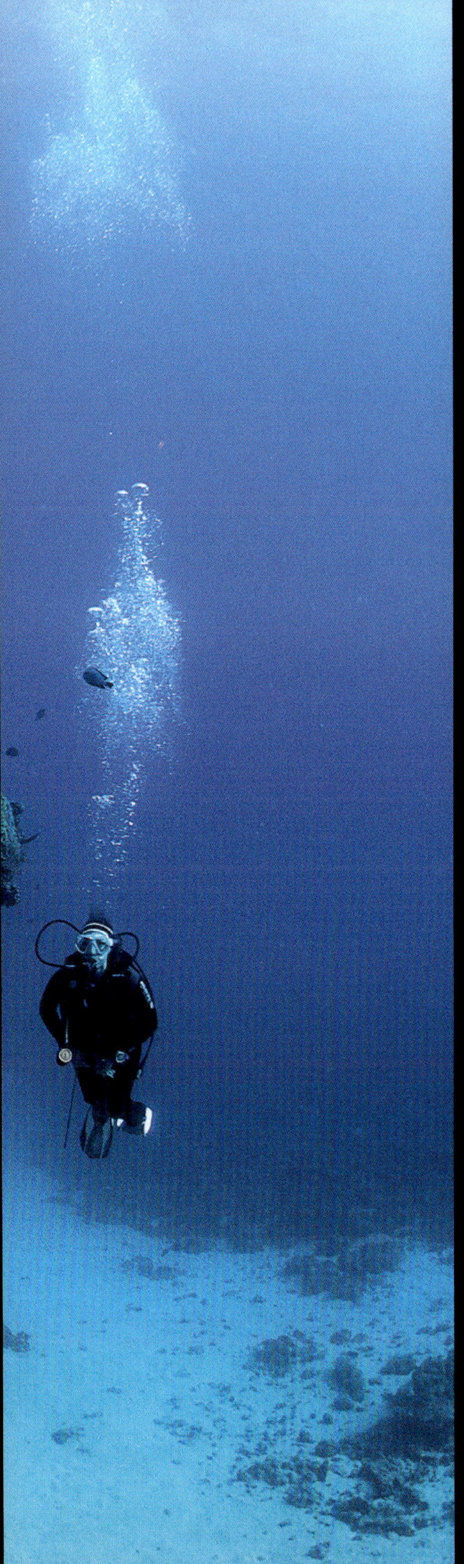

34 *Stella Maru* wreck

Mauritius

In the heart of the Mascarene Mountains, Mauritius stands as one of the most stunning tropical destinations in the world, offering breathtaking views of the Indian Ocean with its unmistakable, vibrant colours.

To the northwest of the island, you'll find Trou aux Biches, renowned for its exquisite beach that gracefully faces the bay of the same name. Just beyond the protective coral reef lies the wreck of the *Stella Maru*, a former Japanese trawler measuring about 30 metres (98 feet) long. This vessel was intentionally sunk in 1987 to create an artificial reef, originally resting on its starboard side.

However, in 2002, the powerful cyclone Dina righted the wreck, surprising divers with its new upright position. Today, it remains largely intact and richly colonised by marine life, making it a must-visit dive site in Mauritius.

Essential info

Located at a depth of seven to 25 metres (23 to 82 feet), this wreck is accessible to divers of all experience levels, making small penetrations into its structure able to be done safely.

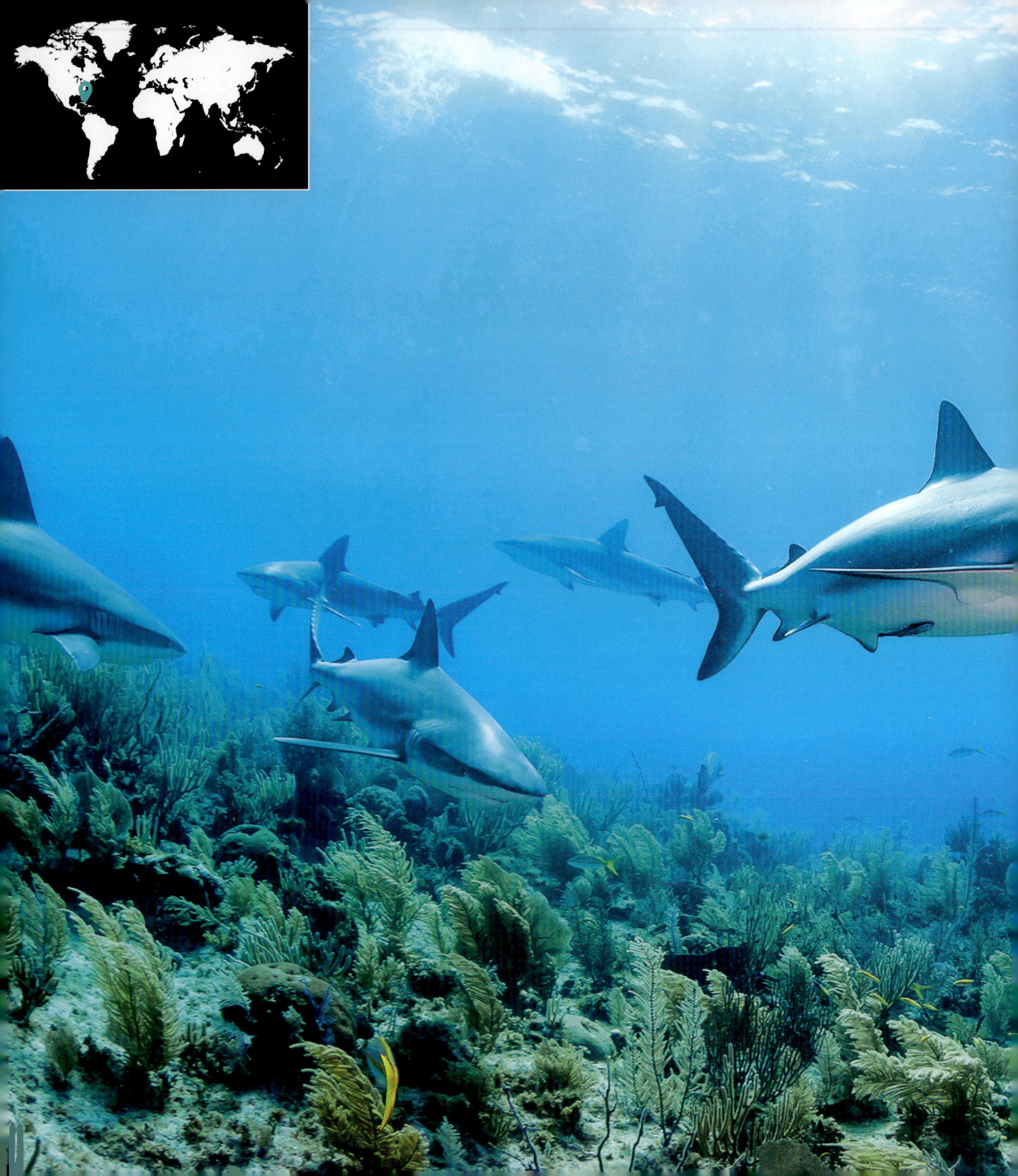

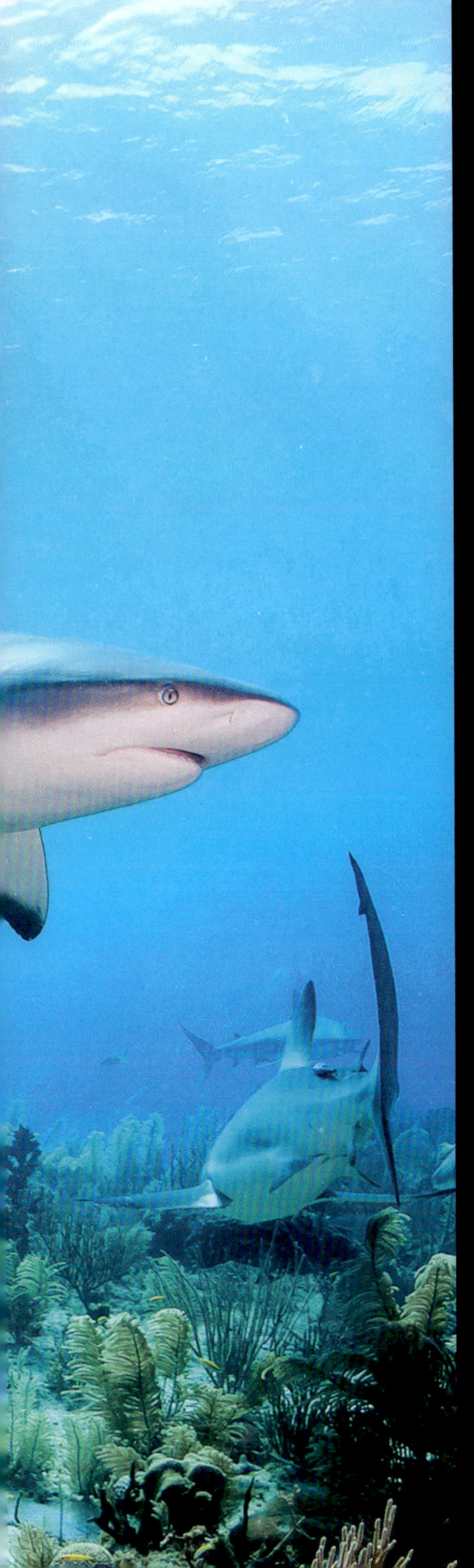

35 Jardines de la Reina

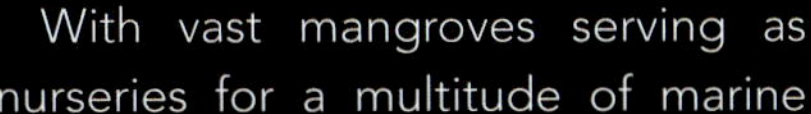

Cuba

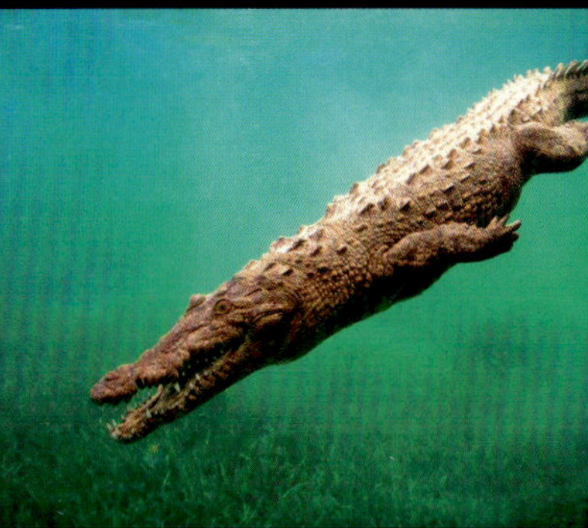

Christopher Columbus discovered this archipelago of hundreds of islands and islets southeast of Cuba and named it in honour of Queen Isabella I of Castile. The famous Cuban political leader Fidel Castro, a passionate diver himself, established a marine park here in 1996 to preserve its unique underwater ecosystem.

With vast mangroves serving as nurseries for a multitude of marine species, these islands are home to some of the richest biodiversity in the Caribbean. Divers are particularly drawn by the presence of various shark species, including silky sharks (see photo), lemon sharks, blacktip sharks, nurse sharks and hammerhead sharks. The reefs are in pristine condition and brimming with life, where large groupers and sea turtles glide through the waters.

For an added thrill, you can venture into the mangroves, where marine crocodiles are occasionally spotted. Exploring this sanctuary, which welcomes fewer than 3,000 divers annually, is a true privilege.

Essential info

With its calm waters, diving at Jardines de la Reina is accessible to all levels. There is only one diving and cruise centre that holds the exclusive rights to operate within the archipelago.

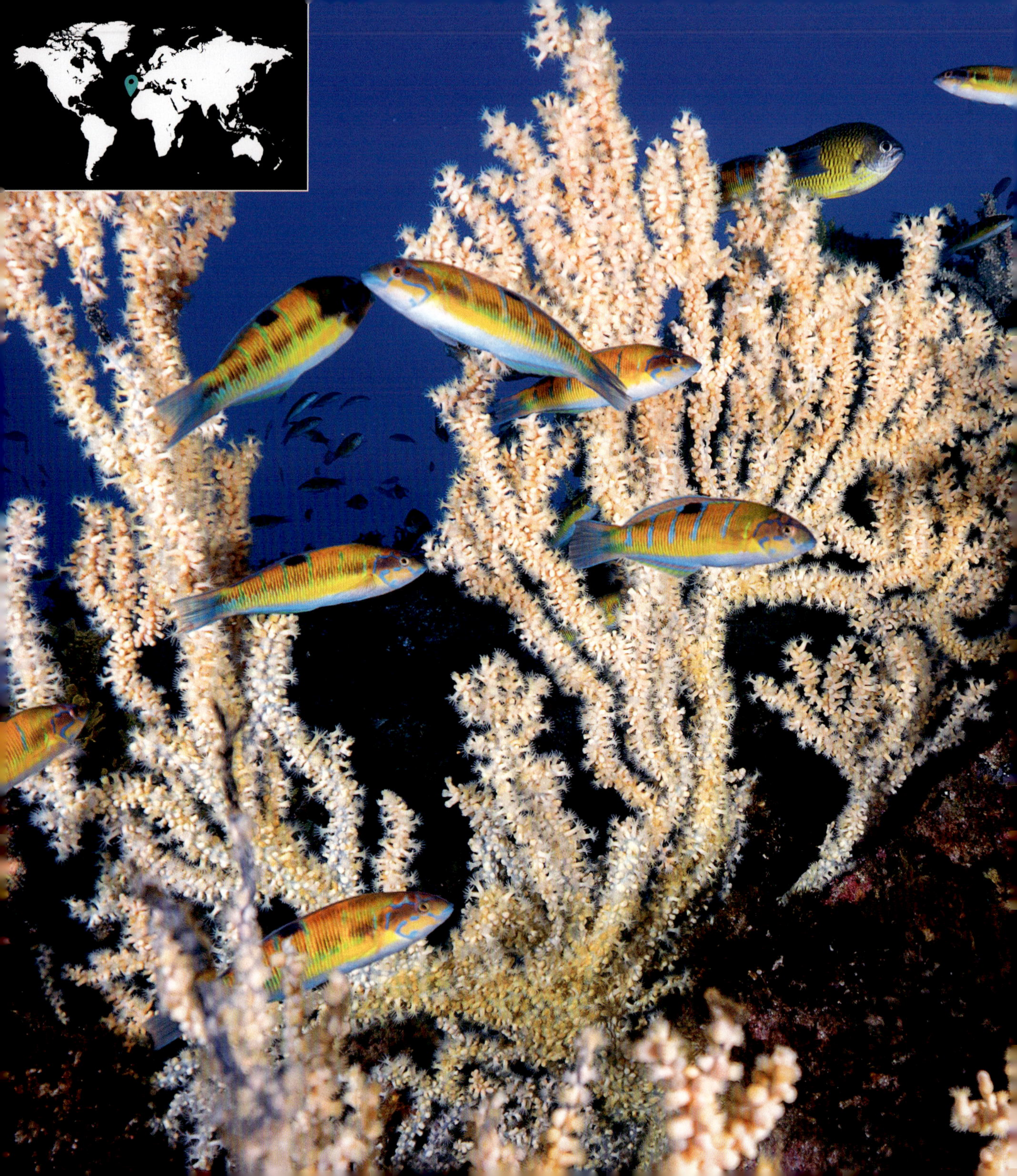

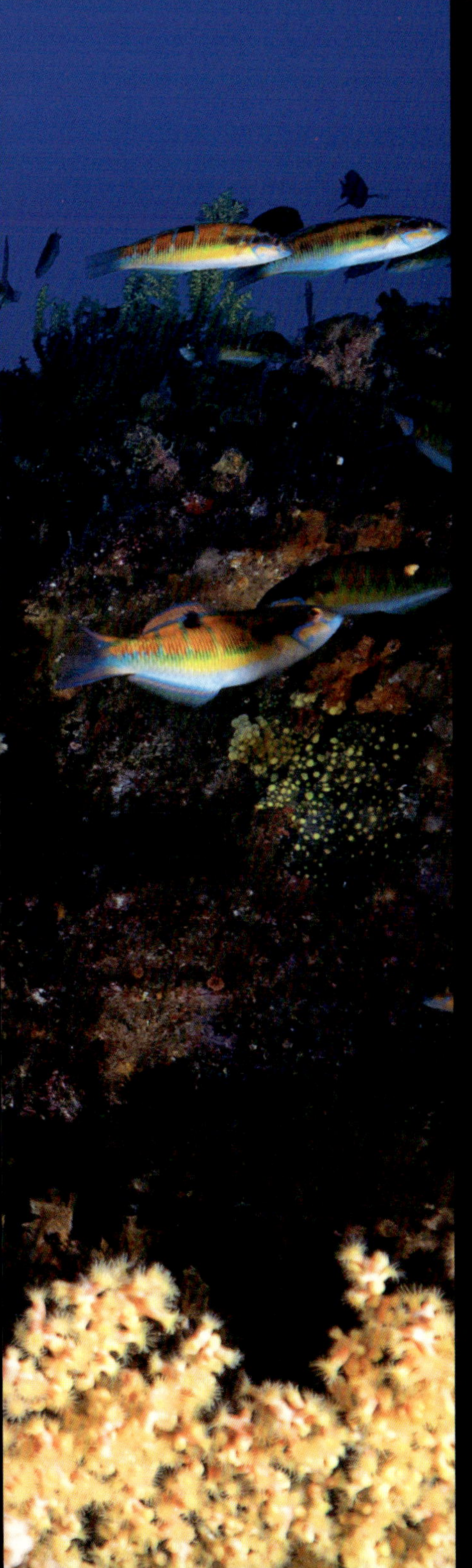

36 La Graciosa

Lanzarote, Canary Islands

The main island of the small Chinijo archipelago, located north of Lanzarote, La Graciosa – with its dirt roads – remains one of the few places in Europe that feels suspended in time. It is also home to the largest marine reserve on the continent. The aridity of the land, dominated by immense extinct volcanoes, contrasts beautifully with the rich, fully protected seabed.

At the Bajo de las Gerardias site, the drop-offs are adorned with vibrant orange branching corals, alongside the largest known concentration of *gerardia* (deep sea gold coral) in the world and bushy anemones, making it a remarkable destination. Around this underwater promontory, groupers reign supreme, occasionally joined by schools of greater amberjack hunting for anchovies. In the azure waters, the distinctive silhouettes of barracudas add an extra touch of magic to this captivating scene.

Essential info

The sites around La Graciosa are not protected and can be quite stormy. Some, like el Bajo de las Gerardias, are also very deep (40–45 metres/130–145 feet).

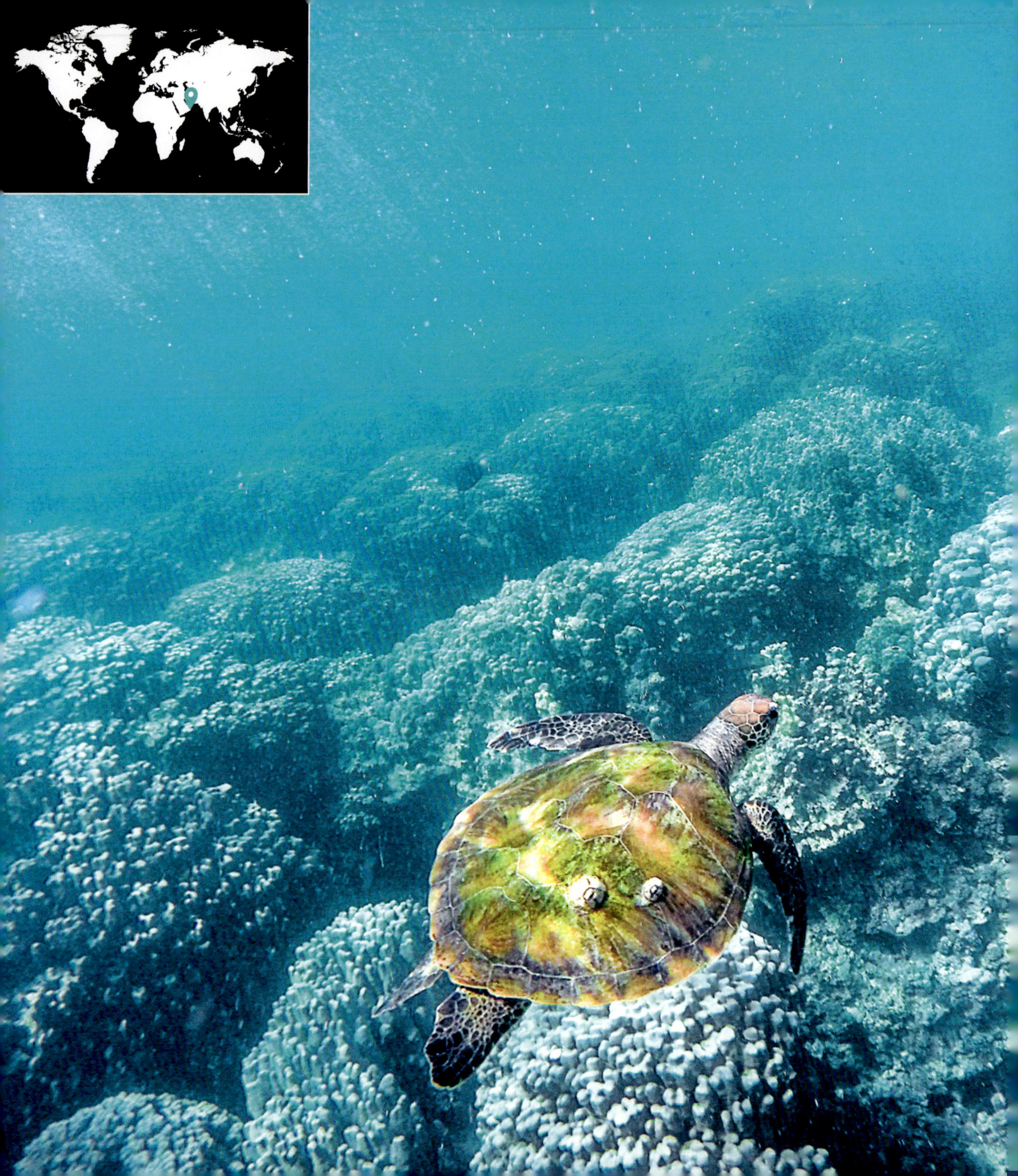

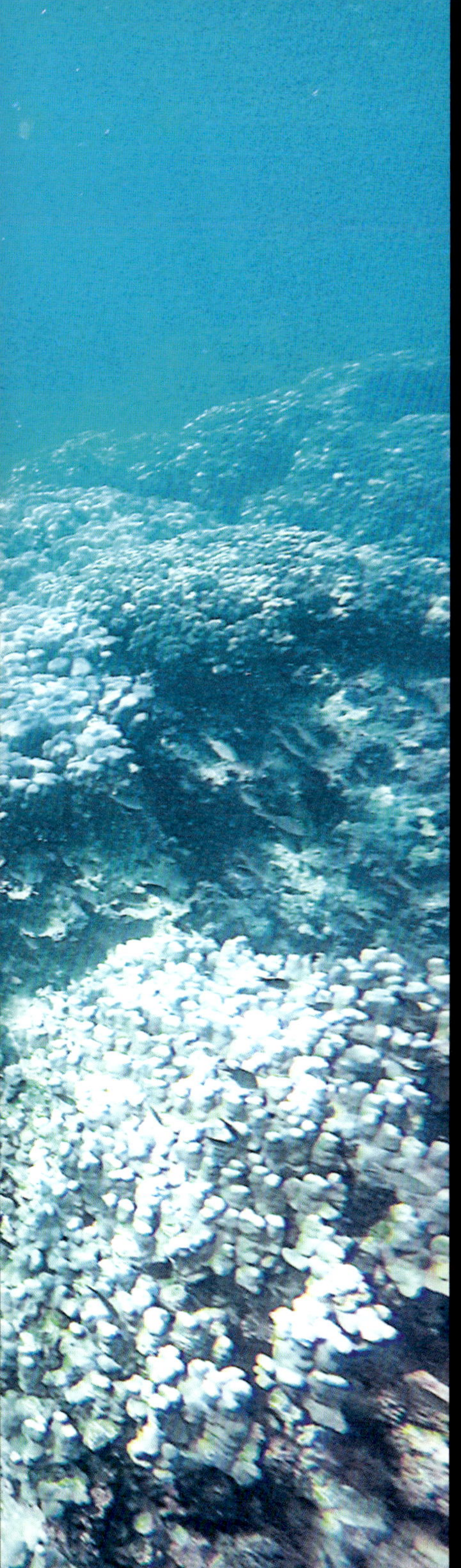

37 Damaniyat Islands

Oman

Nestled between the sea and the desert, the Sultanate of Oman is a multifaceted gem that inspired the *One Thousand and One Nights* tales. Located in the southeast of the Arabian Peninsula, it boasts 1,700 kilometres (1,056 miles) of coastline along the warm, vibrant waters of the Gulf of Oman and the Arabian Sea. To the north lies the stunning Damaniyat Archipelago, a chain of nine aligned islands and several smaller islets.

Listed for potential inclusion in the UNESCO World Heritage List, the Damaniyat Islands Marine Reserve is home to some of the most beautiful dive sites in the country. Despite variable visibility, diving into its emerald waters reveals a magnificent coral reef, boasting nearly a hundred species of hard and soft corals, about 10 per cent of which are endemic. Marine life here is abundant, with sea turtles being part of the scenery, along with blacktip sharks, guitarfish and leopard sharks. Whale sharks visit during the summer months. The rich ecosystem also includes eagle rays, stingrays, eels and playful dolphins, along with a dazzling array of tropical fish in a multitude of colours.

Essential info

Non-divers can easily observe corals and the many fish with a mask and snorkel. Further north, the Musandam Peninsula with its sumptuous fjords is also worth a visit.

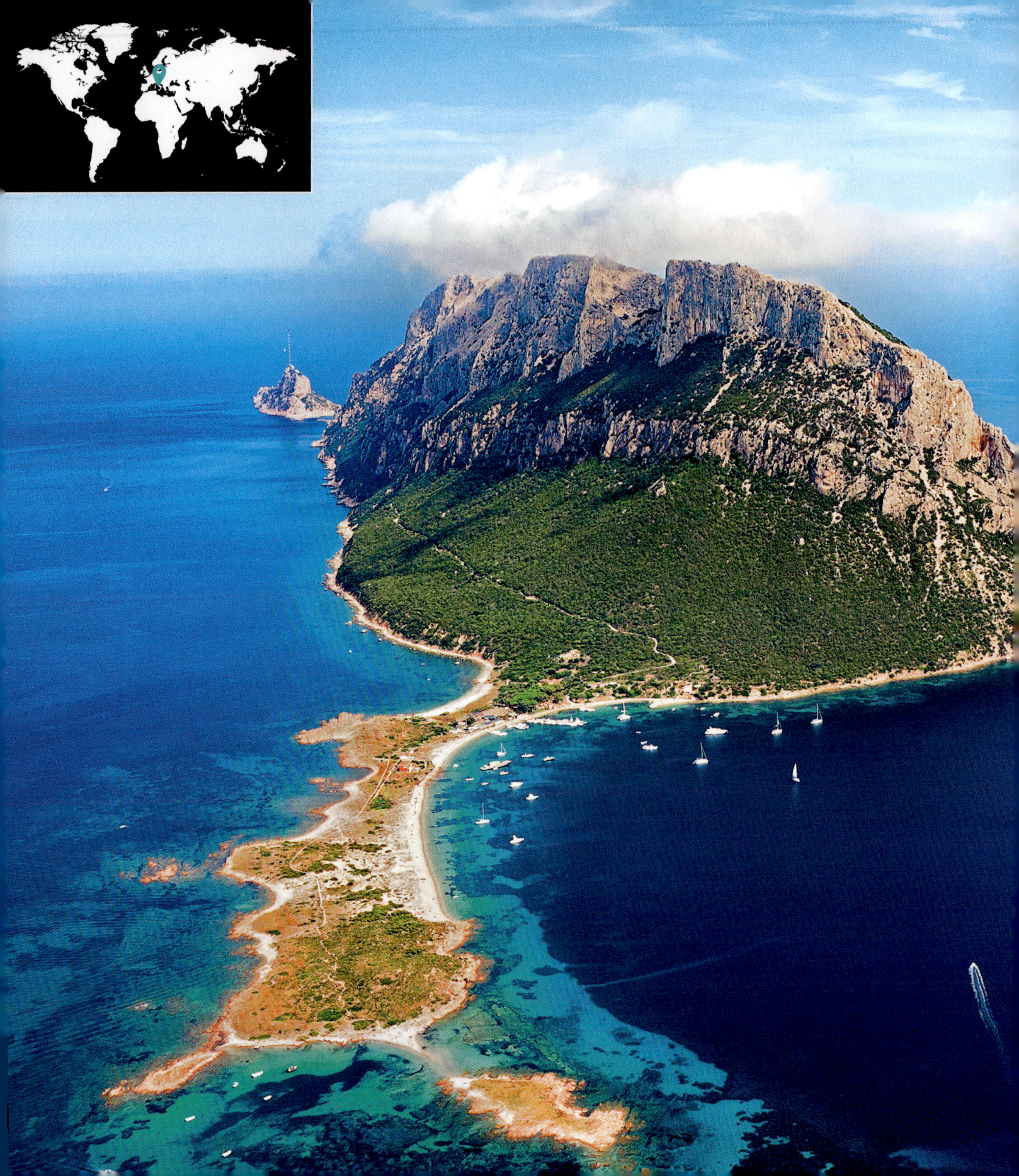

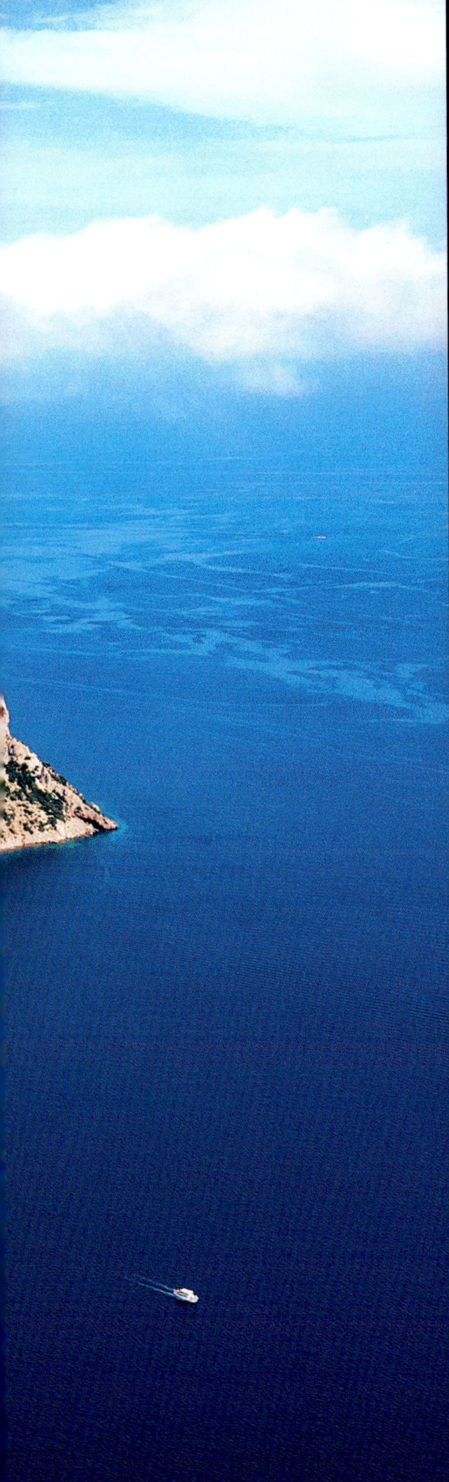

38 Tavolara

Sardinia, Italy

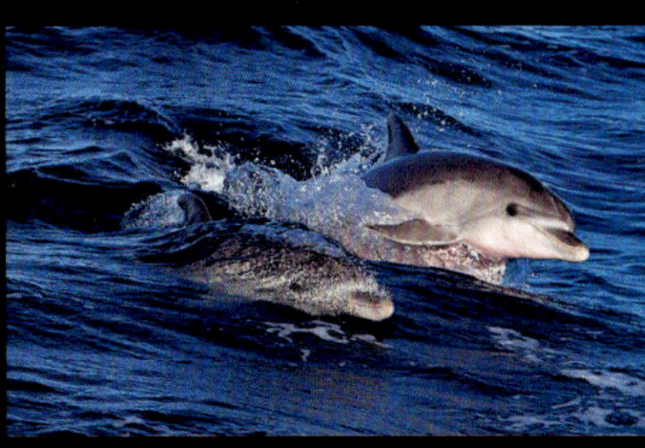

In the middle of the western Mediterranean, between Corsica and Tunisia, the sandy beaches of Sardinia spread out beside turquoise waters.

To the northeast, Tavolara Island resembles a huge limestone mountain emerging from the water. Surrounding this area, 15,000 hectares of sea have been protected since 1997, forming the Tavolara-Punta Coda Cavallo Marine Reserve alongside the Molara and Molarotto islands. This reserve is home to an exceptional array of marine life that beautifully represents the Mediterranean ecosystem.

Vast meadows of posidonia (sea grass) stretch as far as the eye can see, while the dramatic cliffs are adorned with countless species, including gorgonians, sponges, bryozoans and vibrant yellow encrusted anemones. The limestone rock features arches and caves that divers can safely explore, while schools of anthias and castagnoles dance above the majestic brown groupers. Tavolara has been a strategic location for centuries and is also home to numerous shipwrecks that delight metal enthusiasts.

Essential info

With its uncrowded shores, Tavolara Island allows visitors to enjoy its stunning landscapes, including the breathtaking Spalmatore di Terra Beach, which provides a magnificent view of the whole island.

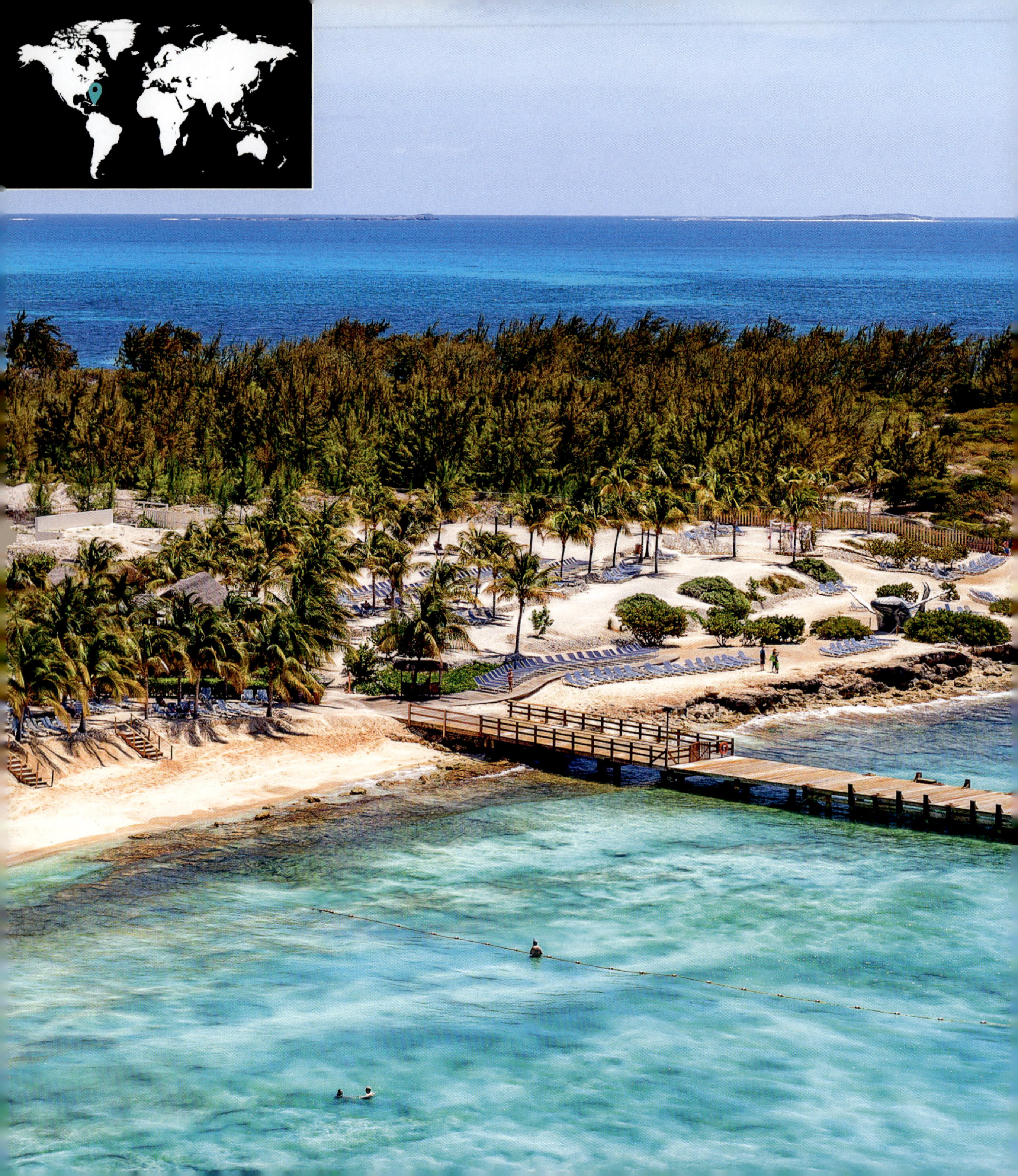

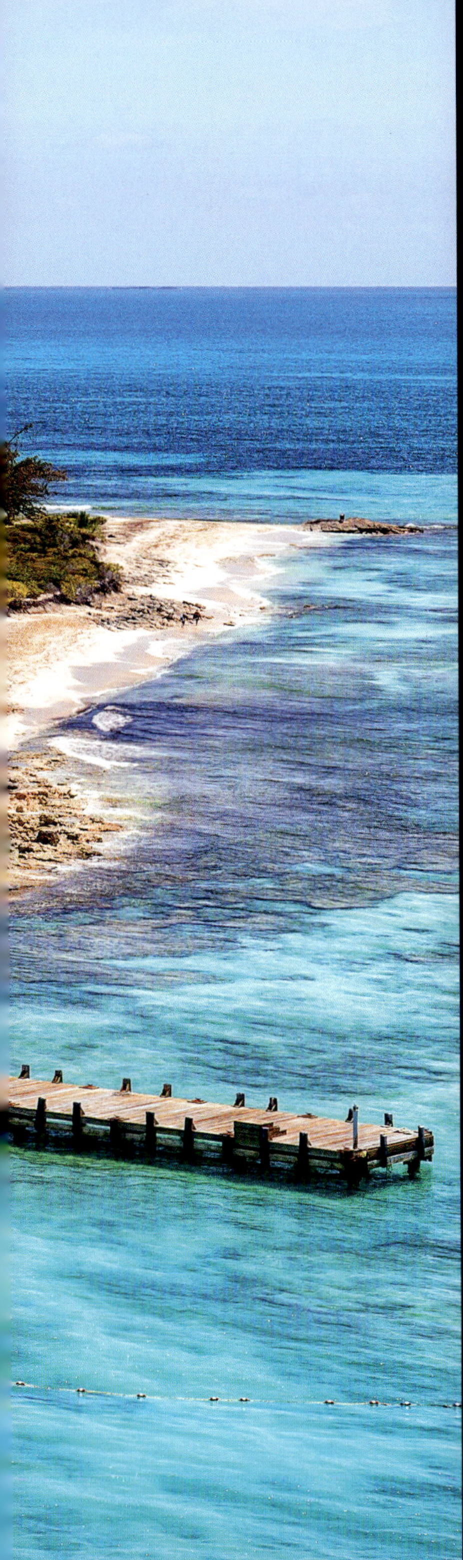

39 Turks and Caicos

Dominican Republic

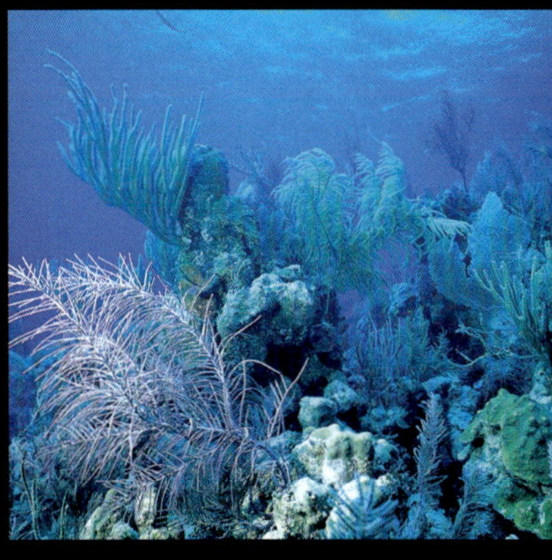

The Turks and Caicos Islands, an extension of the Bahamas located north of the Dominican Republic, are little known by many travellers. They are known as the Turquoise Islands due to the colour and clarity of their waters.

Centuries ago they were a pirate hotspot, but today they offer an idyllic escape, with endless stretches of pristine white sandy beaches bordered by lagoons in every shade of blue. Divers will find colourful underwater scenes and varied marine landscapes – from sandy patches dotted with coral and lush reefs to dramatic drop-offs covered in vibrant gorgonians and plateaus populated by iconic Caribbean sponges. The diverse scenery offers the thrill of spotting abundant marine life, from splendid lobsters, groupers and parrotfish to snappers, rays and turtles. There is also plenty for small animal lovers including multiple species of shrimp and crabs. If you're lucky, you may even spot a shark or two.

Essential info

The months of December to March bring extra excitement, as humpback whales arrive to breed and calve in these serene waters.

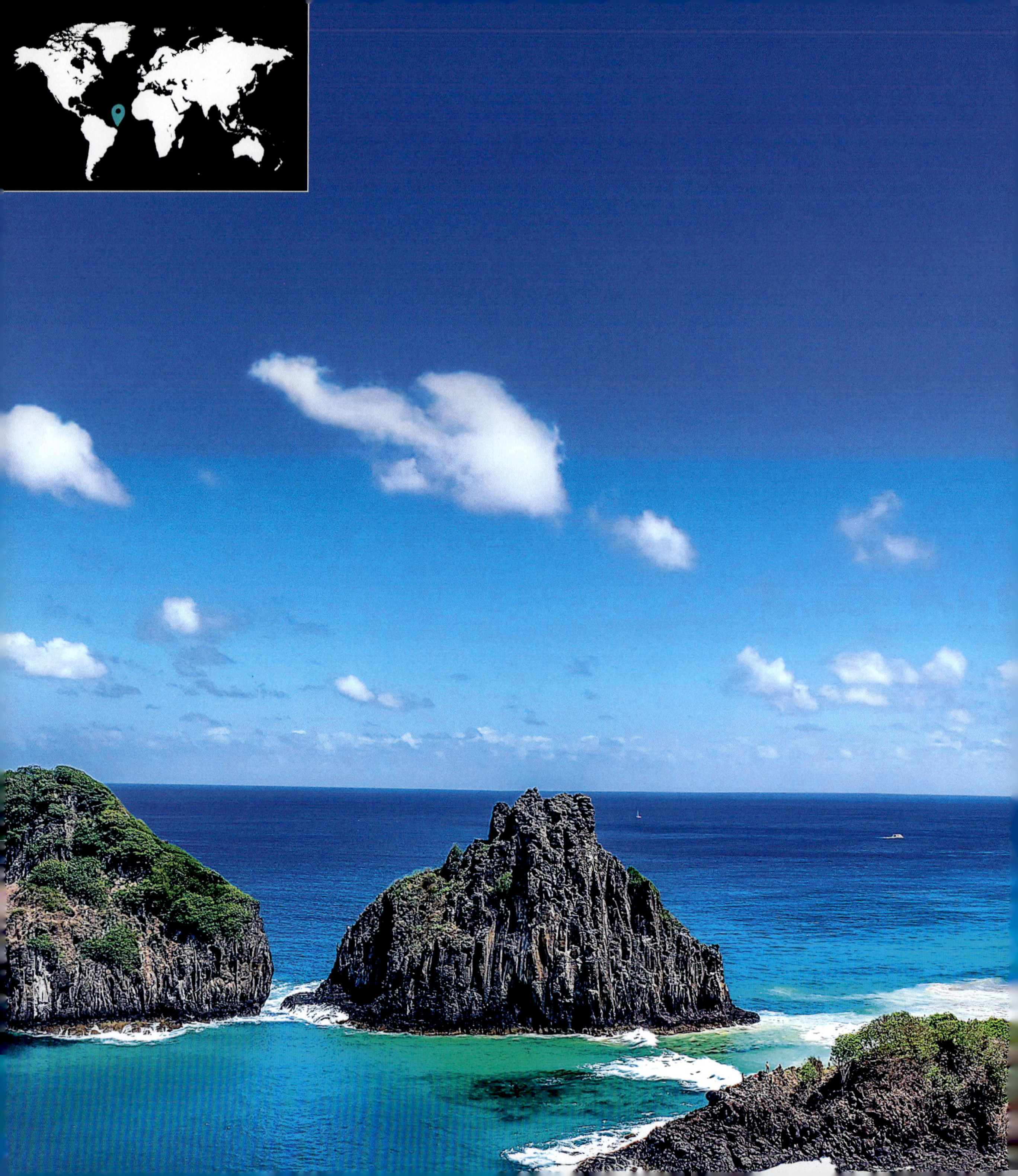

40 Fernando de Noronha

Brazil

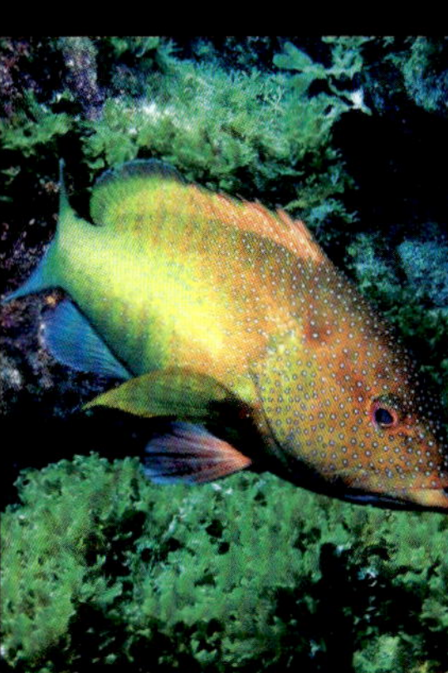

While Brazil is vast and stunning, it isn't typically regarded as a diving destination as such. However, nearly 400 kilometres (250 miles) off the northeast coast the Fernando de Noronha archipelago, consisting of 21 islands and islets, will win over any diver fortunate enough to explore its depths. Designated as a national park and listed as a UNESCO World Heritage Site, these islands enjoy full protection, allowing nature to thrive.

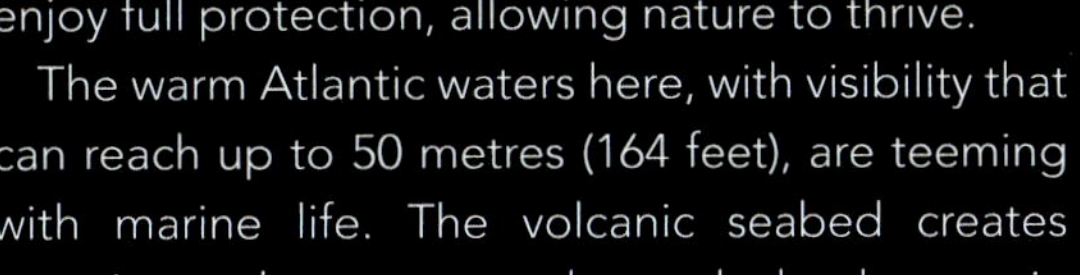

The warm Atlantic waters here, with visibility that can reach up to 50 metres (164 feet), are teeming with marine life. The volcanic seabed creates stunning arches, caves and tunnels that host an incredible array of wildlife.

Among the highlights are the sea turtles and long-beaked dolphins – with the local population estimated to be between 200 and 300 individuals. Diving experiences are enriched by encounters with eagle rays, stingrays, large groupers, reef sharks and a vibrant assortment of tropical fish, their colours rivalling the dazzling costumes of the Rio Carnival.

Essential info

Tech divers will have plenty to keep them busy with several shipwrecks to explore, including the beautiful *Corveta V17*, a military ship resting on the sea floor at a depth of over 60 metres (195 feet).

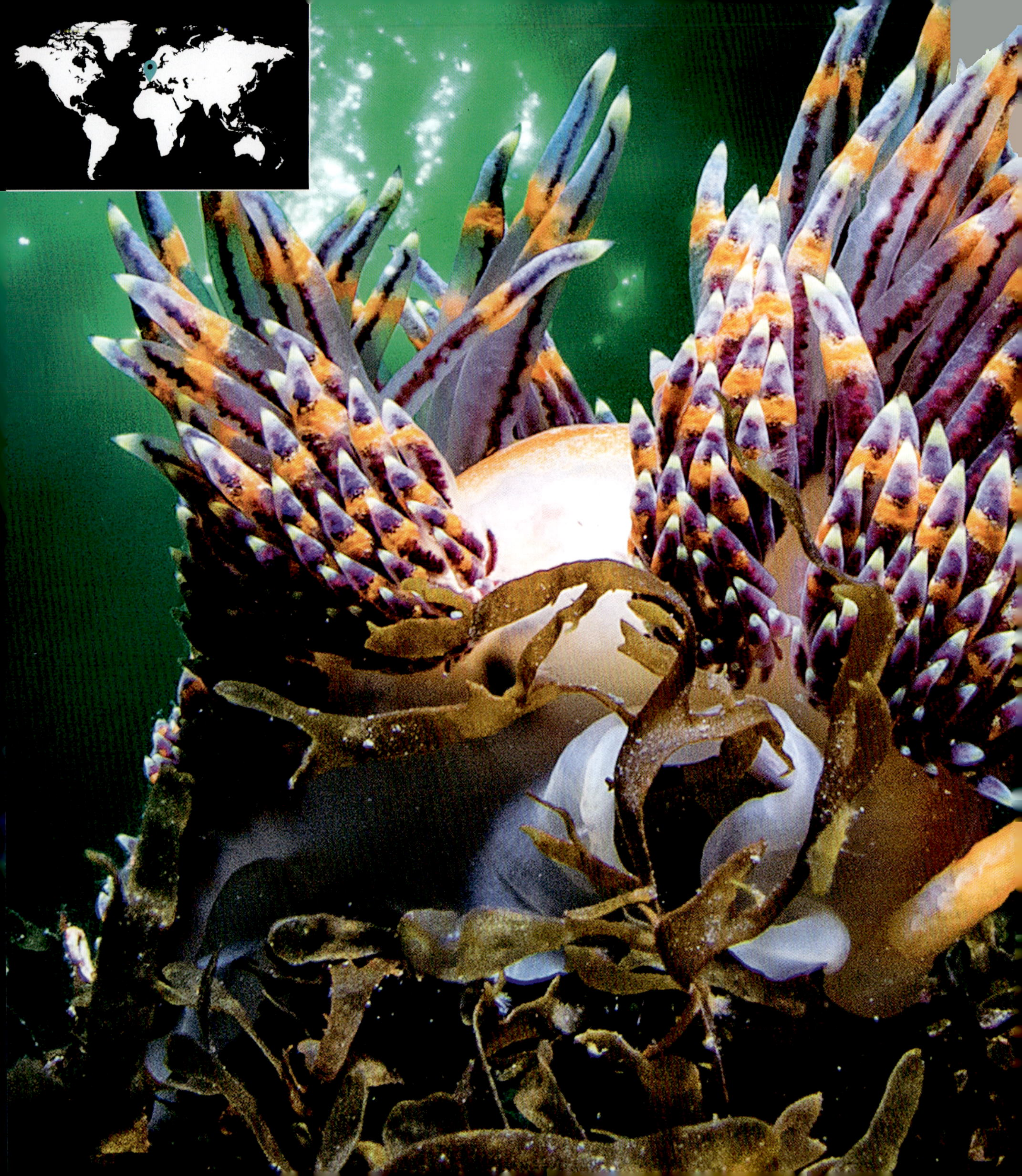

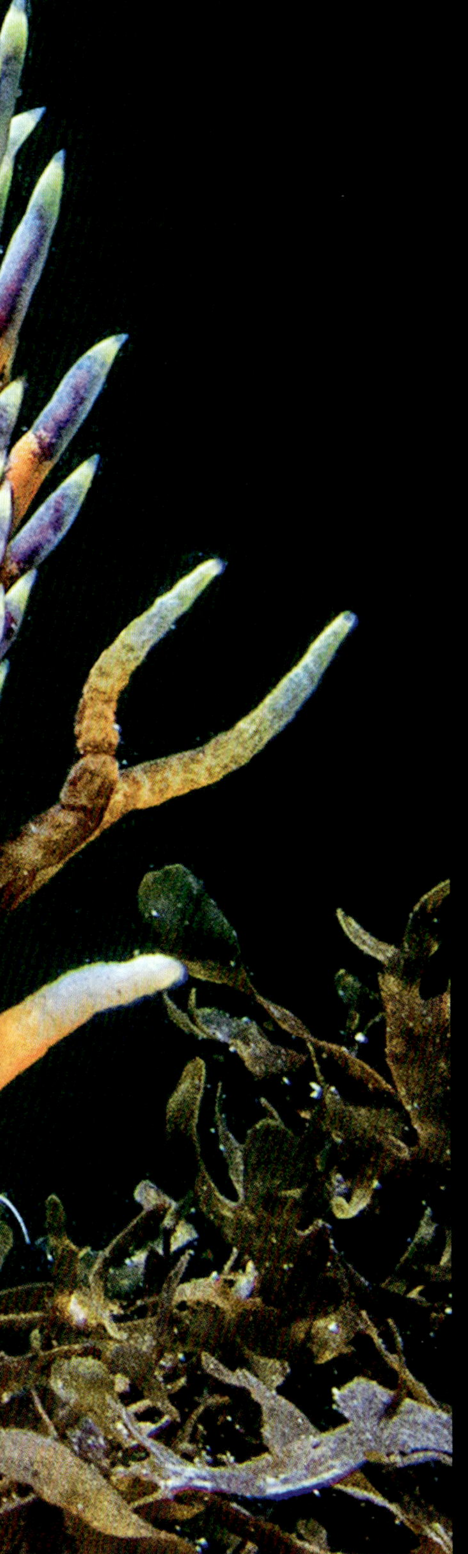

41 Thau Lagoon

Hérault, France

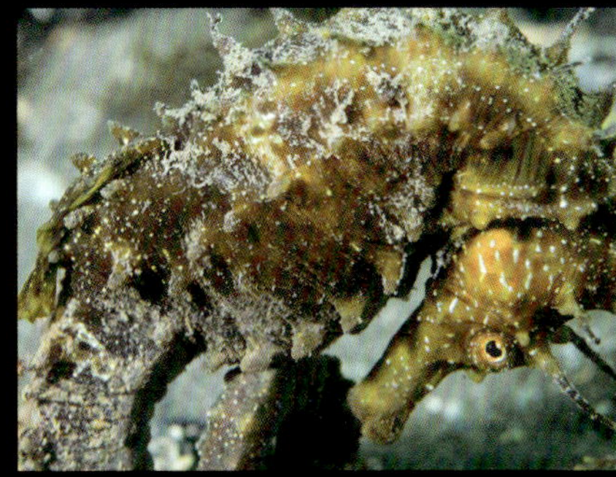

Well known to oyster lovers, the Thau lagoon, located between Sète and Agde in the Hérault region, is an incredibly rich saltwater lagoon. It's no wonder that divers from numerous dive centres, along with independent enthusiasts, regularly come to explore its waters. It is reputed to be one of the best in Europe for observing seahorses in their natural environment, especially long-snouted seahorses (*Hippocampus guttulatus*). This small fish, which has inspired countless myths and legends, is commonly spotted in the shallow waters of the lagoon (see inset photo).

But that's not all. If the water isn't clear, you can easily come across nudibranchs, pipefish and the curious peacock blenny. The Ponton de la Bordelaise is the most famous dive entry point. The handful of shipwrecks here provide shelter for a multitude of Mediterranean species, some of which are far easier to observe than in open waters.

Essential info

The waters of the lagoon heat up faster than at sea, becoming too hot in summer, and making it unsuitable for diving in the hotter months. So it is best to dive here in spring and autumn. This site is easily accessible from the shore and suitable for all skill levels.

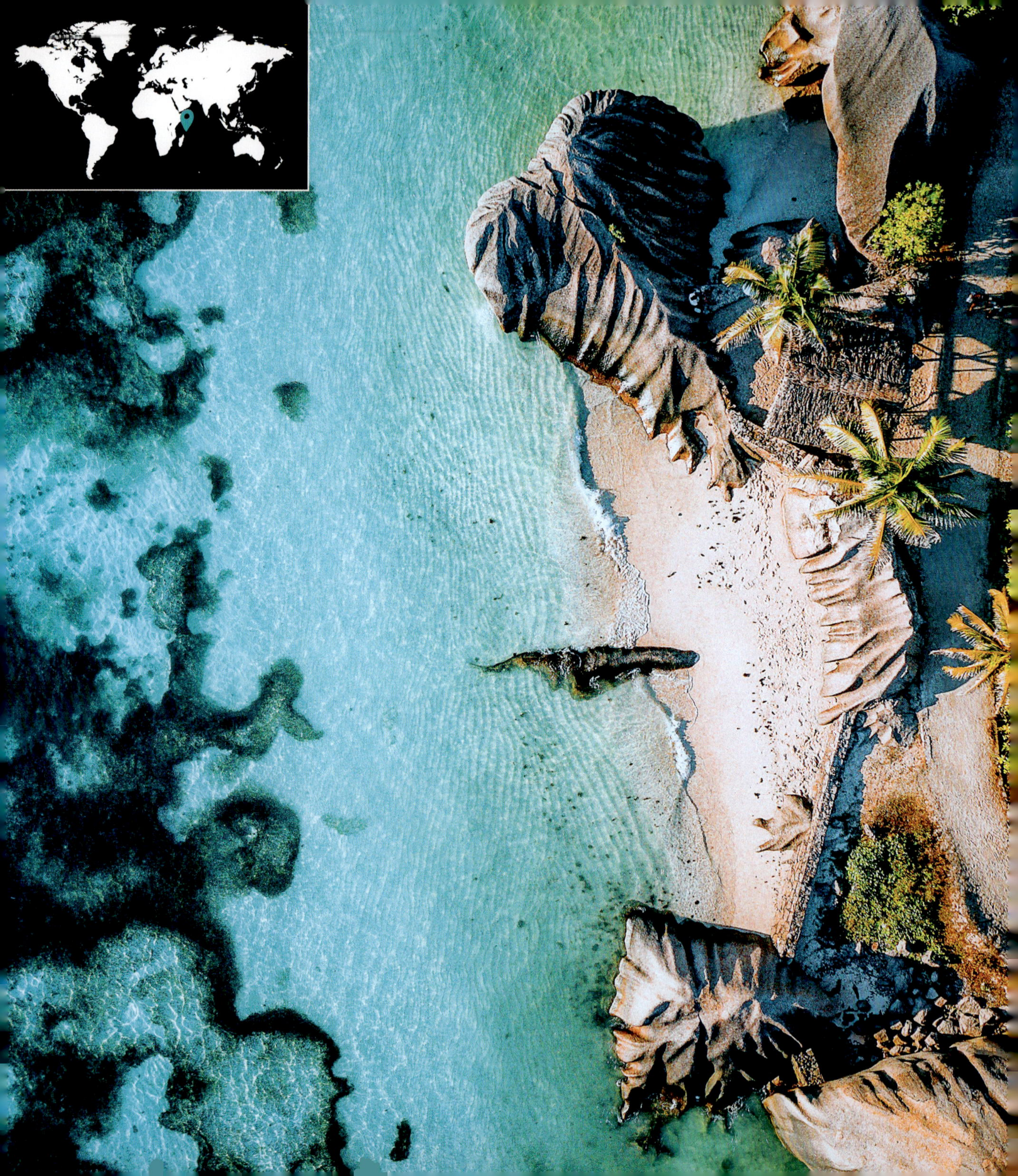

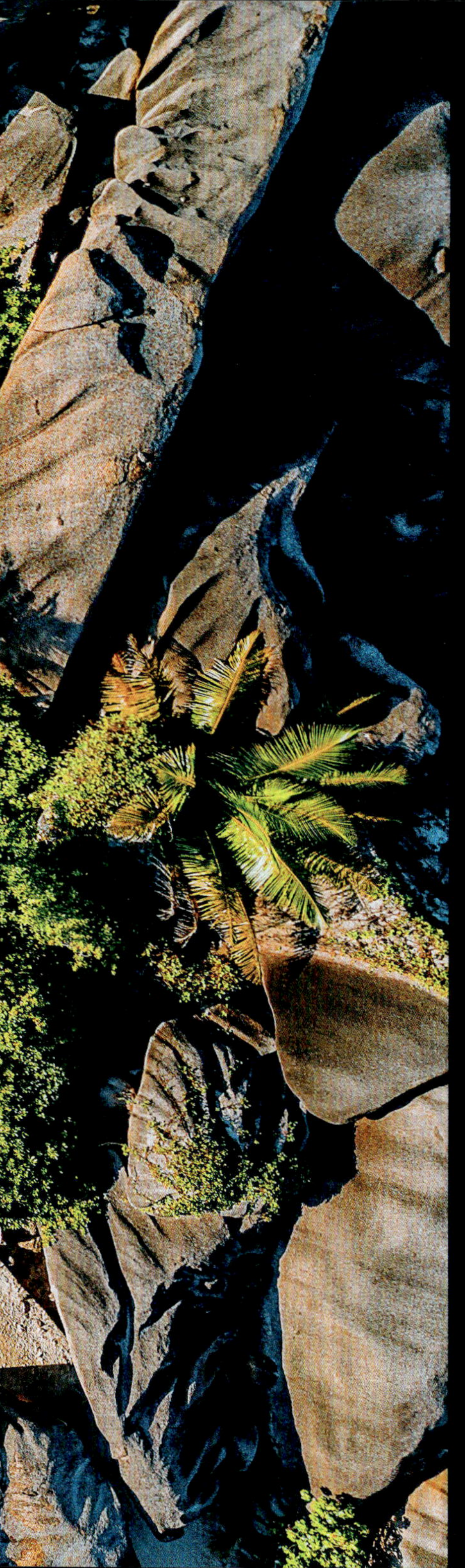

42 La Digue

Seychelles

The Seychelles is one of those corners of the earth with breathtaking natural beauty. Its white sandy beaches lined with tropical forests, coconut palms and huge blocks of granite make this destination nothing short of a dream. La Digue is home to Anse Source d'Argent, often hailed as the most photographed beach in the world. From La Digue, divers have easy access to some of the best dive sites in the region, including Praslin, Félicité, Sister, Marianne and Cocos islands. Whether you're scuba diving or snorkelling, there are experiences for everyone, regardless of skill level.

While the underwater terrain is more granitic than coral-based, marine life thrives in this mineral-rich environment. As you navigate through the pinnacles, labyrinths and canyons, you'll encounter the vibrant wildlife of the Indian Ocean. Expect to see graceful grey sharks, majestic sea turtles and schools of colourful fish, including snapper, fusilier, parrotfish, angelfish and other triggerfish, as well as the stunning Platax, all swimming in crystal-clear waters.

Essential info

At Union State Farm on the island of La Digue, don't miss the largest turtles in the world, weighing up to 300 kilograms (about 660 pounds).

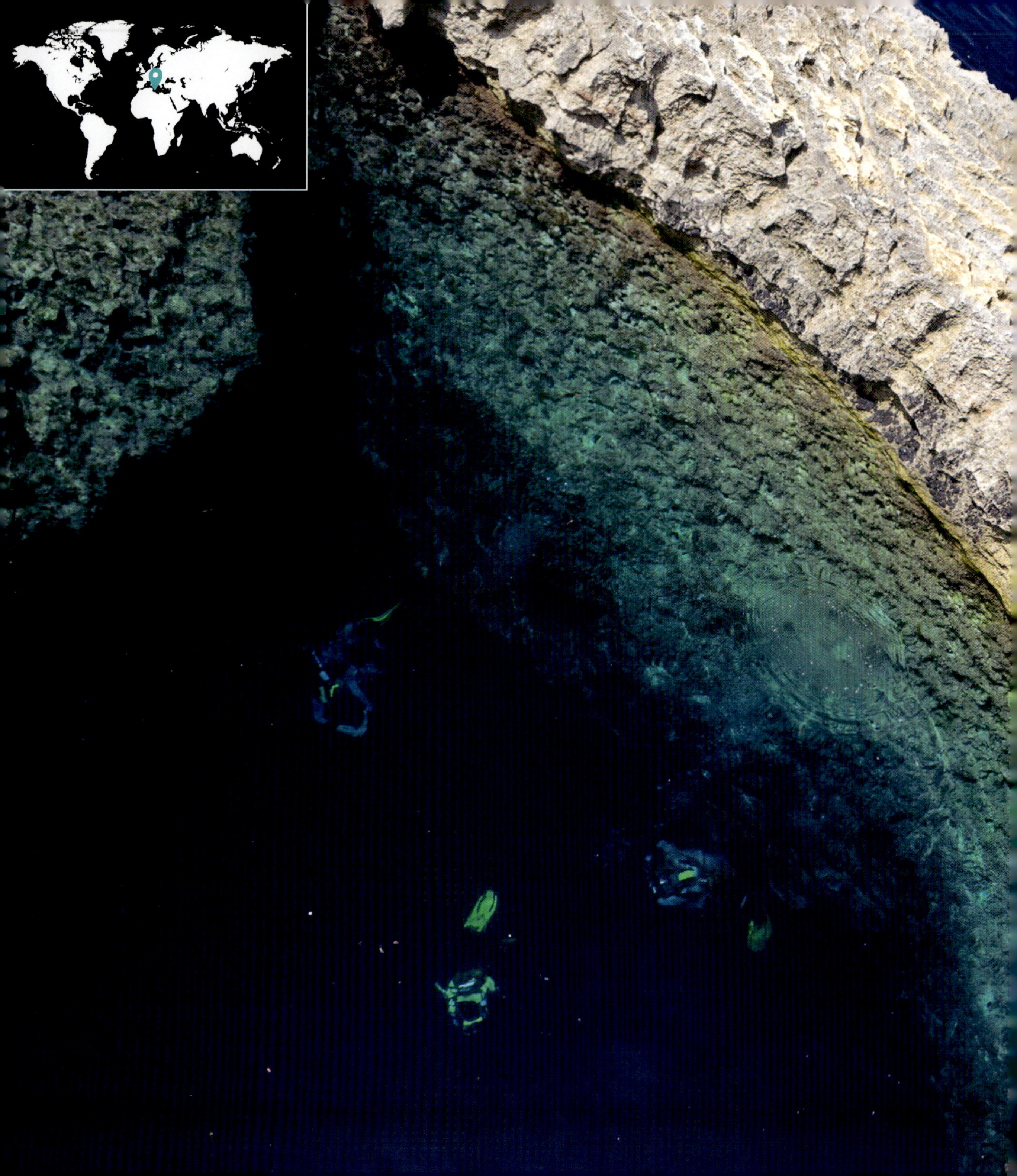

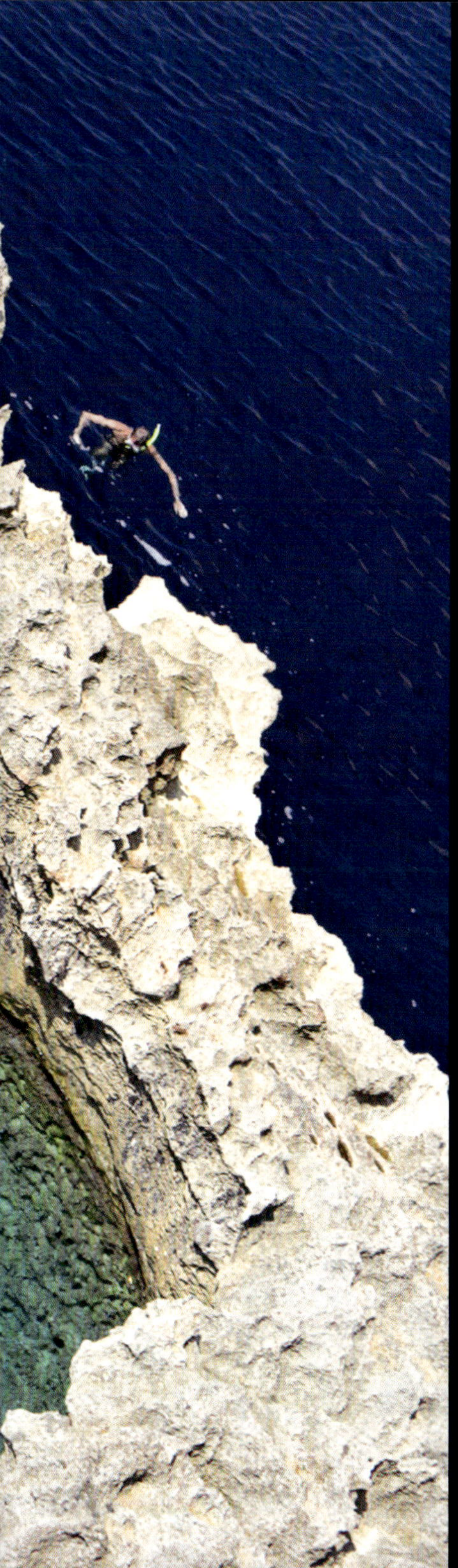

43 Blue Hole

Gozo, Malta

In the middle of the Mediterranean, the Maltese archipelago, formed mainly by the islands of Malta, Gozo and Comino, is renowned for its incredibly clear waters. The seabed features numerous caves, arches, crevices, galleries and impressive geological formations. This makes it a particularly popular destination for caving enthusiasts.

To the west of Gozo Island is one of the most beautiful sites. At the base of the now collapsed Azure Window, a natural arch swept away by a storm in 2017, an immense hole descends into the limestone rock, creating a stunning natural pool. The entry point once offered a splendid view of this arch, but it still remains superb today. The hole, measuring less than 20 metres (65 feet) in diameter, offers a delightful descent to explore two caves and a tunnel that leads to the open sea, allowing divers to continue their adventure among the fallen rocks of the Azure Window. Groupers and moray eels enjoy the multiple hiding places among the rocks.

Essential info

Although diving is accessible to all levels, getting to the Blue Hole site is quite dangerous. Before you can enjoy the dive, there is a long walk through the rocks carrying equipment on your back.

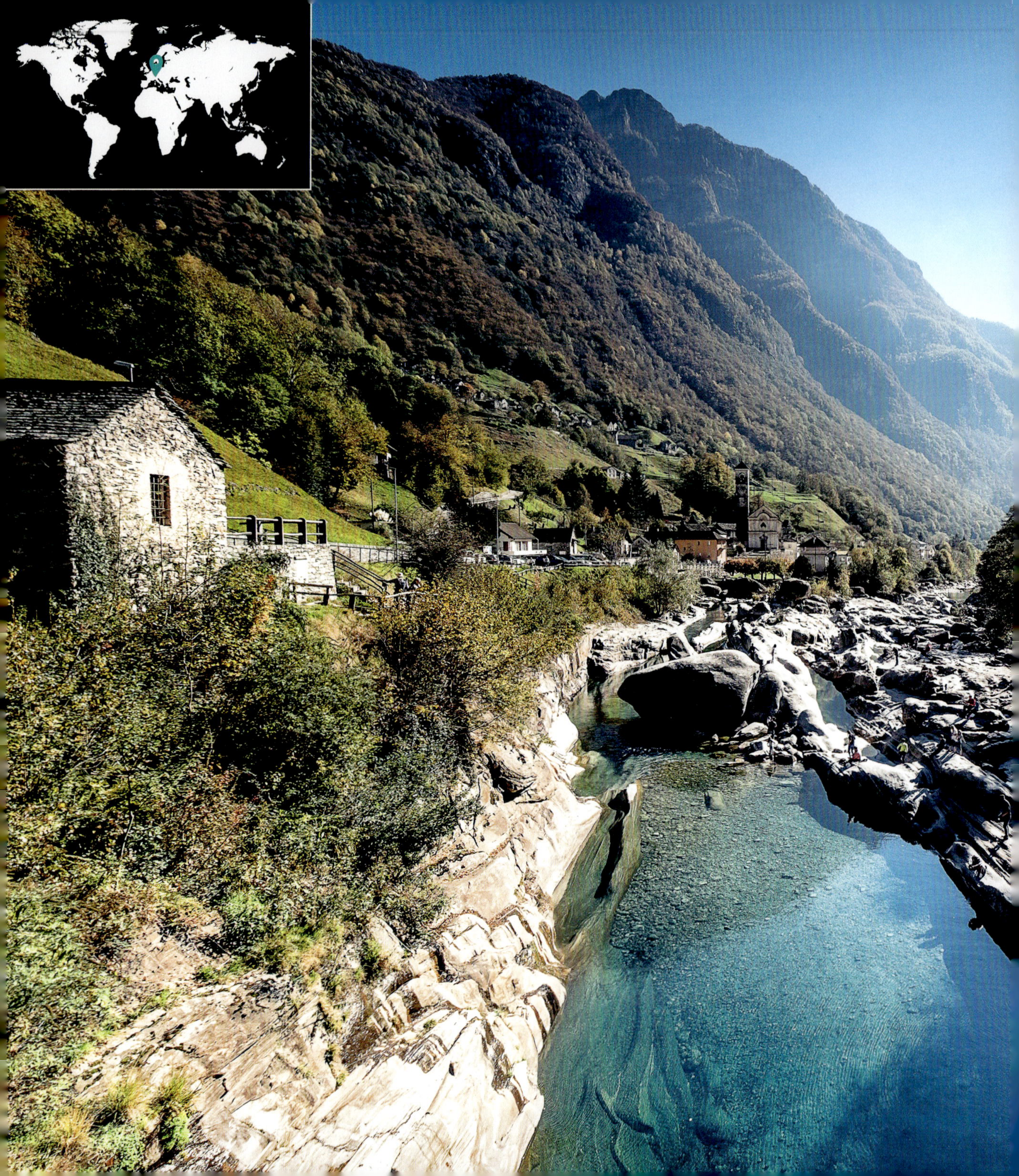

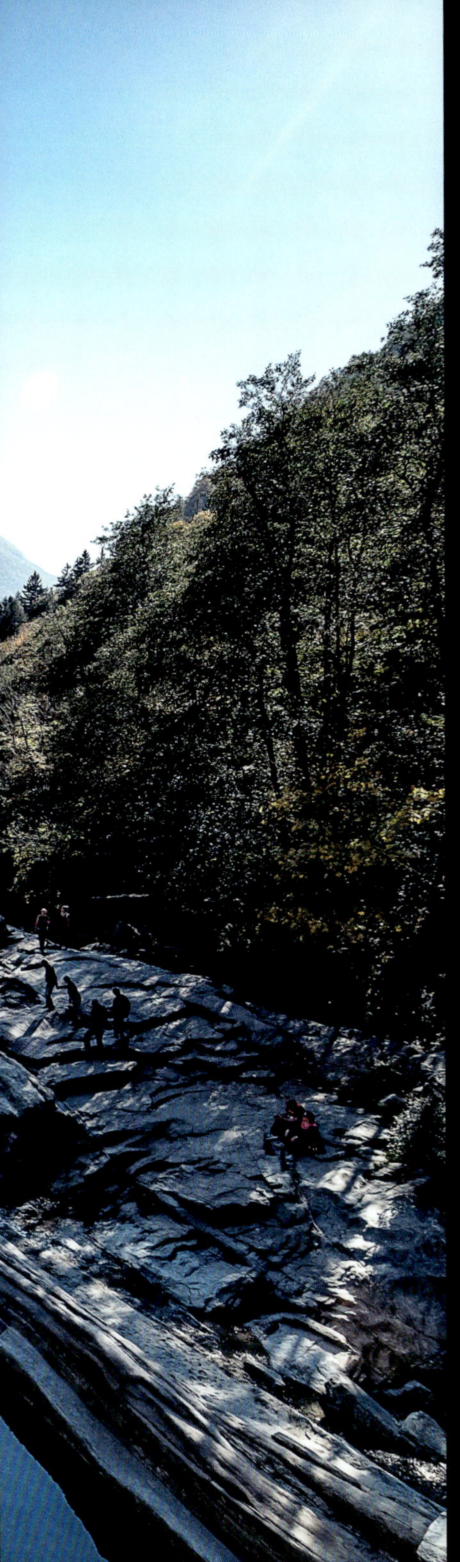

44 Verzasca River

Switzerland

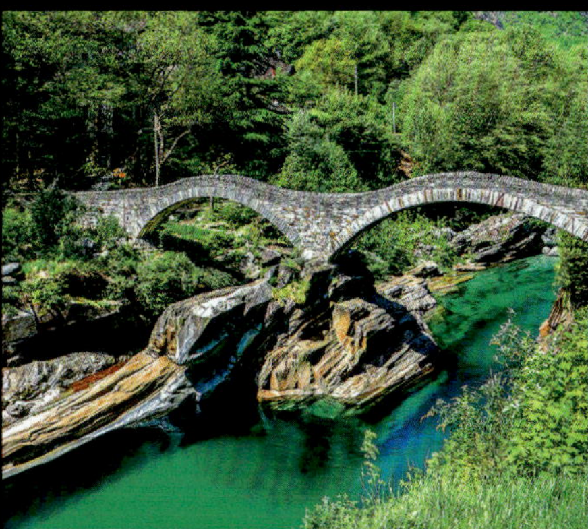

Despite being far from the sea, landlocked Switzerland has a vibrant community of passionate divers eager to brave any conditions to fulfil their desire for underwater exploration. The famous Lake Geneva or Lake Neuchâtel offer many dive sites. But Switzerland also offers other surprising and unique diving spots. In Ticino, close to the Italian border, Verzasca is reputedly one of the most beautiful river dives in the world.

Tucked away between the cliffs, its crystal-clear waters have sculpted the rock over millennia, creating stunning scenery and atmospheres that have earned it the nickname 'Swiss Maldives'. The site of the Roman bridge at Pozzo dei Salti is the most famous, offering a stunning viewpoint where the emerald hues beneath the surface contrast superbly with the two-arched medieval bridge that spans the river (see inset photo). It also provides a breathtaking opportunity to observe a unique geological landscape, shaped by the enduring relationship between water and rock.

Essential info

Depending on the season, currents can be extremely strong in the Verzasca. It is therefore essential to dive with professionals.

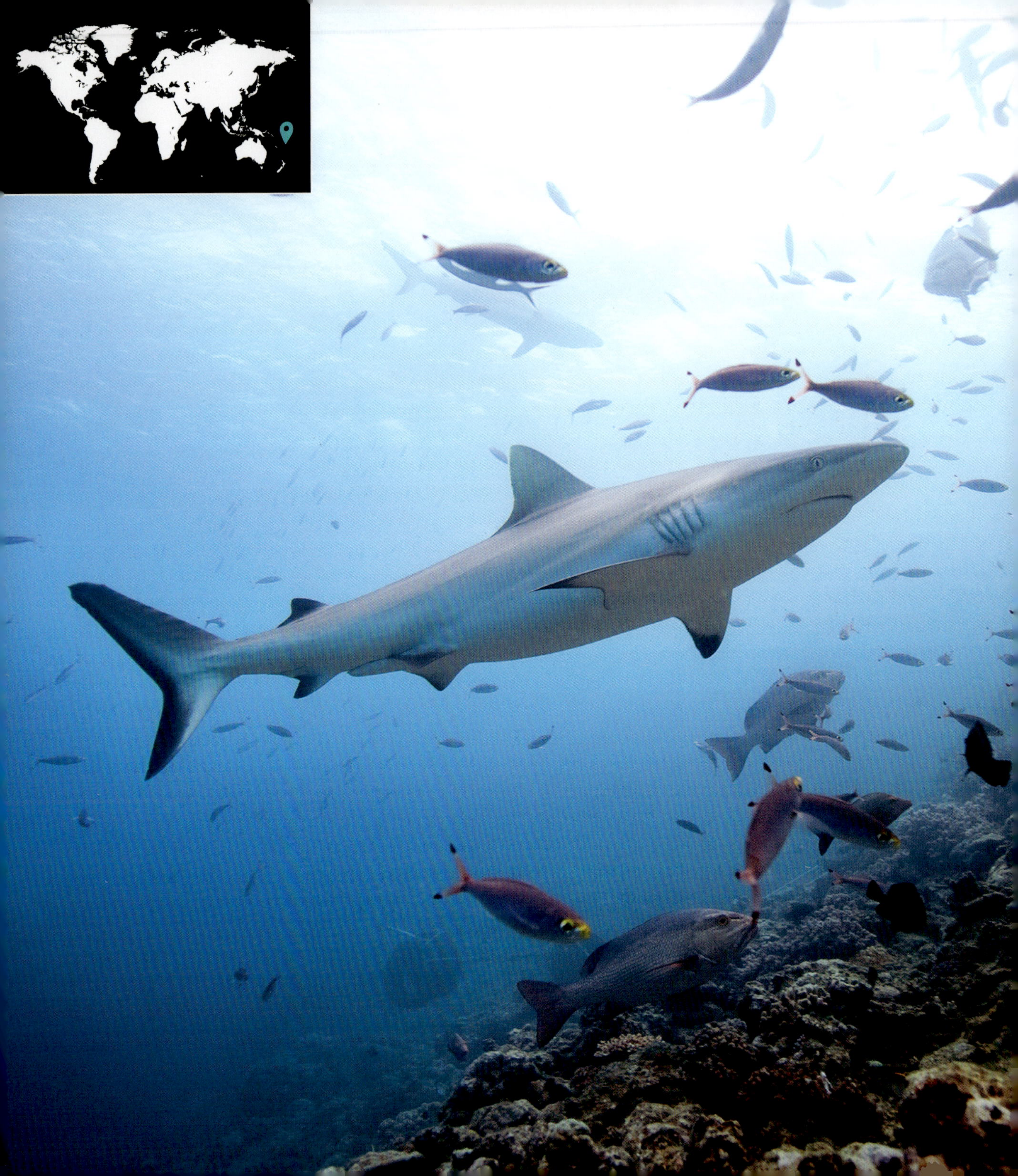

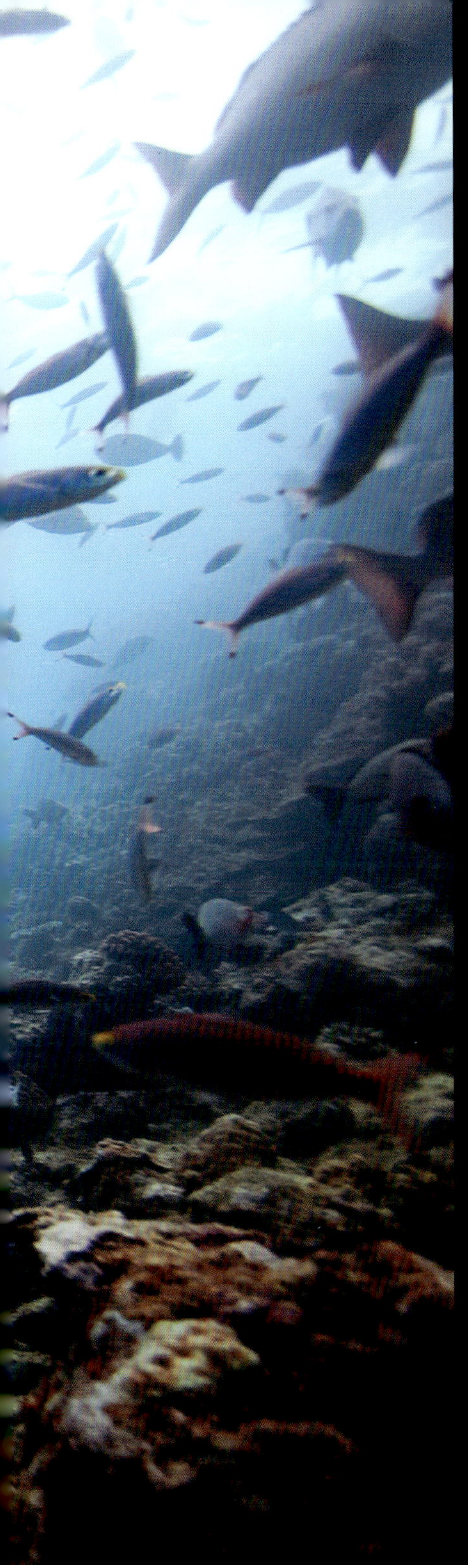

45 Beqa Lagoon

Fiji

In the heart of Oceania, Fiji's archipelago comprises just over 300 islands, each showcasing untamed, pristine beauty. Most are lush with dense tropical forests, including Beqa Island, located south of the main island. This island is the ancestral home of Fiji's legendary fire walkers and birthplace of the shark god Dakuwaqa, considered by the people to be the islanders' guardian.

Encircled by a vast lagoon and coral reef, Beqa boasts nearly 300 kilometres (186 miles) of untouched reefs, where marine life flourishes abundantly. Diving here immerses visitors in vibrant coral landscapes, home to an incredible array of soft corals – *Alcyonaceas* – and brilliantly coloured gorgonians. Perfect for underwater enthusiasts who will discover nudibranchs, shrimps, crabs, ribbon eels and an impressive diversity of tropical fish.

In the channel between Beqa and Viti Levu, thrill-seekers can experience exhilarating dives with up to eight shark species, including bull, lemon, grey (see photo), nurse, whitetip, blacktip and coral sharks, with tiger sharks appearing on occasion.

Essential info

For this shark dive experience, controlled feeding is used. However, the area and dive site are fully protected, with a strict ban on fishing.

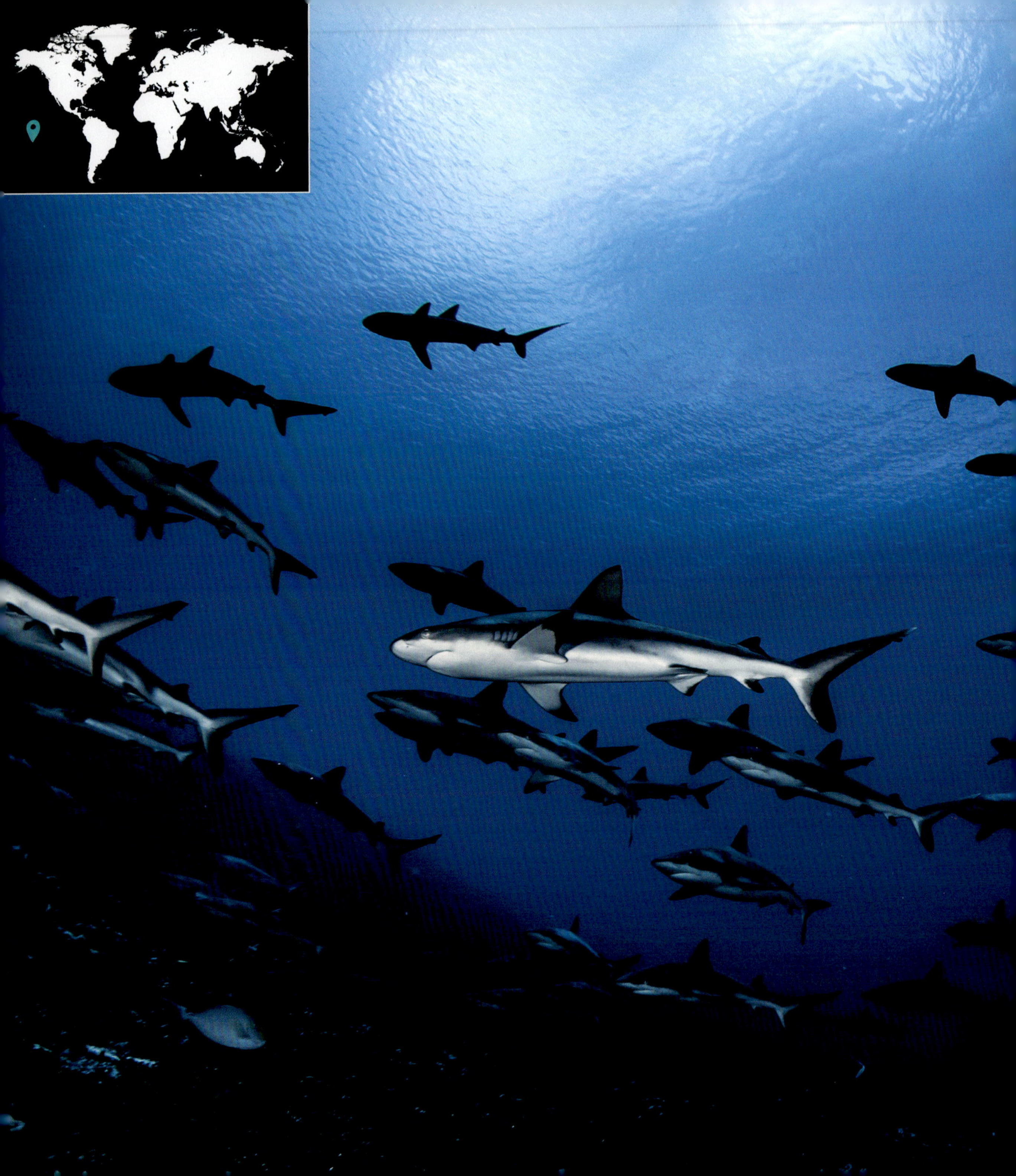

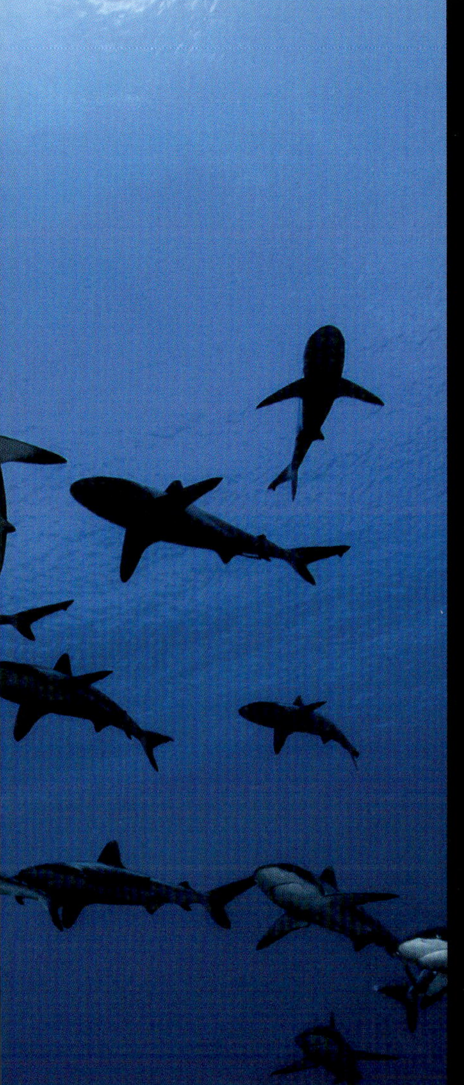

46 Tetamanu Pass

Fakarava, French Polynesia

Arriving in Tahiti, in French Polynesia, feels like reaching the end of the world, deep within the planet's largest ocean. And then there's Fakarava Atoll, a magical place located in the Tuamotu archipelago. This UNESCO Biosphere Reserve is a dream destination for thrill-seeking divers.

At the southern tip of this 60-kilometre (37 miles)-long atoll lies the Tumakohua Pass, or Tetamanu Pass, renowned worldwide for hosting the planet's largest known population of grey sharks. With an estimated 700 sharks, it's no wonder this place is often called the 'wall of sharks'. By day, they drift in open water, riding the currents to conserve energy; by night, the pass transforms into a hunting ground, where survival and predation intertwine in a captivating display. Day or night, the spectacle is unforgettable.

Essential info

The current is generally not excessive and the depth is reasonable,

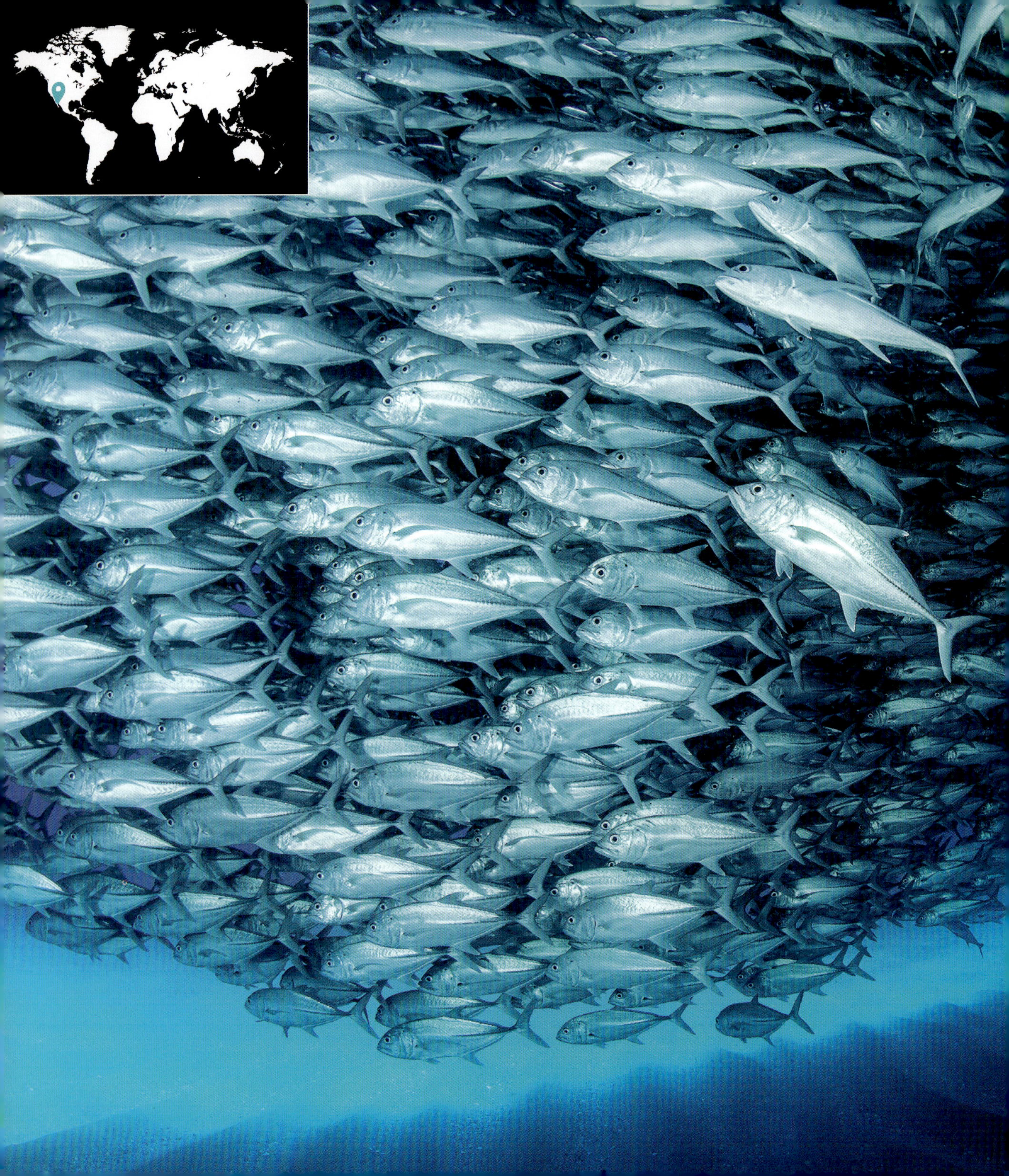

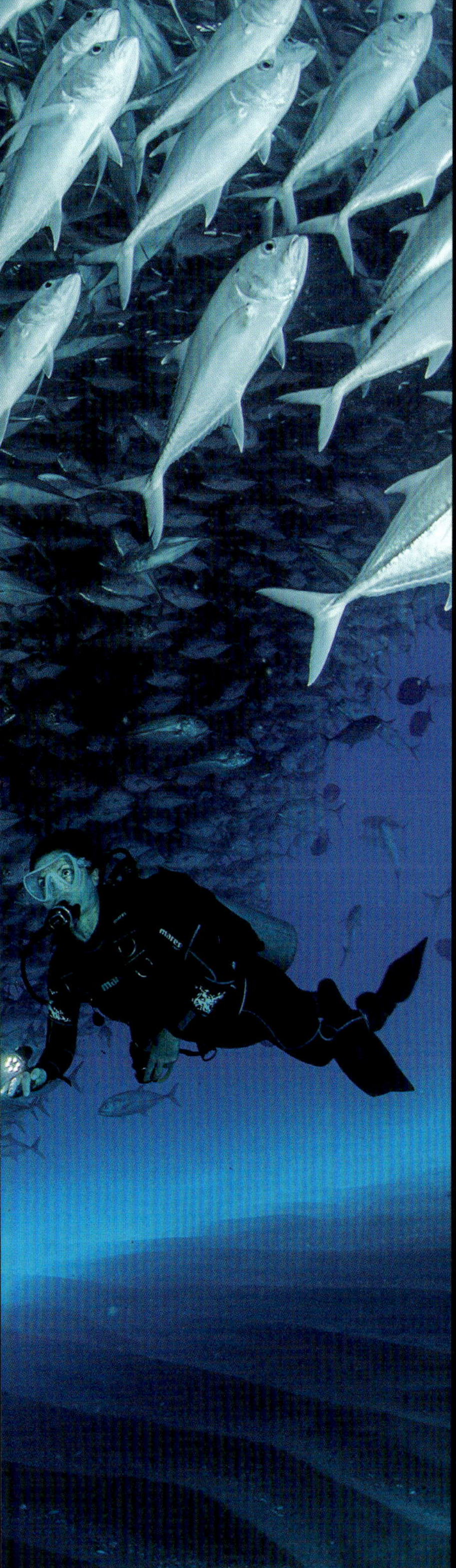

47 Sea of Cortez

Mexico

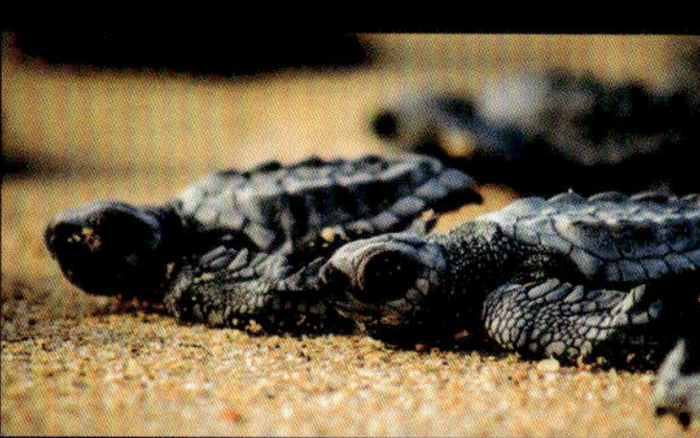

Nestled between the Baja California Peninsula and the Mexican mainland, the Gulf of California – better known as the Sea of Cortez – was a cherished destination for Commander Cousteau, who embarked on multiple expeditions here with his crew aboard the *Calypso*. In awe of the rich biodiversity, he affectionately dubbed it the 'World's biggest aquarium'.

This sanctuary of pelagic life offers encounters that are nothing short of spectacular. From blue whales, the largest of all whales, to fin whales, grey whales, humpbacks and sperm whales, sightings of these giants are common in winter. Divers and visitors can also encounter manta rays, mobula rays, schools of jacks, whale sharks, hammerheads, orcas, dolphins and sea turtles – nowhere else on Earth offers such an array of incredible marine life. The location boasts over 800 species of fish. Cabo Pulmo encapsulates the best of the Sea of Cortez, with an impressive density of fish and marine life. In recognition of its natural wealth, 244 islands and coastal areas were designated a UNESCO World Heritage Site in 2005. Then, in 2009, Cerralvo Island was officially renamed to honour Cousteau himself and is now called Jacques Cousteau Island.

Essential info

The Sea of Cortez offers something for everyone, with dive sites suited to all skill levels. Even non-divers can enjoy snorkelling here, with a wealth of accessible spots to explore.

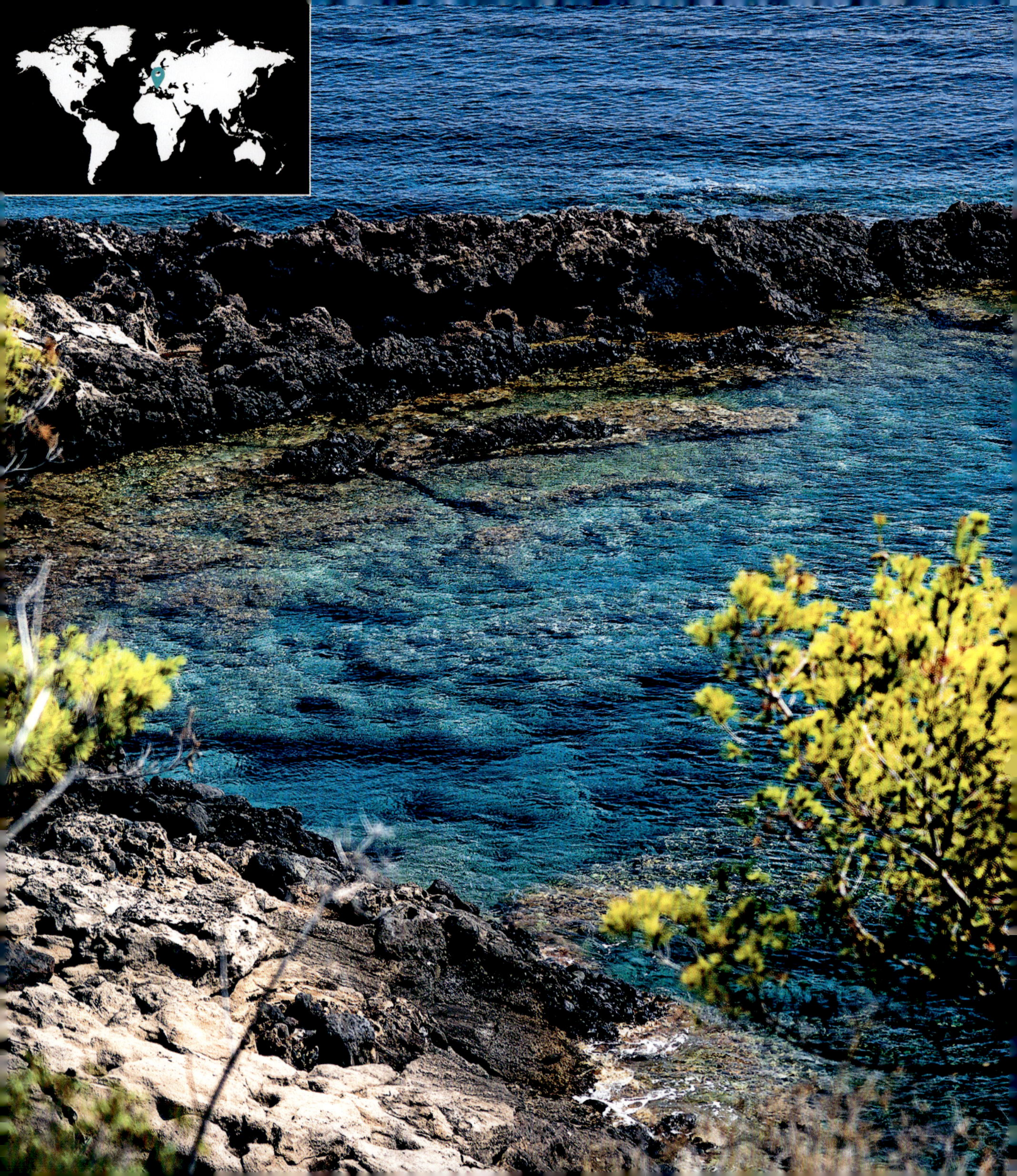

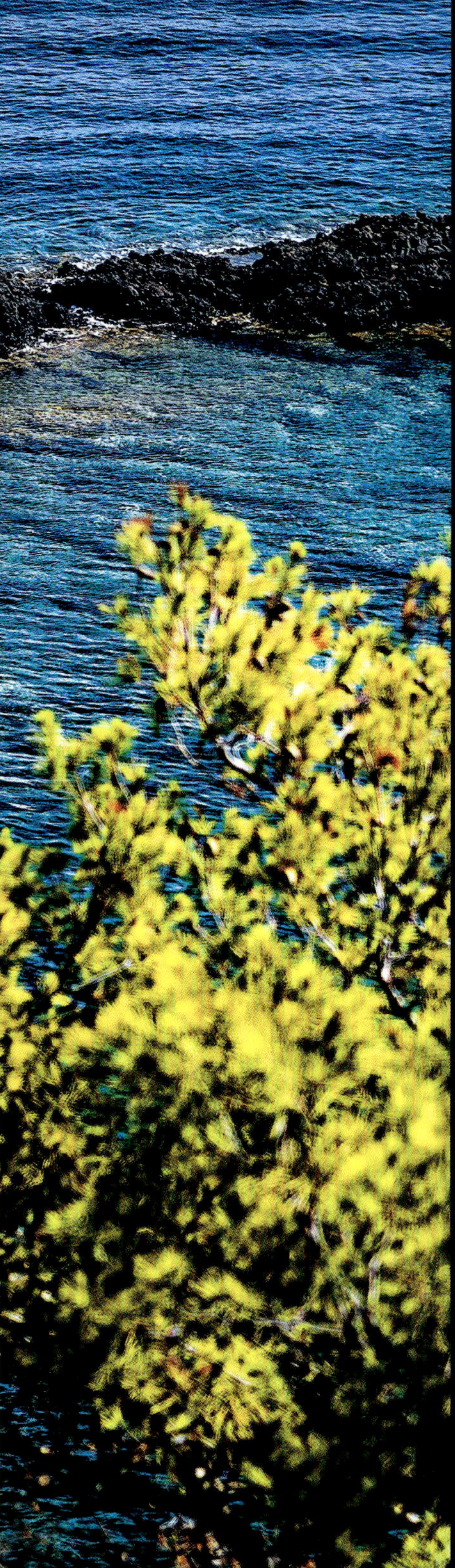

48 Ustica Island

Italy

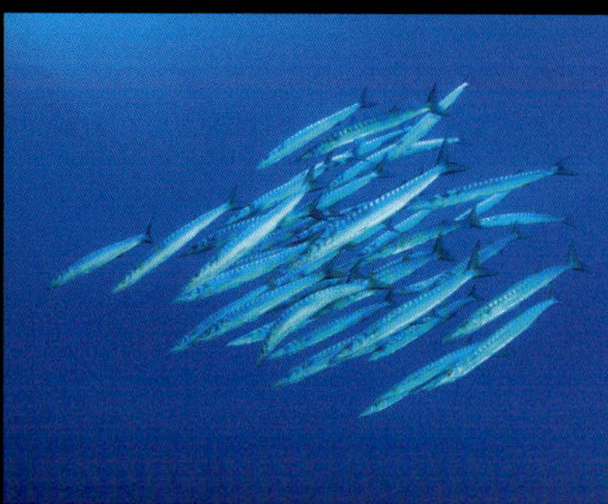

The Mediterranean Sea is dotted with small islands, most of which are unknown to the general public. To the north of Sicily stands Ustica Island, less than 70 kilometres (43 miles) off the coast of the city of Palermo. This tiny volcanic island, home to about 1,300 residents, feels as though time stopped here several decades ago. It boasts a charming and quiet fishing village, enlivened by several excellent restaurants.

Ustica is, however, becoming increasingly popular with divers. The seabed, protected by Italy's first marine nature reserve established in 1986, offers a spectacular showcase for a rediscovery of the Mediterranean.

All the diverse fauna of the Great Blue seems to gather here. Beneath the surface, divers can frequently spot large groupers, abundant lobsters, greater amberjack, sea bream, schools of barracuda (see inset photo), and even triggerfish. The dark caves are inhabited by thousands of shrimp, along with conger eels and moray eels. Once back on land, indulge in the local cuisine to conclude the day, embracing the legendary Italian dolce vita.

Essential info

Ustica offers about 30 dive sites, and all levels will find an option to enjoy.

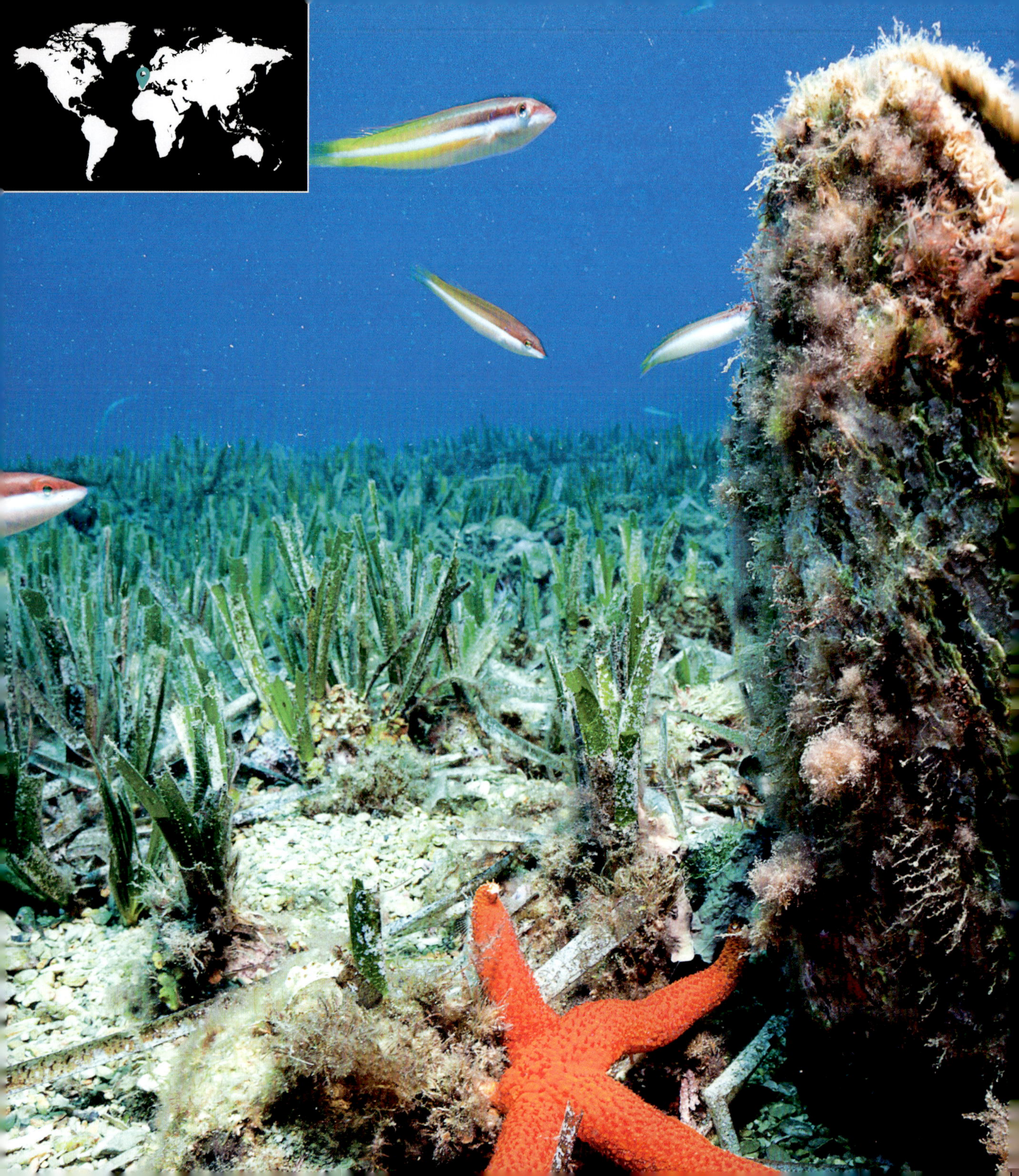

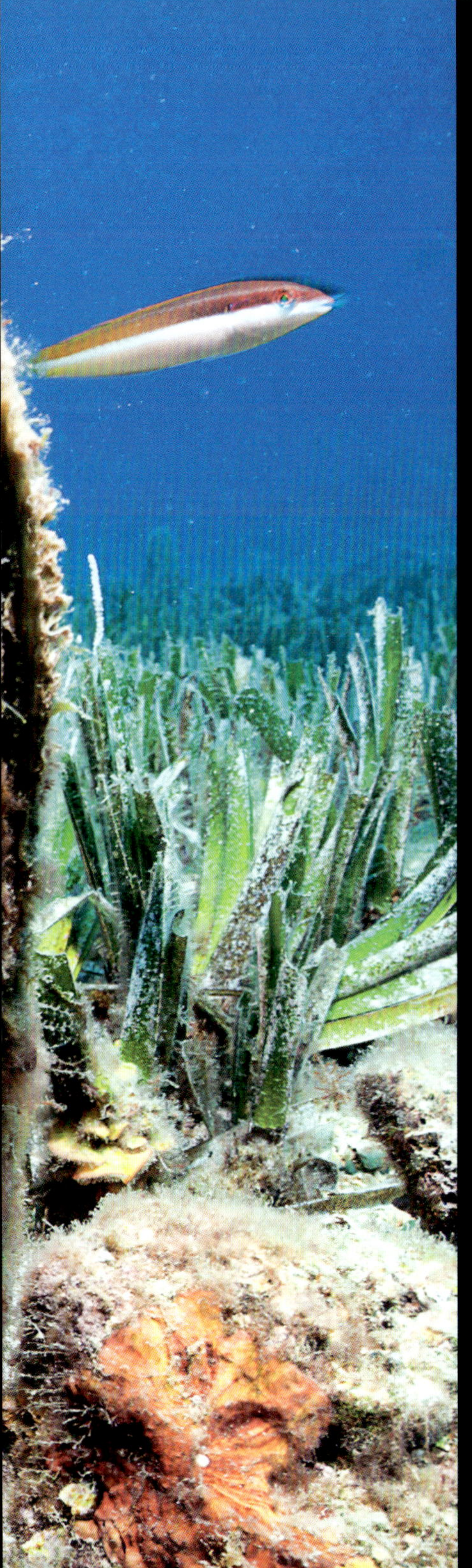

49 Medes Islands

Spain

Nearly 10 per cent of the world's recorded marine biodiversity is found in the Mediterranean. Yet many places are being damaged due to human activity. Fortunately, there are widely designated sanctuary areas where we can experience what the Great Blue looked like several decades ago.

On the Spanish Costa Brava, close to the French border, the Medes Islands have been fully protected since 1983, offering over 500 marine hectares where marine species can live in peace. From L'Estartit, on the coast, it takes just a few minutes by boat to reach this stunning location. Without a doubt, as soon as you dive in, you'll encounter the Mediterranean in all its vibrant glory, teeming with fish. Marvel at the breathtaking drop-offs adorned with red and yellow gorgonians, spot beautiful red scorpionfish, and observe schools of castagnole swimming alongside large octopuses that gracefully move from rock to rock. Those with a keen eye will discover numerous nudibranchs displaying their shimmering colours, while barracudas patrol the upper waters. It's a spectacle that resembles a living painting.

Essential info

This is a dive site for all levels, even beginners. Diving primarily takes place from April to October.

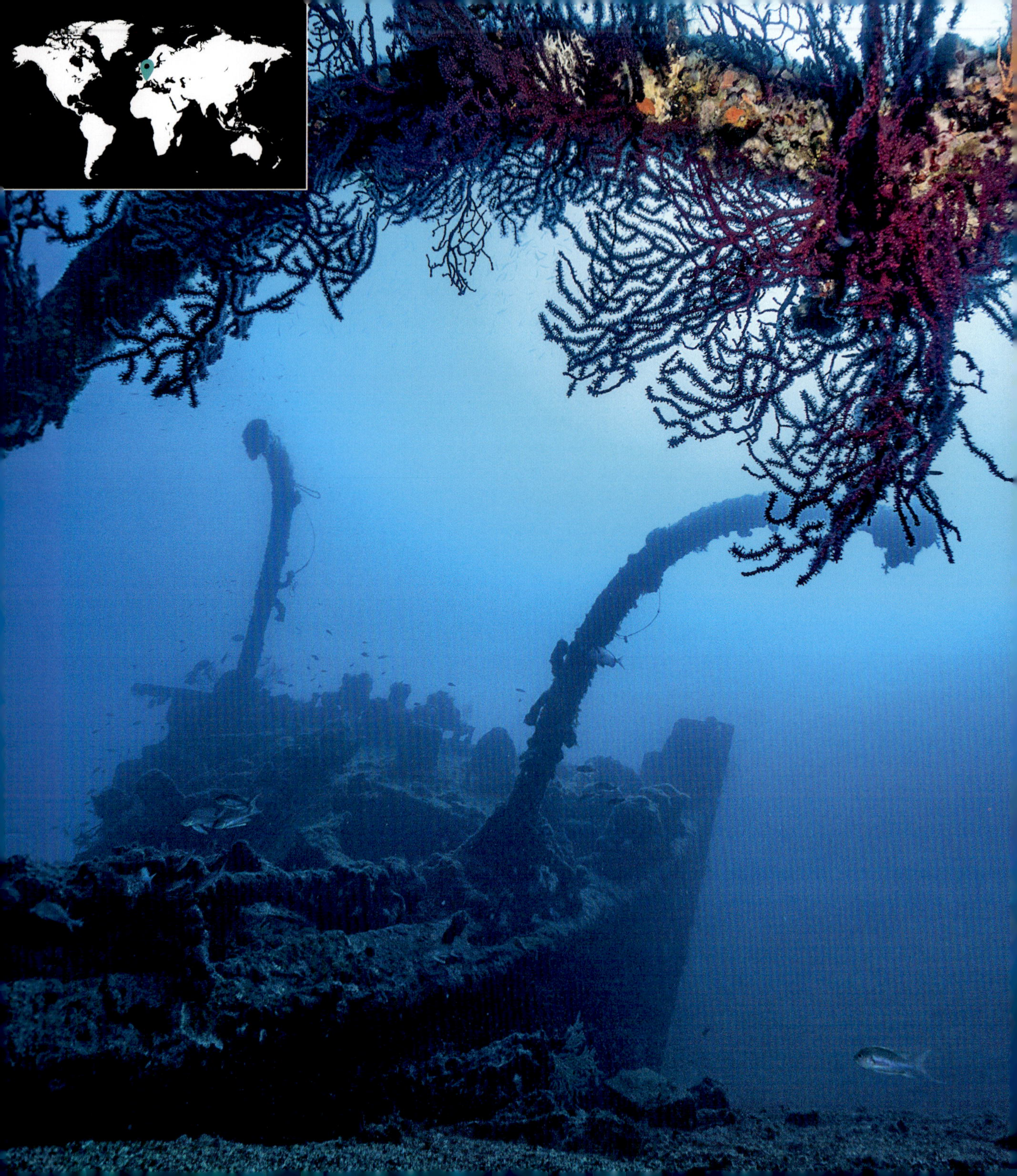

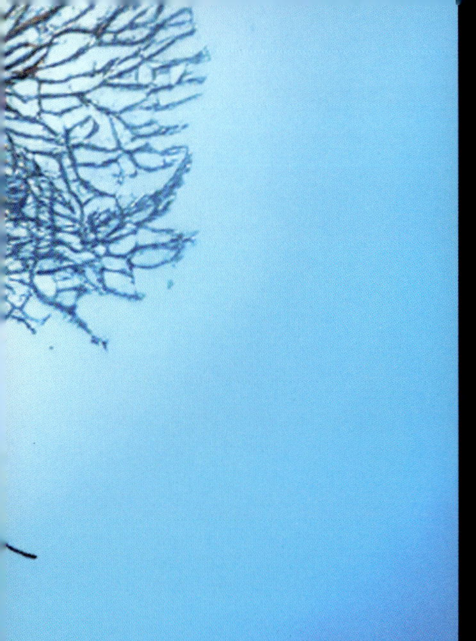

50 *Le Liban* wreck

Marseille, France

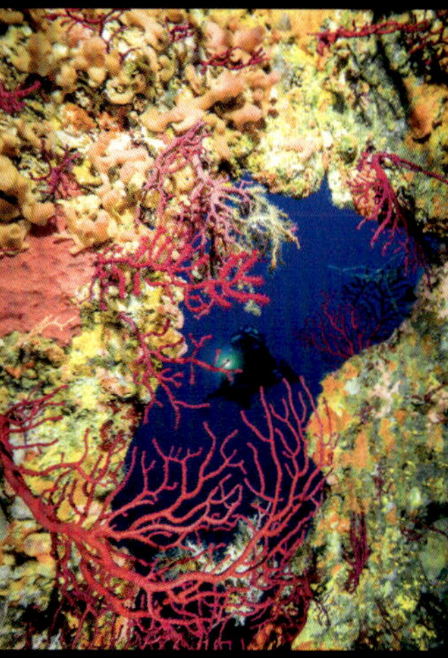

In June 1903, the steamer *Le Liban* set off from the port of Marseille towards Bastia, in Corsica. As it passed the Tiboulen de Maïre Island, it encountered a liner from the same company on its return journey. A miscommunication occurred between the captains during their manoeuvres, which led to a disastrous outcome. A few minutes later, *Le Liban* had already started sinking near the Pharillons, the two islets off the southern tip of Maïre Island.

Nearly 100 people perished, trapped largely under huge shade tarpaulins. Today, nestled within the Calanques National Park, the wreck is among the most popular diving destinations in Marseille. The 91-metre (298-feet)-long ship teems with abundant marine life. Despite its bow being embedded in the rock, it maintains an impressive presence. The still intact davits are covered with stunning red finger gorgonians. Meanwhile, vibrant anthias fish bring splashes of colour to much of this vessel marked by its tragic past.

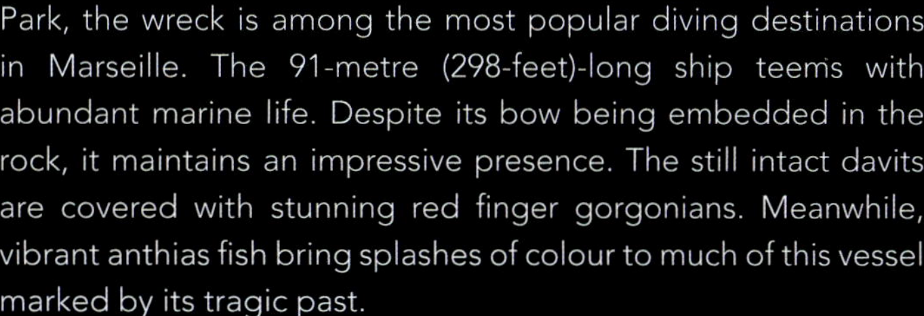

Essential info

At a depth of 32 and 36 metres (104 and 118 feet), this site is perfect for level 2 divers. After exploring the wreck, you can easily stroll to the nearby Pharillons site, with its superb arches.

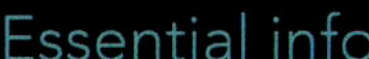

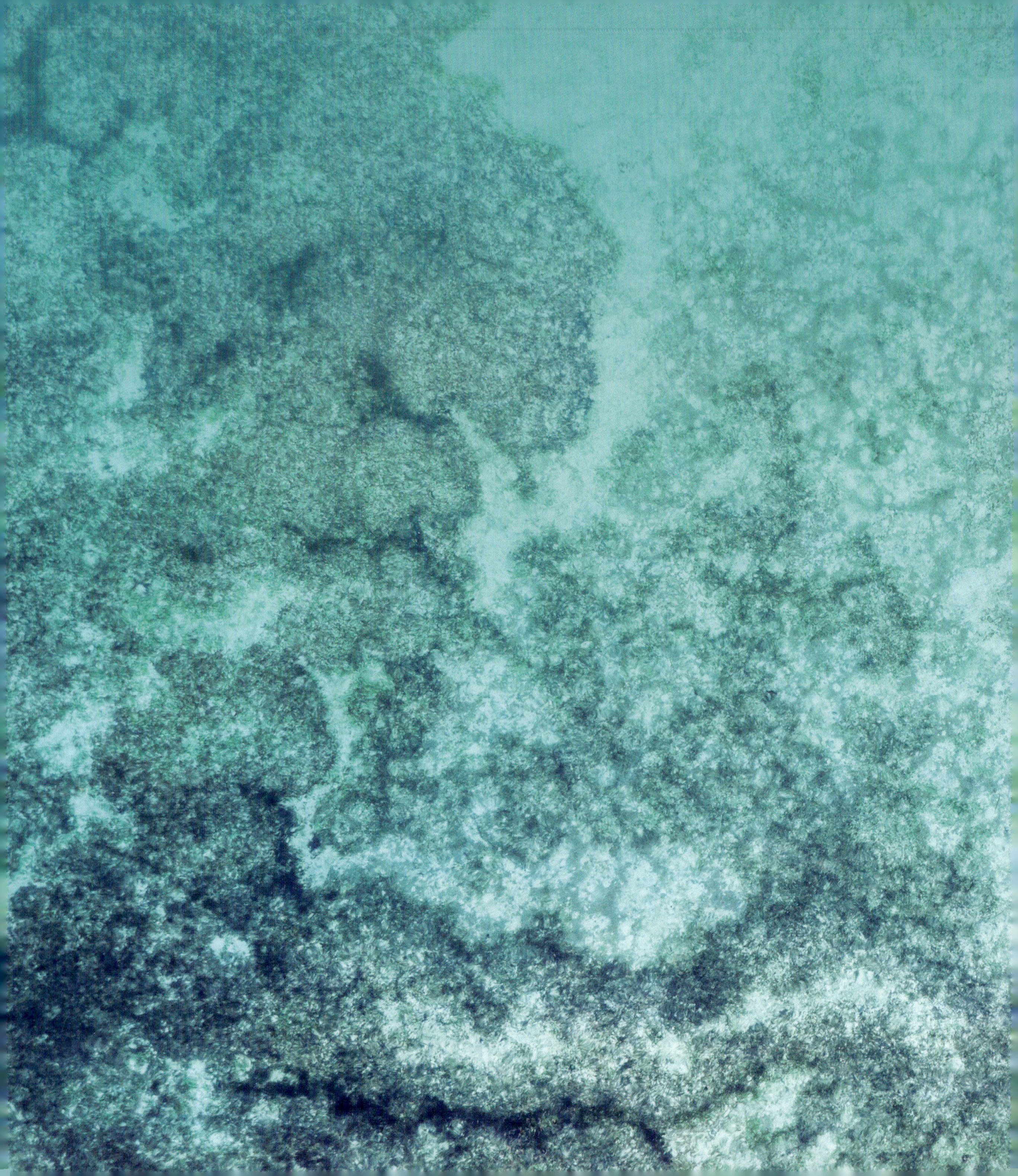

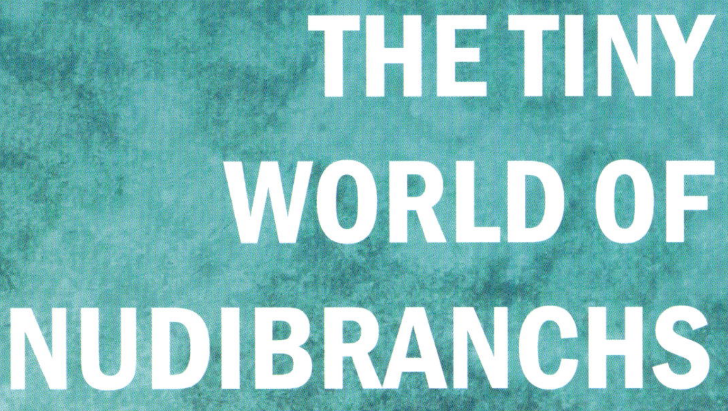
THE TINY
WORLD OF
NUDIBRANCHS

These small creatures adorned with shimmering colours captivate divers and photographers alike. Nudibranchs inhabit all seas and oceans, resembling vibrant jewels to be searched for like treasure.

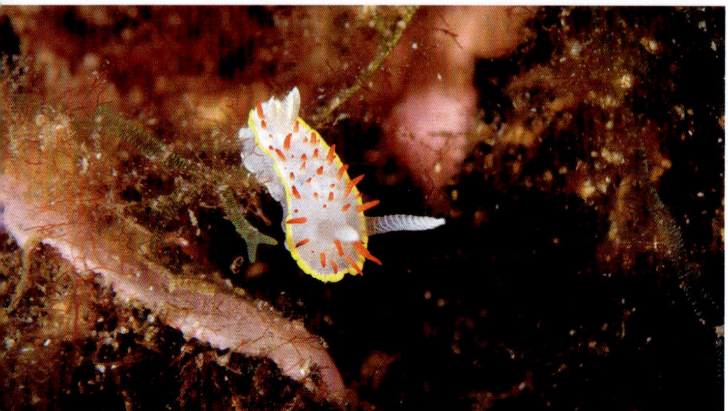

Red-tipped dorid.

Sea slugs?

In the classification of living organisms, nudibranchs belong to the phylum Mollusca species, specifically within the class Gastropoda and the subclass Opisthobranchia. This diverse group boasts over 3,000 known species.

Commonly referred to as 'sea slugs', it's important to note that while nudibranchs are a family within this category, not all sea slugs are nudibranchs. The term 'nudibranch' derives from the Latin word nudus, meaning 'naked', and the Greek word brankhia, which translates to 'gills'.

These fascinating creatures are characterised by their exposed gills or sensory structures that allow them to breathe. Only certain species have gills that are positioned beneath the mantle, making them invisible when the animal is viewed from above.

A wide variety

Their size varies from a few millimetres (0.1 inch) to tens of centimetres. For instance, the Spanish dancer (*Hexabranchus sanguineus*) can reach up to 60 centimetres (24 inches) in length. Boasting nearly every imaginable colour and pattern, nudibranchs are a delight for underwater photographers. Most nudibranchs fall into the two most common categories: dorid and eolid. Dorids are easily recognisable by their plume of gills that encircle the anus on their dorsal side. In contrast, eolids possess dorsal appendages known as 'cerata', which enhance the gas exchange surface area for cutaneous respiration.

Nudibranchs generally have a short lifespan, ranging from a few weeks to about a year for some species.

Adapted to their environment

White *Flabellina.*

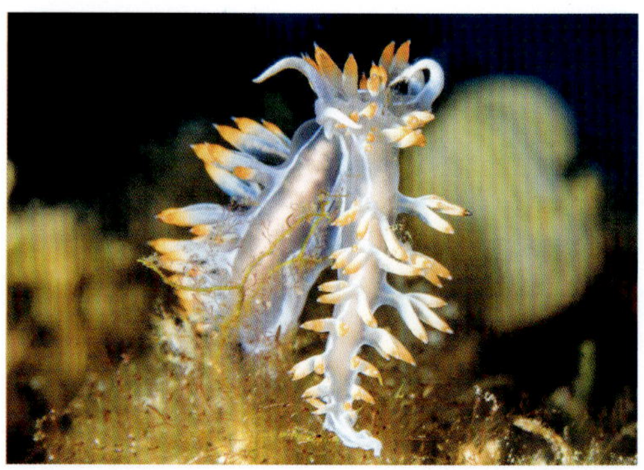

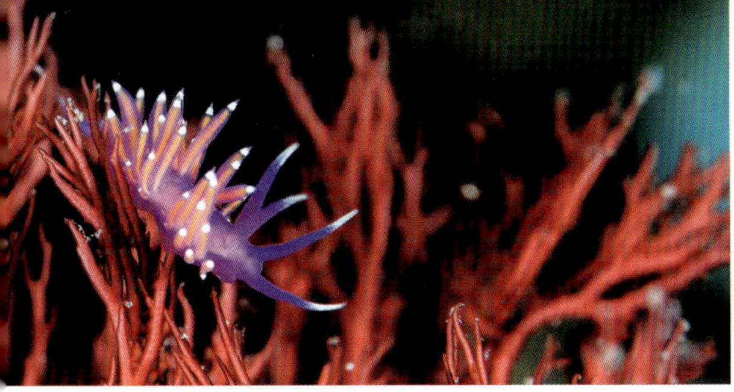

Purple *Coryphella*.

Given their slow movement and short lifespan, optimising reproductive success is crucial for sustaining nudibranch populations. All nudibranchs are hermaphroditic, possessing both male and female genital organs. When two individuals mate, they position themselves head-to-tail and exchange male gametes before depositing banded eggs on substrates like rocks or seaweed.

These species rely on their rhinophores to navigate their environment. These two extensions on their heads are equipped with chemical receptors that help them detect food and locate other individuals.

A unique way of life

Some species store photosynthetic algae inside their bodies from their food, which provides them with energy. These nudibranchs live close to the surface in order to make the most of the sunlight.

Eolids are notable for their ability to store stinging cells within their cerates. They achieve this by consuming cnidarians, particularly hydroids, which are rich in these cells.

Nudibranch laying eggs.

As they move, nudibranchs leave a trail of mucus that can serve multiple purposes, including allowing them to follow the scent trail left by a species mate.

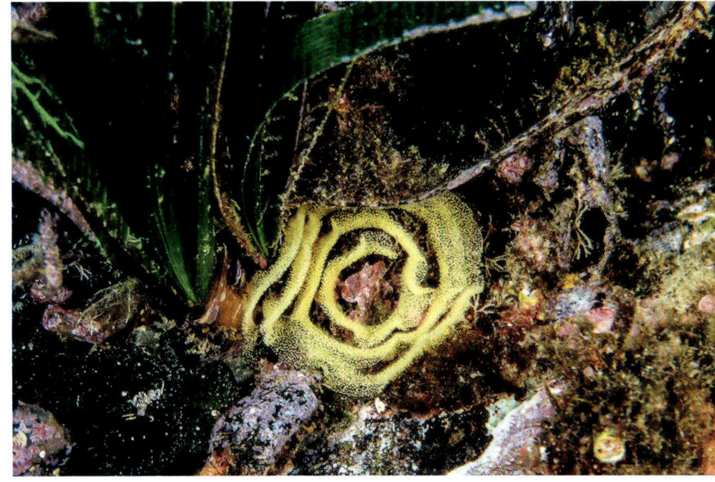

Chromodoris.

Observing nudibranchs

The best way to spot nudibranchs while diving is to use lighting that will reveal their vibrant colours.

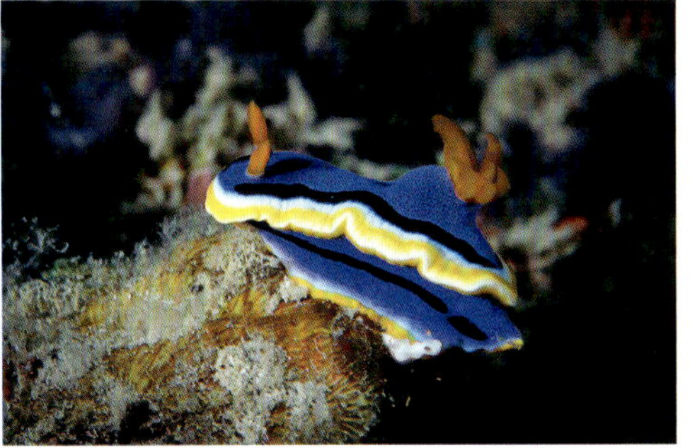

Nembrotha with white streaks.

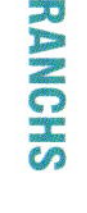

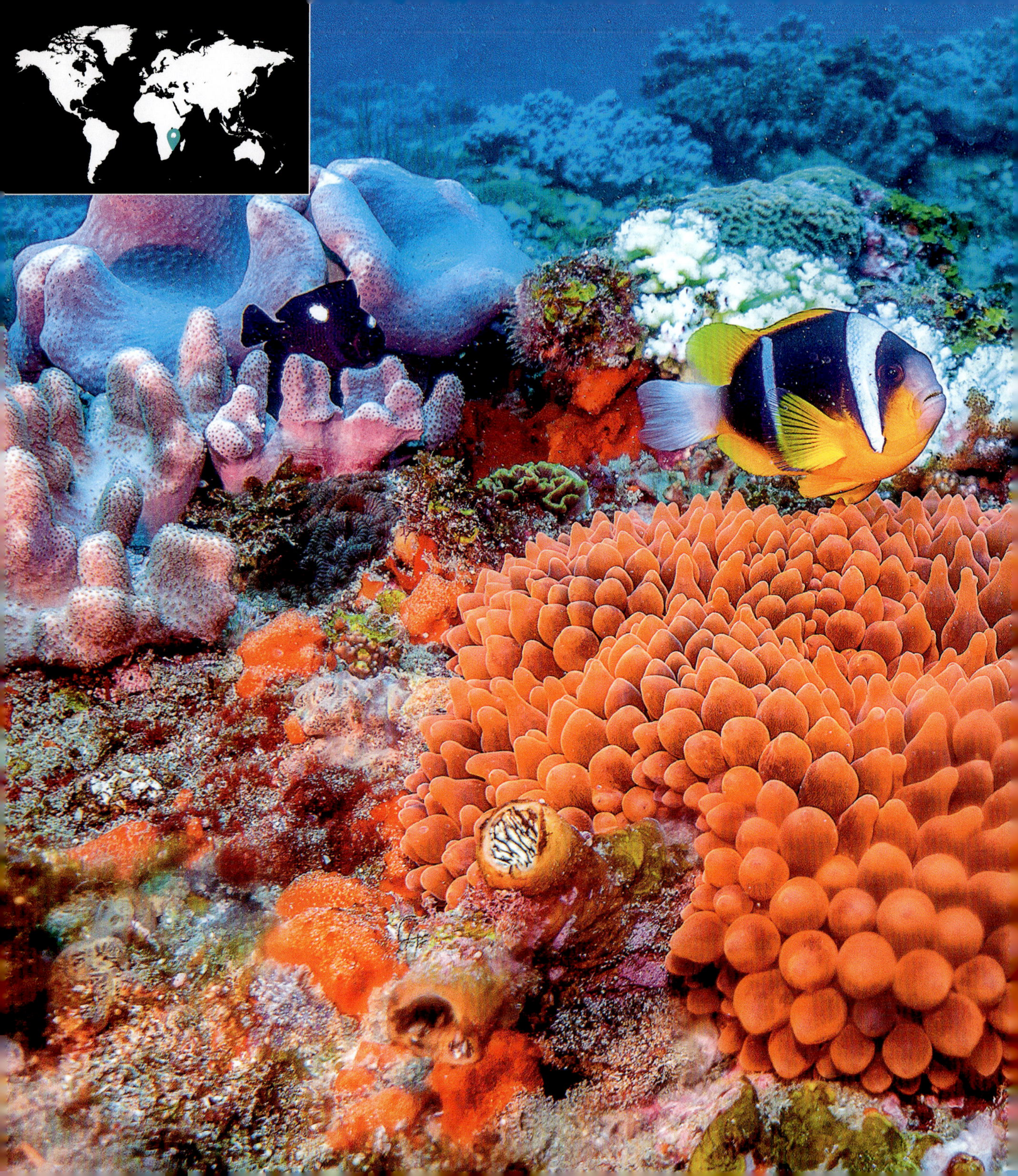

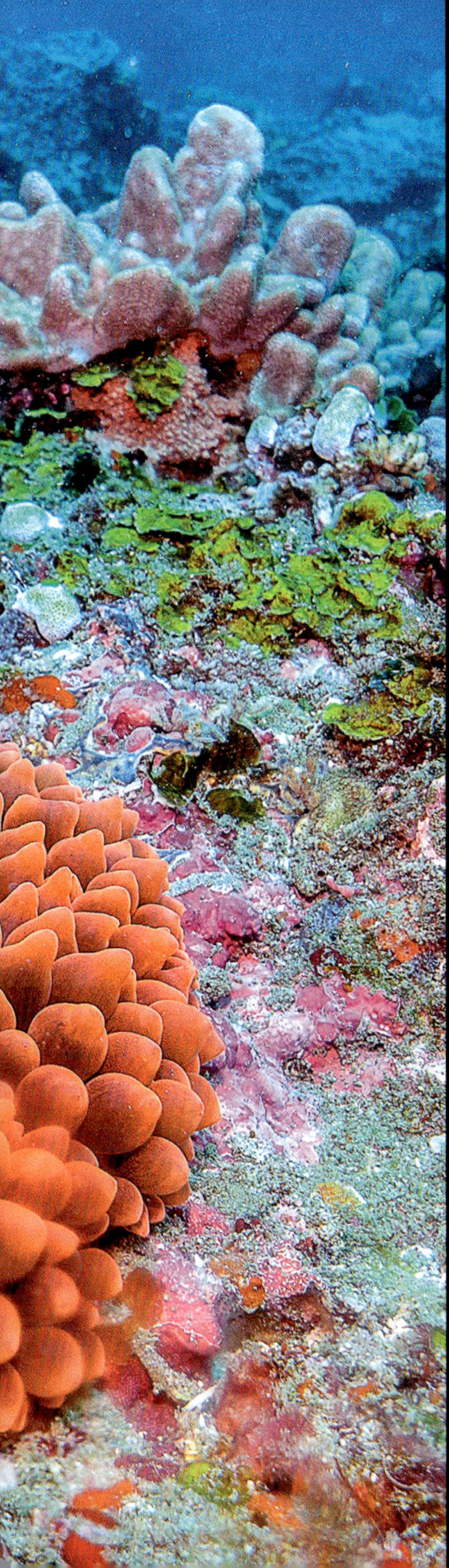

51 Ponta do Ouro

Mozambique

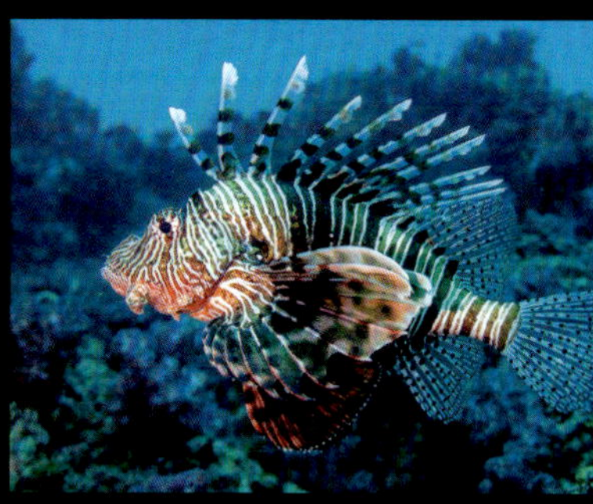

Mozambique, still largely untouched by mass tourism, is increasingly popular with travellers looking to reconnect with nature. A true sanctuary, Ponta do Ouro Bay, just a short distance from the South African border, is one of the country's most stunning locations. Its golden sandy beach stretches for kilometres, where the waves are the only barrier to easily reaching some 20 nearby dive sites.

The rich waters of the Mozambique Channel draw incredible marine life, making it one of the top spots to dive with sharks. Nearly 20 species of sharks roam these waters, offering thrilling encounters for divers. Bull sharks, hammerheads, tiger sharks, grey reef sharks and blacktip sharks are frequently seen here, much to the distress of groupers, who rely on cunning to survive in this challenging environment. Manta rays, lionfish (see photo), whale sharks and even humpback whales can also be spotted. For those who enjoy smaller creatures, nudibranchs, frogfish, pipefish and other leaf fish balance the thrill of finned predators with delicate beauty.

Essential info

The varied dive sites in Ponta do Ouro cater to divers of all experience levels. This adventure is best complemented by a land safari for an unforgettable encounter with Africa's majestic wildlife.

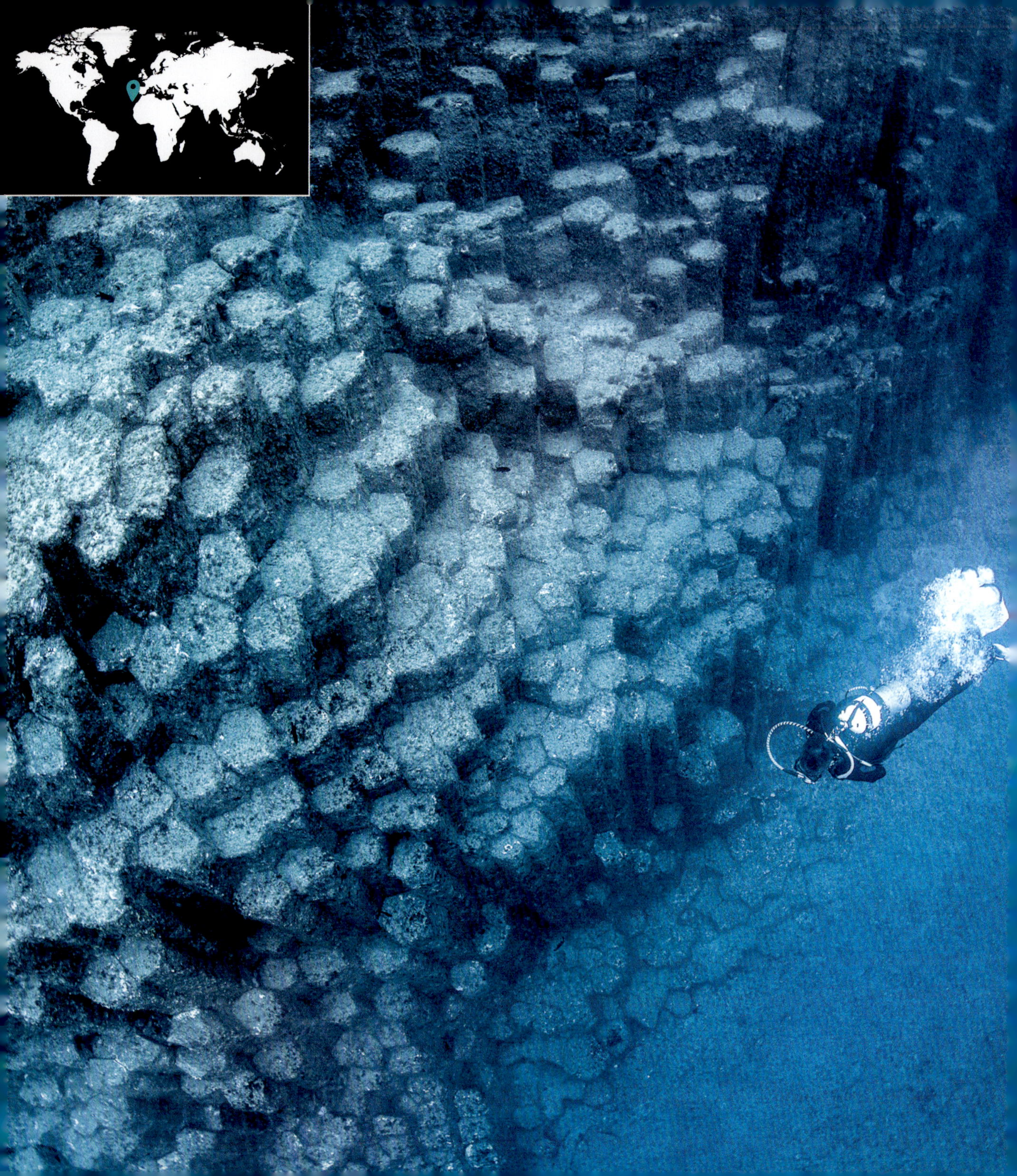

52 La Rapadura

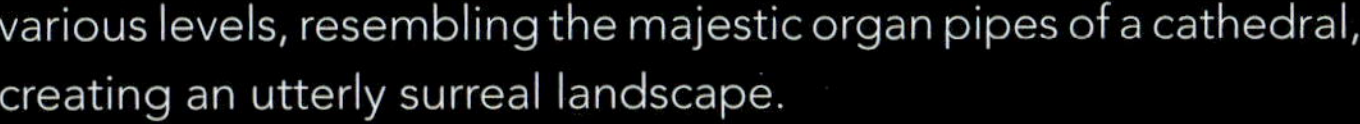

Tenerife, Canary Islands

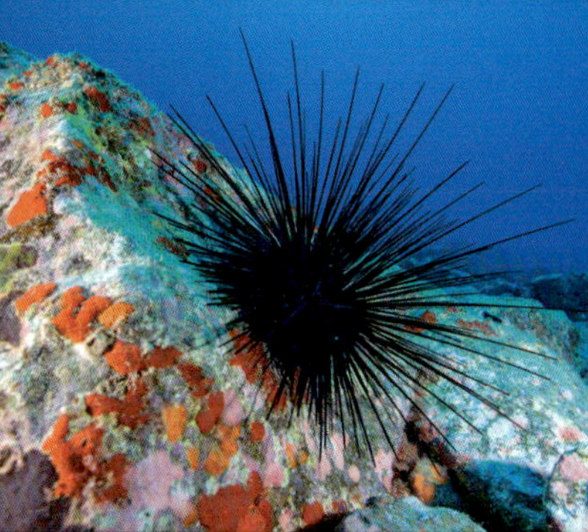

Marine life, shipwrecks and caves are often the primary drawcards for divers, regardless of the location. The Canary Islands offer stunning displays of these underwater wonders, but north of Tenerife lies a truly unique site unlike any other on the planet.

At the foot of the La Quinta cliff, which plunges steeply into the ocean, a basalt flow has cooled into massive, perfectly prismatic blocks that rise at various levels, resembling the majestic organ pipes of a cathedral, creating an utterly surreal landscape.

Marine life is sparse here, with diadem urchins (see inset photo) having proliferated and significantly diminished the algal presence. The site is strikingly mineral and grandiose. At a depth of 25 metres (82 feet), these colossal basalt columns, seemingly frozen in time, evoke the sensation of being a privileged observer of long-extinct volcanic activity.

Essential info

A site for experienced divers, with the upper section of the organ pipes at a depth of 25 metres (82 feet).

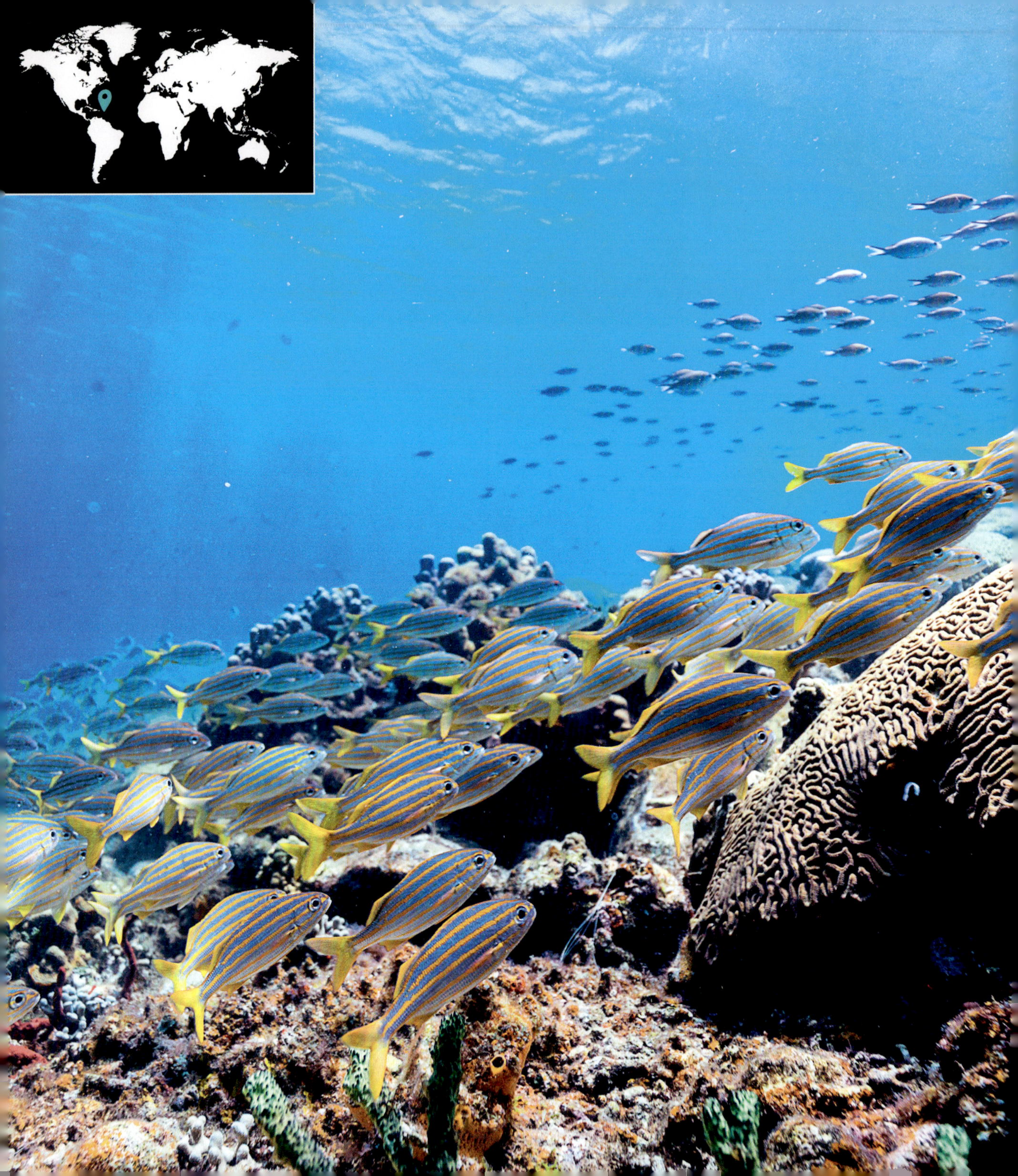

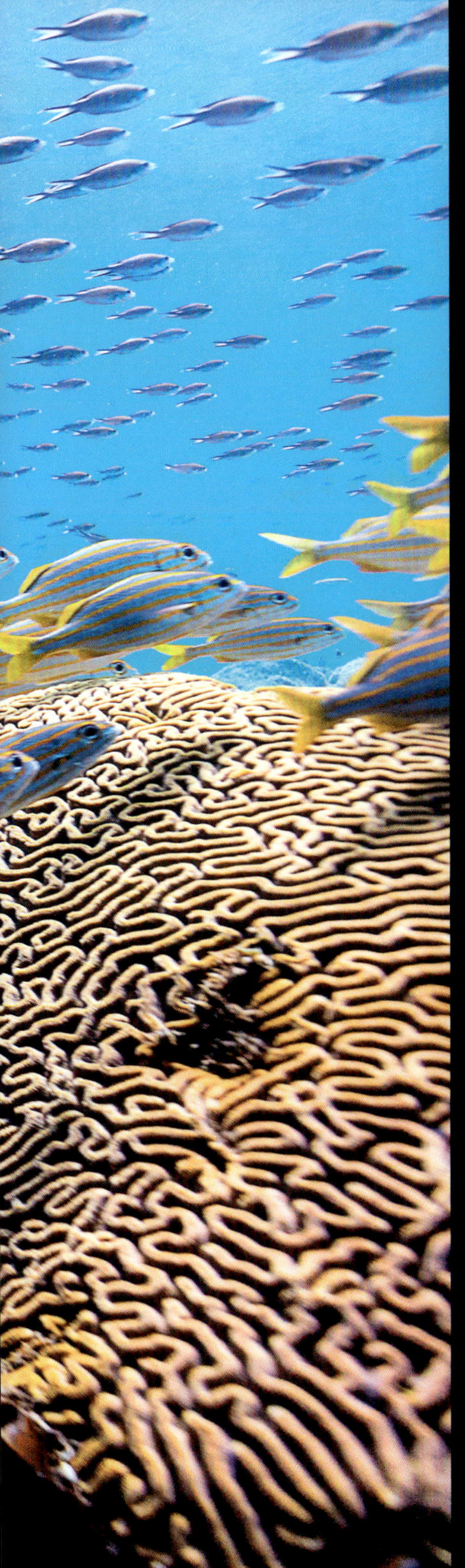

53 Sec Pâté

Guadeloupe, French Antilles

Approximately 13 kilometres (eight miles) south of Guadeloupe and the Trois-Rivières commune, a group of nine small islands and islets make up the archipelago of Les Saintes. There are charming fishing villages adorned with vibrant, colourful huts in a truly delightful and peaceful setting. Beneath the surface lies an underwater mountain, with its base plunging approximately 300 metres (1000 feet) deep and its summit rising through three peaks ranging from 38 to 15 metres (125 to 50 feet).

Sec Pâté is renowned as one of the most stunning dive sites in the Caribbean, attracting divers from around the globe. This remarkable location serves as a haven for diverse local marine life. Schools of giant trevally and barracuda patrol the waters around these majestic peaks, where an abundance of colourful fish thrive. Among them, you may spot the elusive and rare royal angelfish, with its exquisite blue and yellow patterns. The vibrant corals and sponges welcome an array of turtles, lobsters and a multitude of creatures waiting to be discovered.

Essential info

A minimum level 2 certification is necessary to be able to fully enjoy diving at Sec Pâté and its dizzying drop-offs.

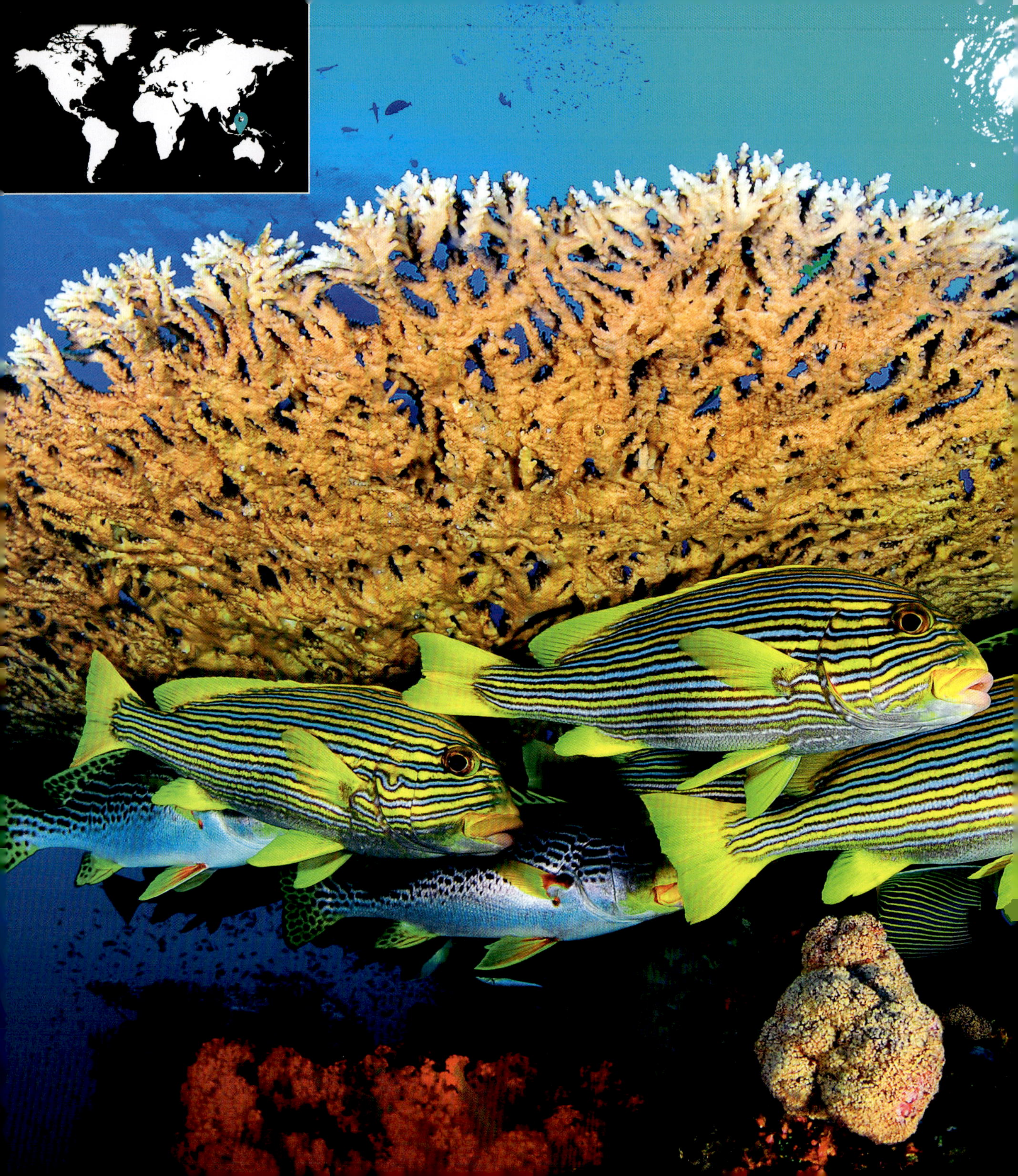

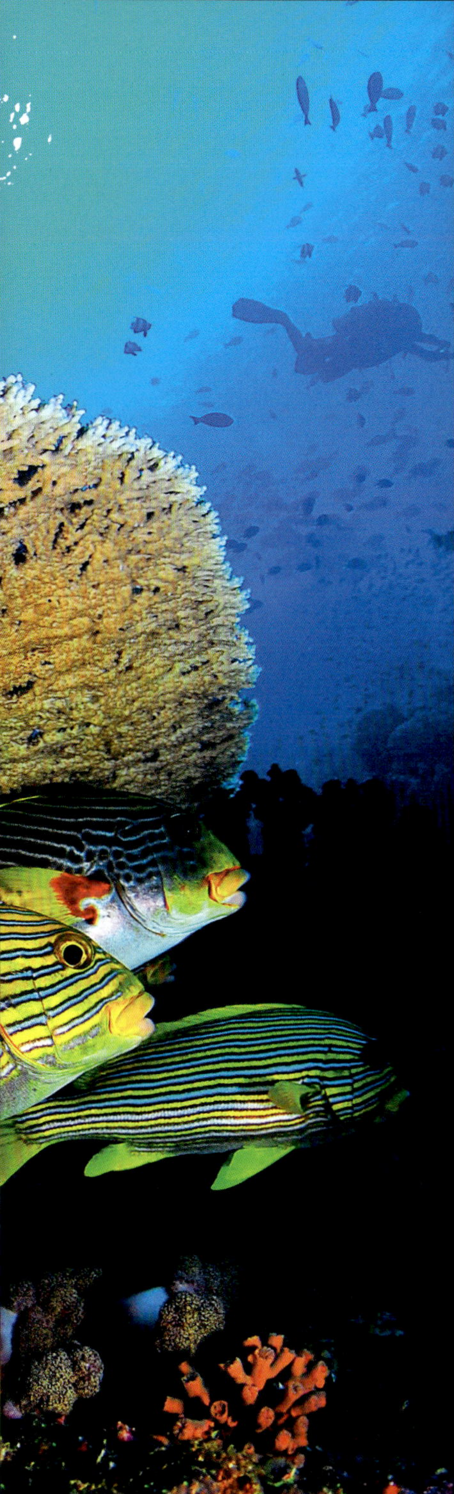

54 Komodo

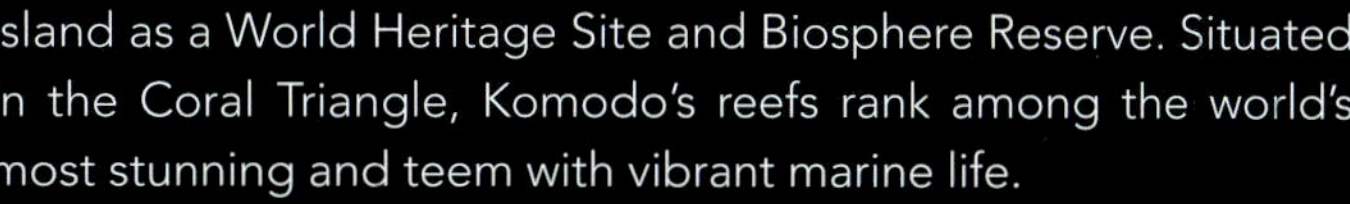

Indonesia

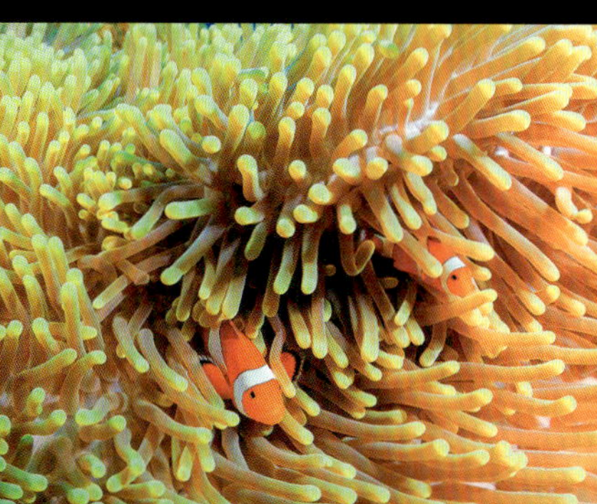

When we think of Komodo, the first image that often springs to mind is that of the iconic Komodo dragons – massive lizards found only on a few islands in central Indonesia.

This unique wildlife, along with Komodo's truly remarkable marine biodiversity, led UNESCO to list the island as a World Heritage Site and Biosphere Reserve. Situated in the Coral Triangle, Komodo's reefs rank among the world's most stunning and teem with vibrant marine life.

Positioned between the Indian and Pacific Oceans, the island's waters are swept by strong currents that bring in nutrients and plankton, making for thrilling drift dives and frequent sightings of pelagic species. Manta rays, sharks, clownfish (see inset photo), tuna and trevallies are regular visitors in these waters. Sheltered dive sites provide calmer conditions for exploring the reef up close, where a kaleidoscope of smaller marine life awaits discovery: multicoloured nudibranchs, various shrimp species and even pygmy seahorses.

Essential info

Many sites are challenging due to unpredictable sea currents, which can change direction suddenly. Strong drift diving experience is essential.

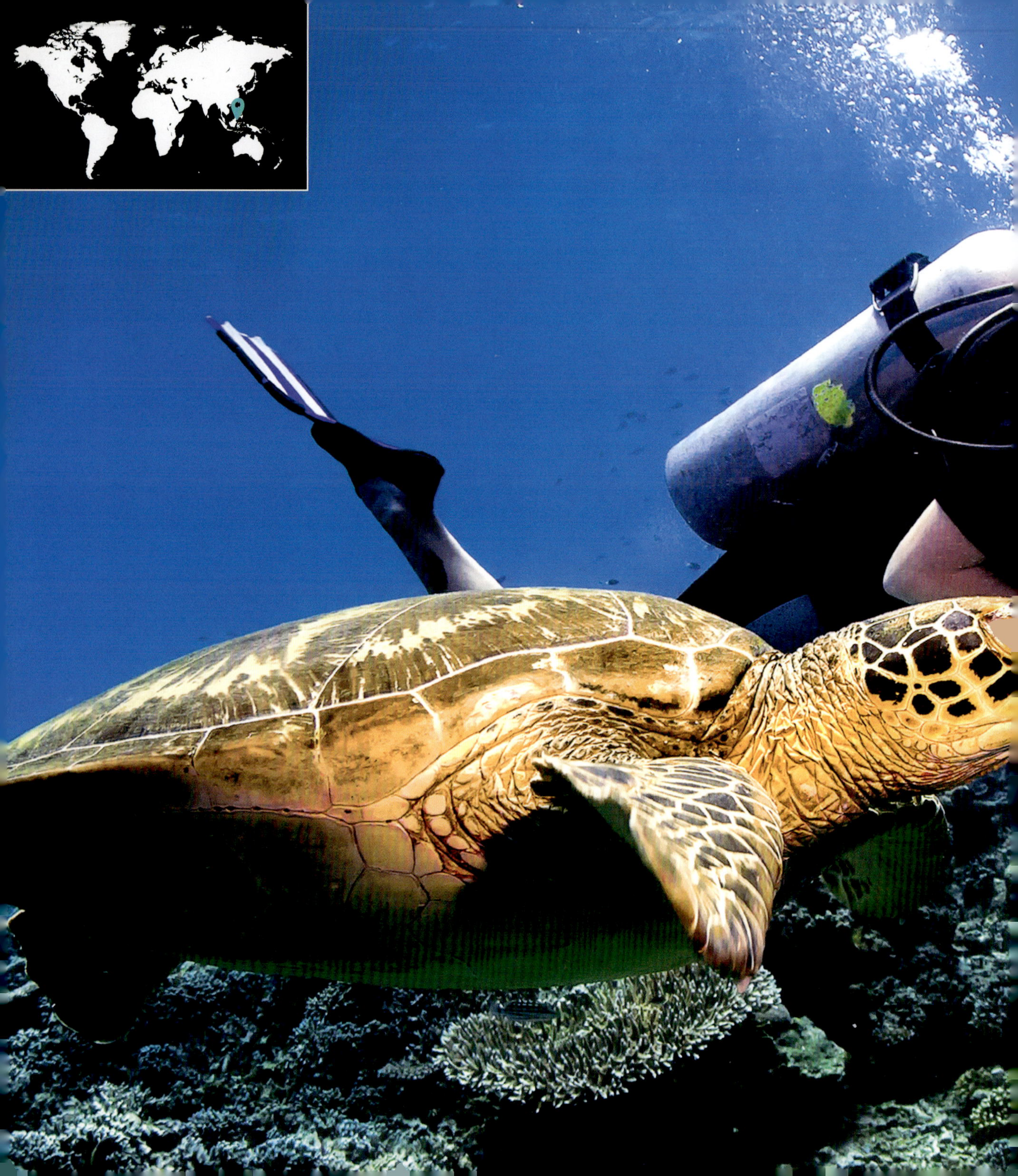

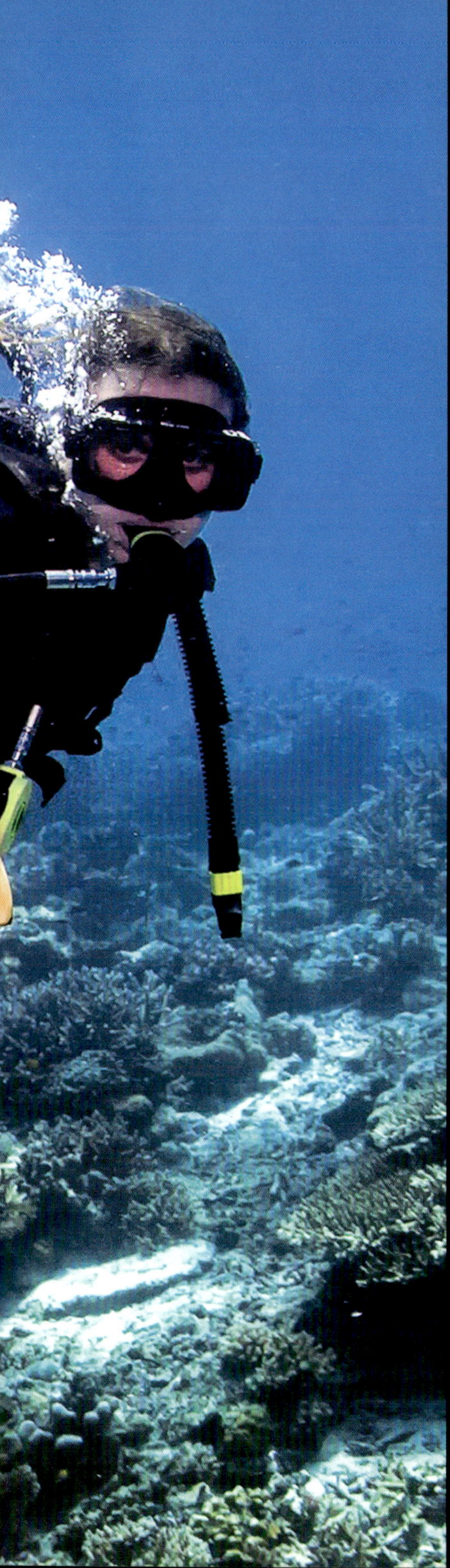

55 Sipadan

Malaysia

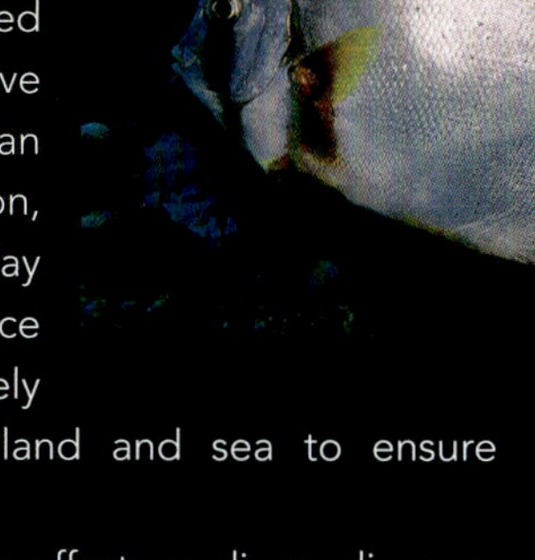

East of Borneo, on the edge of the Celebes Sea, a tiny island has earned a place among the world's top 10 dive sites. Once overrun with divers, Sipadan now operates under strict regulation, allowing fewer than 200 divers per day who must obtain permits in advance for a day's access. The island is closely monitored by military patrols on land and sea to ensure adherence to regulations.

Diving at Sipadan is well worth the effort, as divers discover within minutes of descent. Its dramatic drop-offs shelter a densely packed marine ecosystem, where green and hawksbill sea turtles accompany divers on nearly every dive. The island's beaches also serve as vital nesting grounds for these turtles. Sharks thrive in these fish-rich waters alongside parrotfish, triggerfish (see inset photo) and Napoleon wrasses. At Barracuda Point, arguably the most stunning site, schools of shimmering silver barracudas spiral through the blue waters.

While pelagic species are the main attraction, resident marine life such as nudibranchs and other reef species are widely present.

Essential info

As access is only allowed for the day, it is advisable to stay on the nearby islands of Mabul or Kapalai and apply for a permit well in advance.

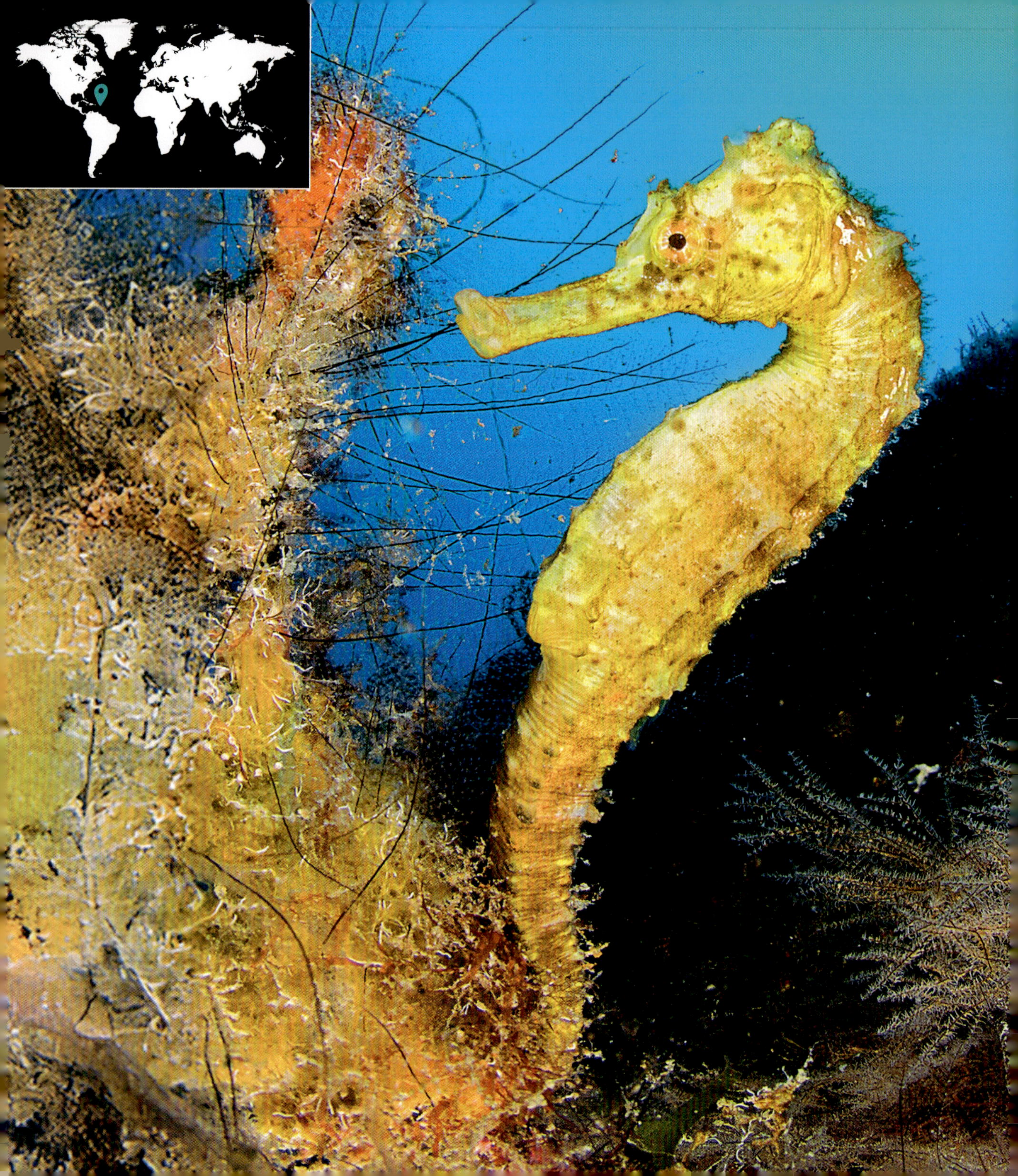

56 *Nahoon* wreck

Martinique, French Antilles

One of Martinique's most renowned dive sites, the three-masted *Nahoon*, celebrated its 30th anniversary in 2023. This vessel was intentionally sunk in 1993 by the Martinique Regional Diving Committee in the bay of Fort-de-France to create an artificial reef and establish a new diving destination.

Spanning 41 metres (135 feet) in length, the *Nahoon* was not chosen by chance; its eventful history motivated the decision. Originally built in 1911 as a beacon ship, it first gained notoriety under its original name, *Quinette de Rochemont*, when it rescued the crew of a ship torpedoed by a German submarine during World War I. In 1941, it was seized by the Germans as war loot. In the 1950s, it was sent to the West Indies and renamed *Caribbean*. It eventually ran aground on a sandbank following a cyclone in 1966. Rescued and converted into a three-masted vessel, it was given the name *Nahoon* in 1976 but was ultimately abandoned in the bay of Fort-de-France.

Today, largely inhabited by marine life, the *Nahoon* is an example of a remarkably successful artificial reef creation, maintaining its grandeur 35 metres (115 feet) below the surface.

Essential info

The wreck is accessible to divers with a minimum certification of level 2 or Advanced Open Water, yet it poses no significant challenges. Marine life thrives here, with the wreck adorned by vibrant corals and sponges, creating a colourful habitat for schools of fish and lobsters.

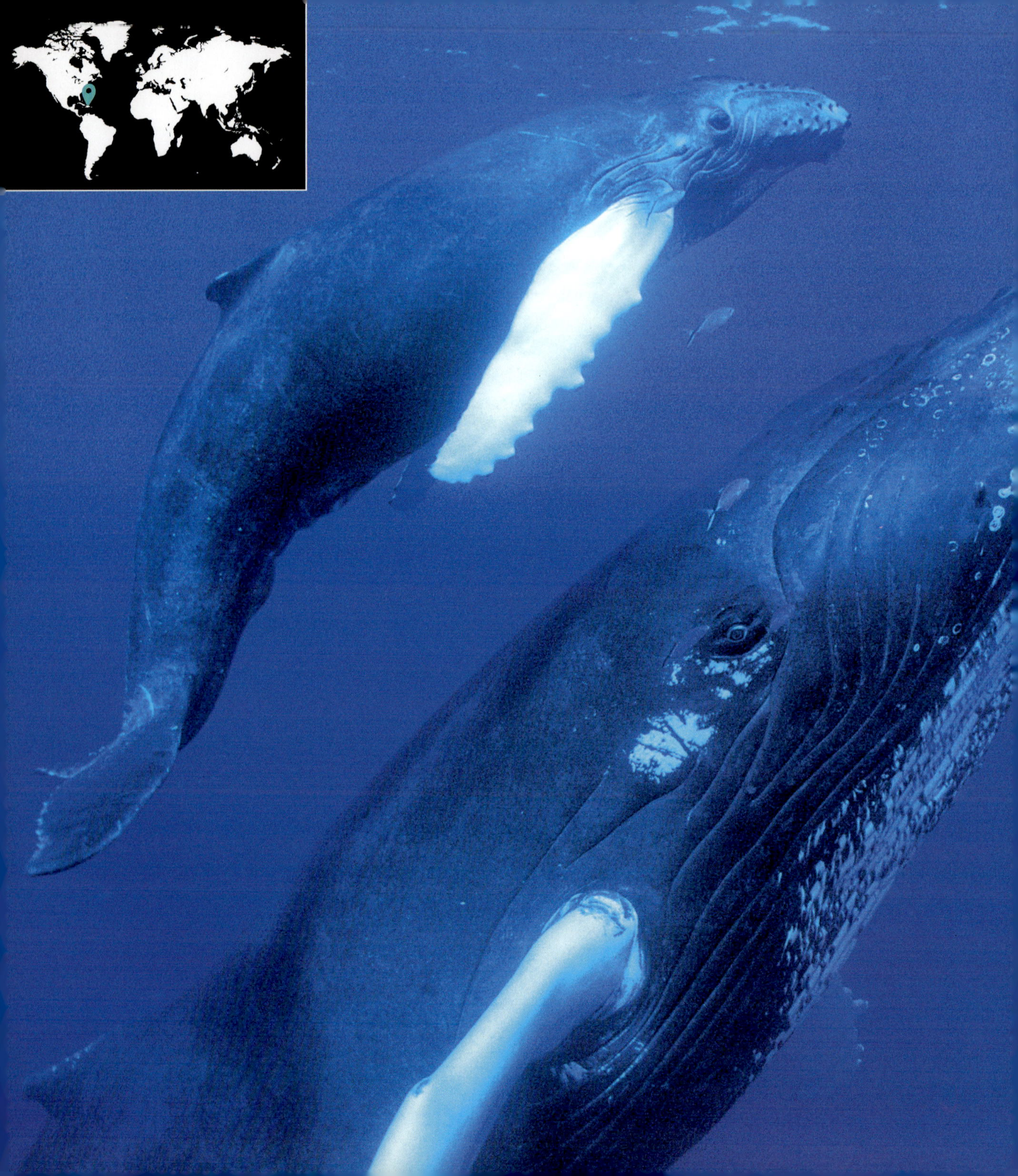

57 Silver Bank humpback whales

Dominican Republic

With its idyllic beaches lined with coconut palms, the Dominican Republic is a prime holiday destination, renowned for its exceptional opportunities to observe humpback whales. Around 90 kilometres (56 miles) north of the mainland, nestled alongside the Turks and Caicos Islands, lies Silver Bank. This vast underwater plateau averages 20 metres (66 feet) in depth and is one of the Atlantic's major breeding and calving grounds for these magnificent creatures. Every year, from January to April, over 5,000 humpback whales gather in the warm, tranquil waters of Silver Bank, offering a rare chance for close encounters with these gentle giants. Access to this incredible sanctuary is strictly regulated to ensure minimal disturbance to the whales and their habitat.

This area was designated a whaling sanctuary in 1986. Respecting the natural world is paramount here, and swimmers are invited to experience the wonder of being approached by whales on their own terms, creating amazing memories.

Essential info

One-week cruises are available to make the most of the whale watching. Snorkelling is the only activity allowed as diving is prohibited out of respect for the whales and their environment.

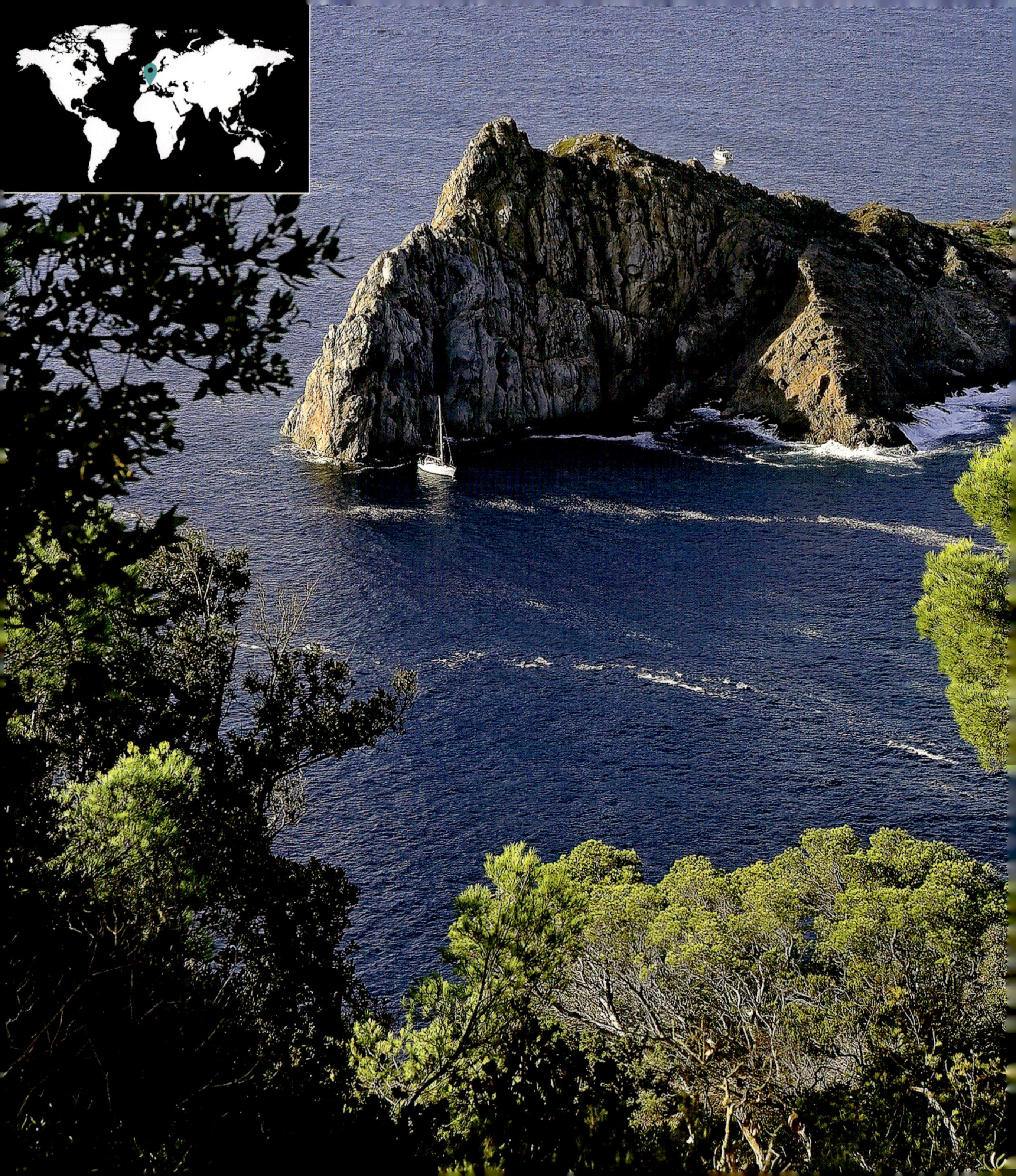

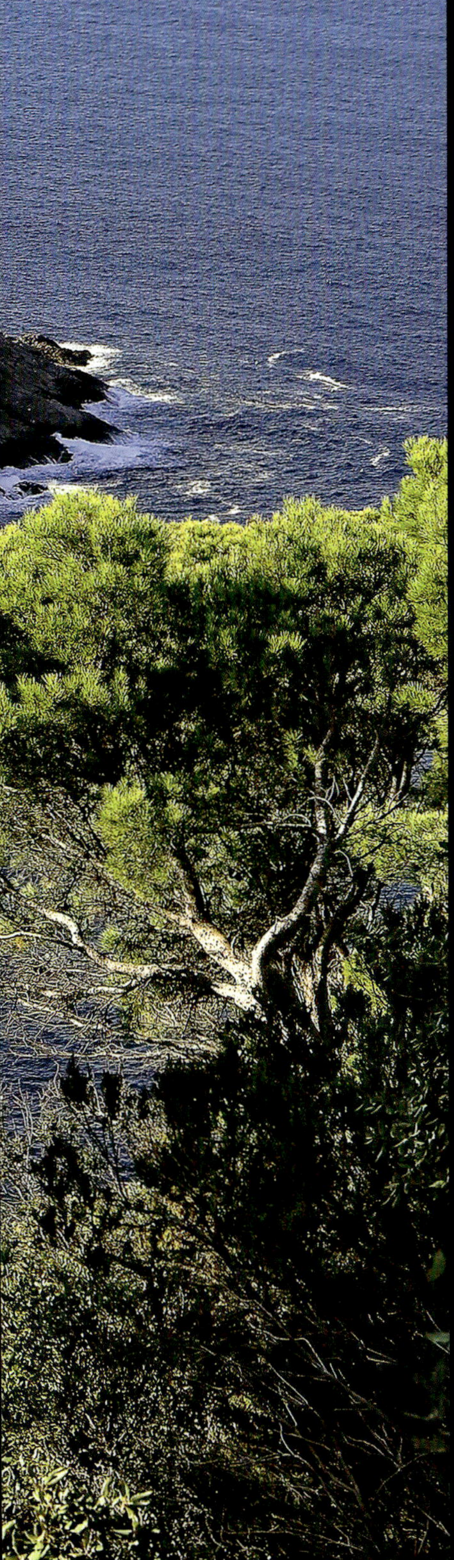

58 La Gabinière

Port-Cros, Var, France

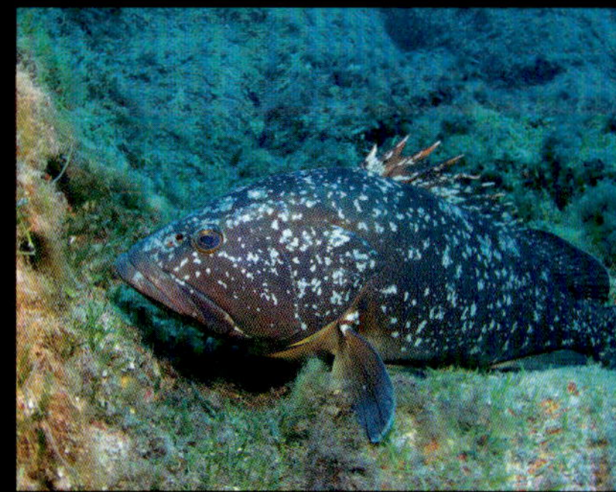

Some places in metropolitan France are scuba diving hotspots. The Mediterranean coasts offer ideal conditions for diving, which explains the high number of divers and diving centres located in the south. Off the coast of Lavandou, the Golden Islands are part of this precious heritage: Porquerolles, Le Levant and Port-Cros.

The island has been a national park since 1963 and is one of the most popular diving spots in the Var region. To the south, an islet called La Gabinière is a site not to be missed. Beneath the surface, schools of barracuda glide gracefully alongside swirling castagnoles, while dozens of groupers peacefully occupy the site.

Brown groupers (see inset photo) are particularly striking, with some reaching over one metre (three feet) in length. They are remarkably gentle and often swim right up to divers, inviting a close encounter like no other.

Essential info

La Gabinière is accessible from level 1 (open water), and groupers can be seen mainly from a depth of 15 metres (49 feet). It is a relatively easy dive in calm weather. The best months for diving are September and October, when the water is warmest.

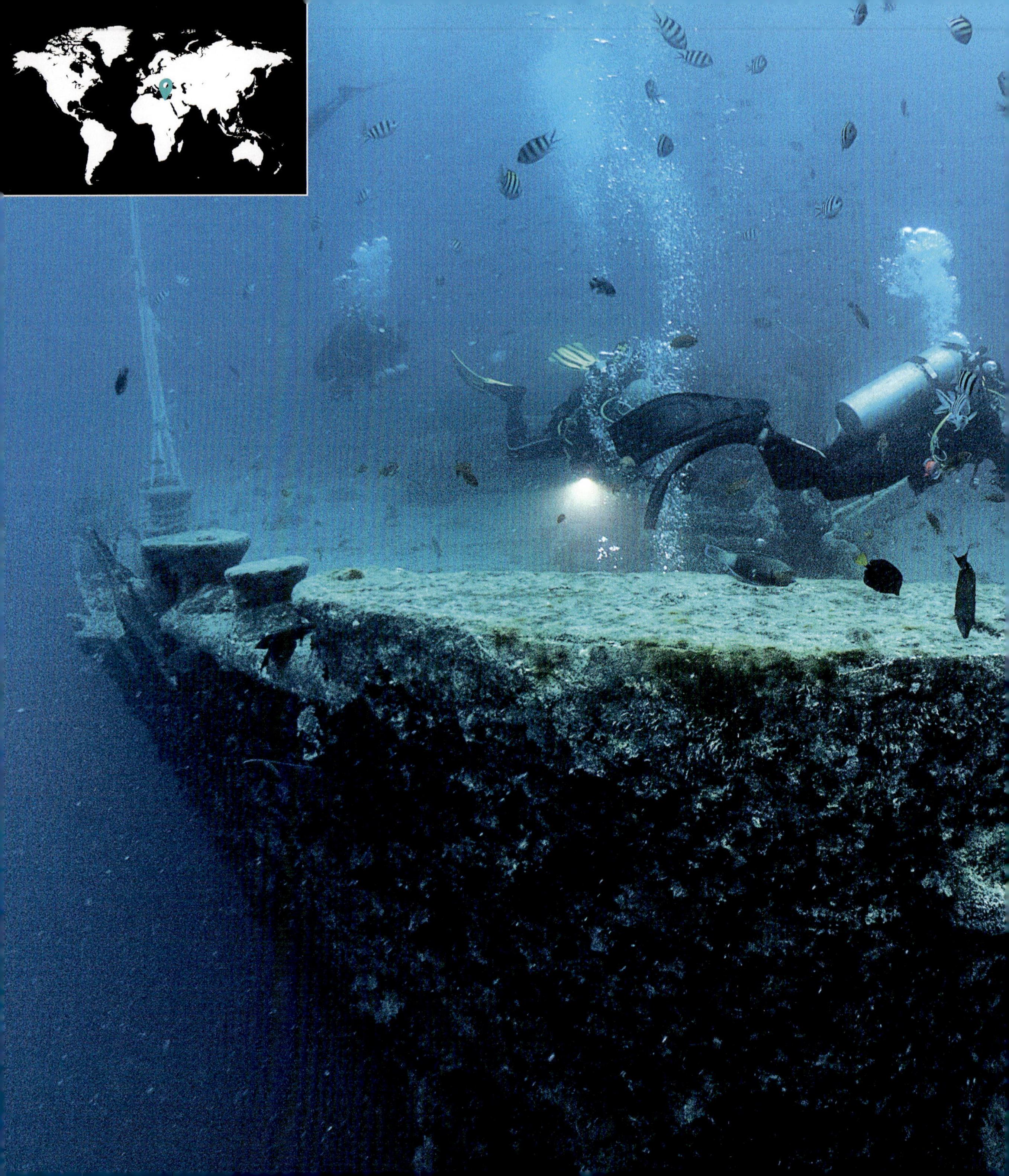

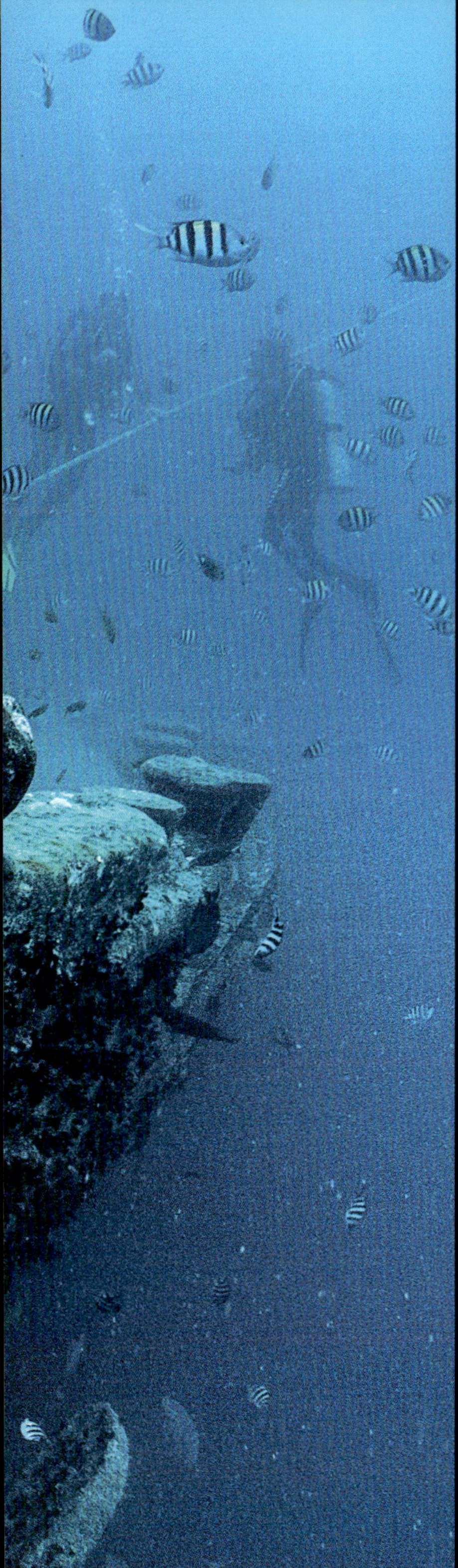

59 SS Thistlegorm wreck

Egypt

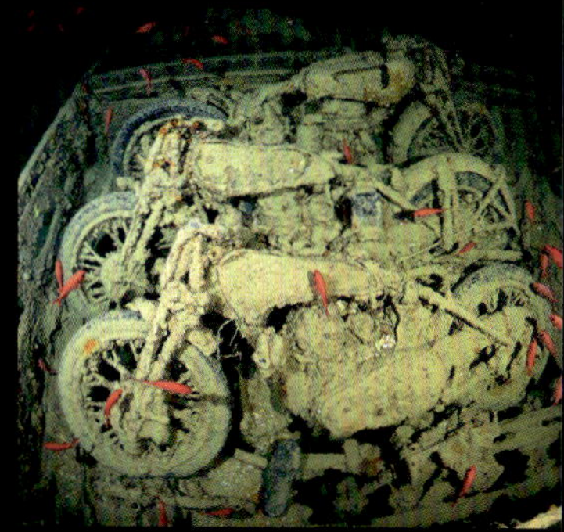

Renowned for its world-class wrecks, northern Egypt attracts metal enthusiasts from across the globe. The wrecks of *Rosalie Moller, Ghiannis D, Carnatic* and *Dunraven* are accessible even to novices in this field. However, one wreck stands out above the rest: the *SS Thistlegorm*. Brought to light by Commander Cousteau in his documentary *The Silent World* in 1956, this British cargo ship was bombed by German aircraft on 6 October 1941.

Exploring this historic vessel and traversing its holds filled with military equipment is an unforgettable experience. Trucks, armoured vehicles, motorcycles and rifles remain frozen in time, now serving as a habitat for shadowy species like hatchetfish and soldierfish. From the outside, the imposing wreck can be admired in its entirety, showcasing its anti-aircraft gun, locomotives, bow and the impact zone from the bombing. When the current permits, divers can venture to observe the magnificent bow up close.

Essential info

Resting on the sandy bottom at a maximum of 32 metres (105 feet), the upper section of the *Thistlegorm* is accessible for level 1 and 2 divers. Ideally, divers should complete two dives: one exploring the exterior and another venturing inside the wreck.

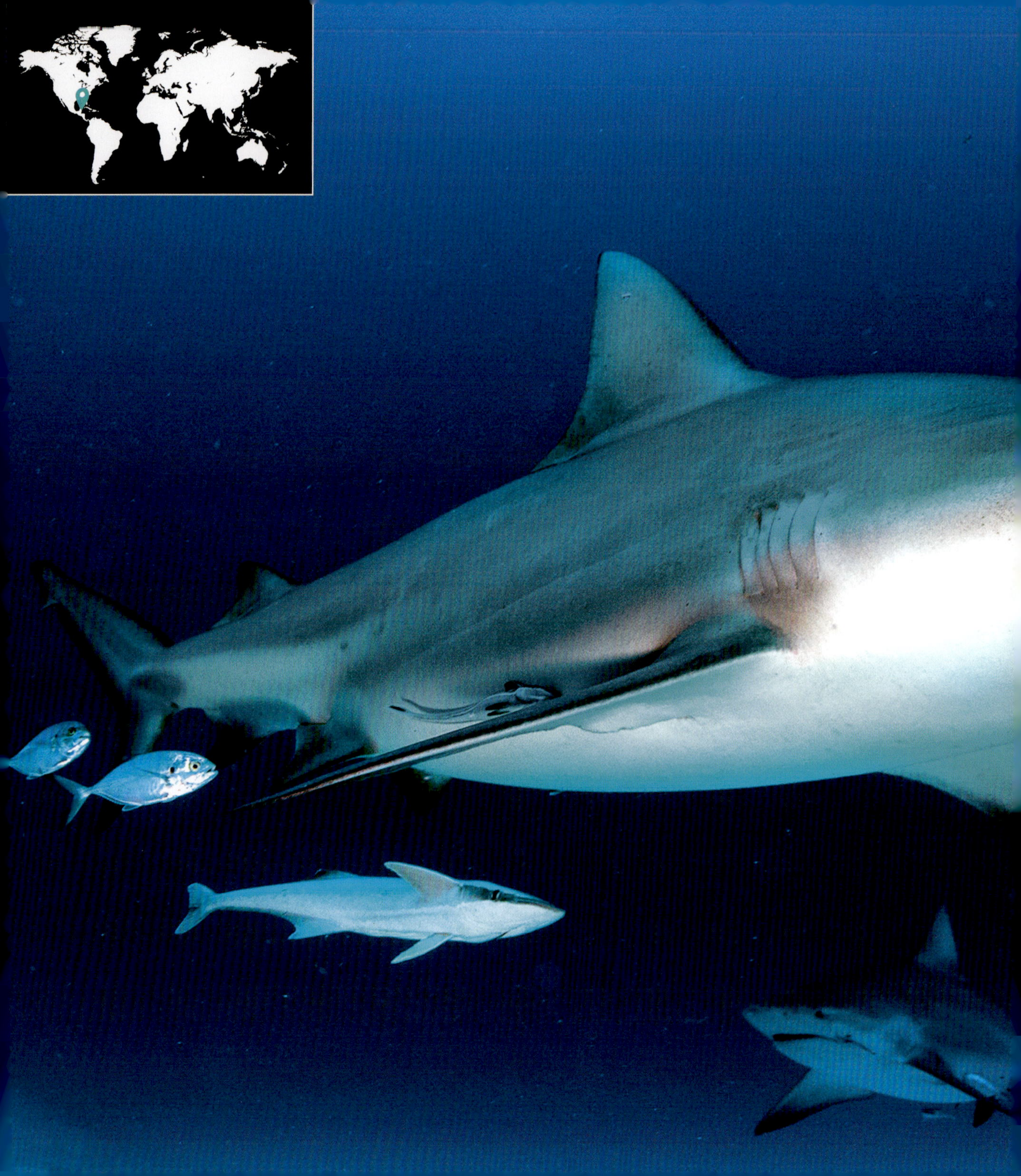

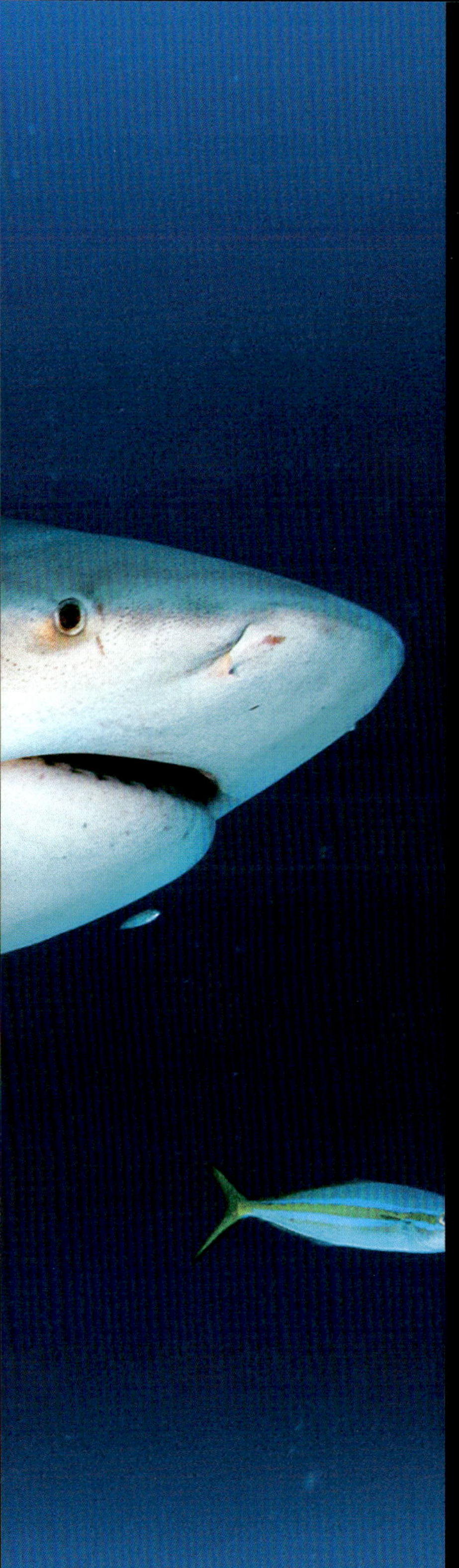

60 Playa del Carmen bull sharks

Mexico

The Yucatán Peninsula is renowned for diving into the cenotes, where the combination of surreal atmospheres and underwater caving creates an unforgettable experience. However, the pinnacle of thrill diving may very well take place off the coast of Playa del Carmen.

Between November and March, a nearby sandbank draws divers' attention. Just a short boat ride away, divers descend to around 25 metres (82 feet) and settle on the seabed on their knees, adrenaline coursing through them as the moment approaches. Characteristic silhouettes start to emerge – first one, then several. Bull sharks glide gracefully close to the divers, creating a mesmerising experience that leaves them in awe of these powerful creatures. Large pregnant females gather in these tranquil waters during this time to rest before giving birth, offering a truly unforgettable encounter for those brave enough to take the plunge.

Essential info

This dive requires excellent buoyancy control and composure, as these wild animals can be both majestic and intimidating.

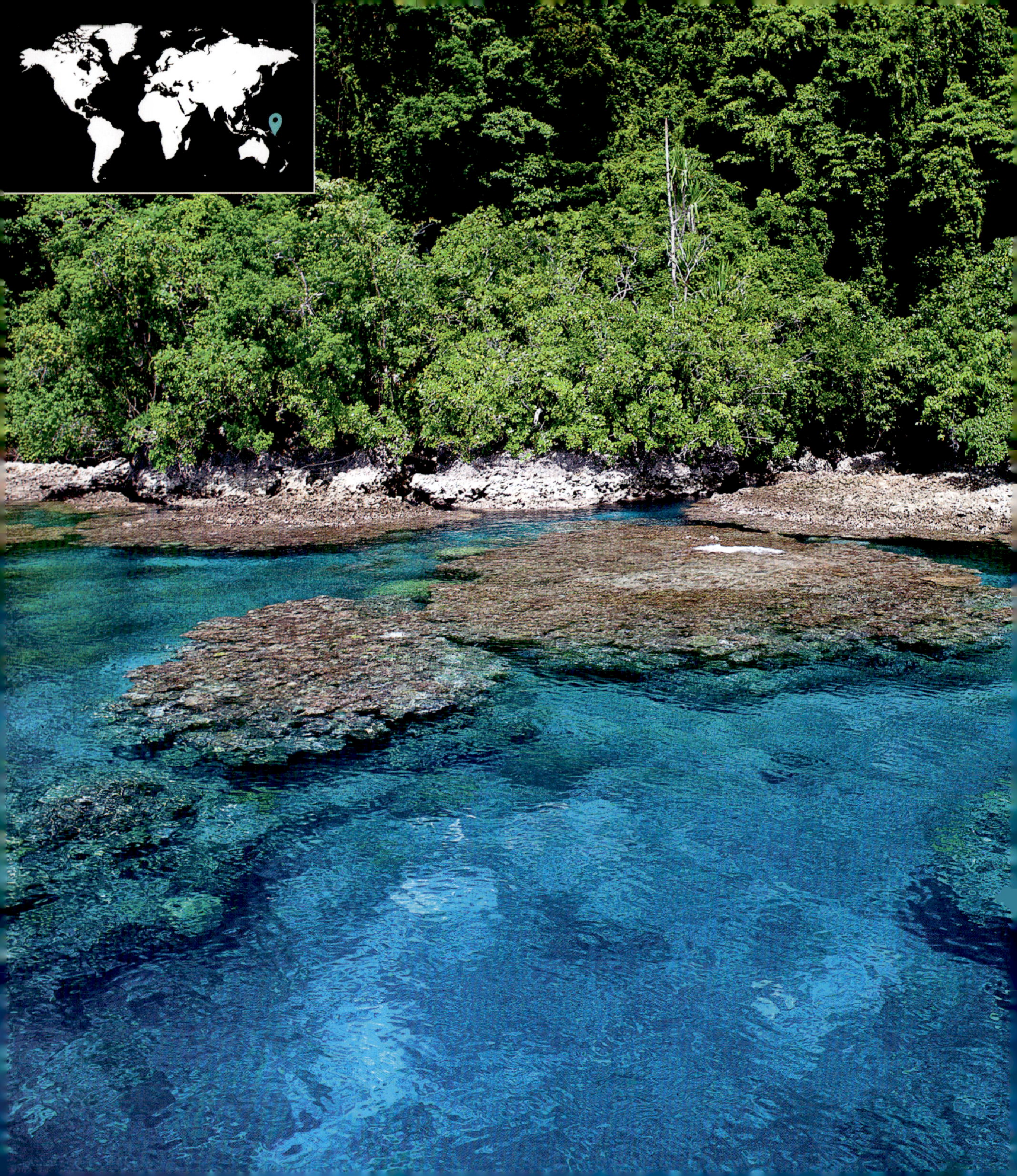

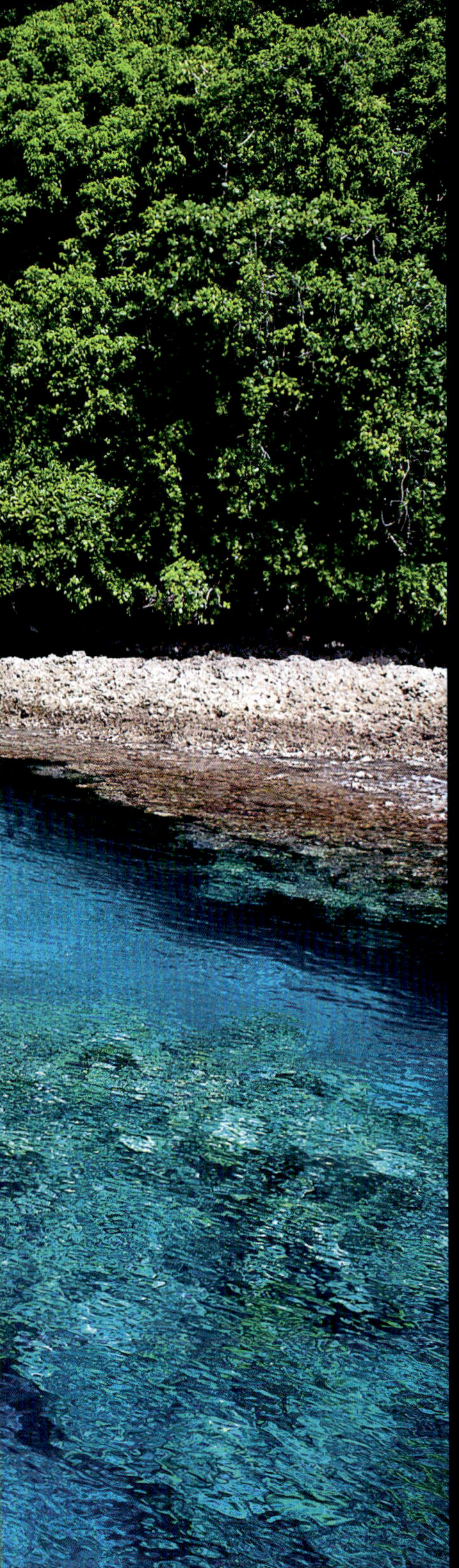

61 Solomon Islands

Oceania

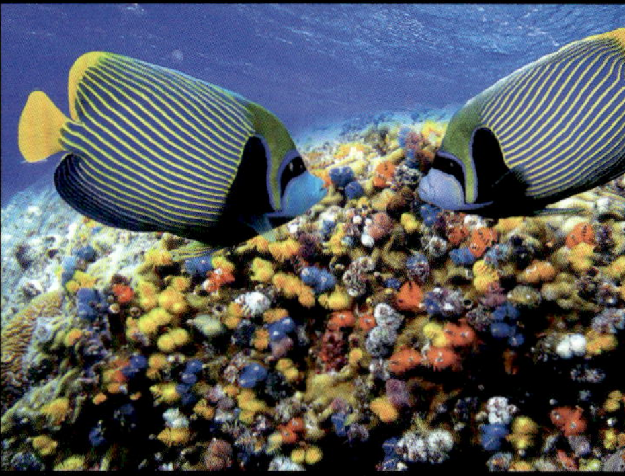

Extending from Papua New Guinea, the Solomon Islands archipelago features pristine landscapes of tropical forests, stretches of white sand and expansive lagoons with turquoise waters. Most tourists visit the Solomon Islands to explore their enchanting underwater environments, from snorkellers and novice scuba divers to experienced and technical divers – it's a paradise for everyone.

The Marovo Lagoon, dotted with small islets, is ideal for those wishing to explore with fins, mask and snorkel, offering encounters with vibrant tropical species. These rich waters teem with marine creatures great and small, from manta rays and reef sharks to dolphins and sea turtles. The region is also perfect for those who appreciate the smaller marine wildlife. Additionally, the Solomon Islands were the site of fierce battles during the Pacific War, leaving behind numerous shipwrecks that are a major drawcard for technical divers.

Essential info

The wrecks of Guadalcanal are among the most famous, with several hundred remnants, including ships, planes and other military artefacts to explore.

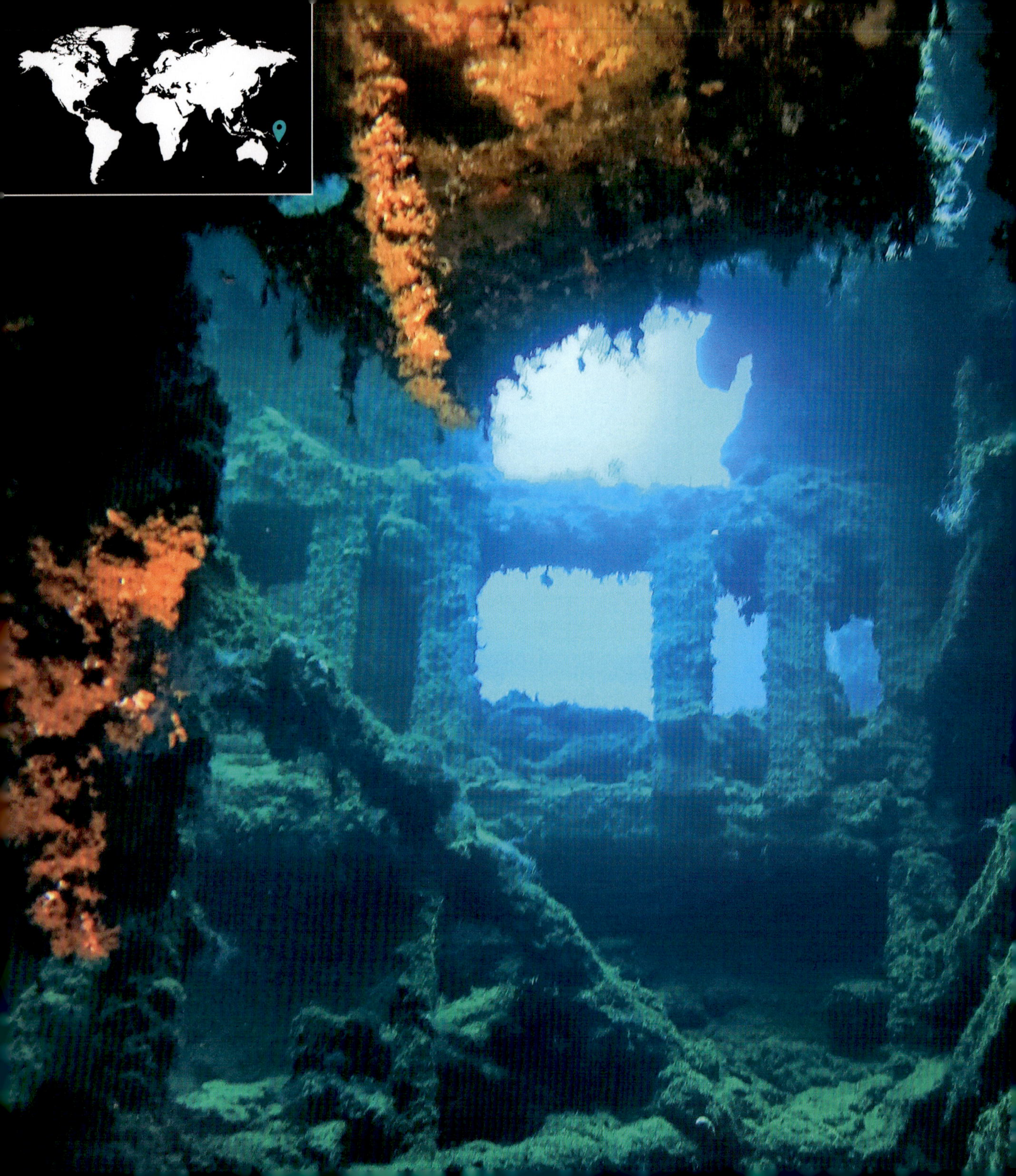

62 SS President Coolidge wreck

Vanuatu

The Vanuatu archipelago lies just a few hundred kilometres (186 miles) northeast of New Caledonia. During World War II, the luxurious American cruise ship *SS President Coolidge* was requisitioned for troop transport in the Pacific. On 26 October 1942, it arrived in the Luganville Channel, south of Espiritu Santo, carrying nearly 5000 GIs. Though there was no combat in the area, the ship struck two American mines intended to protect against Japanese submarines due to a lack of accurate information. Fortunately, it ran aground near the shore, allowing the soldiers to escape, with only five reported missing. Eventually, the *SS President Coolidge* sank and now rests at depths between 20 and 70 metres (65 and 230 feet).

This wreck has become a major diving destination in Vanuatu, renowned as the largest World War II wreck accessible from the shore. The ship is remarkably well-preserved, as the remote location of the archipelago prevented salvage operations, leaving almost everything in place. However, the wreck is nearly 200 metres (656 feet) long, requiring multiple dives to fully explore its hidden treasures.

Essential info

Easily accessible from the shore, this wreck offers a piece of history for everyone – from beginner divers to advanced ones who can explore its deeper sections.

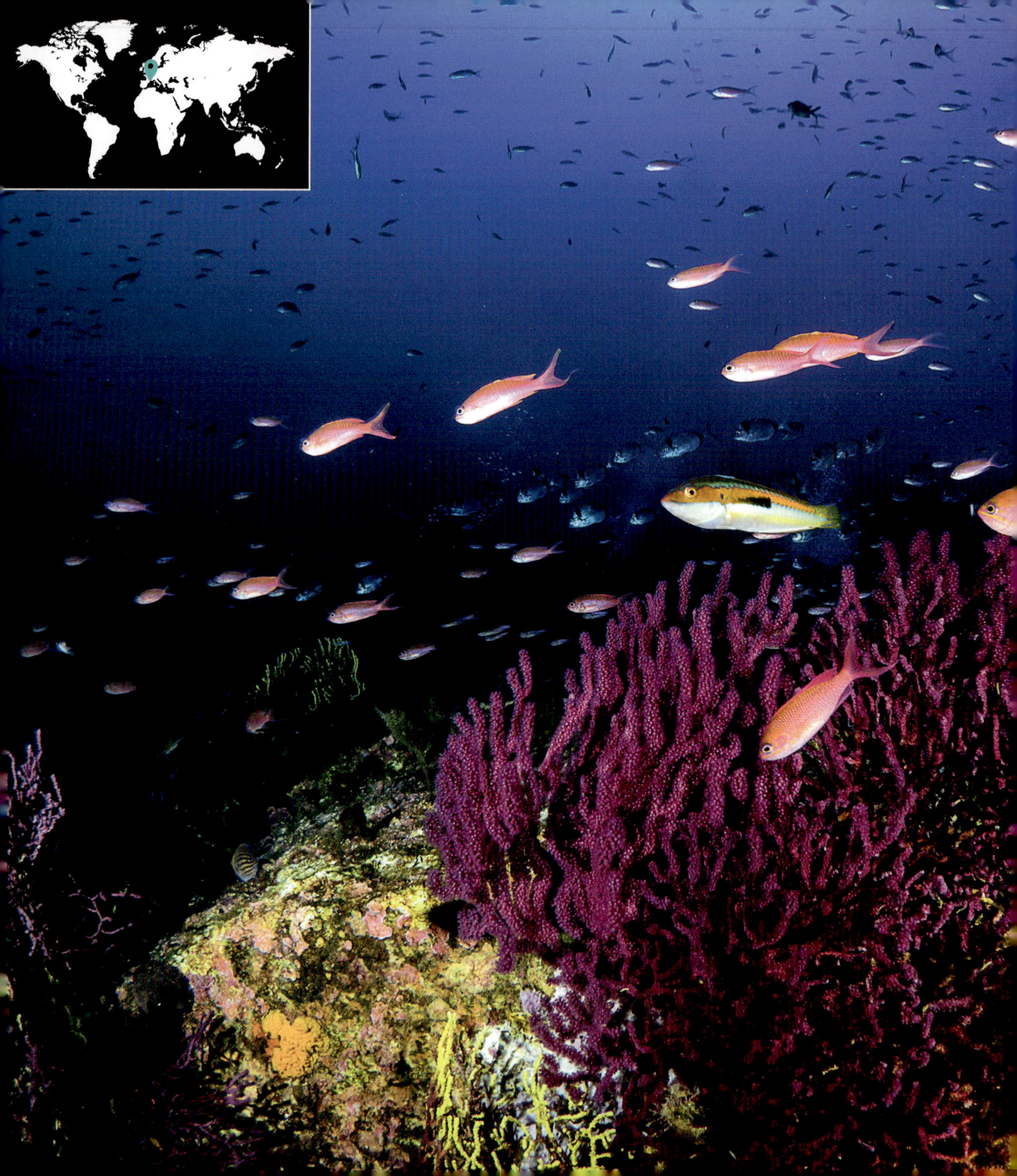

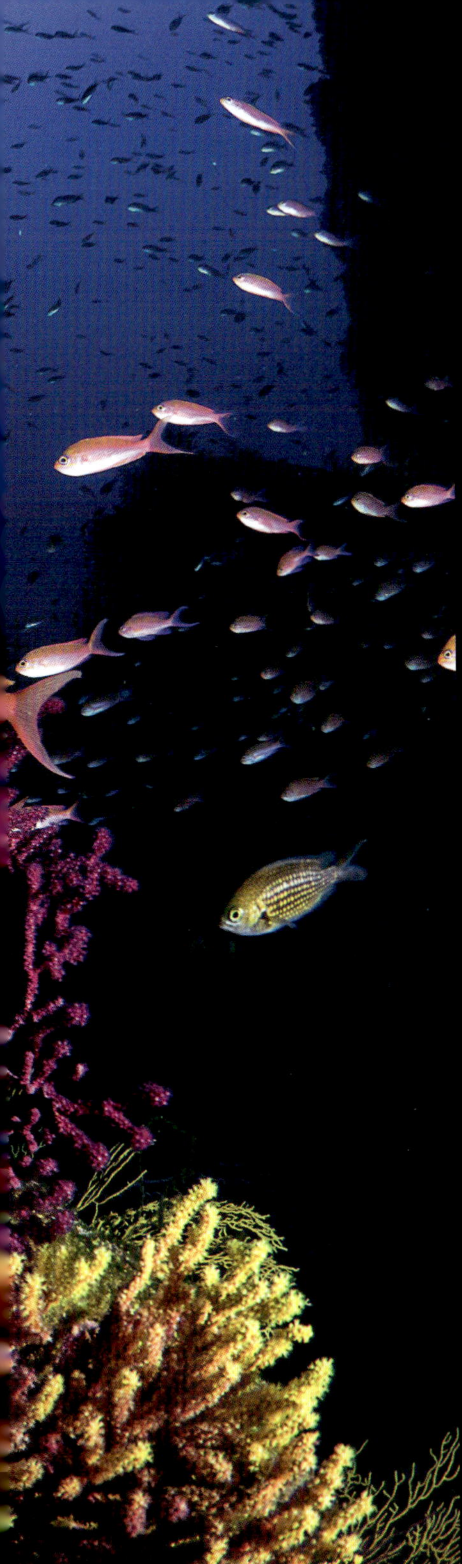

63 Donator wreck

Var, France

With the end of World War II, the Schiaffino shipping company had only one remaining ship from its pre-war fleet of 20 vessels. On 10 November 1945, the *Prosper Schiaffino*, better known as the *Donator*, was returning from Algeria with a load of wine as it approached Porquerolles Island, in the Var.

The conditions were bad, with strong winds and mines in the region not yet fully cleared. An explosion sounded and destroyed the bow. Water rushed into the ship and it quickly sank. Now resting on the sand at a depth of 51 metres (167 feet), the *Donator* is considered one of the most beautiful shipwrecks in the Mediterranean. Covered by huge purple and yellow gorgonians, this amazing artificial reef is home to impressive schools of sars, anthias and castagnola, as well as sea bream and striking brown groupers who have taken up residence.

Essential info

Deep and frequently subject to currents, this wreck is exclusively suited to experienced divers, requiring a minimum certification of level 3 to explore its depths safely.

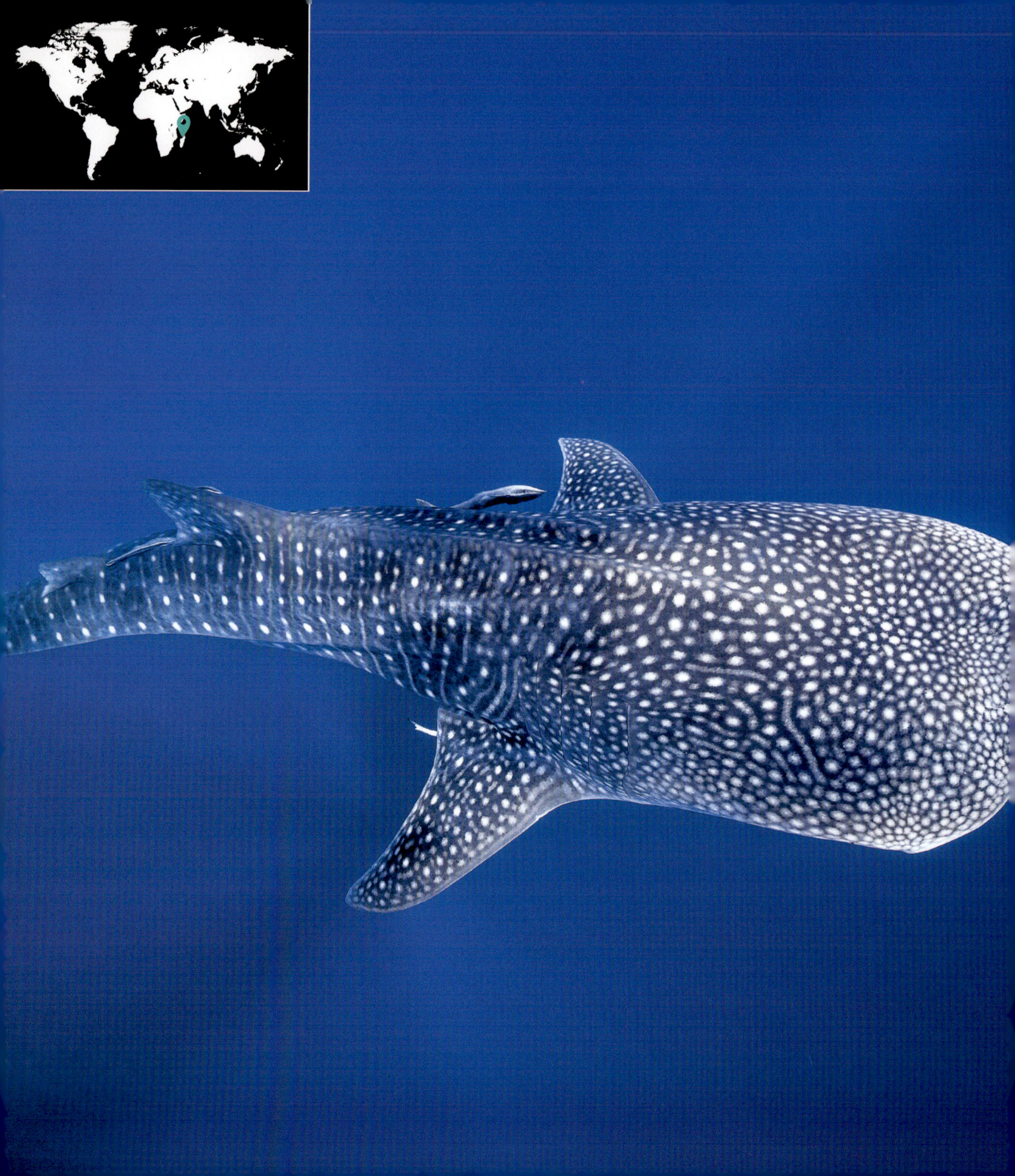

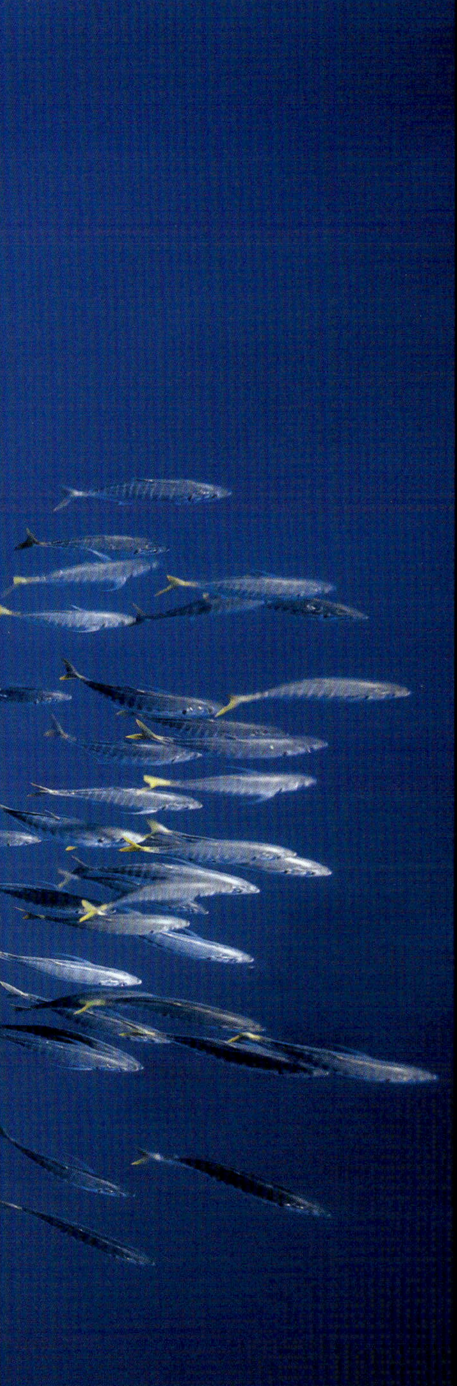

64 Nosy Be

Madagascar

As one of the world's largest islands, Madagascar offers a range of enriching experiences. To the northeast lies Nosy Be Island, renowned as the most beautiful destination in the Indian Ocean, celebrated globally for its exceptional underwater landscapes. Known as 'the island of perfumes' due to its fragrant ylang-ylang and spice plantations, Nosy Be has preserved its authentic charm, making it an ideal place to reconnect with nature.

The coral reefs here are breathtaking and bursting with life, offering a diverse range of dive sites where you can encounter both tiny creatures and majestic marine animals. From nudibranchs, frogfish and ghostfish to impressive schools of jackfish, tuna and manta rays, the variety is astounding. If you're lucky, you might even spot whale sharks (see photo) and humpback whales at certain times of the year. Each dive promises to be a complete and exhilarating experience.

Essential info

There are other equally exceptional islands near Nosy Be, such as the Mitsio Archipelago, Nosy Komba or Nosy Iranja. You will be spoiled for choice.

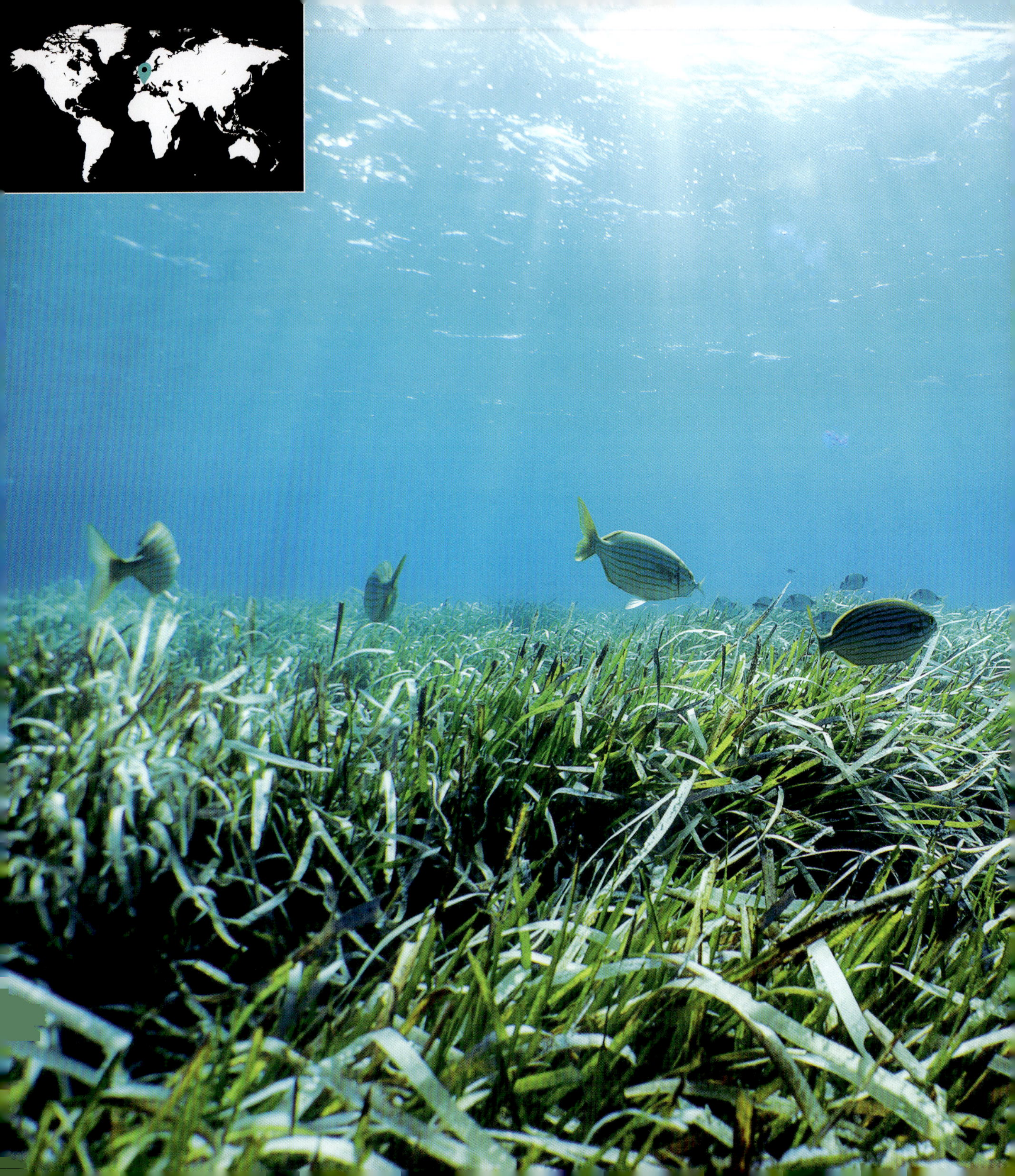

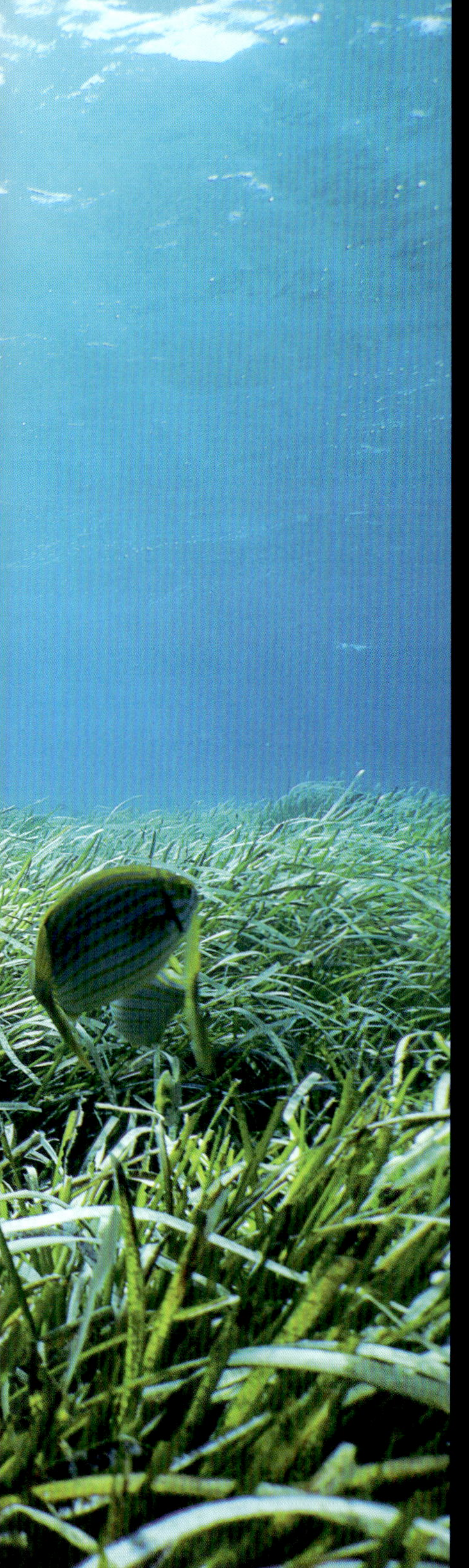

65 Rascas Islet underwater trail

Port-Cros, Var, France

Nestled off the Var coast, Port-Cros Island has been under robust protection since the establishment of its national park in 1963. This diver's paradise boasts a vibrant seabed teeming with life, particularly its gentle brown groupers. The island is also popular with swimmers and snorkellers.

After a 45-minute walk along a shaded path that winds between the charming small port and the beautiful bay of La Palud, visitors are greeted by a beautifully designed underwater trail. Bordered by a small sandy beach overlooking Rascas Islet, the sheltered seabed offers an ideal opportunity to explore a stunning array of Mediterranean marine life. With thriving beds of posidonia (seagrass) stretching as far as the eye can see, schools of saupes and sars cross paths with a kaleidoscope of vibrant wrasses. Seabass and large sea breams roam under the watchful eyes of red mullets sifting through the sandy bottom, foraging for their next meal.

Essential info

Well-protected, the bay is quiet with often excellent visibility, making it an ideal spot for even the most novice snorkellers. More seasoned divers will gladly explore the whole island.

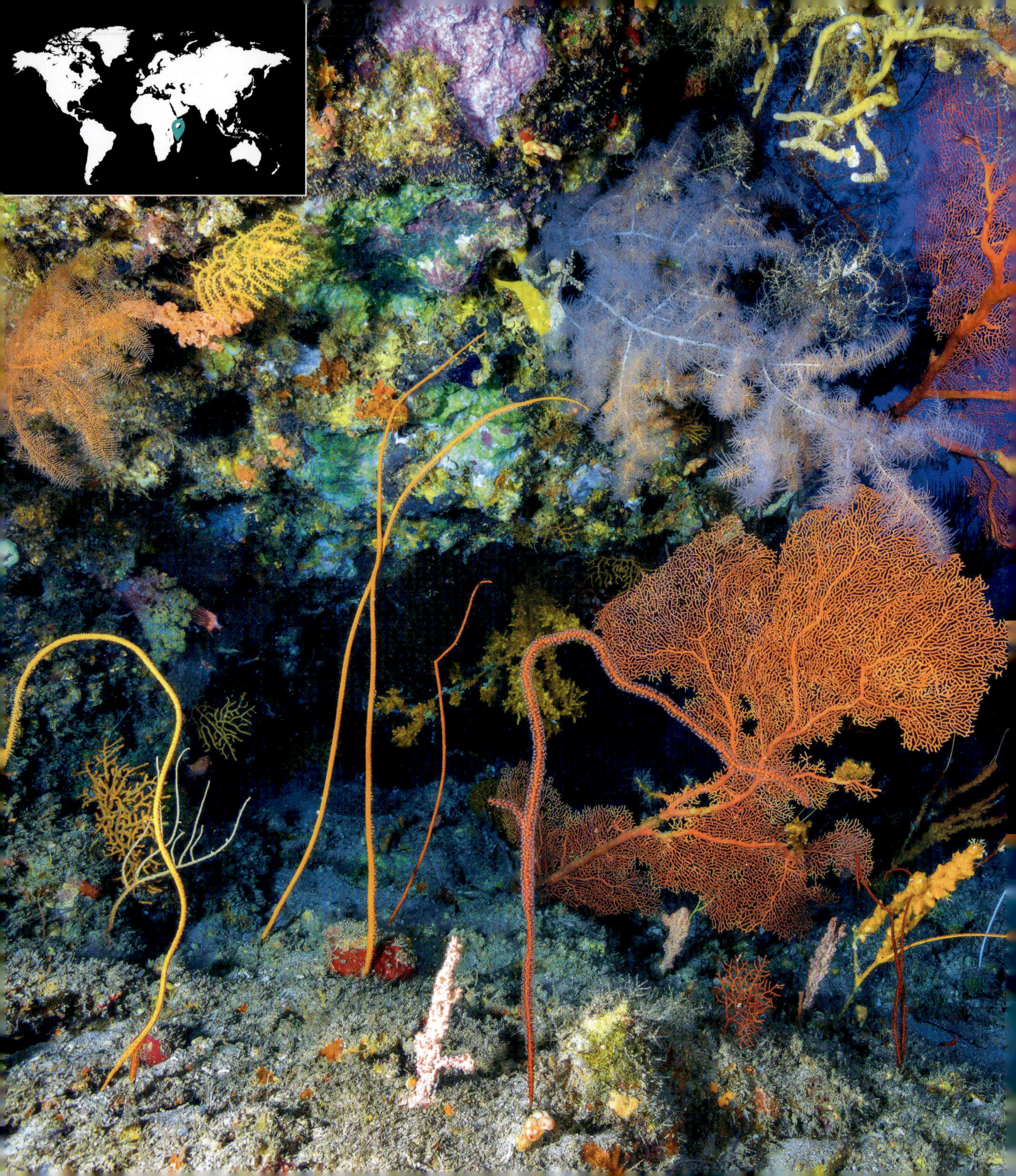

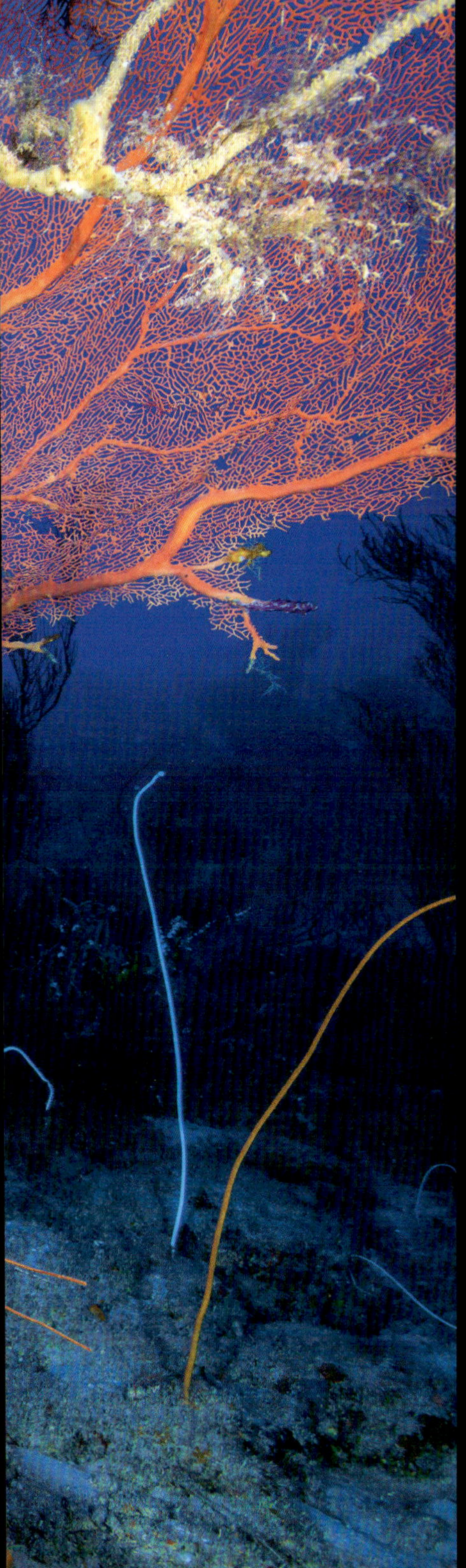

66 The S Pass

Mayotte

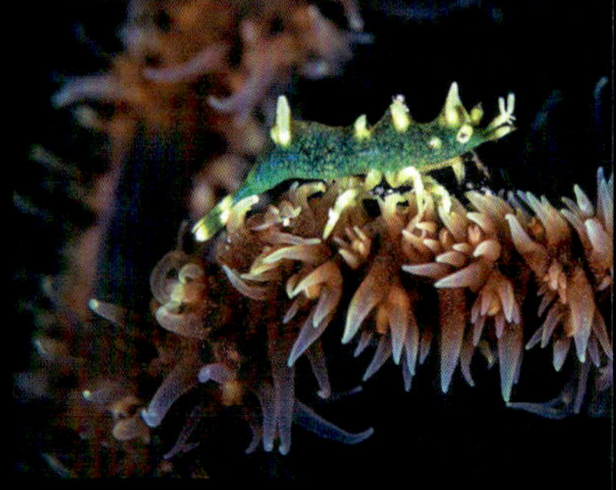

The department of Mayotte is a true gem of the French territories in the Indian Ocean. With its double coral reef, the island boasts one of the largest lagoons on the planet, protected by the Mayotte Marine Natural Park.

This vibrant ecosystem features mangroves, seagrass beds and coral reefs, all teeming with extraordinary marine life. In the western region, a winding passage known as the S pass bisects the reef, earning its reputation as Mayotte's most famous dive site.

Designated as a protected marine reserve since 1990, this remarkable stretch spans four kilometres (2.5 miles) and is dotted with 17 mooring buoys, providing countless dive opportunities for enthusiasts of all levels. Diving here feels like a journey through the Indian Ocean's diverse wildlife, with marine life flourishing in every direction. A dazzling array of colourful fish is just the beginning of the spectacle; divers may encounter grey sharks, parrotfish, humpback whales and numerous sea turtles navigating this channel carved by an ancient river.

Essential info

During the months of July to October, it is possible to observe humpback whales coming to calve in the lagoon before returning to the cold waters of Antarctica.

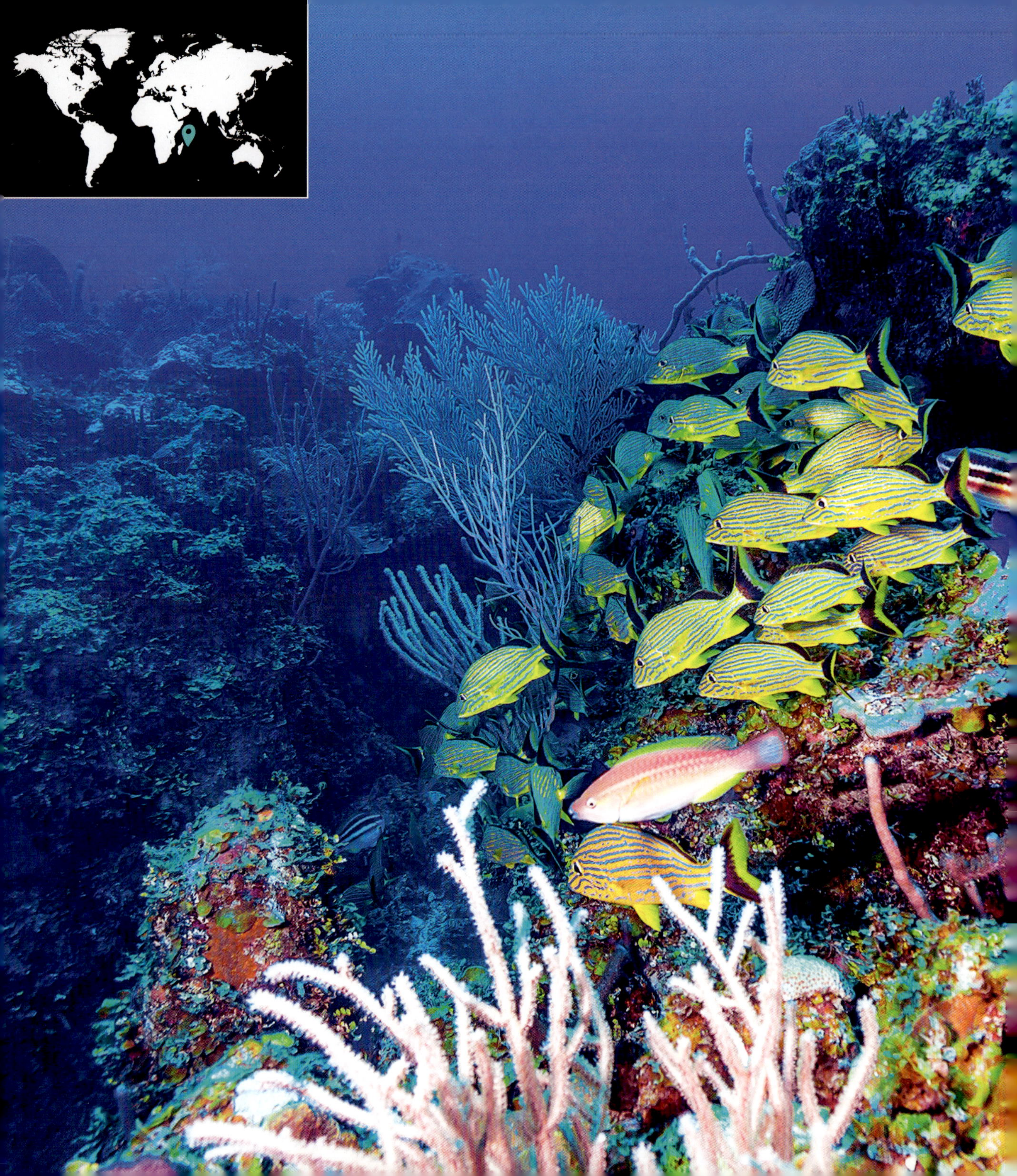

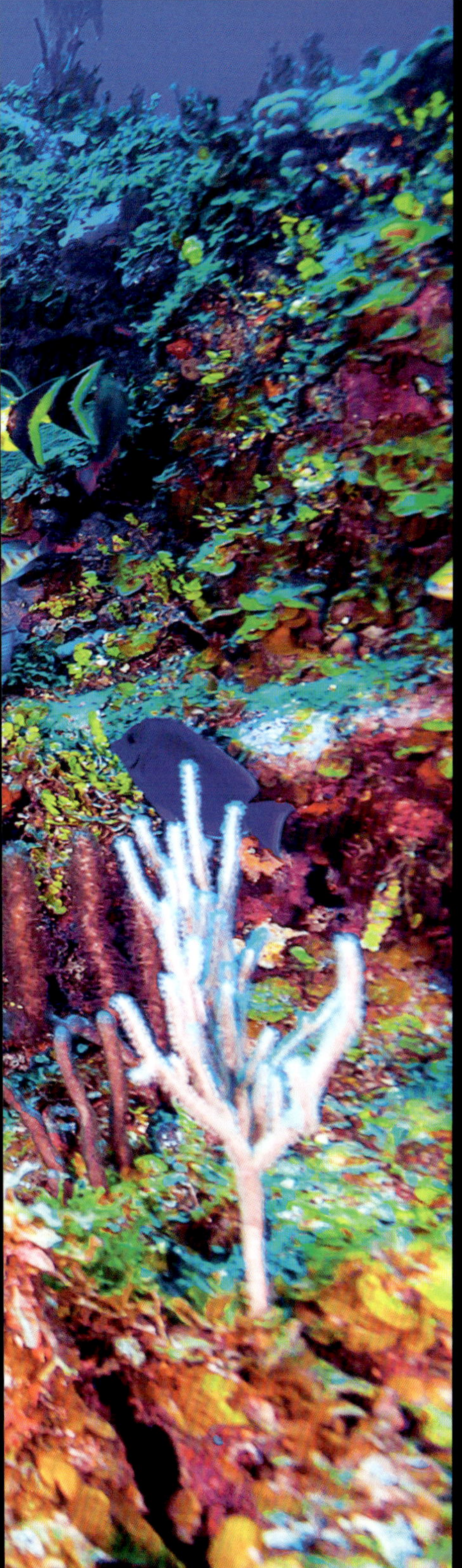

67 Saint Brandon

Mauritius

The Mascarene archipelago in the Indian Ocean offers stunning surprises. Beyond the islands' shimmering blue lagoons lies a hidden gem nearly 500 kilometres (310 miles) northeast: the remote Saint Brandon archipelago. Comprising numerous islets and sandbanks, this Robinson Crusoe-worthy setting remains virtually untouched, with only a few hundred visitors allowed each year, strictly on guided cruises.

Centuries ago, pirates found a perfect hideout here for their treasures. Nowadays, Saint Brandon serves as an incredible sanctuary for birds and marine life. Its seldom-visited dive sites teem with vibrant biodiversity, featuring pelagic species that signal a thriving ecosystem. Various sharks, including lemon, reef, hammerhead and occasionally tiger sharks, patrol these coral reefs. Divers can enjoy a lively spectacle, with passing schools of giant trevally and tuna, sea turtles and countless colourful tropical fish.

Essential info

The number of cruises and seats is very limited each year, so you'll need to book in advance for the opportunity to discover this lost paradise.

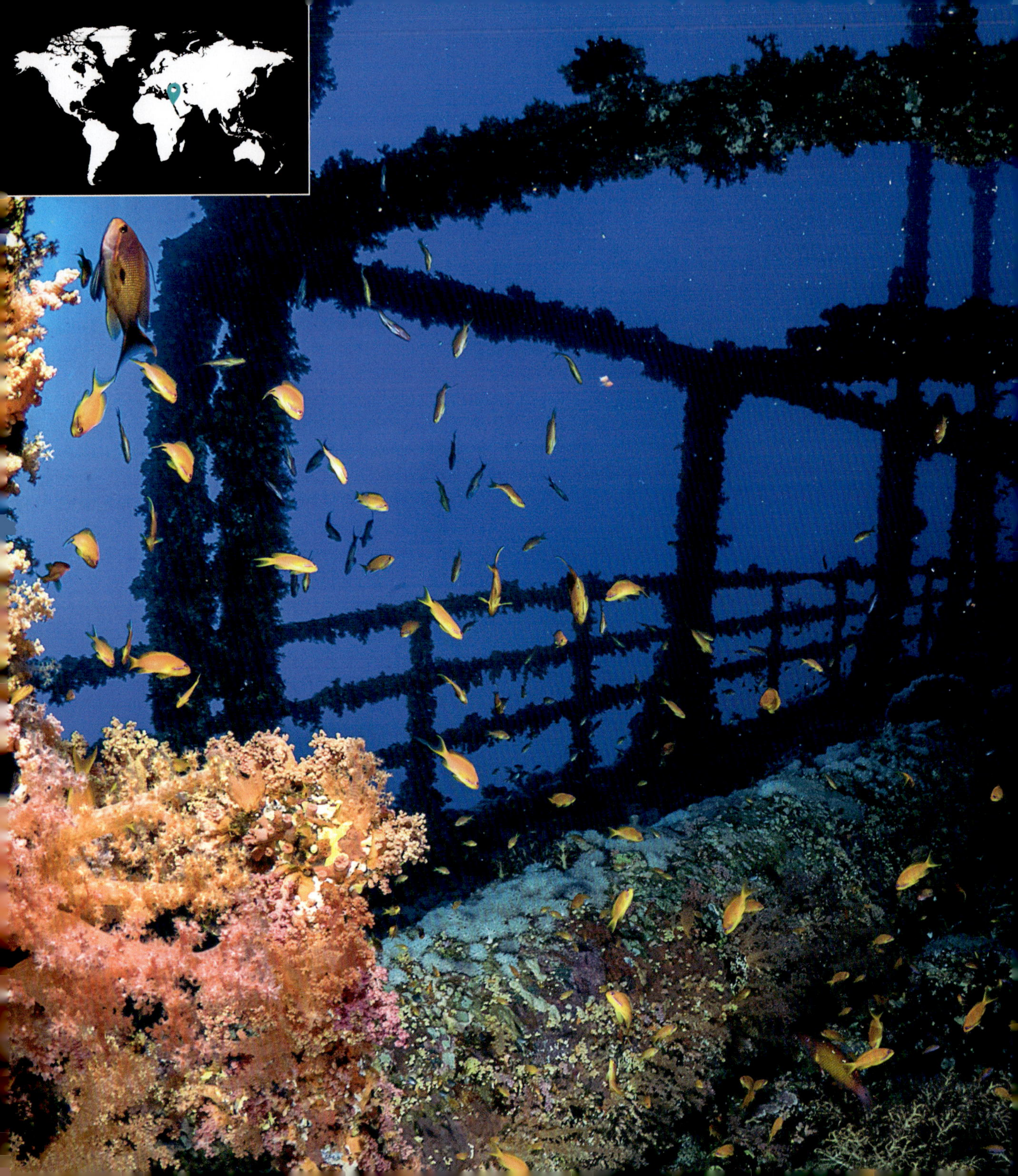

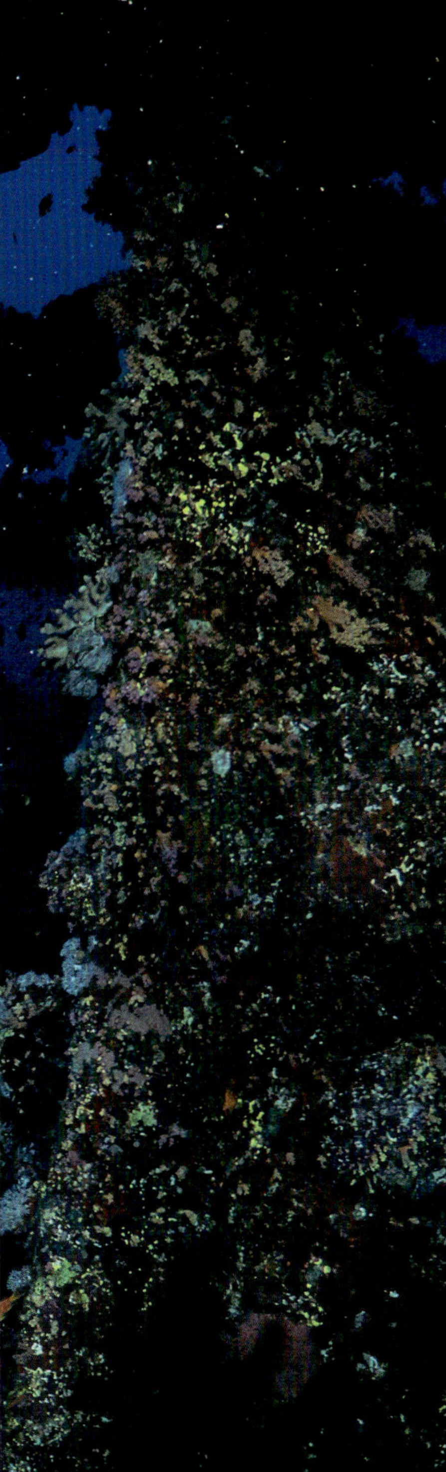

68 *Numidia* wreck

Brothers Islands, Egypt

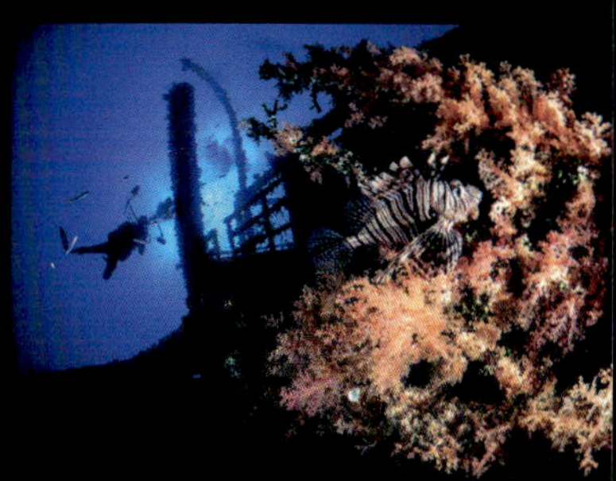

The Brothers are two islands, desolate and lost in the heart of the Red Sea. Far from everything, divers confront the elements – swells, currents and drop-offs plunging into the abyss – while encountering a rich array of pelagic life, particularly various species of sharks.

At the northern tip of Big Brother, waves crash against the reef, where beneath the surface lies one of Egypt's most impressive shipwrecks: the *Numidia*. This cargo ship, launched from Glasgow shipyards in February 1901, met its fate during its second and final voyage in July of the same year, departing from Liverpool bound for Calcutta.

On the night of 19 February, it struck the northern island with tremendous force, allegedly due to the officer on watch falling asleep. The *Numidia* sank, taking with it a cargo of railway equipment. Positioned vertically at a depth of between 10 and 85 metres (33 and 279 feet), this wreck provides divers with a unique and original configuration. Constantly buffeted by northward currents, it teems with marine life, watched over by the pelagic creatures that pass by regularly.

Essential info

Diving in the Brothers is worth it. Experience is essential to navigate the swell and drift dives, but the encounters are always spectacular.

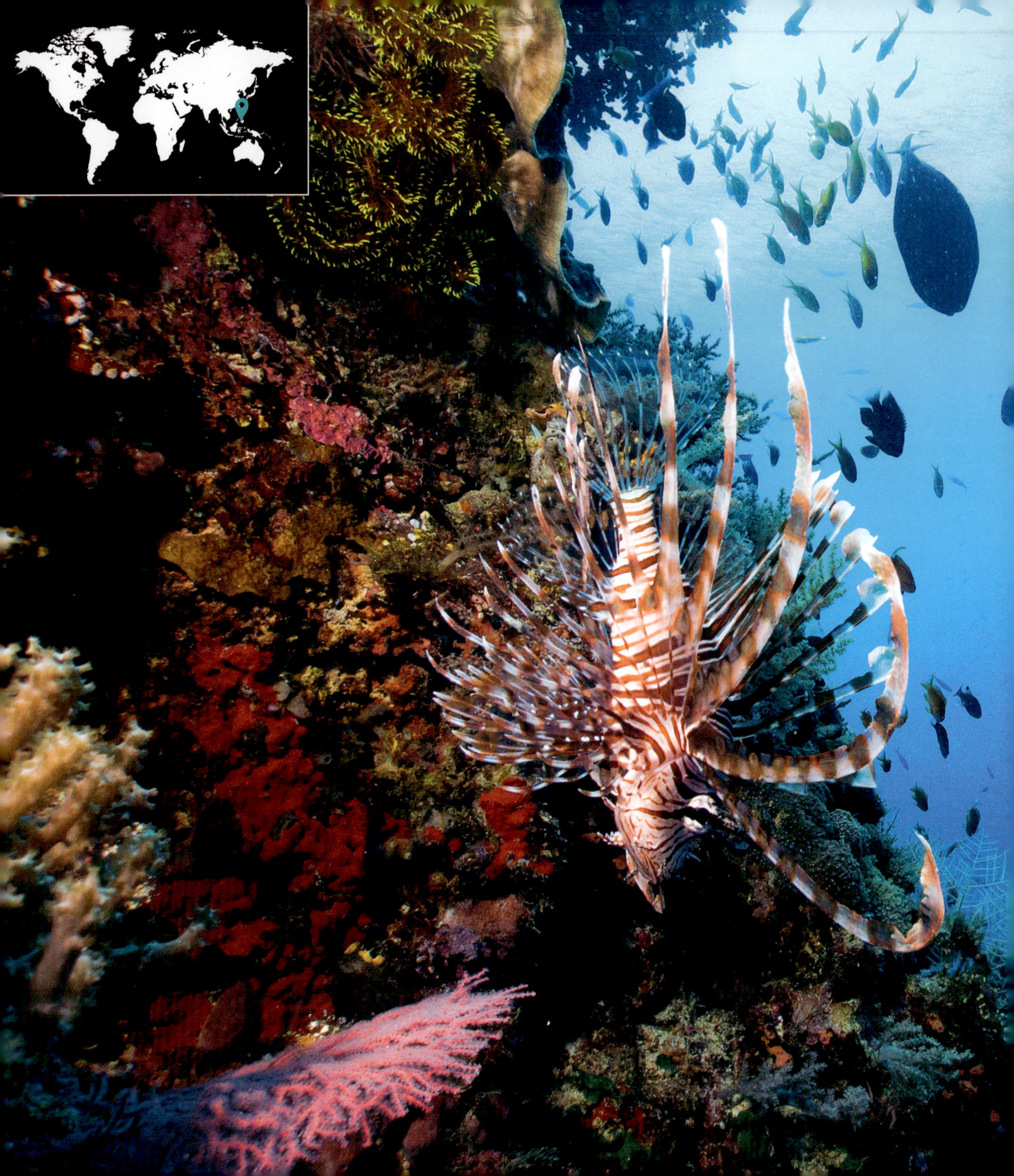

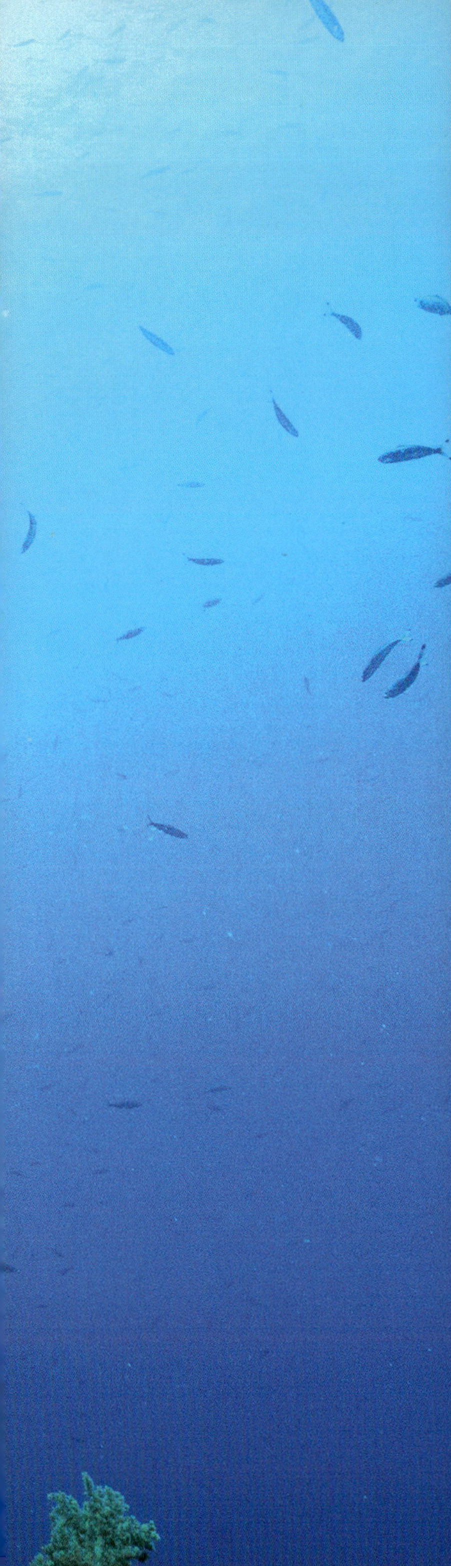

69 Cabilao Island

Visayas, Philippines

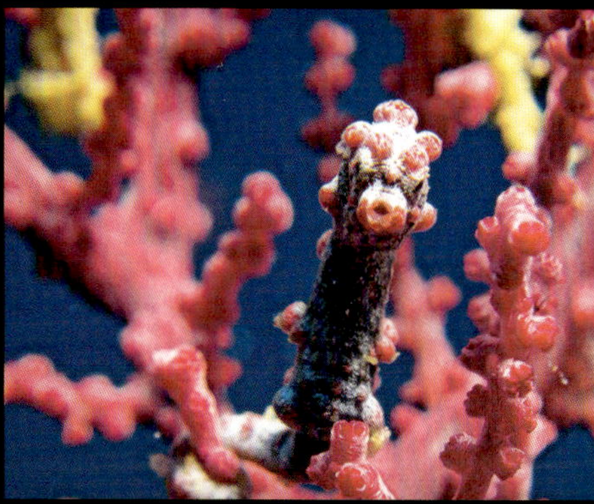

In the central region of the Philippine archipelago, known as the Visayas, lies the small island of Cabilao, nestled in the warm waters near Bohol Island. The journey to get here may be long, but as soon as the local banka (a traditional outrigger canoe) lands on the sandy shores, you'll quickly realise that this destination is truly worth the trip. Underwater photographers will be in their element here, as the sheer abundance of subjects to capture is staggering. Situated in the heart of the Coral Triangle, Cabilao boasts extraordinary biodiversity.

Surrounding the island, you'll encounter some of Asia's most iconic marine species: pygmy seahorses (see inset photo), nudibranchs, ghost pipefish and mandarinfish, all waiting to be observed during twilight dives.

This location is a true paradise for wildlife lovers, offering countless opportunities for encounters with every dive.

Essential info

With relatively little current, dives are accessible at all levels. However, divers should exercise caution with their buoyancy to avoid making contact with the reefs which are everywhere.

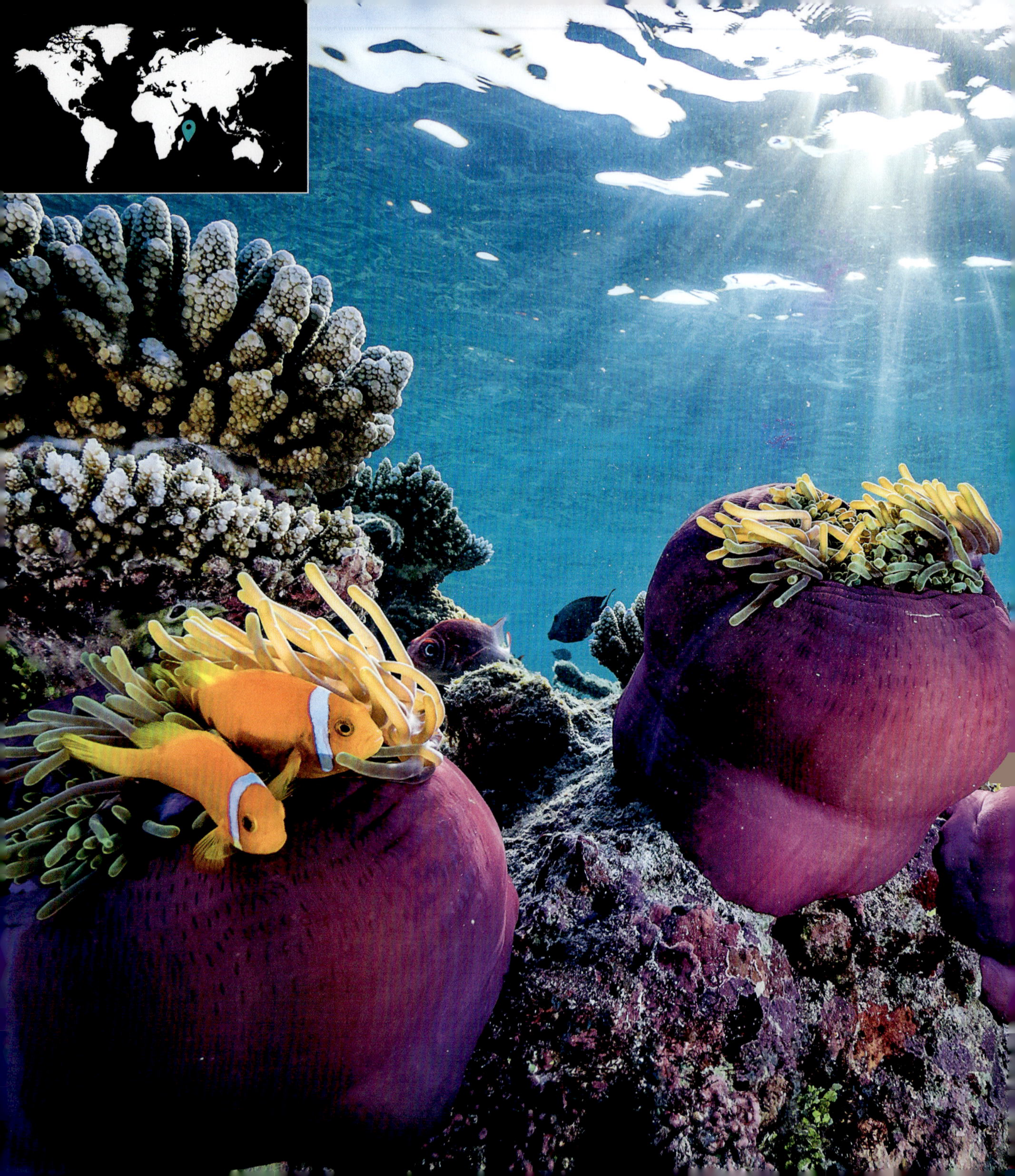

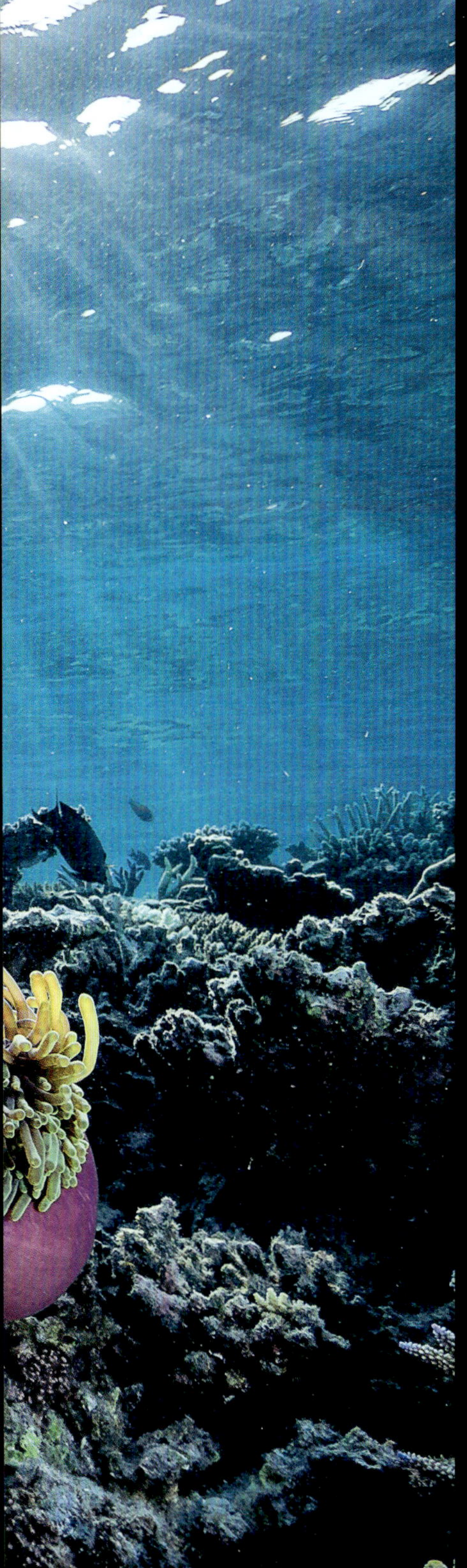

70 Rodrigues

Mauritius

The smallest of the main islands of the Mascarene archipelago in the Indian Ocean, Rodrigues is a place that seems to have been forgotten by time and tourists alike. Many bypass it in favour of its more famous neighbour, Mauritius. As a result, this island boasts rare and exceptional tranquillity; the perfect place to enjoy the Indian Ocean's calm waters. With a shallow lagoon stretching over 200 square kilometres (125 square miles), it is a paradise for kitesurfers. Protected by a coral reef, it boasts over 40 seldom-frequented dive sites. Nearly 280 coral species have been recorded here, creating stunning coral gardens alive with vibrant tropical fish in unique colours.

The sites have arches, faults and underwater caves as well as magnificent drop-offs covered with giant Gorgonia.

In the passes, drift dives bring divers face-to-face with formidable giant trevally (*Caranx horribilis*) reaching up to 1.8 metres (six feet) in length. Parrotfish, ghost pipefish, butterflyfish, surgeonfish and reef sharks add to the rich tapestry of marine life, and the most observant may even spot the rare Pegasus fish walking on the sand.

Essential info

There are two main areas for diving in Rodrigues: Pointe Cotton in the north and from Grande Passe in the south. On land, a visit to the François-Leguat reserve with its giant turtles is a must-see.

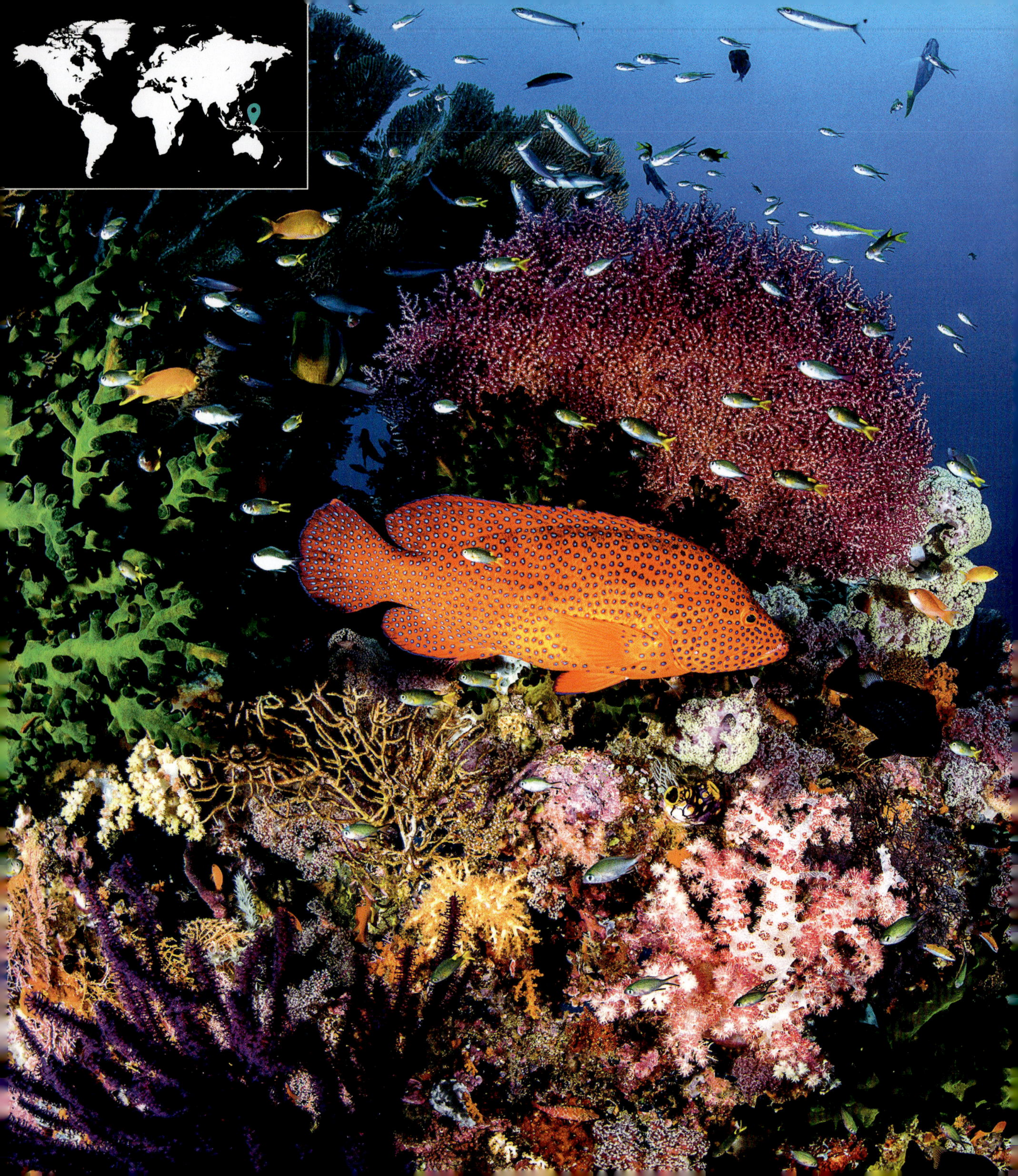

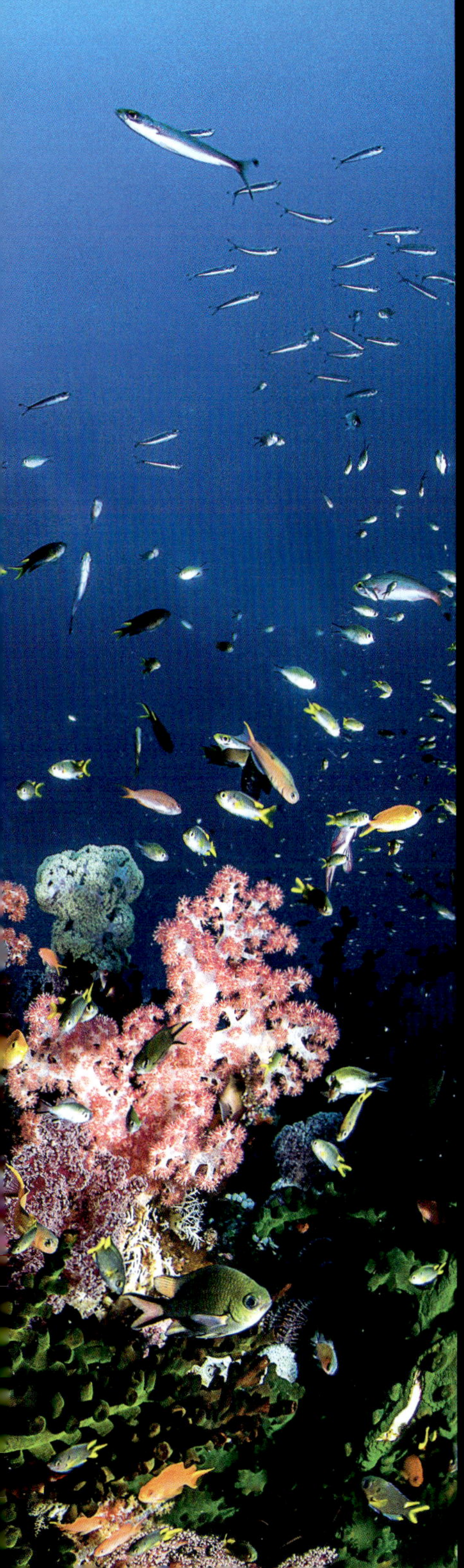

71 Raja Ampat

Papua, Indonesia

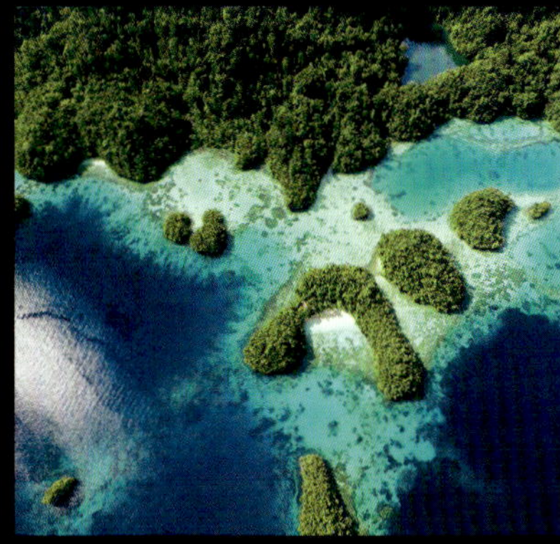

For most divers, this is the ultimate dream. Raja Ampat, the archipelago of the 'Four Kings' and famously called the 'last paradise on Earth', is renowned for its awe-inspiring landscapes, where lush green islets are surrounded by the intense blue sea.

Set in the heart of the Coral Triangle, this location is home to the planet's richest marine biodiversity. With over 540 coral species and more than 1,400 types of fish, its coral reefs are among the most thriving in existence. The biomass and the concentration of species per square metre are simply phenomenal. Raja Ampat is a diver's paradise, offering extraordinary opportunities for underwater photographers and scientists alike. Encounters range from the tiniest creatures, like pygmy seahorses, mandarinfish, ghost pipefish and frogfish, to majestic manta rays, hammerhead sharks and the iconic wobbegong shark (or carpet shark). This 'Holy Grail' of marine life will undoubtedly be the adventure of a lifetime.

Essential info

While conditions are typically favourable, some dive sites experience strong currents, so getting good experience under your belt is recommended to make the most of your Raja Ampat adventure.

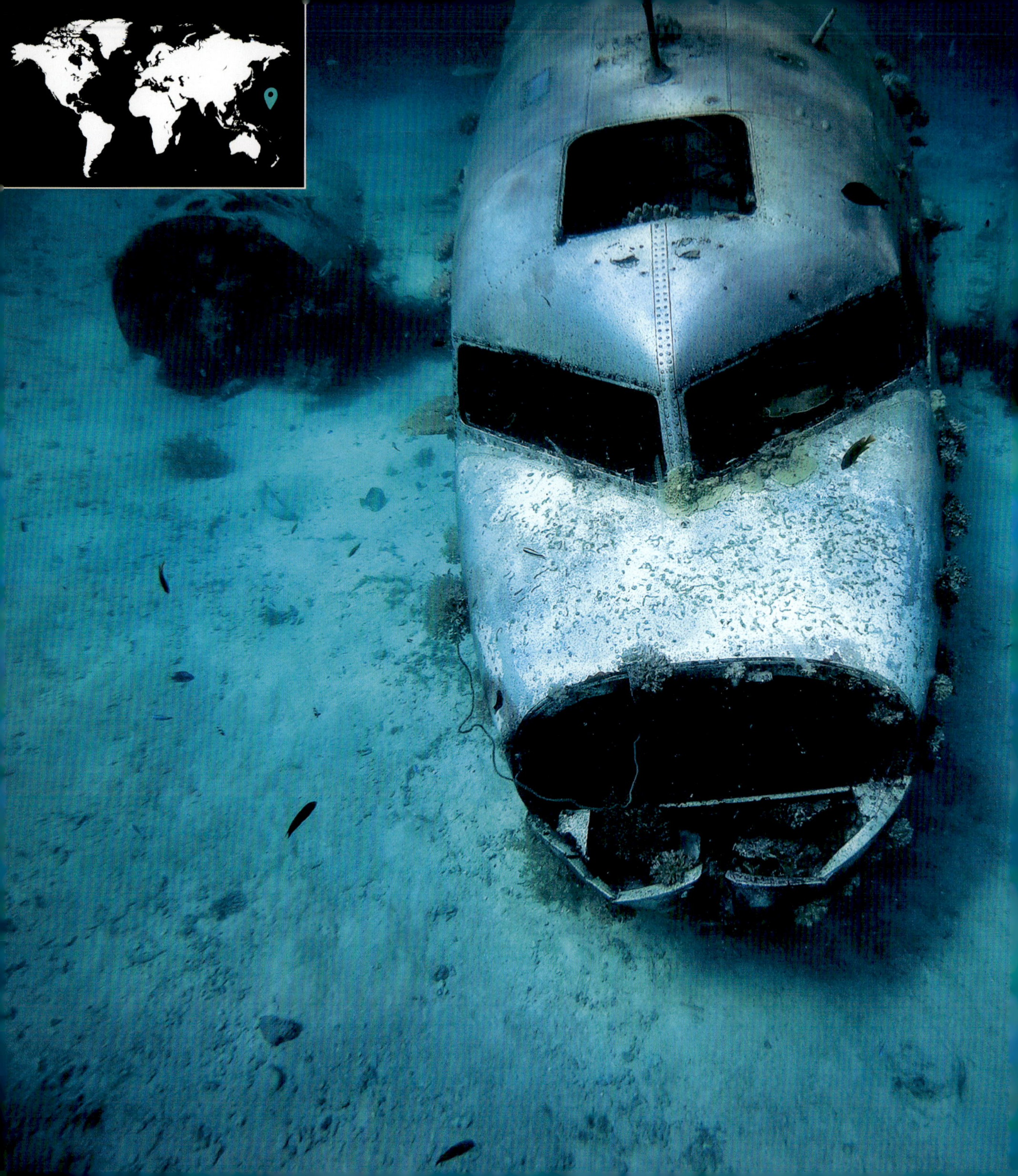

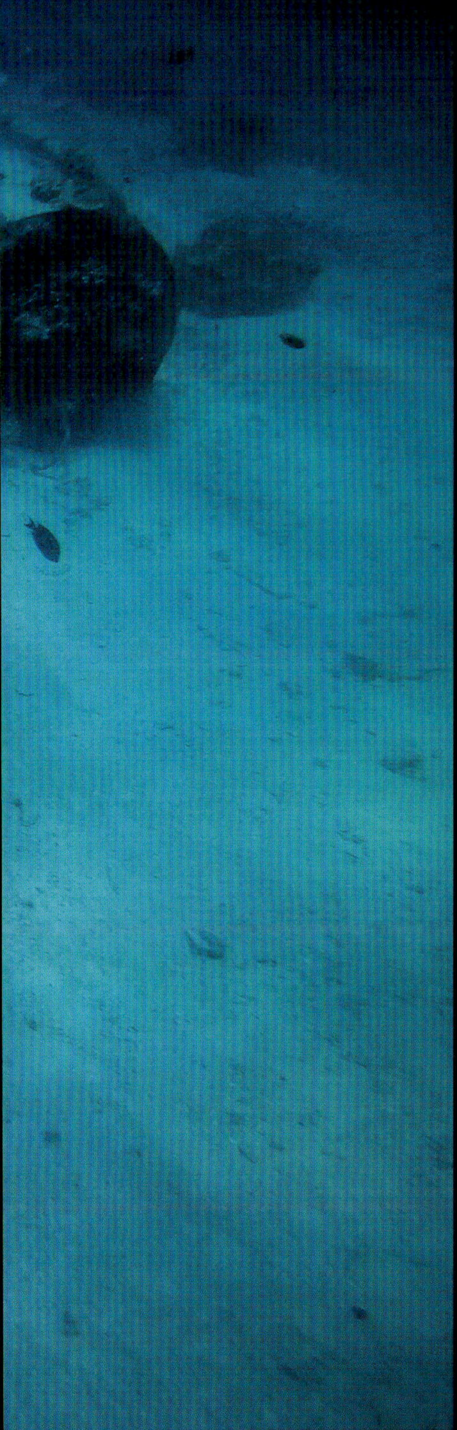

72 Bikini Atoll

Marshall Islands

The Marshall Islands: a collection of remote atolls in the heart of the Pacific Ocean. Following World War II, the United States selected Bikini Atoll as a testing site for newly developed atomic bombs, far more powerful than the bomb dropped on Hiroshima. A mock fleet of nearly 100 warships was deployed and then sunk in these tests. Over 23 detonations created a massive crater, two kilometres (1.25 miles) in diameter and extending to a depth of more than 70 metres (230 feet).

Since it was opened for diving in 1996, Bikini Atoll has become one of the most awe-inspiring underwater shipwreck sites accessible to divers. Nature has since reclaimed the area and the seabed around the atoll is beautiful. Vibrant corals, gorgonians and schools of fish now cover the wrecks, while various shark species have made these famed waters their own. With many sites at depths exceeding 40 metres (131 feet), Bikini Atoll is a haven for technical divers with a passion for shipwreck exploration. Interestingly, this UNESCO World Heritage Site, designated in 2010, lent its name to the iconic swimsuit introduced by French fashion designer Louis Réard in 1946, inspired by the idea that his design would create an 'explosive' impact.

Essential info

Diving at Bikini Atoll is available exclusively on dive cruises and is only accessible to experienced divers with certifications beyond 40 metres (131 feet), which is level 3 + Nitrox certified, ideally with trimix or rebreather qualifications.

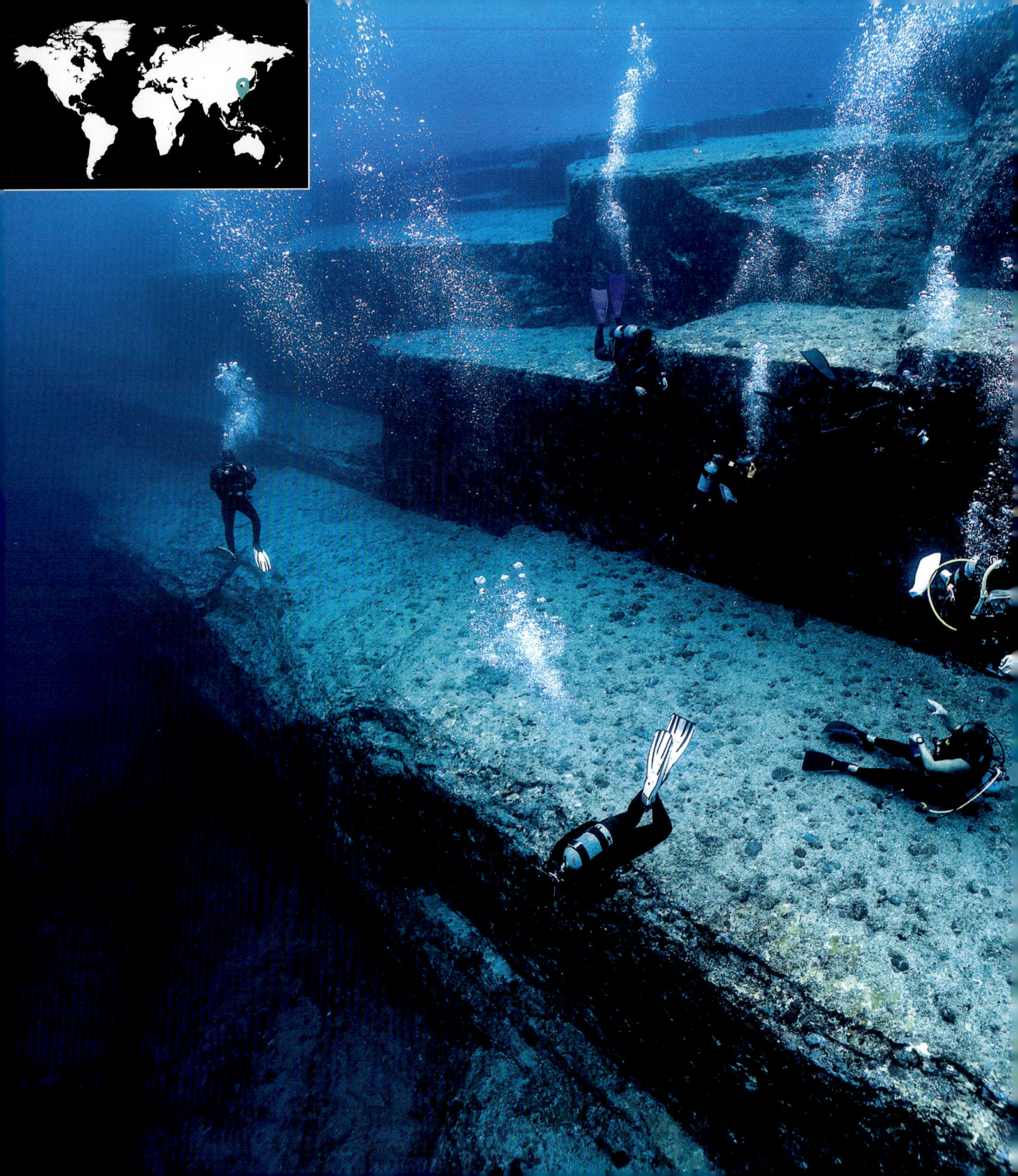

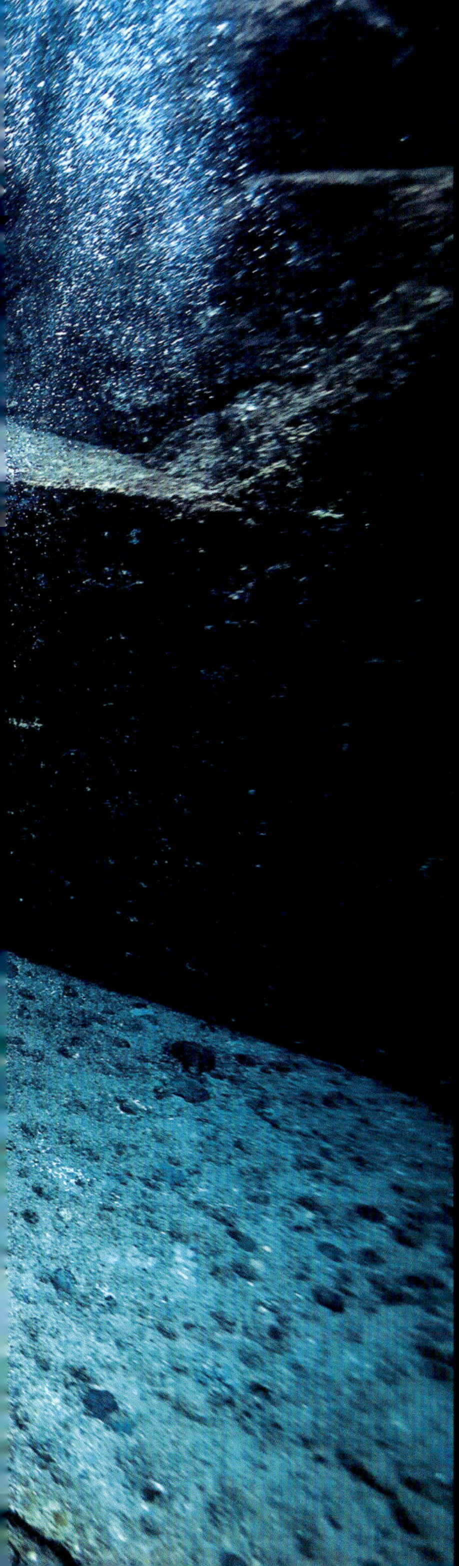

73 Underwater city of Yonaguni

Japan

Japan, often called the Land of the Rising Sun, is a country steeped in mystery. Although little known to Westerners for diving, it hides many underwater treasures, particularly in the Okinawa region with its crystal-clear waters and lush coral reefs.

At the southernmost point of the Japanese archipelago lies Yonaguni Island, famed for the vast numbers of hammerhead sharks that gather there from November to March. However, the island's most unique underwater attraction is an enigmatic, monumental rock structure discovered by a diver in 1985 while scouting for sharks. This single, colossal stone formation spans over 75 metres (246 feet) in length, rising from around 25 metres (82 feet) to just three metres (10 feet) below the surface. Resembling a submerged city, the site features terraces, an arch, giant steps and even a sculpture of a turtle – a breathtaking sight that remains a mystery. To this day, experts are still undecided as to whether this site was sculpted by human hands, formed by natural forces or even shaped by otherworldly means.

Essential info

This is an unusual dive, shallow, yet often accompanied by strong currents.

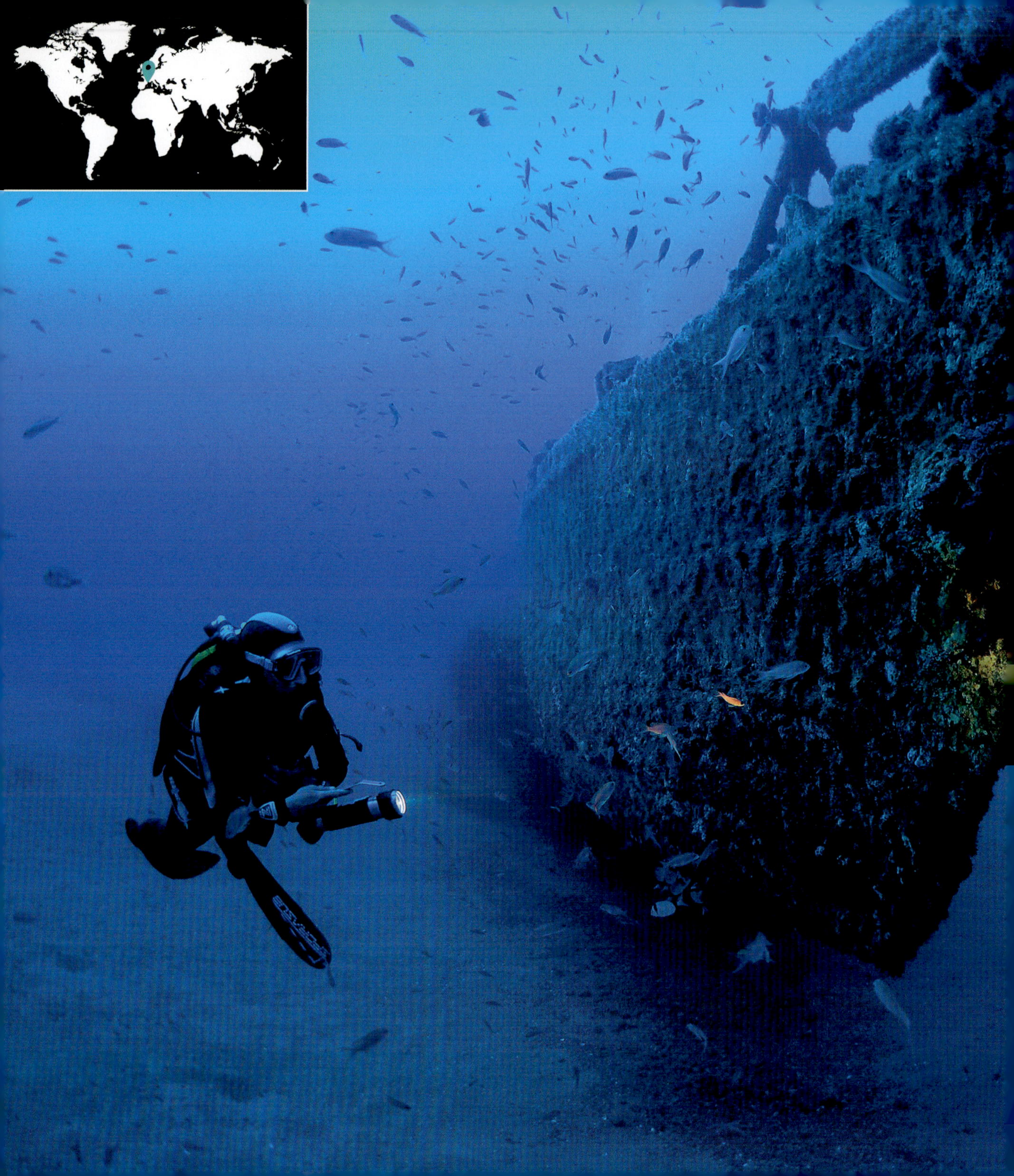

74 *Rubis* wreck

Var, France

The south of France, with its majestic Mediterranean coast, is home to some of the most beautiful ocean dives. The sheer number of dive sites, each as diverse as they are accessible, is truly remarkable. Shipwreck enthusiasts will jump at the opportunity to dive in the Var region. Among all the dive sites available, one stands out as particularly unique: the *Rubis* wreck at Cape Camarat, one of the few submarine wrecks recorded in the world.

This minelaying submarine, built in Toulon in 1931, was particularly distinguished during the Second World War, sinking no less than 18 enemy vessels. Unscathed at the end of the war, she was disarmed in 1945 and used as a training ship for a few years. In 1958, it was decided to sink the vessel, allowing her to settle on a sandy seabed located 40 metres (131 feet) beneath the surface. Divers now come to visit regularly and meet this hero of the Resistance, which is preserved in perfect condition. Today, the guardians of this underwater realm are the impressive groupers, conger eels and moray eels that inhabit every nook and cranny of the artificial reef.

Essential info

A wreck accessible for divers who are at least at level 2, and which requires some experience to descend into the deep blue. Note that the current can be strong.

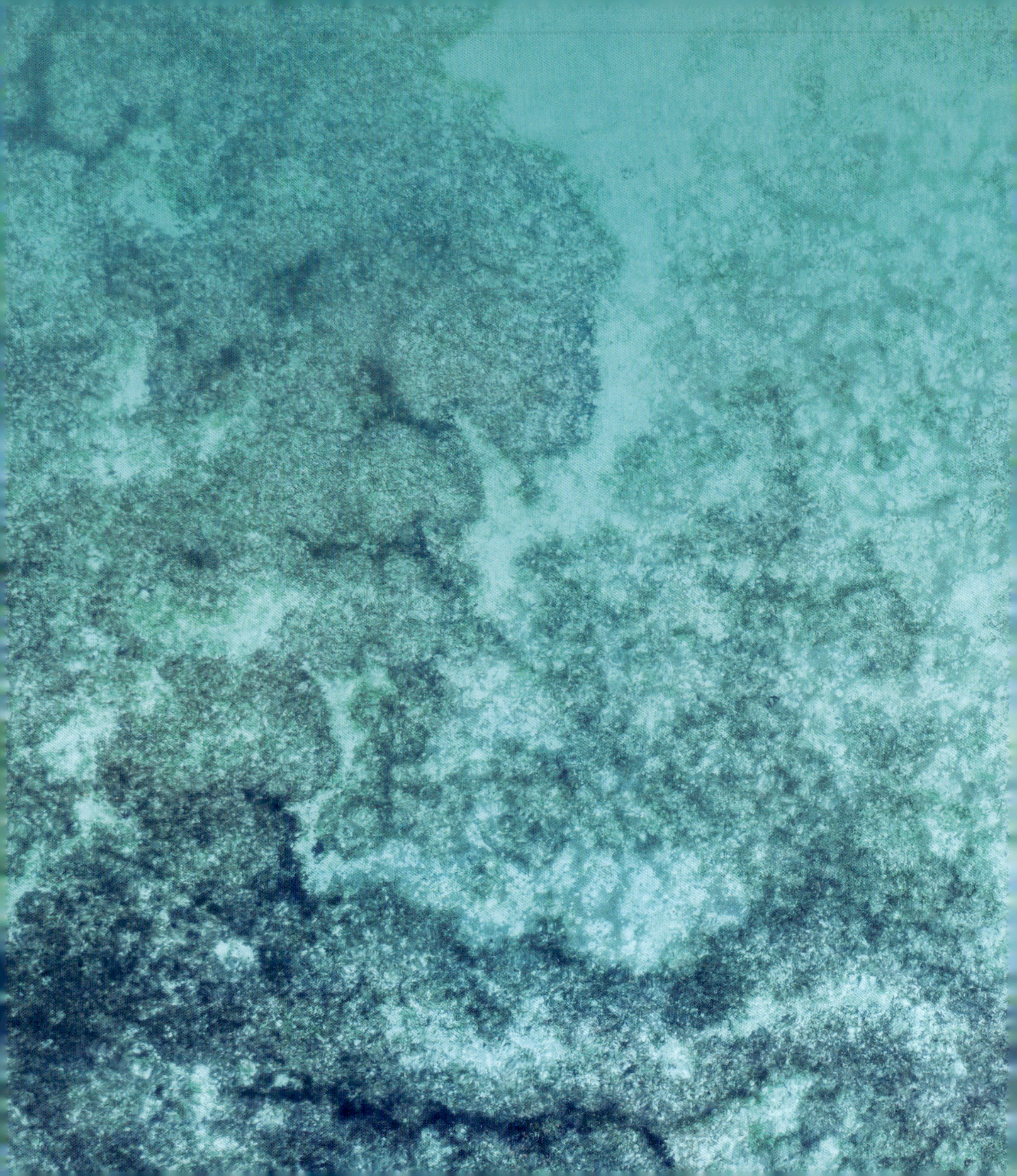

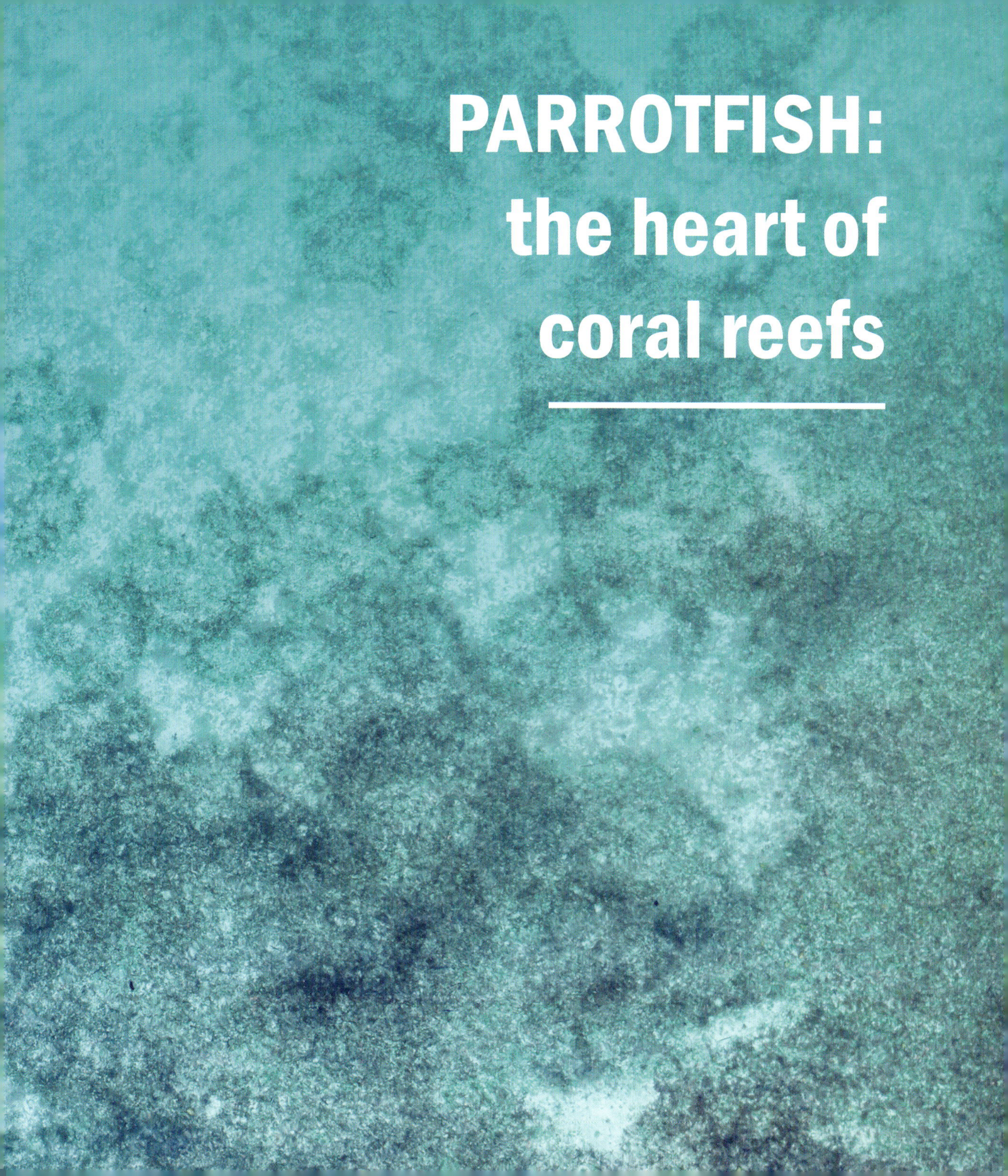

PARROTFISH: the heart of coral reefs

Beautifully coloured and proudly displaying their powerful beak, parrotfish play an essential role in the balance of coral ecosystems.

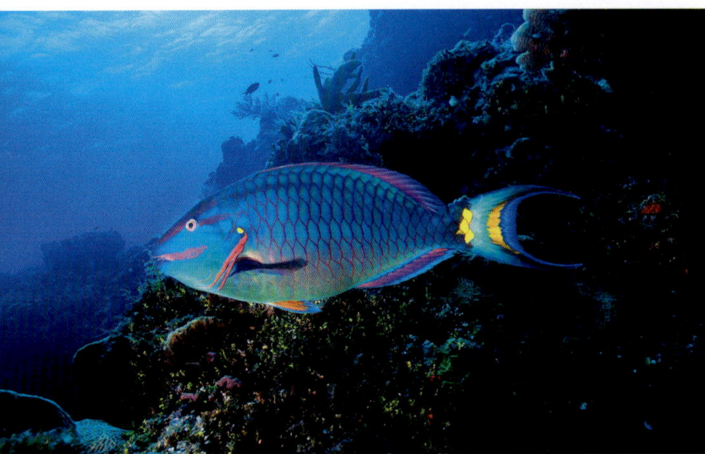

Fire parrotfish.

Fish from distant seas

Parrotfish are fascinating tropical and subtropical residents, belonging to the Scaridae family, with around 100 species spanning 10 genera. Present in all seas in tropical or subtropical zones, they are particularly well represented throughout the Indo-Pacific and the Red Sea. There is even one species found in the Mediterranean called 'Mediterranean parrotfish'.

The humphead parrotfish is the largest, reaching up to an impressive 1.3 metres (four feet) long. This species, with its prominent forehead hump, is often mistaken for the similarly sized Napoleon wrasse.

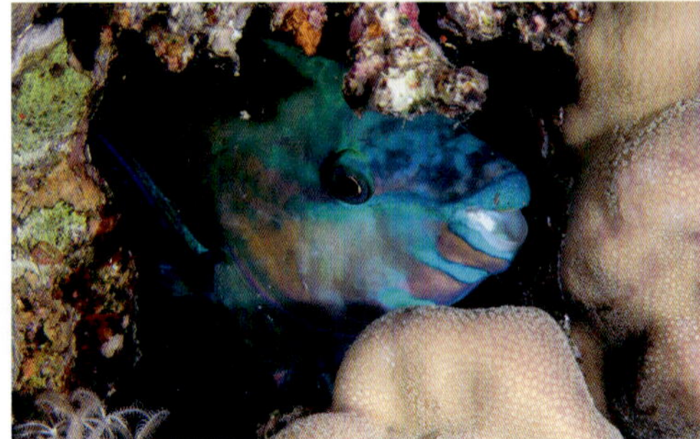

Five-saddle parrotfish.

They are rather fierce towards divers and can form groups of several dozen individuals.

In their bubble

One of their most remarkable traits is their ability to create a protective cocoon. As night falls, parrotfish secrete a protective mucus from glands near their gill covers, enveloping themselves in a bubble that protects them from the outside world.

Their fused teeth form a hard beak-like structure made of fluorapatite, one of nature's toughest biominerals, even stronger than some metals. Despite being considered herbivores – and certain parrotfish species do graze on algae – some consume coral, ingesting not only plant material but also the tiny coral polyps that are, in fact, animals.

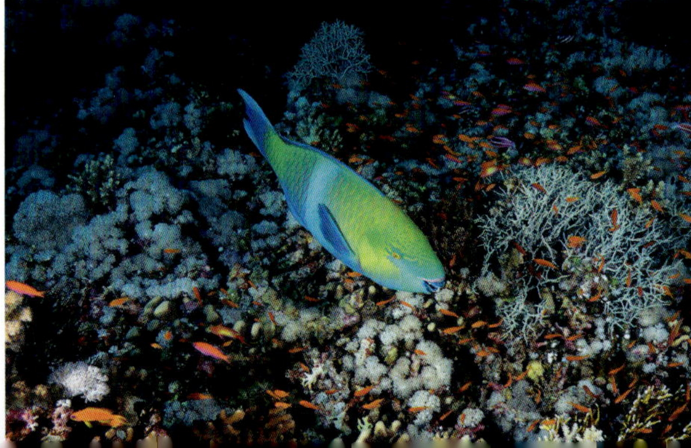

Rusty parrotfish.

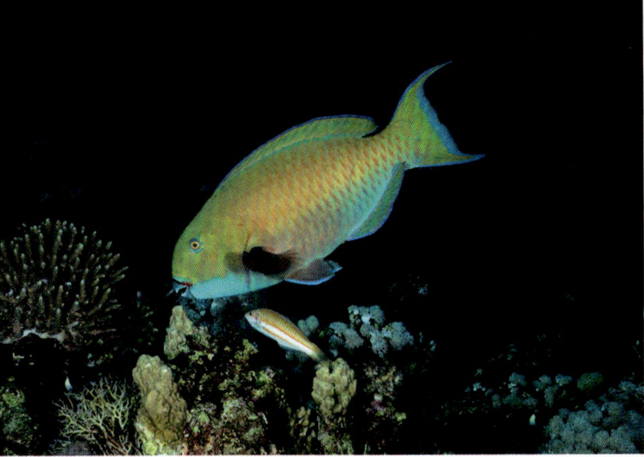

Heavybeak parrotfish.

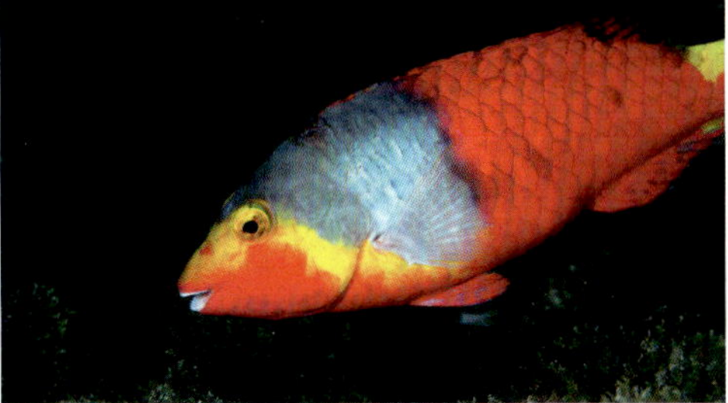

Mediterranean parrotfish.

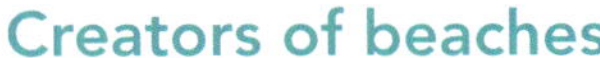

Creators of beaches

Parrotfish play an incredible role in beach formation due to their constantly growing teeth. Their pharyngeal teeth are specially adapted to grind pieces of coral, allowing them to extract the algae within.

Astonishingly, a single parrotfish can transform up to a ton of coral each year into coral sand. This sand, primarily composed of parrotfish waste, helps stabilise coral reefs as it settles on the seabed. Parrotfish also contribute to the formation of beautiful white sandy beaches.

Despite their coral consumption, these fish are far from being a threat to reefs; in fact, they're essential for coral health. By grazing on algae that could otherwise suffocate coral, parrotfish help corals thrive, with research proving that coral ecosystems with large parrotfish populations promote healthy coral and faster coral growth.

Remarkable behaviour

Identifying parrotfish species can be quite a challenge, especially in regions where multiple species coexist, as their colours and patterns shift throughout their lives. Parrotfish go through various colour changes as they progress from the initial juvenile phase, the early adult phase and the final adult phase. They also display intermediate shades, particularly during sexual transition.

Parrotfish possess a fascinating and complex sexuality. Depending on the species, some are born male (primary males), others begin as females and later transform into males (secondary males), while some remain female throughout their lives. In certain species, only primary males exist, whereas in others, both primary and secondary males are present. Typically, a dominant male maintains a harem of several females.

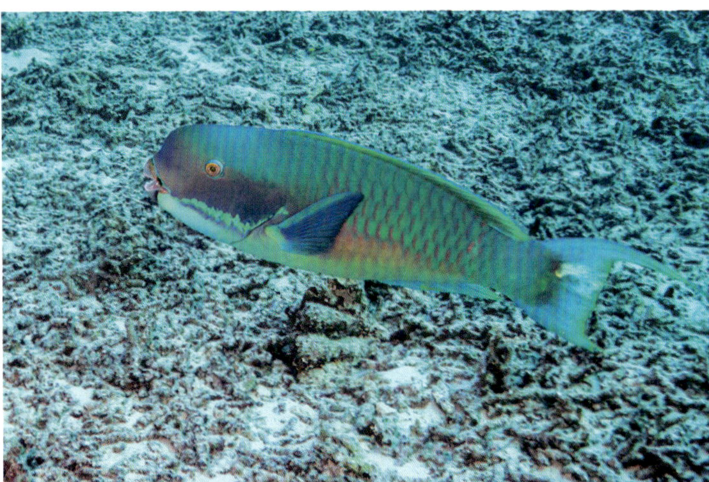

Blue parrotfish.

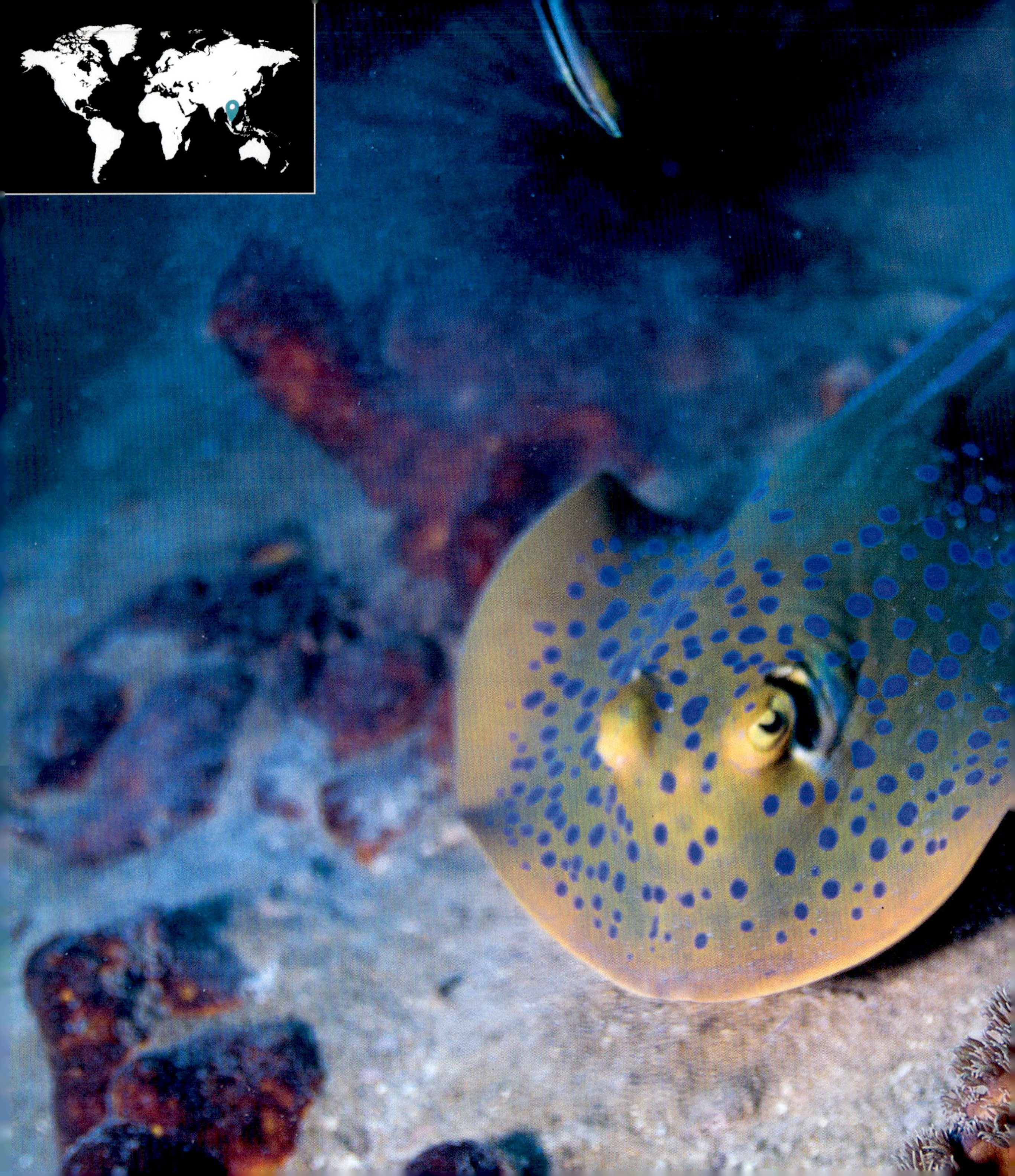

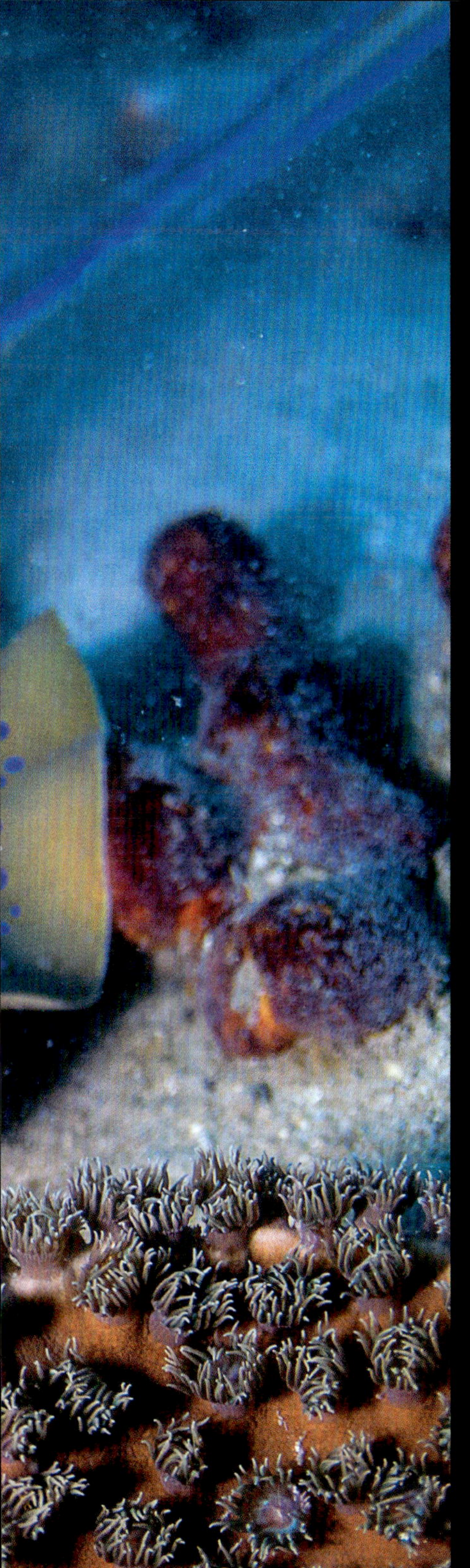

75 Perhentian Islands

Malaysia

The Malaysian peninsula is bordered by the Strait of Malacca on one side and the Gulf of Thailand and the China Sea on the other. To the northeast, opposite the small town of Kuala Besut, sit the Perhentian Islands – just 10 kilometres (six miles) from Thailand and a short 30-minute speedboat ride that transports visitors to this true haven. There are no roads on these islands and the only ways to travel are on foot or by water taxi. The islands boast beaches, cosy hotels, dive centres and jungle landscapes.

Known as a top snorkelling destination, the Perhentians are celebrated for their proximity to remarkable marine life: snorkellers can easily spot large green turtles, blacktip reef sharks and a dazzling array of tropical fish just a few metres (10 feet) from shore. With around 20 dive sites nearby, divers also enjoy a rich underwater playground. The famed Tokong Laut, or 'Temple of the Sea', stands out for its abundant marine life and vibrant coral reefs, including blue-spotted stingrays. The water here is so densely populated that it can make visibility challenging.

Essential info

Divers and snorkellers alike will appreciate the Perhentians' underwater world and breathtaking white sandy beaches. However, be mindful of the titan triggerfish, which can be particularly territorial during the reproduction season.

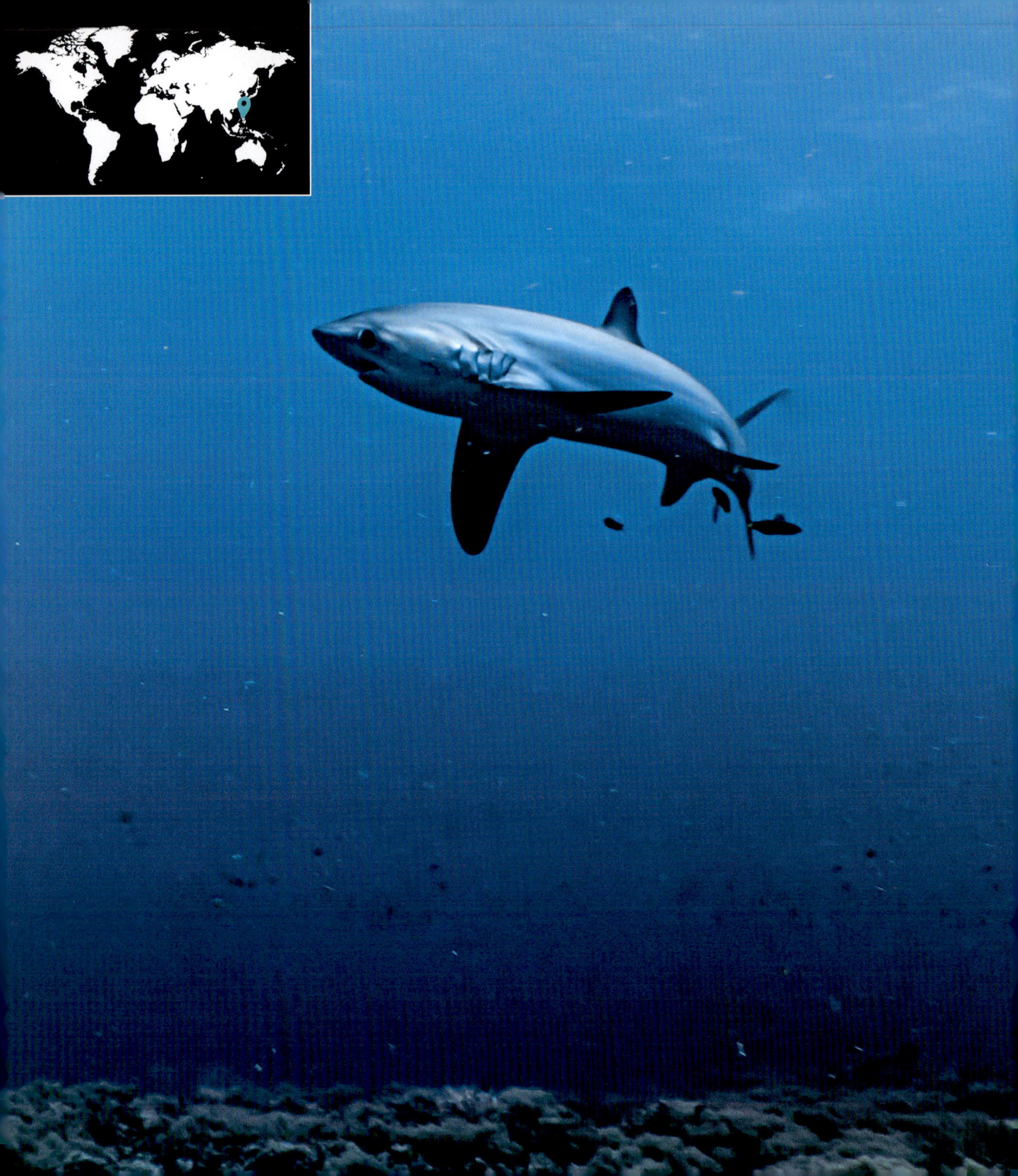

76 Malapascua Island

Visayas, Philippines

For shark enthusiasts, a dive trip to the Philippines would be incomplete without a visit to Malapascua. This small island, sited northeast of Cebu in the Visayas archipelago, is renowned as the world's premier destination for spotting thresher sharks. Typically found at greater depths, these magnificent creatures ascend to shallower waters in the early morning to visit their cleaning stations, where they undergo a de-parasitising ritual.

To catch a glimpse of these sharks, divers must rise early, with dive centres organising excursions to Monad Shoal at dawn. At depths between 12 and 30 metres (39 and 98 feet), divers settle on the ocean floor and patiently wait for the sharks to appear. As the silhouettes emerge, their long tails – equivalent in length to their bodies – whip through schools of smaller fish that they feast on.

Essential info

Departures are typically around five am. Once in the water, it's crucial to remain behind the designated rope barrier to avoid startling the sharks.

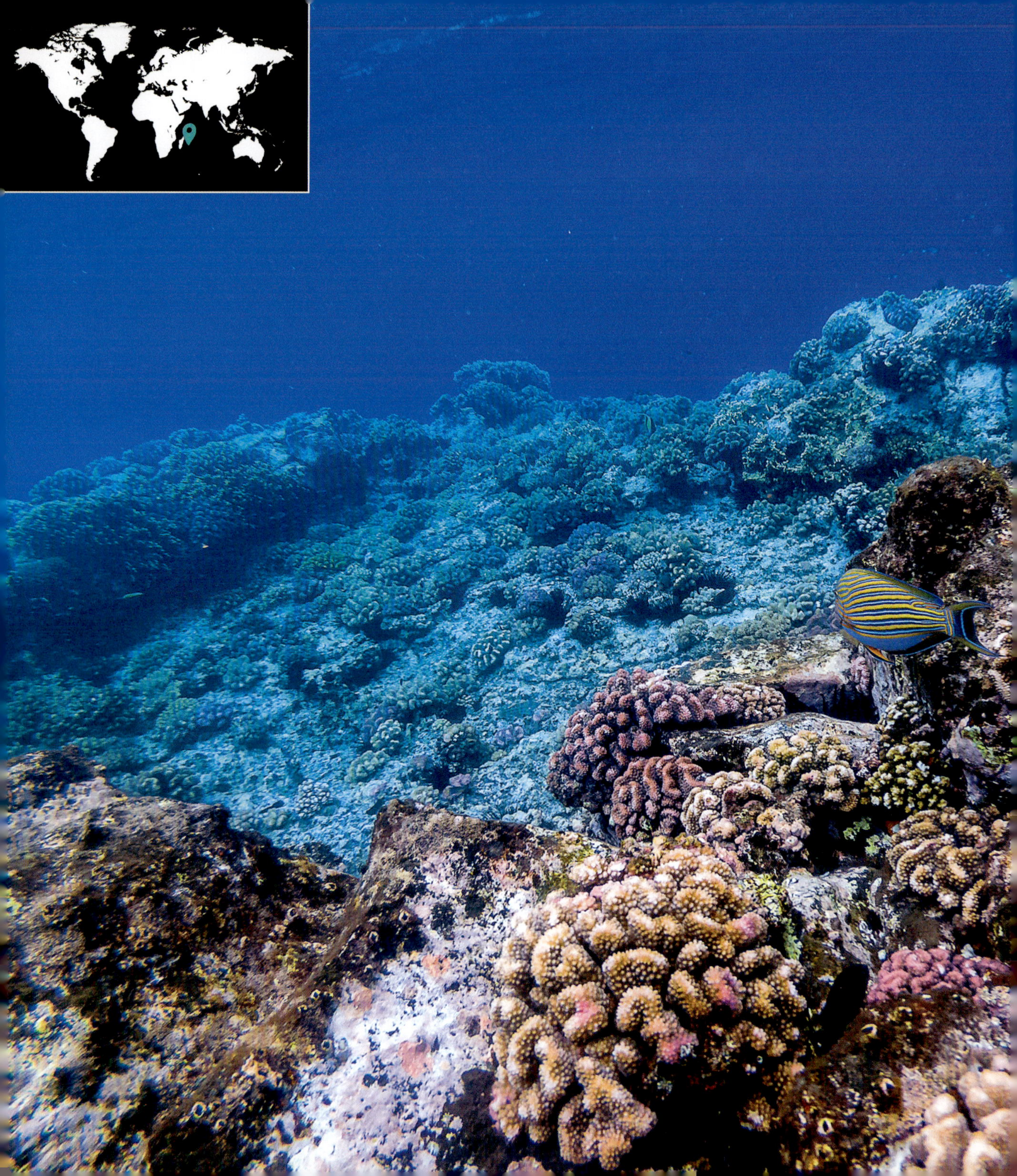

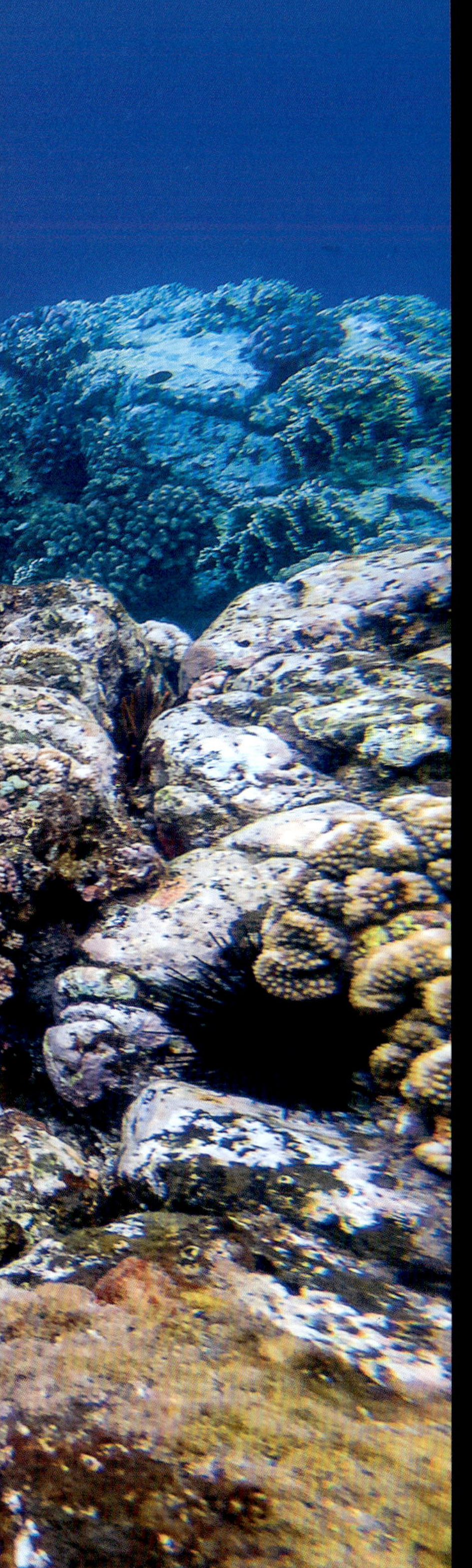

77 Réunion Island marine reserve

Réunion

Réunion Island, a gem of the Indian Ocean, offers an exhilarating blend of lush landscapes and underwater treasures, making it a dream destination for nature lovers. Known for its dramatic volcanic cirques, it attracts hikers and trekkers eager to experience its breathtaking green valleys. Beyond its famous surf spots, Réunion's fringing coral reef also offers several dive sites.

In the west, a vast marine reserve established in 2007 preserves precious coral ecosystems from damage due to human activity. Most of the island's stunning dive sites are located in this area. Over 1,200 fish species are present in these waters, 30 shark species have been sighted and graceful sea turtles are often encountered by divers. From colourful clownfish and butterflyfish, boxfish, scorpionfish, surgeonfish to damselfish, triggerfish or even groupers, Réunion's marine biodiversity is truly remarkable. From June to October, the island's warm waters welcome migrating humpback whales that can be seen just metres from the shore. With a bit of luck, divers may even swim alongside these gentle giants.

Essential info

For non-divers (and even divers), the marine reserve offers many sites in the lagoon for snorkelling, including an underwater trail located at L'Ermitage.

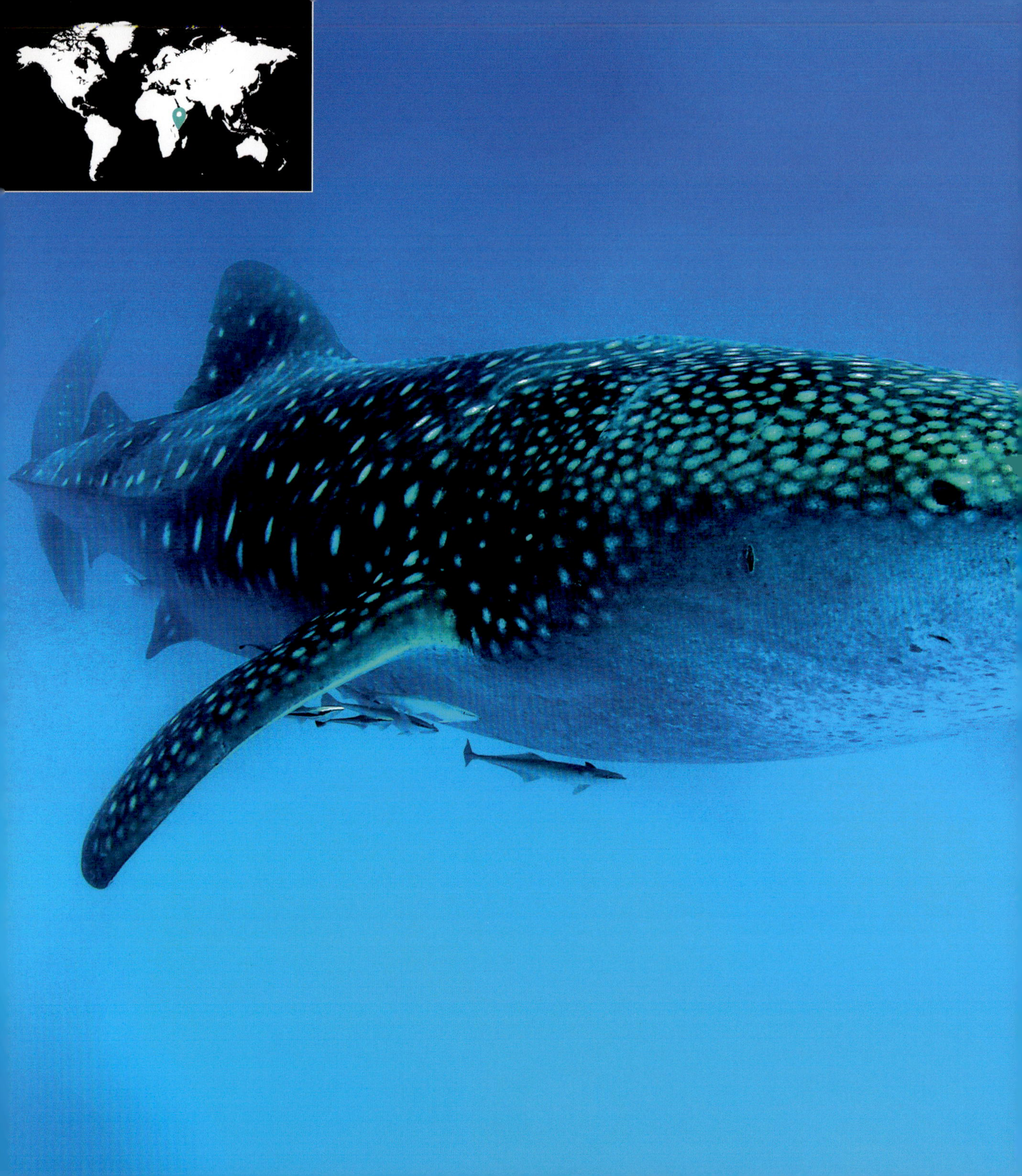

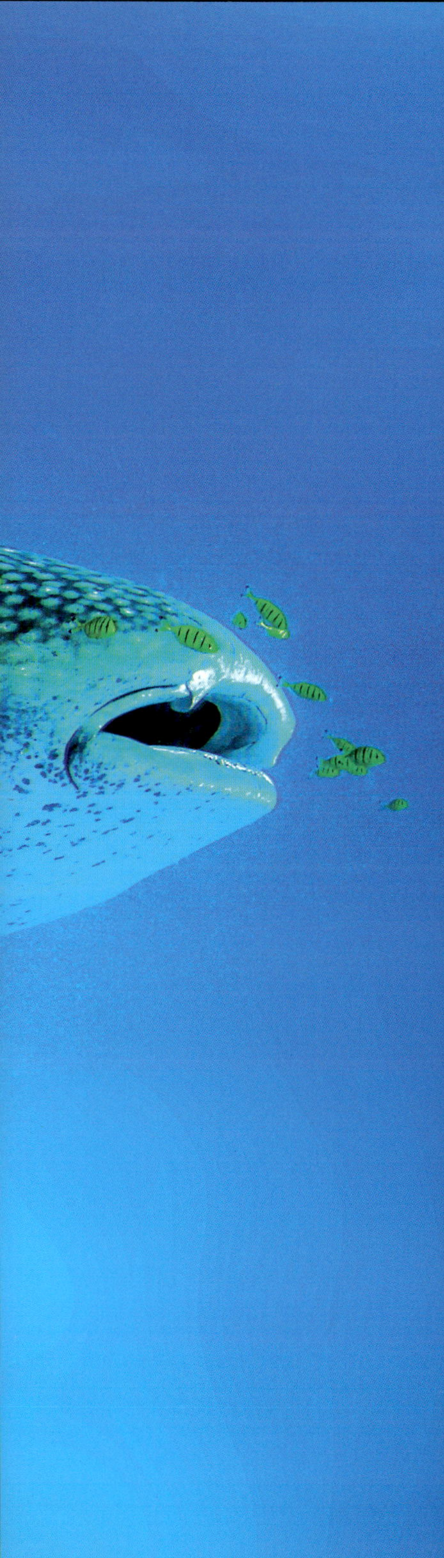

78 Mafia Island

Tanzania

Tanzania is a paradise for nature lovers, both on land and underwater. On land, a safari brings you face-to-face with the iconic 'Big Five' – elephants, rhinos, lions, buffalo and leopards.

Meanwhile, the marine world is just as thrilling, with the Mafia Island Marine Park offering some of East Africa's most pristine dive experiences. Far removed from mass tourism, this idyllic island is encircled by vibrant, untouched coral reefs. Macro photography enthusiasts will delight in finding rare and colourful species like nudibranchs and vivid shrimp of all kinds of amazing shapes and sizes, while larger marine life also abounds. Barracudas, jacks, giant potato groupers, turtles, rays and tuna are common sights, with whale sharks (see photo) making seasonal appearances from October to March. Witness the hatching and emergence of sea turtles or watch humpback whales breaching from July to August.

Essential info

Mafia Island offers something for everyone, and advanced divers can explore the more challenging sites. For non-divers, the snorkelling is equally remarkable, providing a stunning glimpse into the vibrant underwater world.

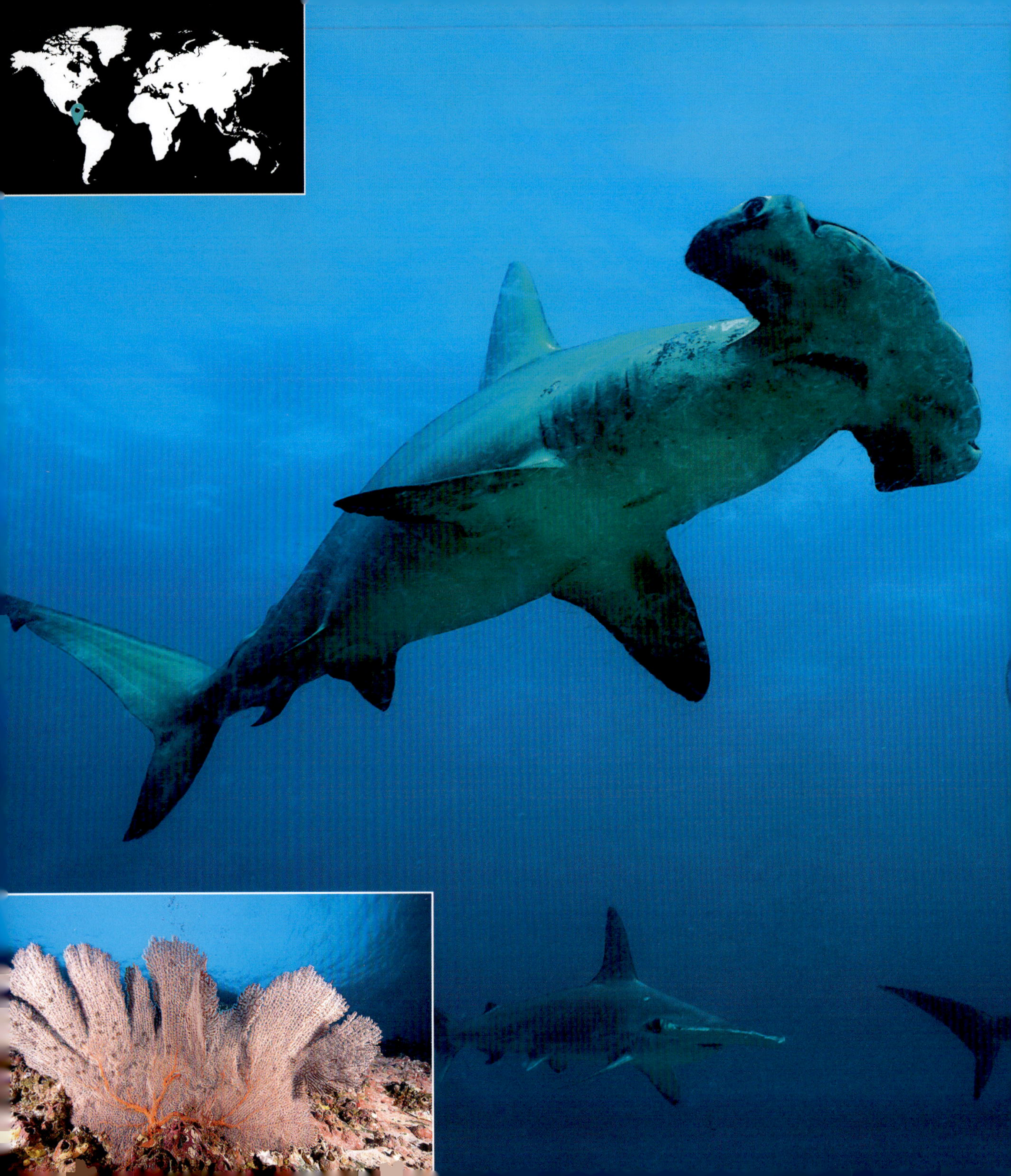

79 Malpelo Island

Colombia

Some remote places on the planet serve as natural sanctuaries, with strategic locations that attract an abundance of marine life.

Remoteness plays a crucial role in creating a natural sanctuary, especially in a world where human impact is so widespread. Over 500 kilometres (310 miles) off Colombia's west coast, Malpelo Island exemplifies this phenomenon. Rising from an underwater mountain range that converges with multiple marine currents, Malpelo is home to an extraordinary diversity of pelagic species. This site boasts the world's largest concentration of silky sharks and remarkable schools of hammerhead sharks (see photo). Divers can also encounter the elusive Galápagos shark and the rare deepwater short-nosed ragged-tooth shark, also known as the 'fierce shark', species usually confined to deep waters due to their reclusive habits.

The dive sites around Malpelo feature dramatic drop-offs and about a dozen pinnacles, offering breathtaking underwater landscapes. While the primary appeal is the deep blue, the island's warm seas also host a variety of vibrant corals, many of which are unique to the region (see inset photo). Diving in Malpelo is the experience of a lifetime.

Essential info

Malpelo is accessible only by cruise and is recommended for experienced divers due to its strong currents. The island has been a UNESCO World Heritage Site since 2006.

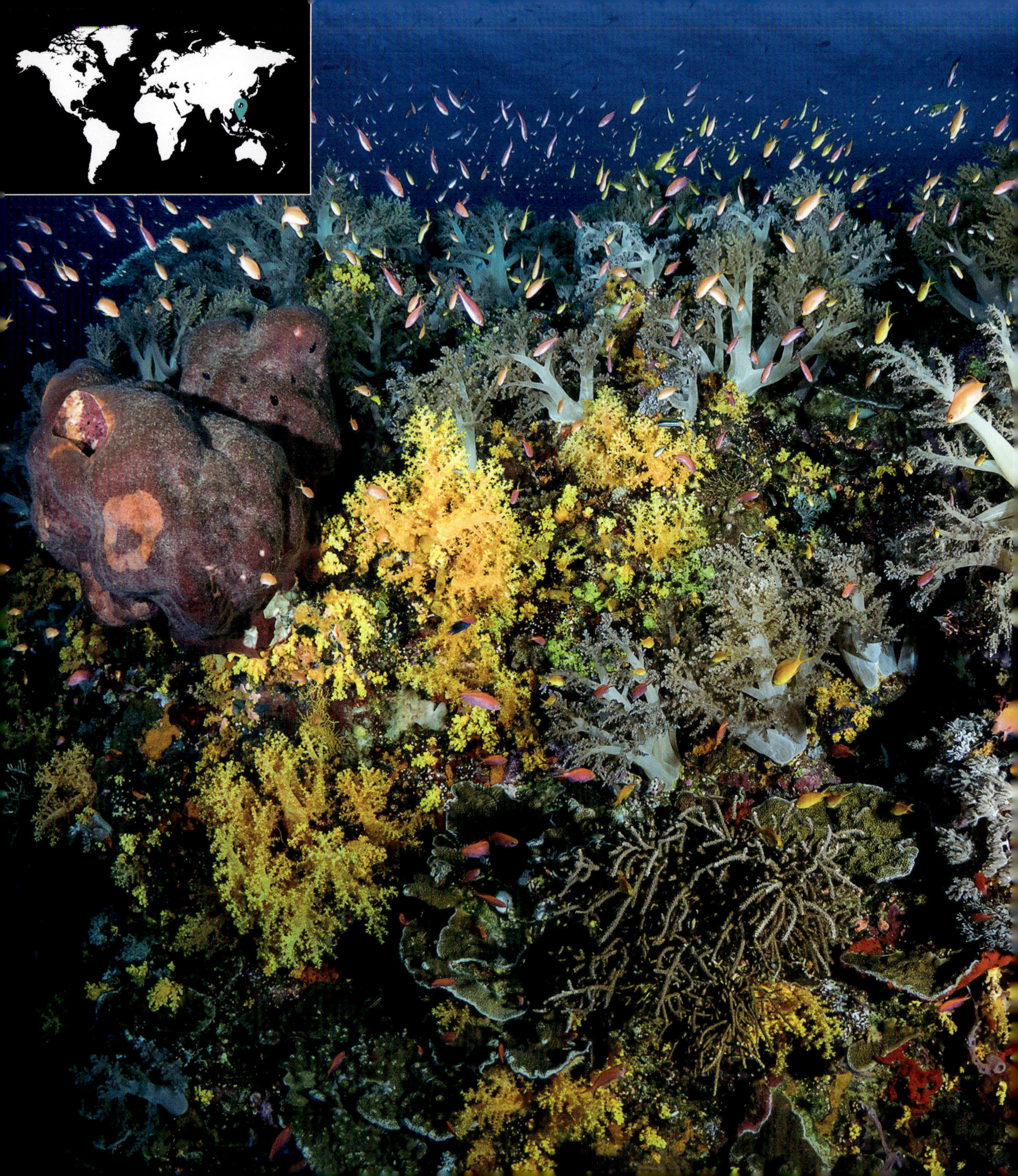

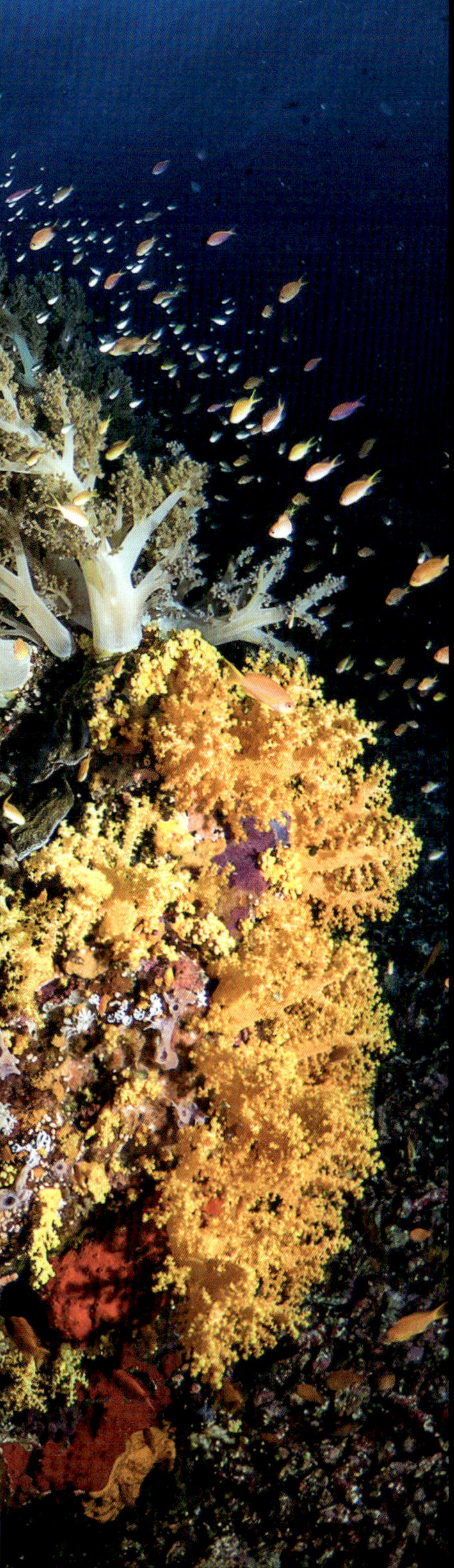

80 Tubbataha Reef attols

Philippines

Tubbataha Reef, the only atolls in the Philippines' archipelago of 7,641 islands, lies in the tranquil waters of the Sulu Sea, within the Palawan region. Reaching this remote paradise requires a 10-hour boat journey from Puerto Princesa, where the horizon forms a continuous, broken line between sky and sea in every direction.

Designated a UNESCO World Heritage Site in 1993, Tubbataha is under strict protection all year round. A dedicated team of around 12 rangers – including military personnel, scientists, divers and local officials – work tirelessly to preserve this paradise. Access for divers is permitted only during the three months from March to June, when the weather is at its most favourable. Nestled in the heart of the Coral Triangle, renowned for its extraordinary marine biodiversity, Tubbataha is home to an impressive array of life, with over 350 species of coral and nearly 500 species of fish recorded. Every dive offers the chance to encounter numerous shark species, with more than a dozen regularly spotted, including the majestic whale shark, a notable visitor to these waters.

Essential info

Most dives here are drift dives, often with strong currents, including occasional downward flows, making solid diving skills essential. It is strictly forbidden to touch marine life or make contact with the seabed in Tubbataha, with rangers and dive guides always on the lookout to ensure compliance with these rules.

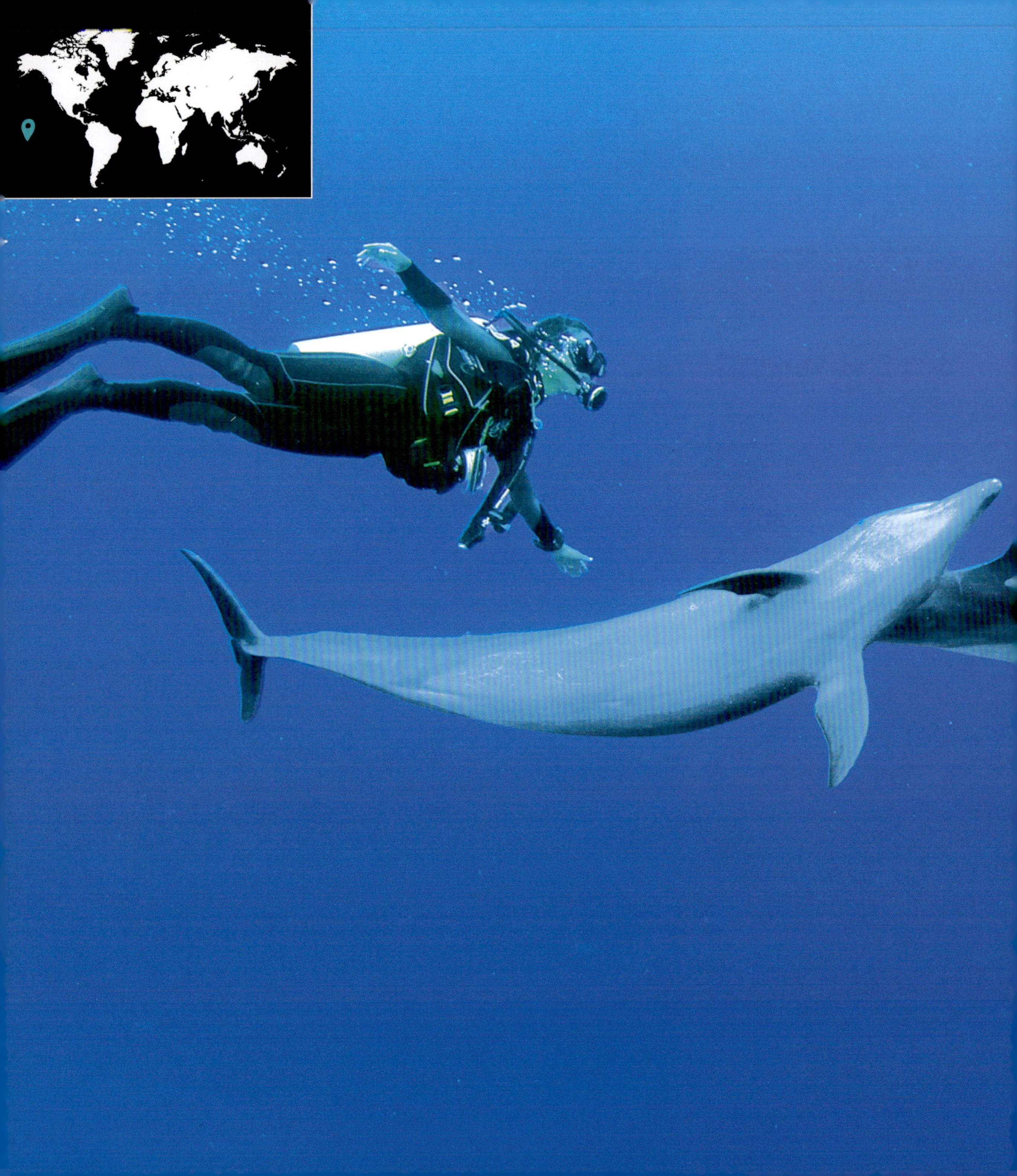

81 Tiputa Pass

Rangiroa, French Polynesia

French Polynesia is somewhat of a diver's Holy Grail, standing alongside renowned destinations like Raja Ampat and the Galápagos. These small islands, scattered across the vast South Pacific, cover an area as large as Europe. From Tahiti, many divers make their way to the Tuamotu Archipelago, particularly to Rangiroa and its iconic dive site, the Tiputa Pass – often hailed as the most famous site in all of Polynesia.

Located on the northern side of the atoll and deeper than Fakarava's Tetamanu, Tiputa offers one of the world's most stunning dives. Drifting with the current, divers are treated to mesmerising schools of fish. It's also common to dive alongside bottlenose dolphins, descend to encounter hammerhead sharks on the hunt, and even spot some grey reef sharks. Giant manta rays and magnificent Napoleon wrasse are also frequent companions on this breathtaking immersion.

Essential info

Tiputa dives are usually done during incoming currents, requiring good buoyancy control. The strong flow creates a thrilling sensation, almost as if you're flying.

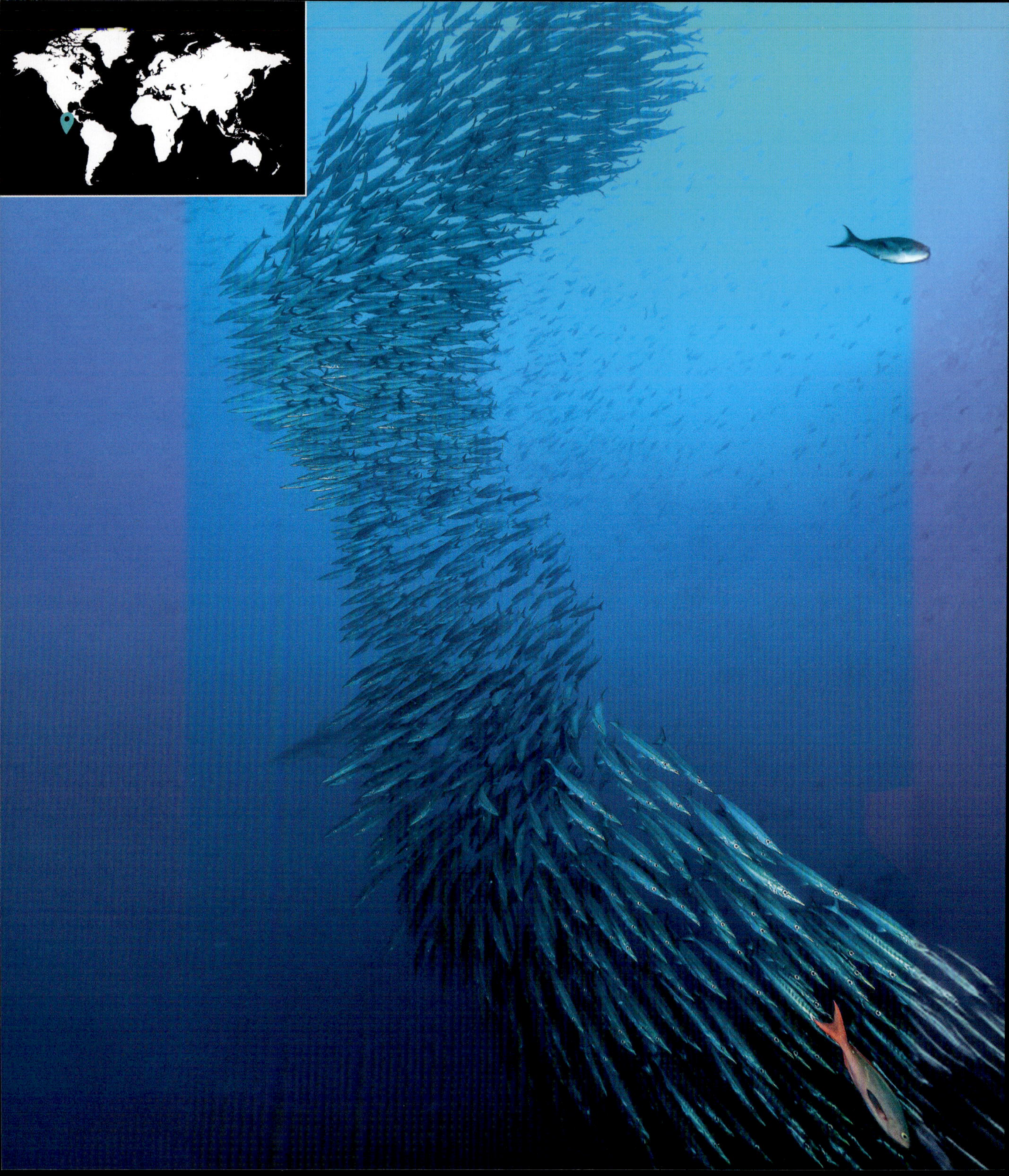

82 Darwin and Wolf Islands

Galápagos archipelago, Ecuador

Closely associated with the renowned British naturalist and palaeontologist Charles Darwin and his work, the Galápagos Islands are among the last great protected sanctuaries where nature thrives with minimal human impact. Situated nearly a thousand kilometres (620 miles) off the coast of Ecuador, this archipelago is home to numerous species that have either migrated here or evolved to be unique to the islands. For divers worldwide, the Galápagos represent a diving utopia, with iconic sites like Darwin and Wolf Islands being particularly noteworthy.

Here, visitors are greeted by vast schools of hammerhead sharks, often accompanied by impressive numbers of barracudas. The cooler waters of this region host a remarkable variety of marine life, including Galápagos sharks, whale sharks, silky sharks and the occasional giant manta ray. Playful sea lions and curious dolphins often approach divers, adding to the experience. The underwater schools of fish, particularly carangids (see photo) and snappers, create an exhilarating spectacle. Describing the Galápagos experience is challenging; it truly must be lived to be fully appreciated.

Essential info

With strong currents and sometimes reduced visibility, these dives require training and are intended for experienced divers.

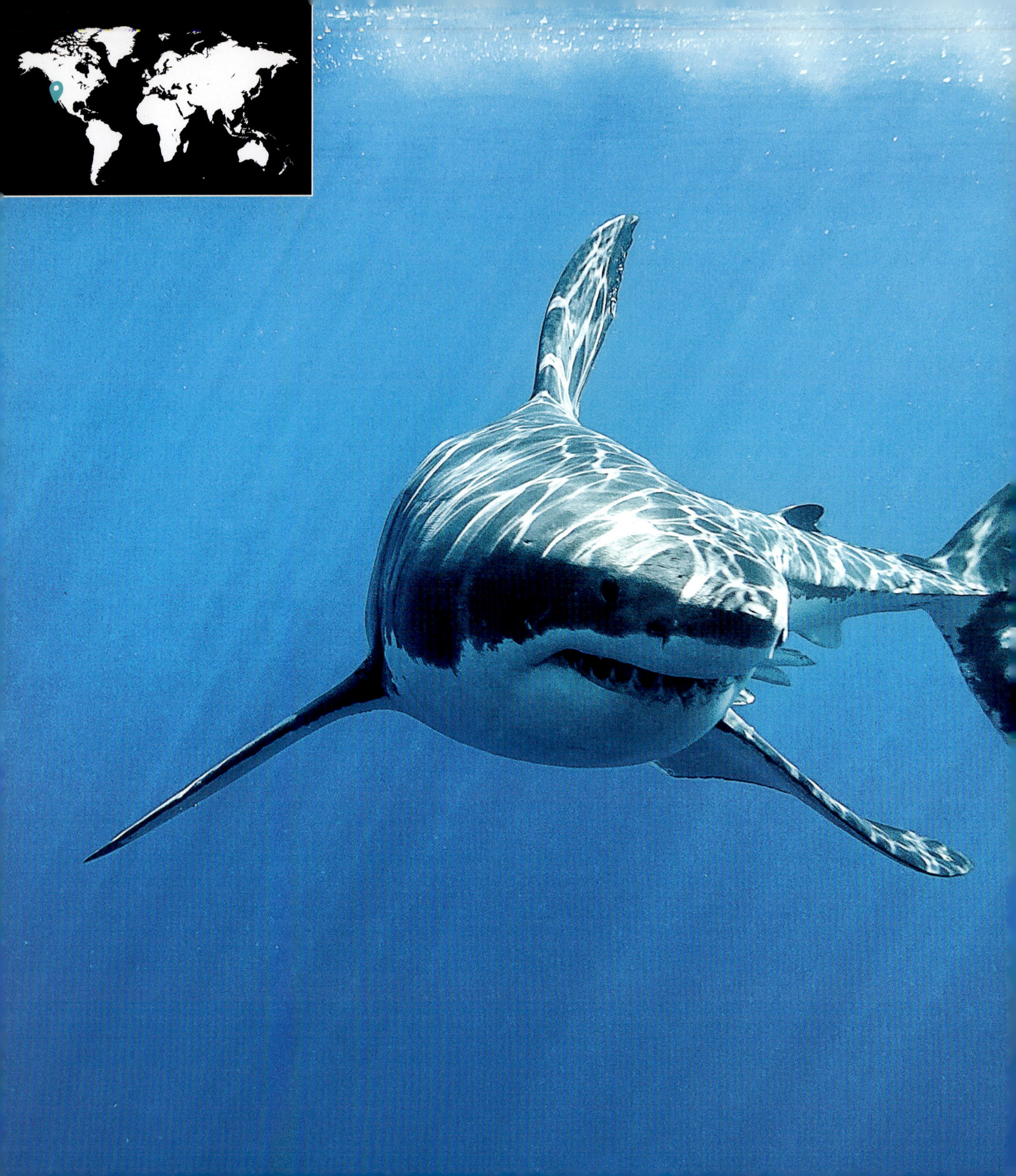

83 Guadalupe Island

Mexico

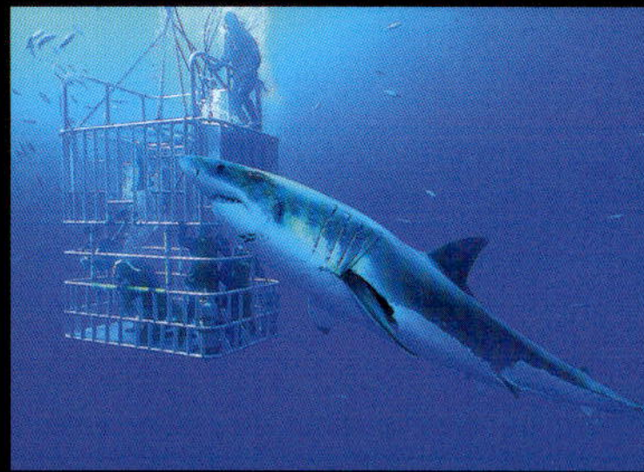

Located about 250 kilometres (155 miles) off the coast of Baja California, Guadalupe Island rises as the highest point of a submarine volcanic chain in the Pacific Ocean. Guadalupe: a place that instantly conjures a vivid, unmistakable image. It's renowned as the premier destination for observing great white sharks in their natural habitat, and the best spot on the planet to observe them in their natural environment.

Reaching the island requires a 20-hour boat journey, but once divers arrive, they are often greeted almost immediately by these majestic predators.

From August to November, the waters around Guadalupe become a breeding ground for these giants, drawn here by the abundant resident populations of seals and sea lions. Divers can safely observe these impressive sharks from within sturdy cages, which sometimes allow for direct contact, creating an unforgettable experience. For the thrill-seekers, there's the option to venture outside the cage for an exhilarating adrenaline rush.

Essential info

Two types of cages are available on cruise ships: one positioned at the surface, accessible to non-divers, and another located about 10 metres (33 feet) deep for certified divers.

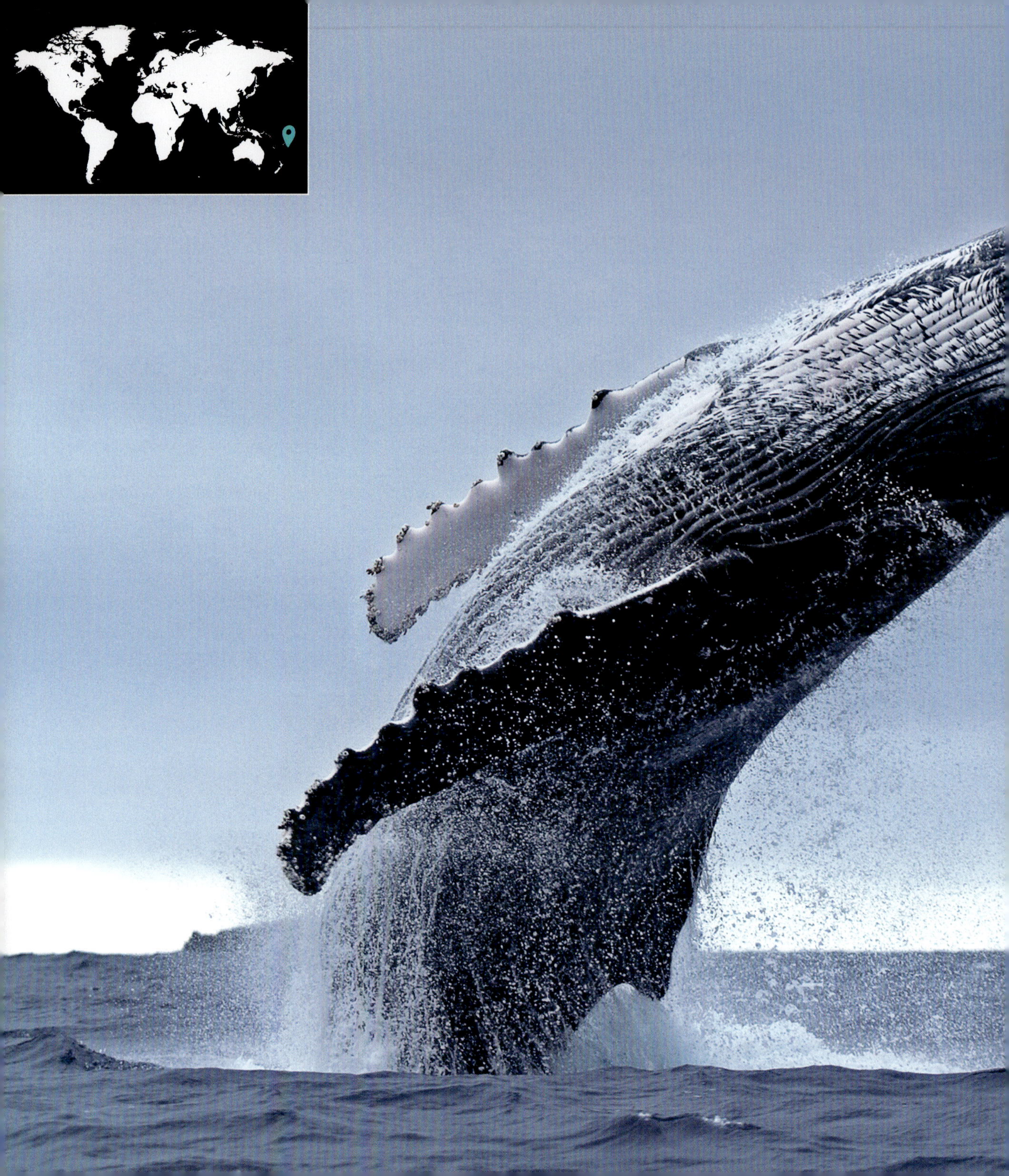

84 Vava'u humpback whales

Kingdom of Tonga, Polynesia

In the South Pacific, the Kingdom of Tonga spans 170 islands and islets across three archipelagos. Tourism is not very widespread, giving the islands a peaceful atmosphere. The underwater scenery is especially stunning around Vava'u, the main northern island known for its exceptional dive sites. Yet it's not only the vibrant seabed that draws visitors to Tonga. Each year from July to October, humpback whales migrate from Antarctica to these warm waters, creating a rare chance to observe them up close in their natural environment. Hundreds of whales arrive, and their dramatic surface breaches help spot them from hundreds of metres away. Spectators can witness large male whales vying for the attention of females – many of which have recently given birth – and even glimpse young calves up to five or six metres (16 or 20 feet) long.

Essential info

Whale watching is regulated in Tonga. Be sure to select operators that respect the whales, avoiding those that allow physical interaction. Sightings while snorkelling are accessible to anyone who can swim.

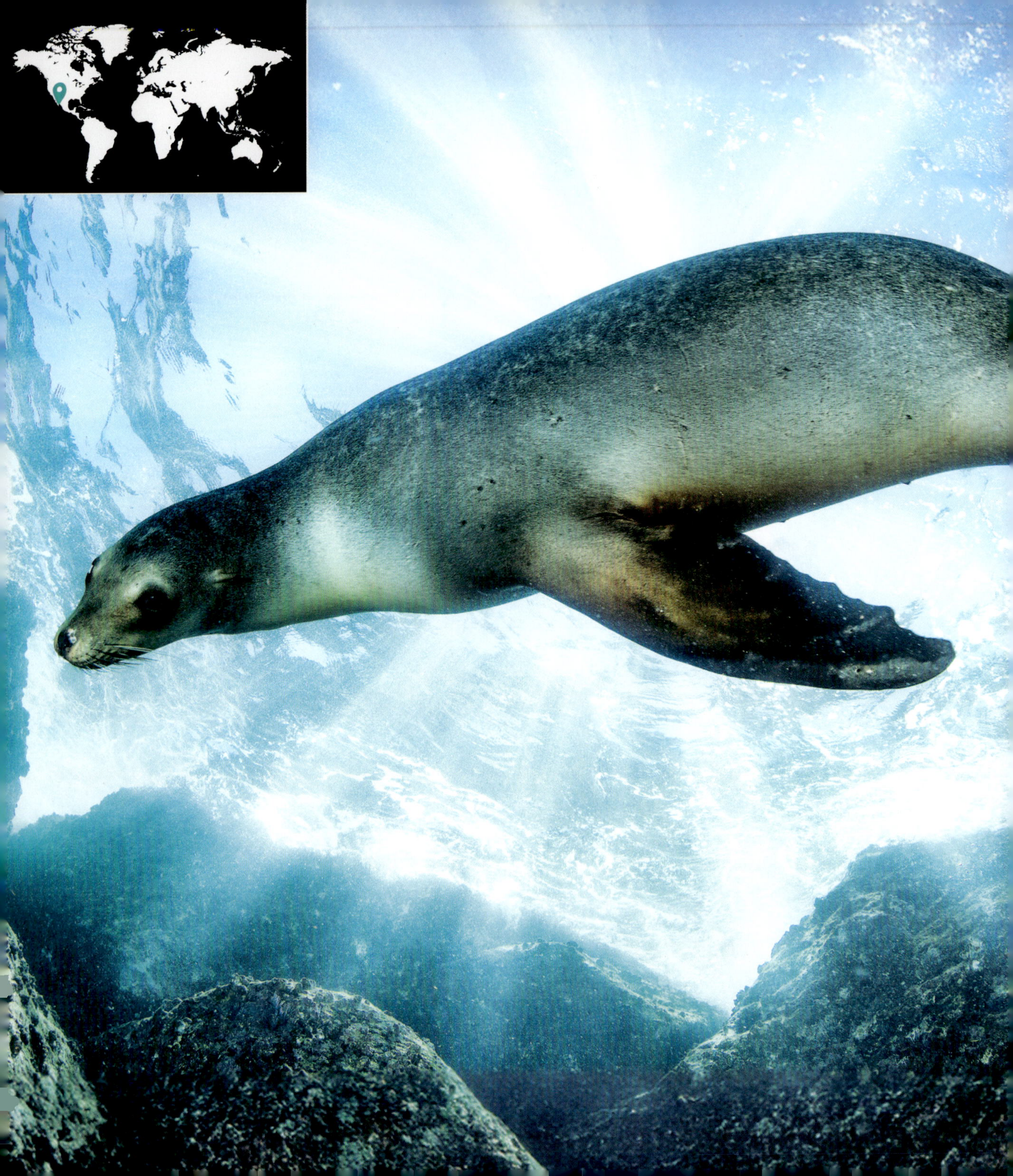

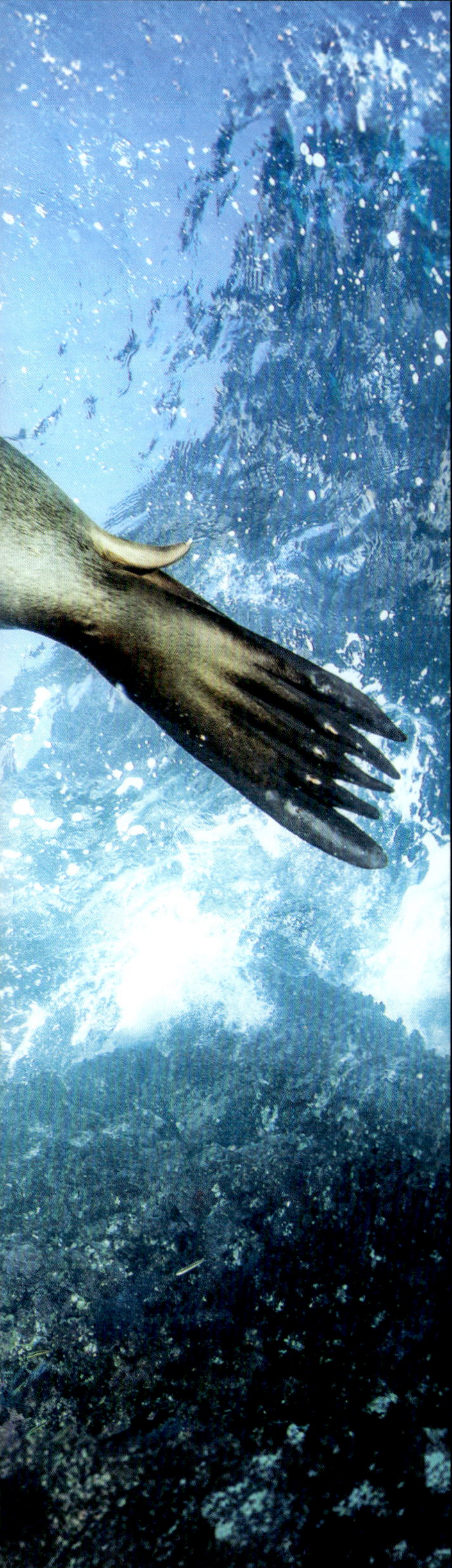

85 Los Islotes sea lions

Sea of Cortez, Mexico

The Gulf of California offers countless surprises, with an extraordinary variety of marine mammal species. In southern Baja California, the town of La Paz serves as the gateway to an unforgettable experience.

Just north of Espiritu Santo Island, the small islets of Los Islotes host a remarkable colony of California sea lions. These sea lions are present year-round, often swirling playfully through the water at the sight of a diver, approaching without hesitation. Known for their agility, they spin and twist gracefully, often surrounding divers in a lively display. Photographers might be delighted – and surprised – to find a sea lion peering into their camera lens. Others may nudge fins or gently nip wherever they want. Male sea lions can be territorial during the breeding season, occasionally showing assertiveness if they feel their female target is giving preference to a diver.

Essential info

Young sea lions are the most playful and curious, often nibbling at anything within reach. It's wise to keep fingers tucked away to avoid their gentle but spirited investigations.

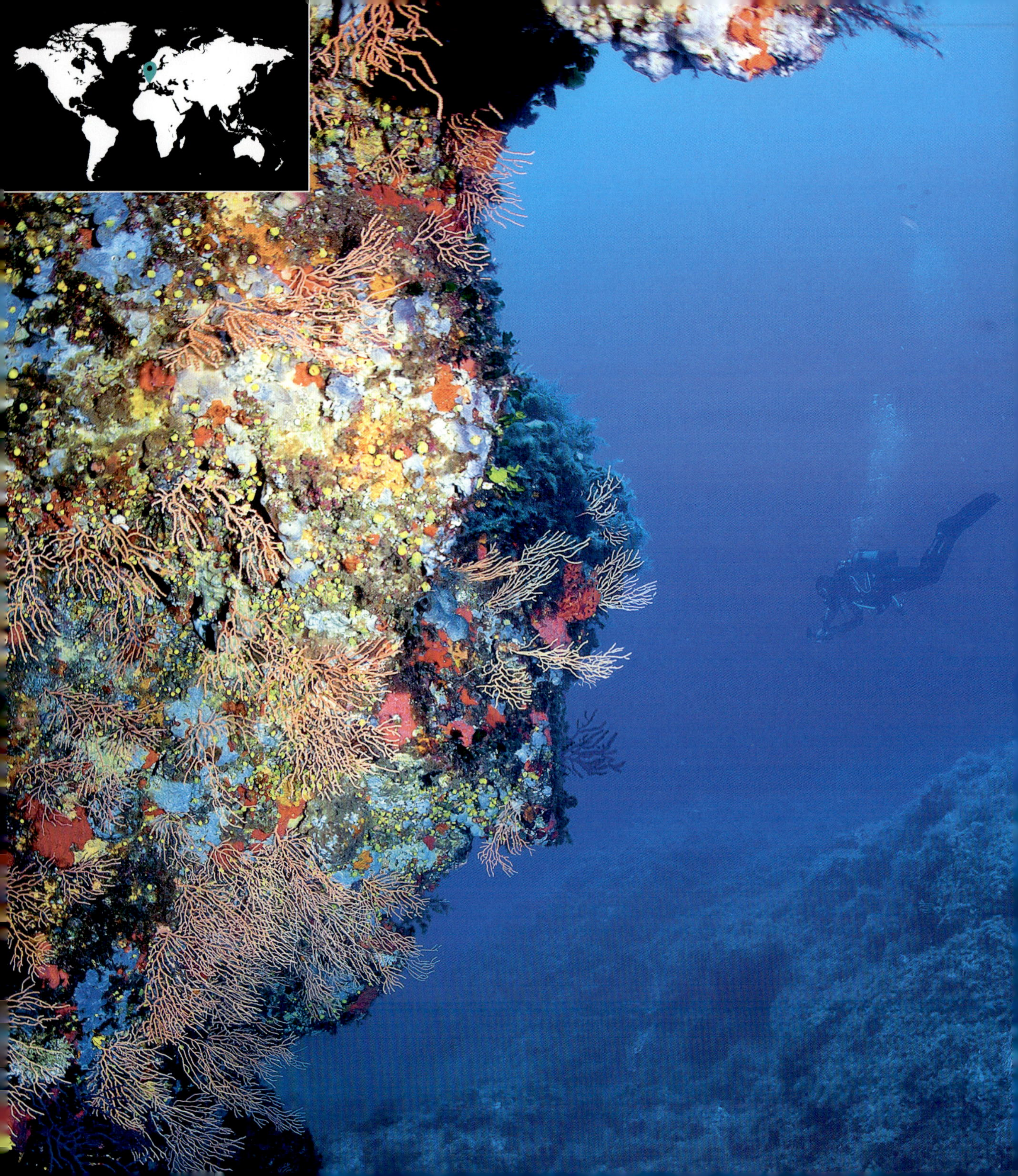

86 La Revellata

Corsica, France

When a Corsican diver is asked what the best dive site on the island is, they are likely to answer: La Revellata. While there are countless dive sites surrounding Corsica, the deep waters of this cape near Calvi are renowned for being among the most stunning.

While the land portion of the peninsula is home to numerous rare and endemic species, the cliffs dramatically descend into the azure waters, offering a breathtaking view. Beneath the shimmering surface lies an extravagant and rugged underwater landscape, characterised by its caves, drop-offs and canyons. There's no better habitat for the majestic brown groupers, which leisurely navigate between the rocks. Schools of brown meagre gracefully swim along the sea floor while barracudas spin like silver arrows. You'll also find dentex, moray eels, sea bream, lobsters and more. Bathed in crystalline waters, La Revellata teems with life from every angle. This enchanting realm appears to pause for a moment as an elegant mobula ray, eagle ray or stingray glides by.

Essential info

This huge site is accessible to all levels, offering depths starting at 10 metres (30 feet) and extending to over 40 metres (131 feet).

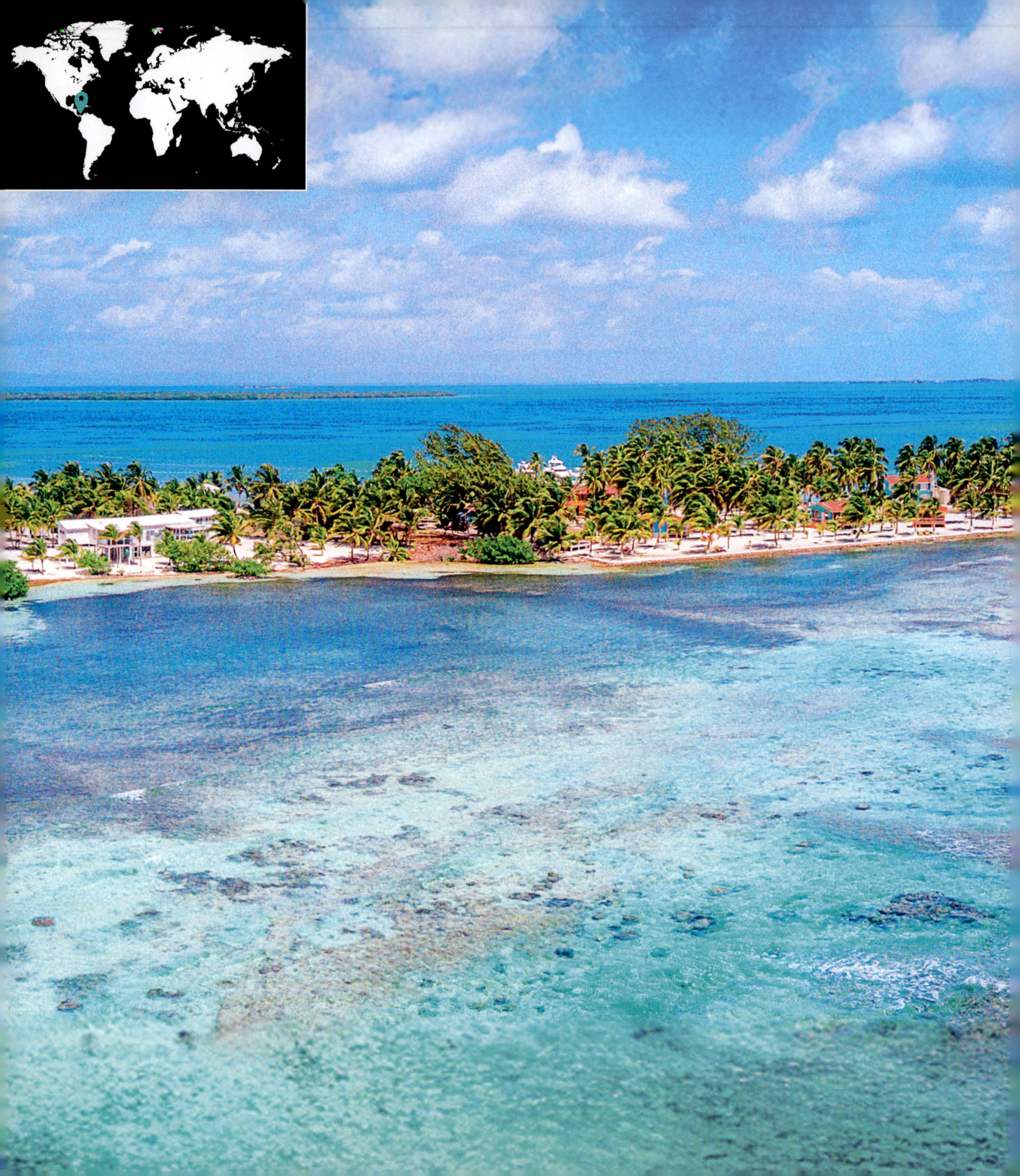

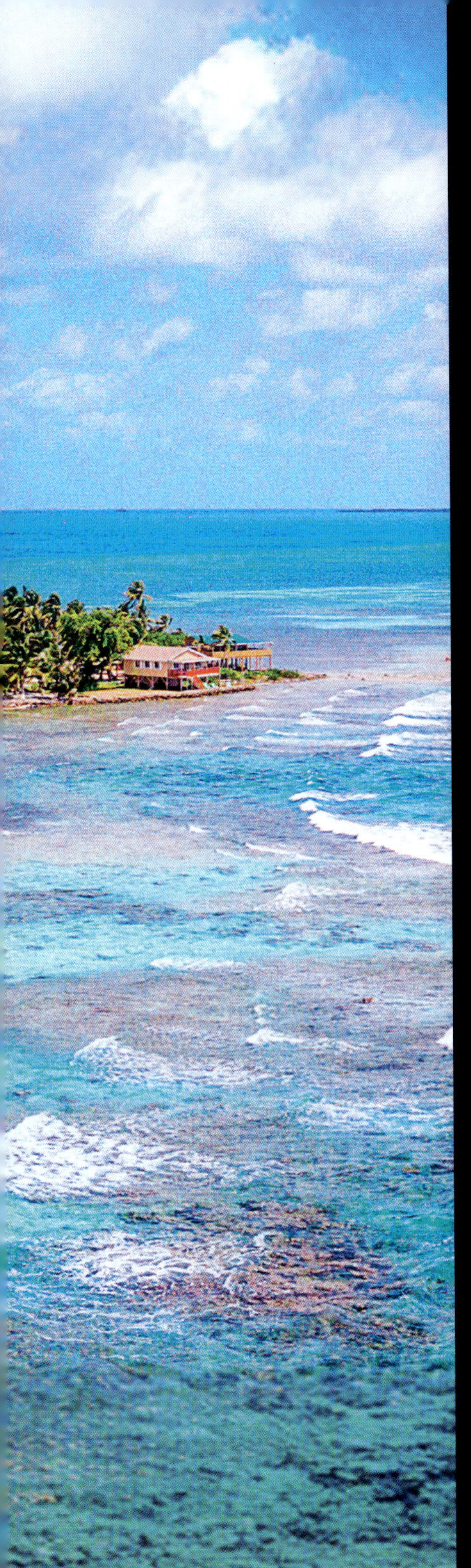

87 Roatán Island

Honduras

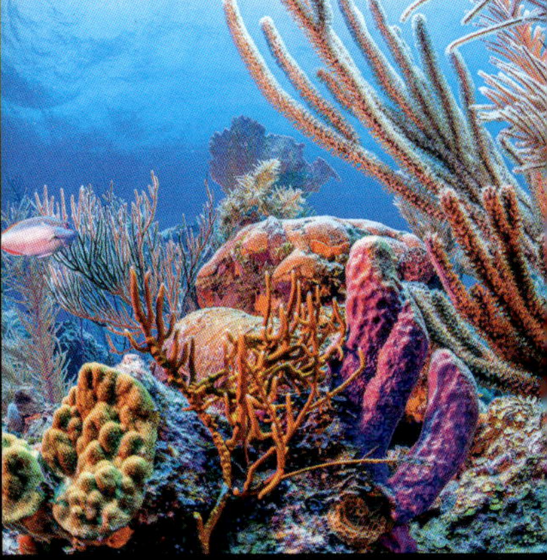

Off the northern coast of Honduras in the heart of Central America, Roatán Island stretches 83 kilometres (51 miles) long and just eight kilometres (five miles) wide in the Caribbean Sea. Surrounded by a coral reef, it forms part of the Mesoamerican Barrier Reef – also known as the Great Mayan Reef – which spans over 1,100 kilometres (684 miles), making it the second-largest coral reef system after Australia's Great Barrier Reef.

Roatán's underwater landscape is incredibly diverse, offering divers stunning drop-offs, coral-covered plateaus, impressive sponges, caves and several wrecks. The marine life, typical of the Caribbean, is abundant and vibrant.

Divers often spot graceful eagle rays gliding over the reefs, impressive eels weaving through the coral, iconic tarpons, schools of vibrant snapper and an array of tropical fish. There are sea turtles, groupers and other jackfish to be spotted as well. It's also possible to enjoy a spectacular dive alongside reef sharks, and although they're attracted by bait, the thrill is guaranteed.

Essential info

Roatán also has a large number of snorkelling sites, making it perfect for a family trip. You can even swim close to dolphins.

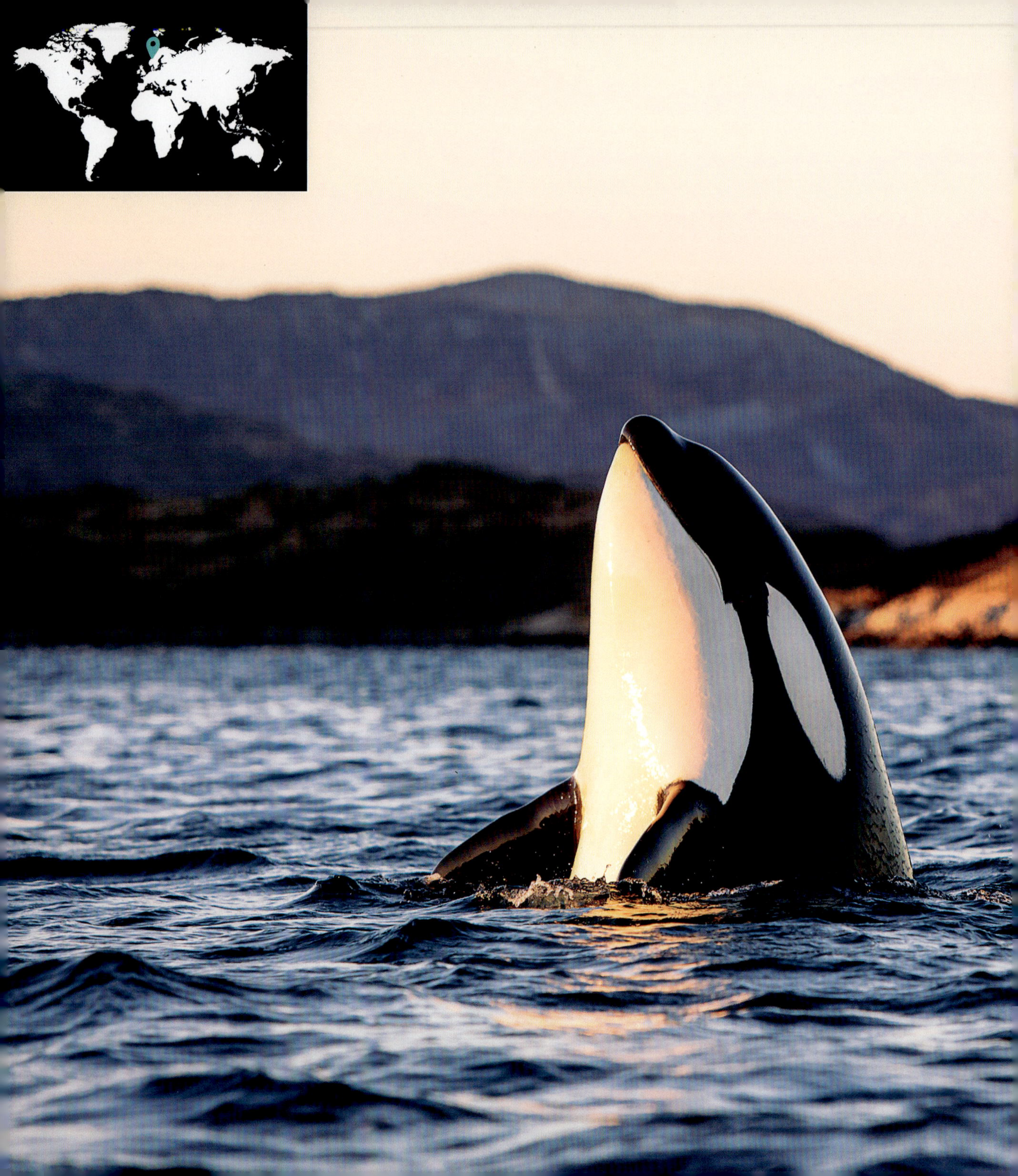

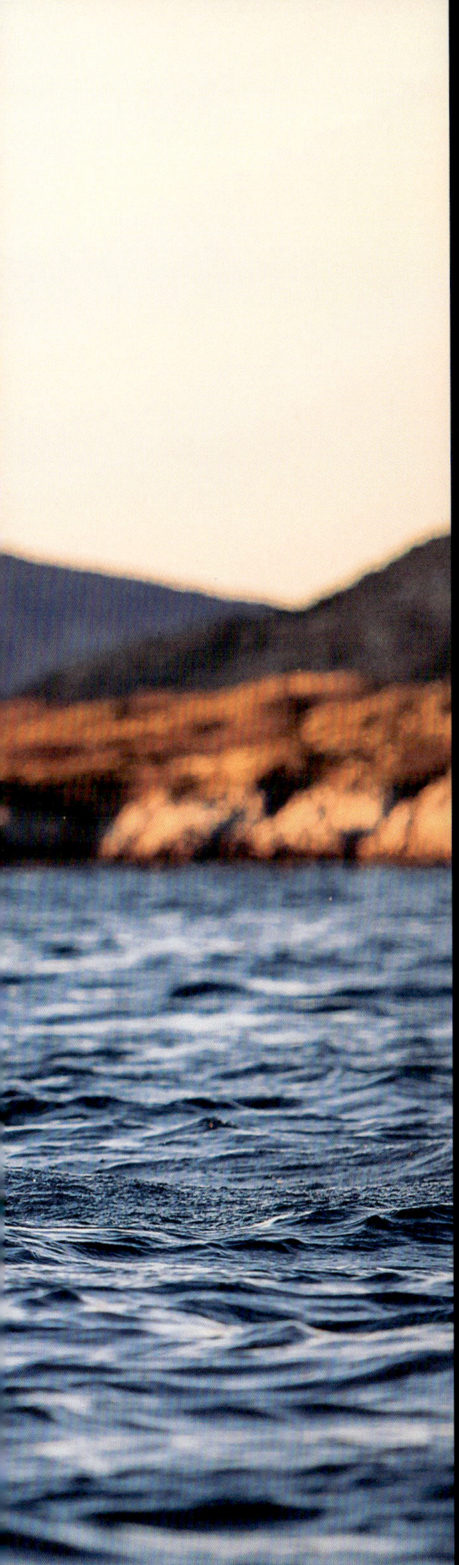

88 Fjord orcas

Norway

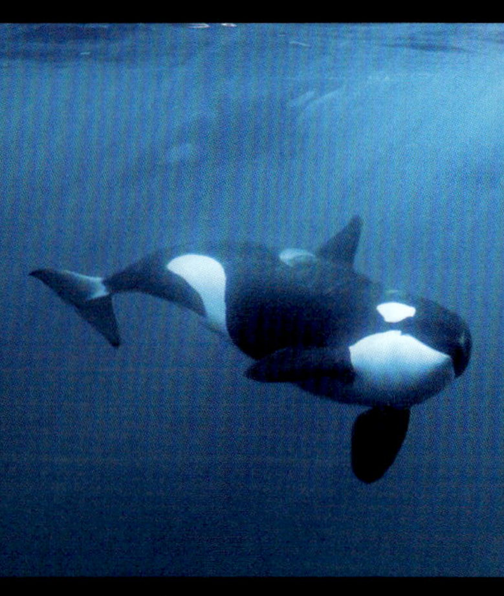

Many unforgettable marine encounters unfold in breathtaking locations – think idyllic islands, white sandy beaches and vibrant coral reefs.

However, to truly experience the most spectacular interactions, you often need to venture off the beaten track and step out of your comfort zone. From November to January each year, millions of herring swim into the frigid waters of northern Norway's fjords. This massive concentration attracts orcas, creating the largest known gathering of these majestic creatures on the planet.

In the crystalline yet dim waters – due to the limited light during this season – wildlife enthusiasts eagerly plunge in to share a few special moments with these powerful killer whales. Showing no aggression towards humans, these cetaceans can reach nearly nine metres (30 feet) in length and often swim close to divers, promising exhilarating encounters and unforgettable memories.

Essential info

These expeditions are open to everyone, provided they are strong swimmers and in good health. Orcas are not fond of bubbles, so scuba diving is not permitted.

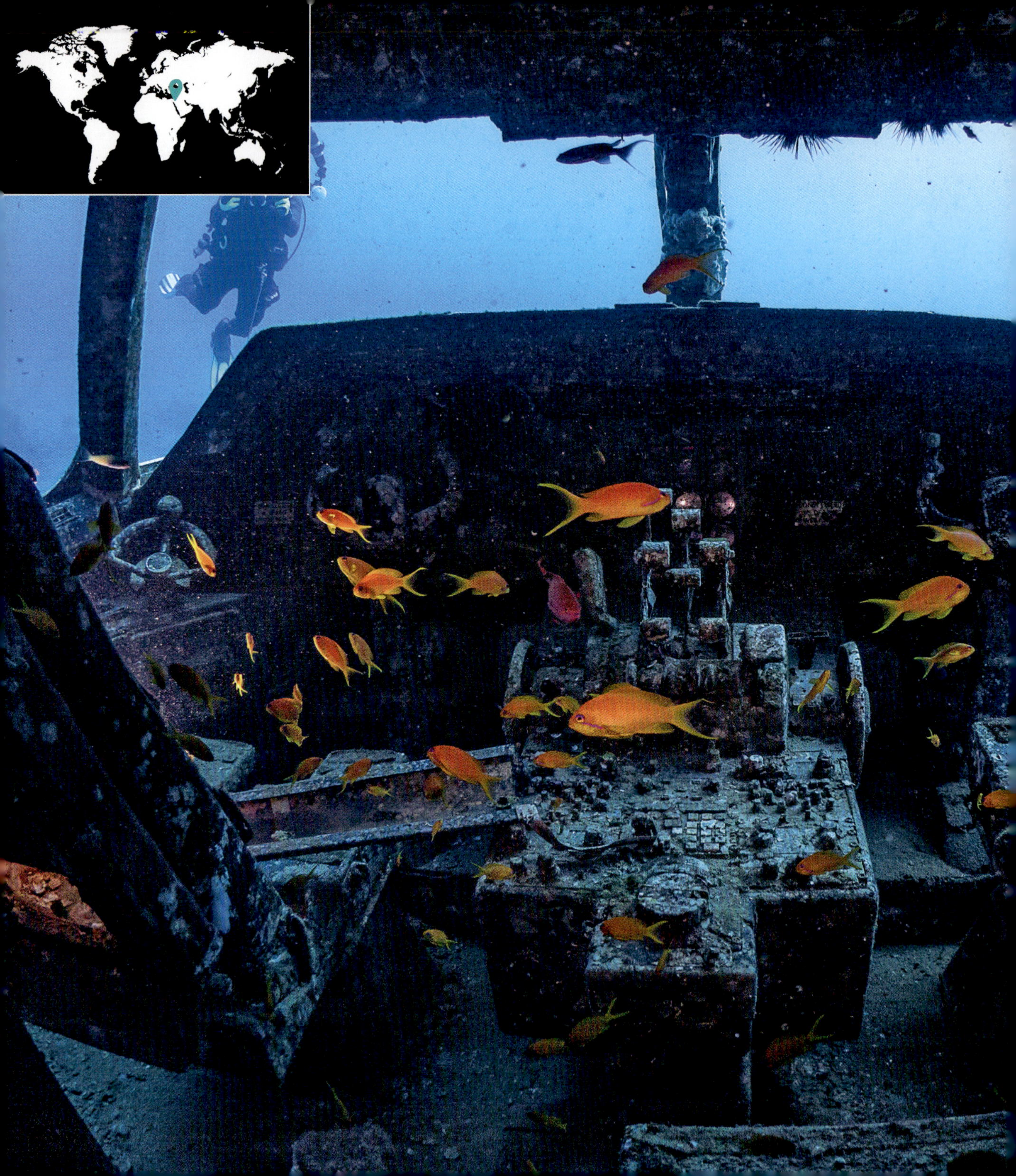

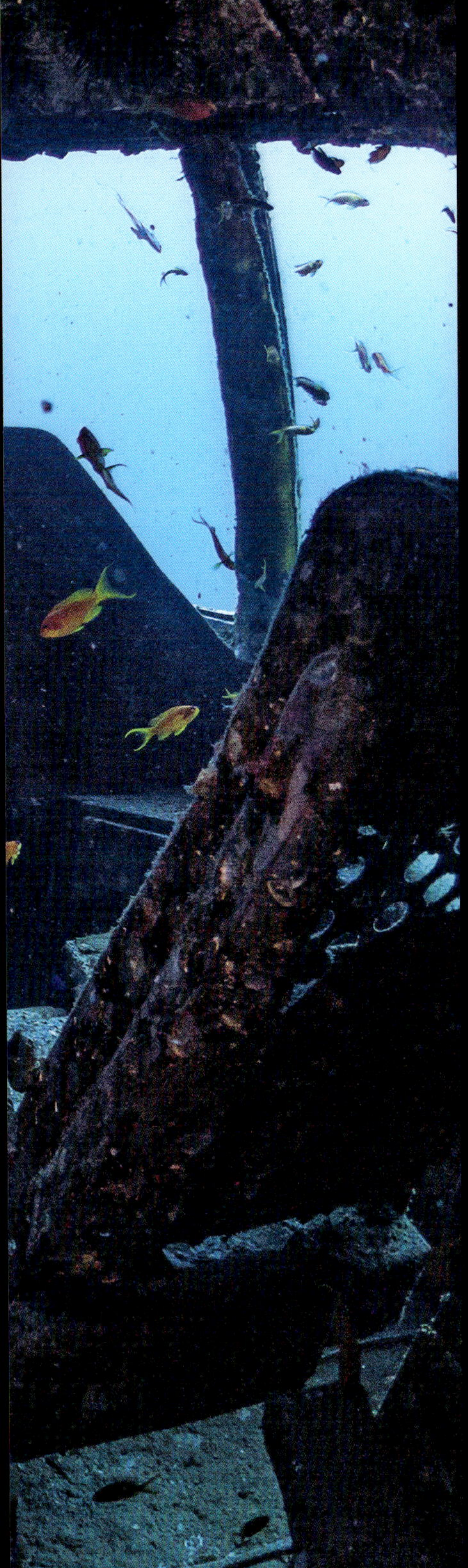

89 *Tristar* wreck

Aqaba, Jordan

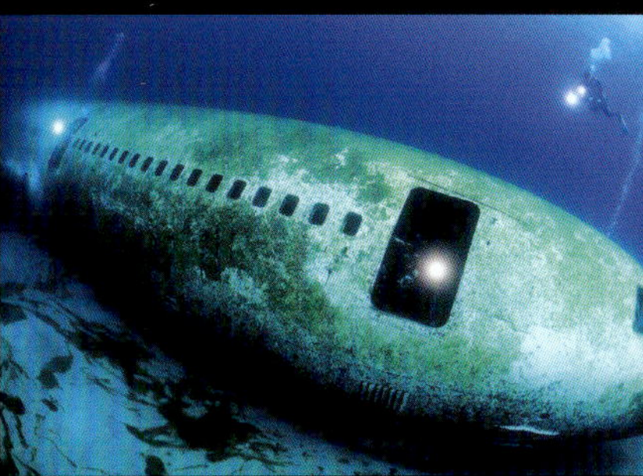

A wreck often evokes a sense of mystery, igniting the imagination and reminding us of childhood stories. What is its history? What happened to it? Did it carry treasure? The list of questions is endless.

Not all divers are fans of wreck diving – but when it comes to exploring one that is really out of the ordinary, why not let yourself be drawn in by the experience? Diving on a World War II plane is almost commonplace, but experiencing an airliner is a much rarer adventure.

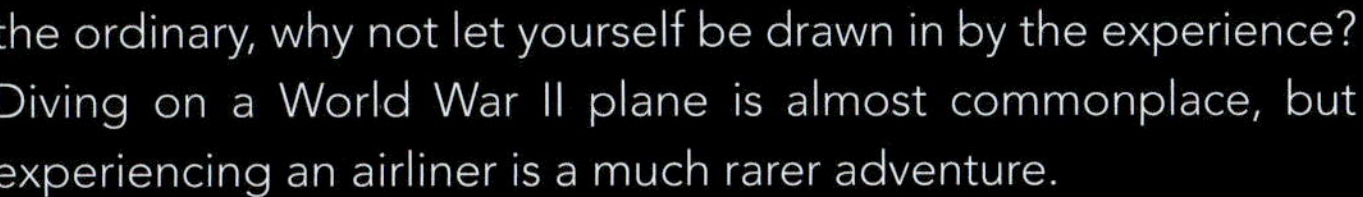

In Aqaba, a stunning *Lockheed L-1011 Tristar* – an impressive 54-metre (177-feet)-long long-haul tri-jet airliner – awaits divers as part of the many shipwrecks intentionally sunk to create artificial reefs and enhance scuba diving appeal. Submerged in 2019 at a depth of 27 metres (88 feet), the aircraft has been stripped of its doors and middle rows of seats, offering a unique glimpse into its interior. Few can say they have ventured into the passenger compartment of an airliner, and even fewer have explored the cockpit, along with a few fishy friends.

Essential info

Easy diving, on a sandy bottom, the plane is accessible at a depth of between 15 and 27 metres (49 and 88 feet). There is not yet much marine life on this young wreck.

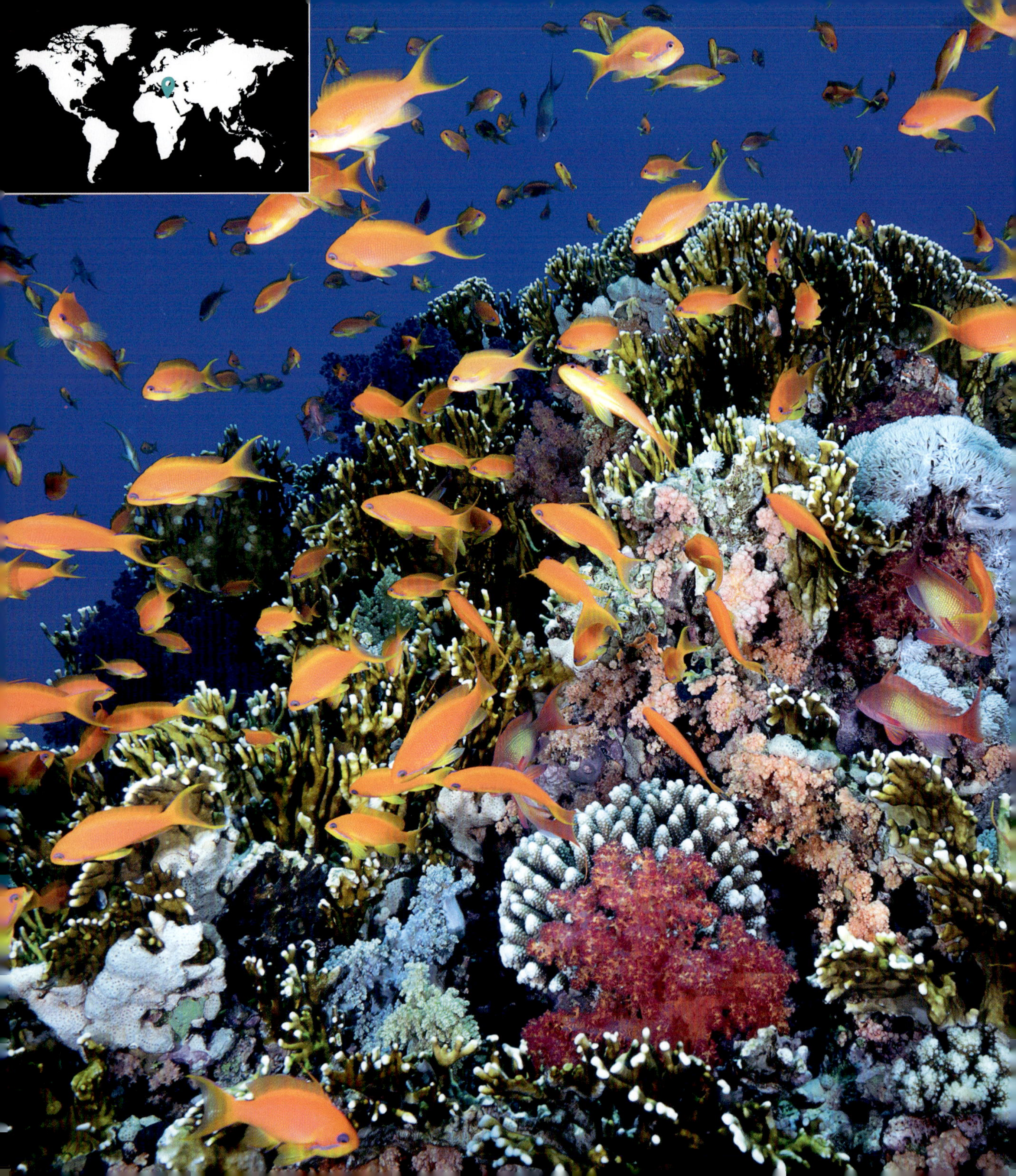

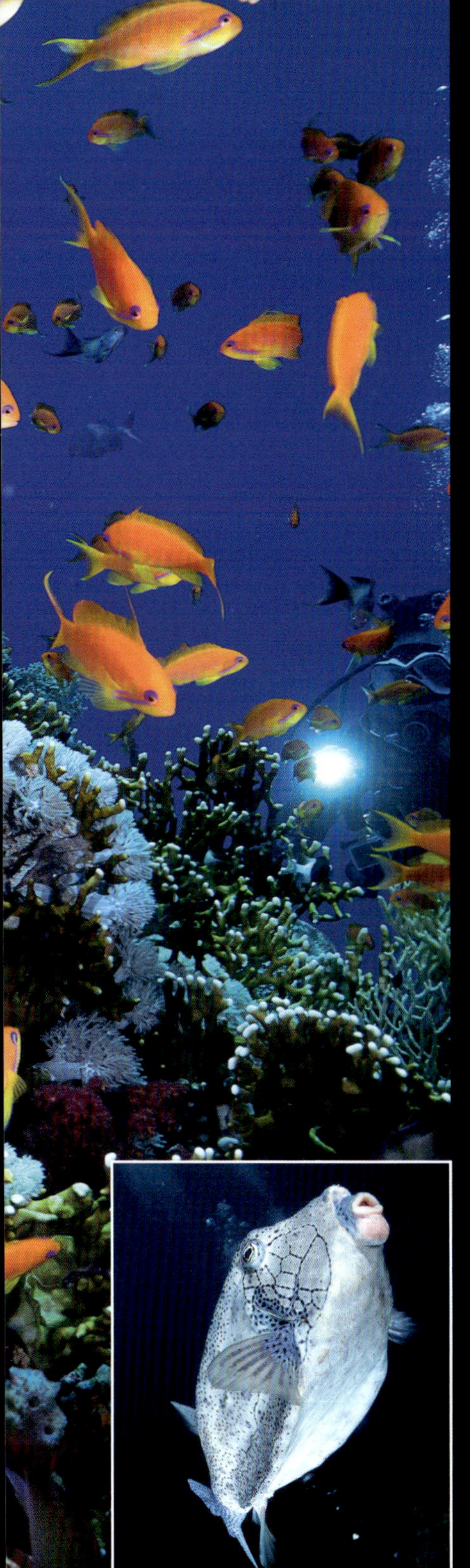

90 Ras Mohammed

Egypt

South of the Sinai Peninsula, the tip of Ras Mohammed plunges into the depths of the Red Sea, with an impressive drop of nearly 700 metres (2,300 feet), making it one of the most breathtaking on the planet. Designated as a national park since 1983, Ras Mohammed is renowned as one of the finest dive sites in the world. As soon as you enter the water the spectacle is nothing short of stunning.

As divers descend along the wall adorned with flourishing gorgonians and corals, they are welcomed by large schools of fish. At times, thousands of snappers swim alongside barracudas and other Platax.

Two magnificent pinnacles, Shark Reef and Yolanda Reef, separate the drop-off from a breathtaking coral garden teeming with life. Here, divers can encounter turtles gliding alongside impressive Napoleon fish (see photo), as well as the most vibrant angelfish, butterflyfish and parrotfish. Occasionally, a graceful stingray sweeps through this underwater paradise, captivating the eyes of awestruck divers. Yolanda Reef takes its name from a ship that ran aground nearby in 1986, spilling its cargo of mainly toilets and bathtubs into the depths. While the ship itself slipped into the deep, part of its unusual cargo remains, providing an unexpected encounter for novice divers.

Essential info

Ras Mohammed is accessible to all levels, even if the currents can sometimes be quite strong. Part of the dive is a drift dive to arrive at the peaceful coral garden area. June–July is magical.

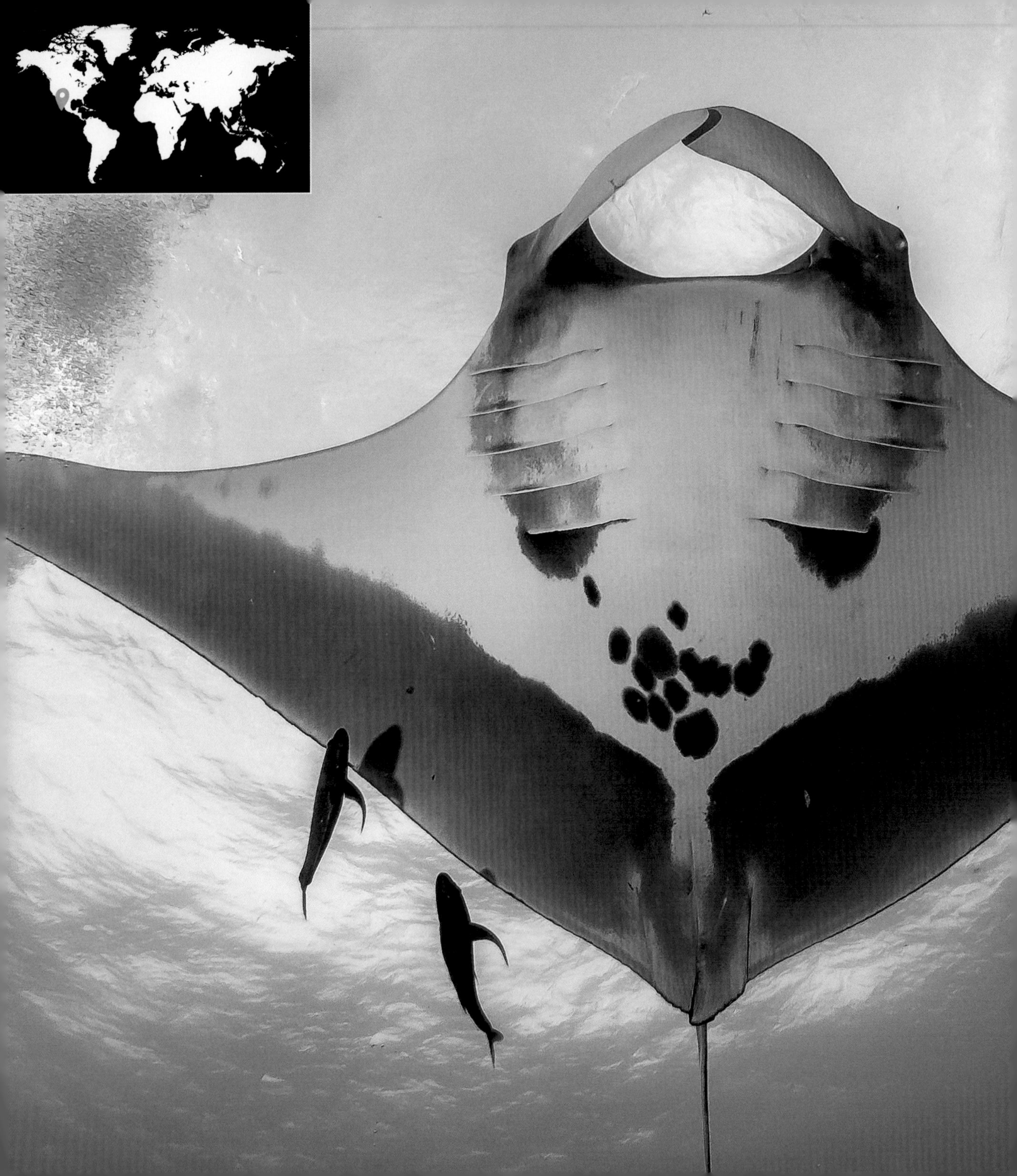

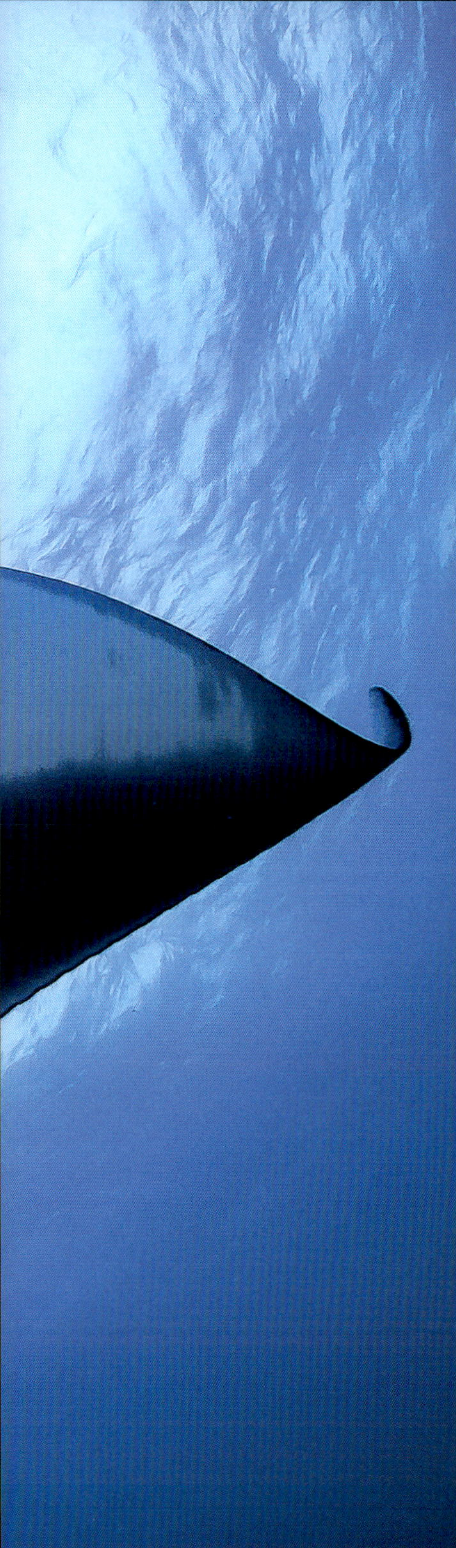

91 Socorro Island

Mexico

Mexico, a country with coastlines stretching along both the Caribbean Sea and the Pacific Ocean, is a prime destination for divers seeking vibrant underwater experiences paired with rich cultural discovery.

Off the west coast, the Revillagigedo Archipelago – comprising four islands – offers exhilarating dives amidst a stunning array of pelagic species. The renowned waters of Socorro Island draw divers from around the world for exceptional encounters with oceanic manta rays (see photo). Powerful ocean currents sweeping through the area make it a true 'pelagic highway'. Giant manta rays glide alongside hammerhead sharks, silky sharks, Galápagos sharks, schools of dolphins and even the occasional whale shark. These waters come alive with breathtaking hunting scenes, similar to those seen in the most beautiful wildlife documentaries.

Essential info

Due to the sometimes-strong currents and challenging entry points, these dives are reserved for experienced divers only.

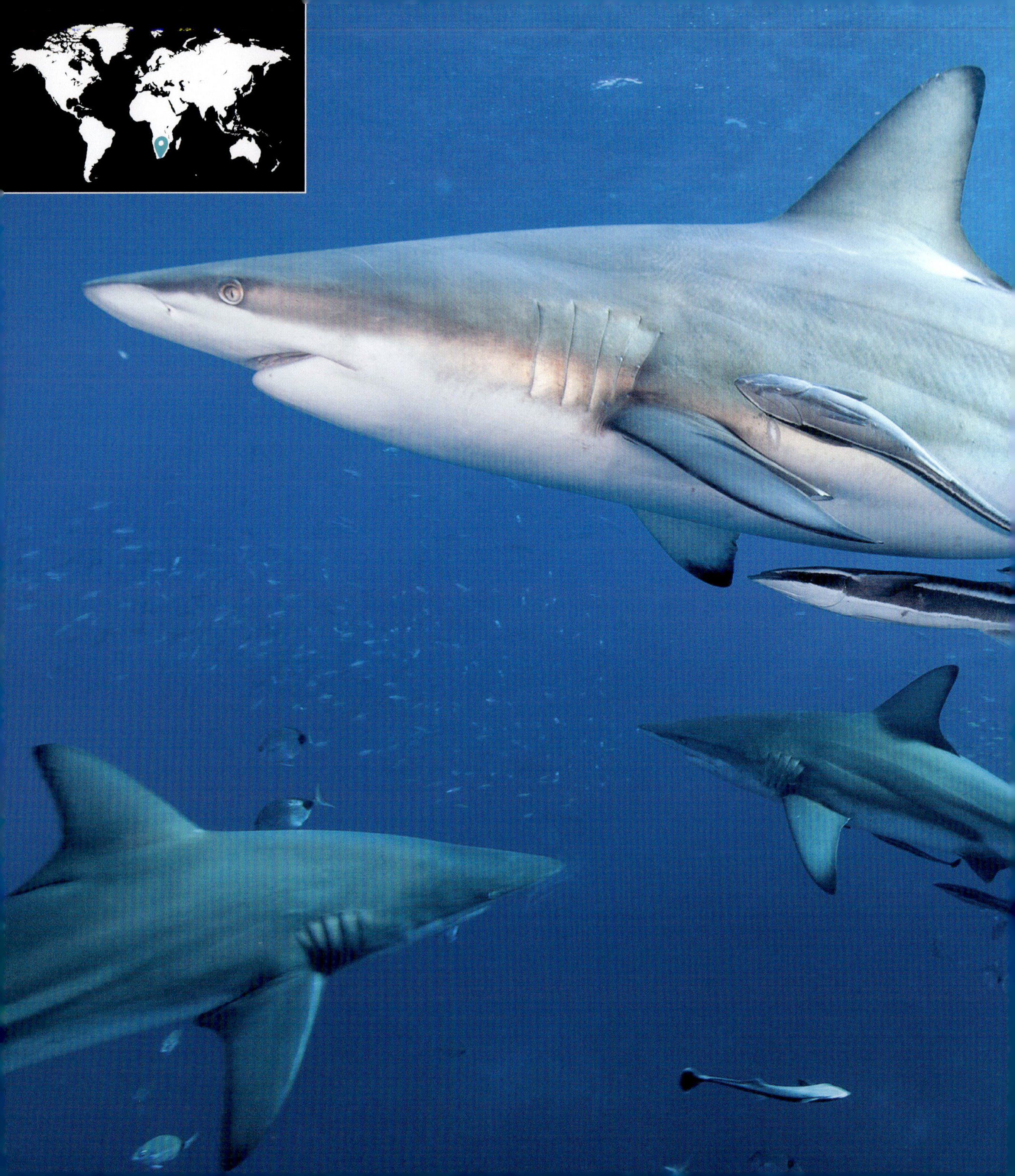

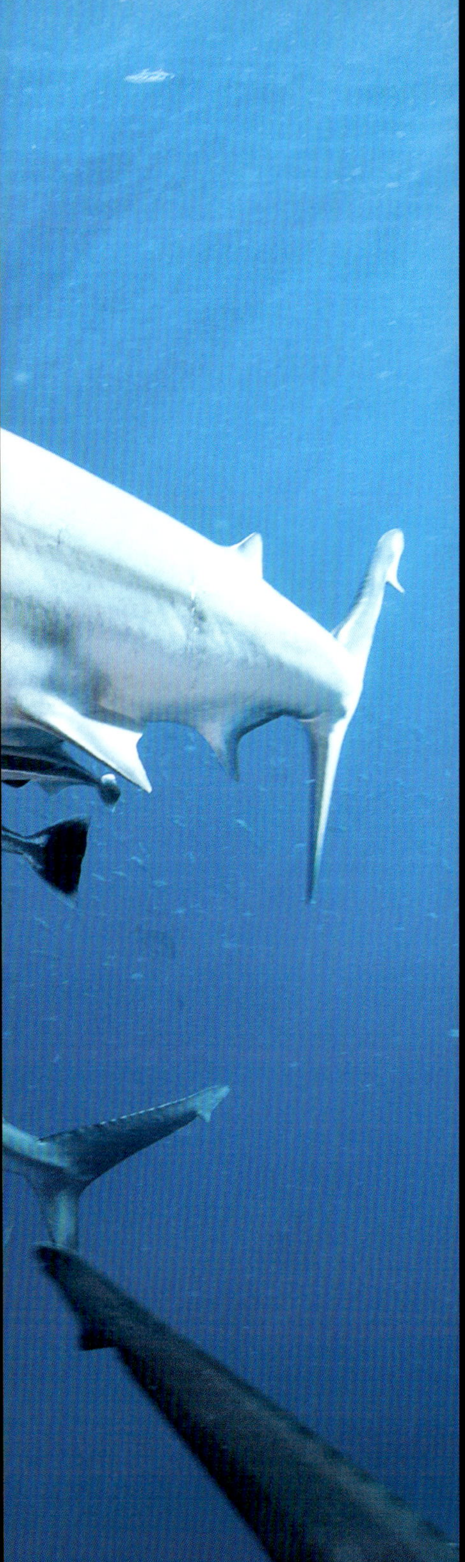

92 Aliwal Shoal

South Africa

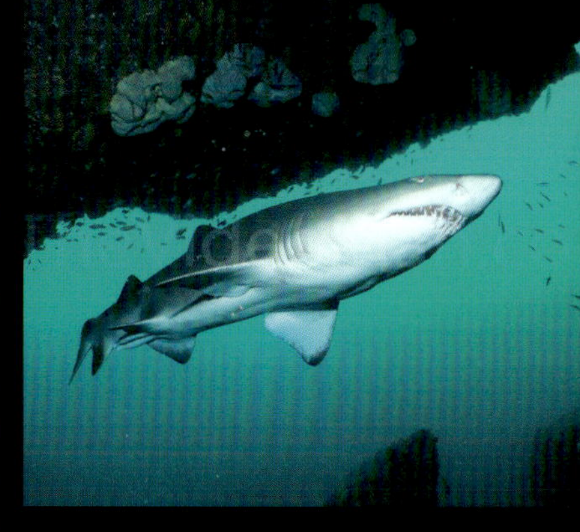

In the diving community, South Africa is synonymous with shark encounters. This region is a prime habitat for the great white, while the waters here host a variety of other fascinating shark species.

Off the coast of Umkomaas, near Durban, lies the renowned Aliwal Shoal, an extensive reef that is bathed in the warm waters of the Indian Ocean and renowned for its shark-diving experiences. This site is home to a range of shark species, though the local stars are the impressive 'raggies' or sand tiger sharks (see inset photo), often seen in large numbers between June and November. Though they may bare their teeth, these sharks are remarkably indifferent to the presence of divers. Cathedral and Raggies Cave are the best-known sites for seeing them up close. Aliwal Shoal also attracts hammerheads, tiger sharks and bull sharks (see photo), adding to the site's reputation for exhilarating dives.

Essential info

With its powerful currents and challenging navigation, Aliwal Shoal is best suited to seasoned divers. Sharks can come into contact with divers.

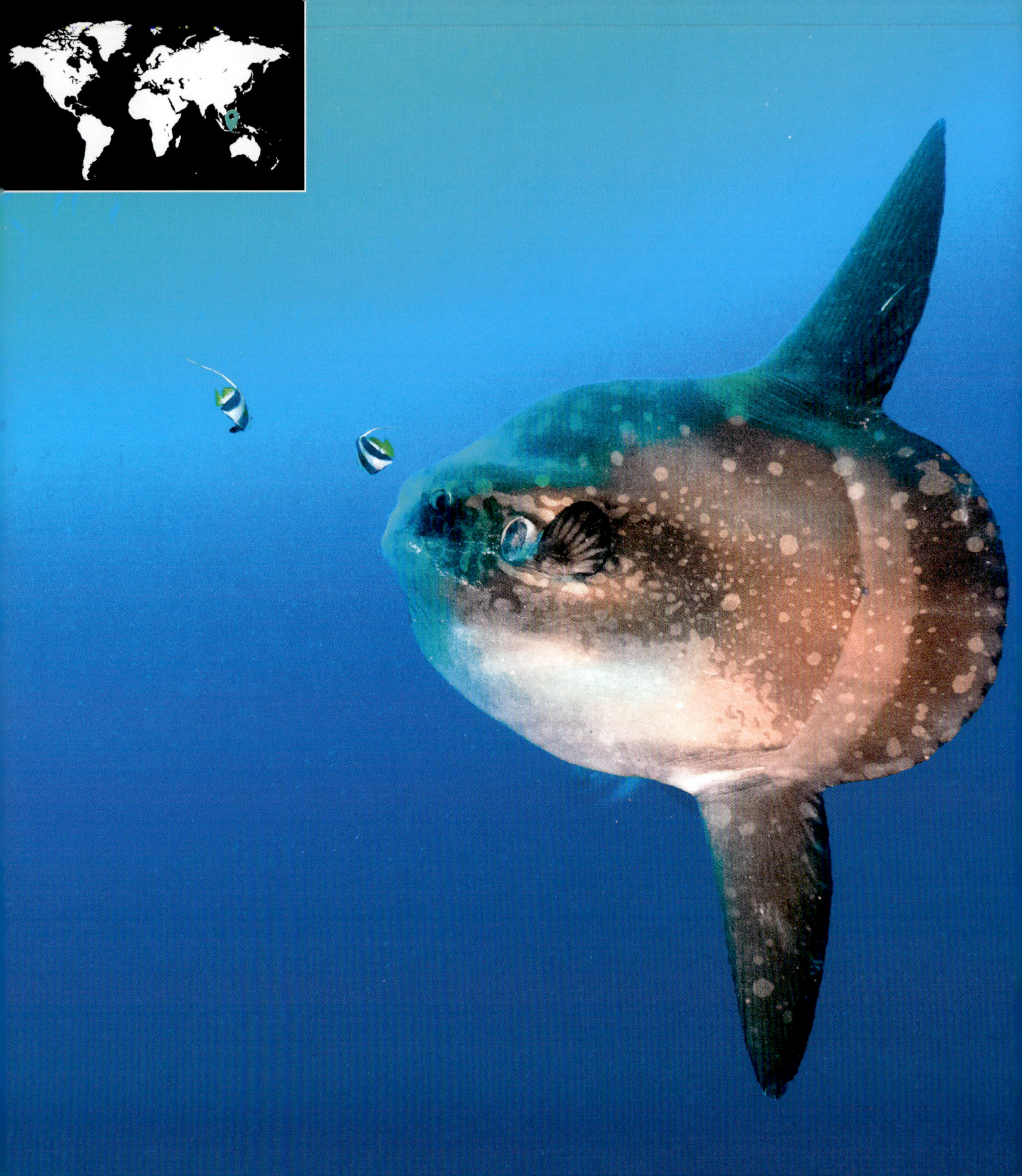

93 Nusa Penida

Bali, Indonesia

In Hindu belief, respecting the balance of power is crucial. While Bali is often referred to as the island of the gods, the more rugged Nusa Penida is seen as the island of demons. Once largely overlooked due to its scarcity of fresh water, this island has gained attention as scuba diving has flourished in nearby Bali. The incredible waters surrounding Nusa Penida have quickly earned a stellar global reputation for diving. Nestled between Bali and Lombok, Nusa Penida is exposed to powerful currents that flow from the depths, resulting in cool waters of remarkable clarity.

The island's most famous dive spot is Crystal Bay, where divers can encounter the majestic sunfish, known scientifically as *Mola mola*. These creatures, often found at greater depths, rely on the currents to come and have their parasites removed by cleaner wrasses and other angelfish. These fascinating placid giants can grow up to three metres (10 feet) in length and weigh nearly two tons. The adventure doesn't end there – just a short distance away is Manta Point, where divers can witness numerous manta rays as they come for a clean as well. It's an exhilarating experience that promises unforgettable encounters.

Essential info

Moonfish are present between July and October, and the Crystal Bay site is sometimes subject to strong currents during this period. Good diving experience is essential. The manta ray cleaning station welcomes divers of all skill levels.

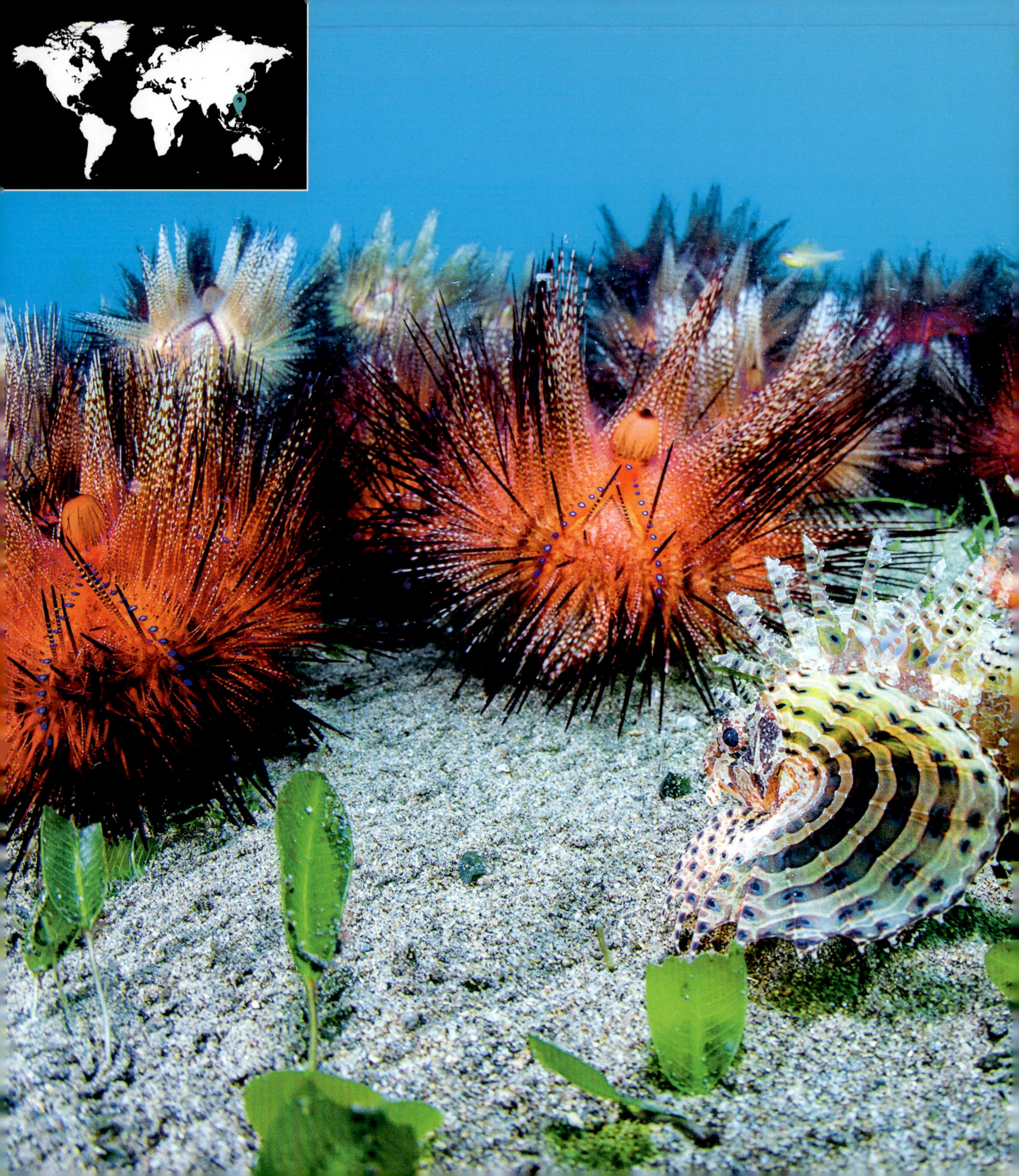

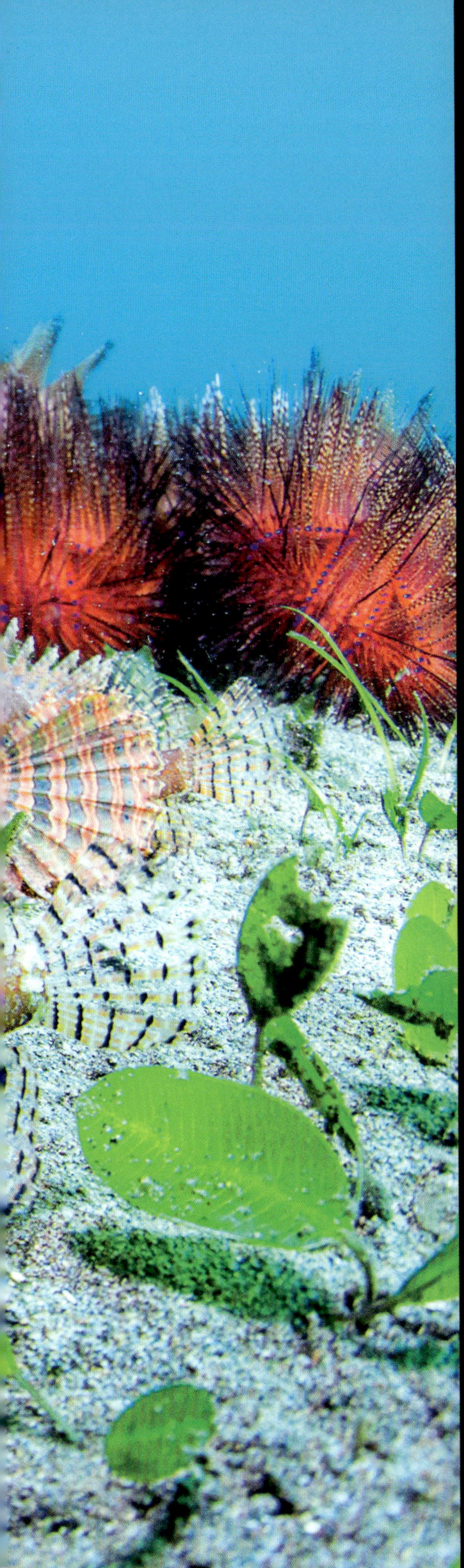

94 Dauin

Visayas, Philippines

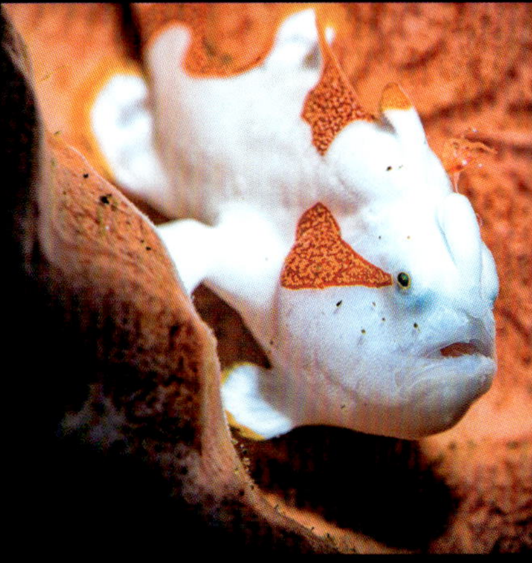

Nestled south of Negros Island in the central Philippines, the charming town of Dauin draws divers from around the globe seeking to experience its stunning marine biodiversity and idyllic landscapes.

This area is particularly renowned for muck diving, a term that reflects the sediment-rich environments found at many dive sites. The seabed, covered in brown sand, serves as a habitat for an astonishing array of marine life, making it a veritable playground for underwater photographers. As soon as you go under, you'll encounter a plethora of species, including seahorses, *Syngnathidae*, vibrant nudibranchs (see inset photo), flamboyant cuttlefish, ghost fish and tiny frogfish – no larger than a fingernail – often expertly spotted by local Filipino guides. As night falls, the show is stunning, even from the beach. Just across from Dauin lies Apo Island, a captivating destination where a vibrant festival of turtles and sea snakes await.

Essential info

A true paradise for underwater photography enthusiasts of all skill levels, this spot offers ideal conditions with gentle currents and shallow dives.

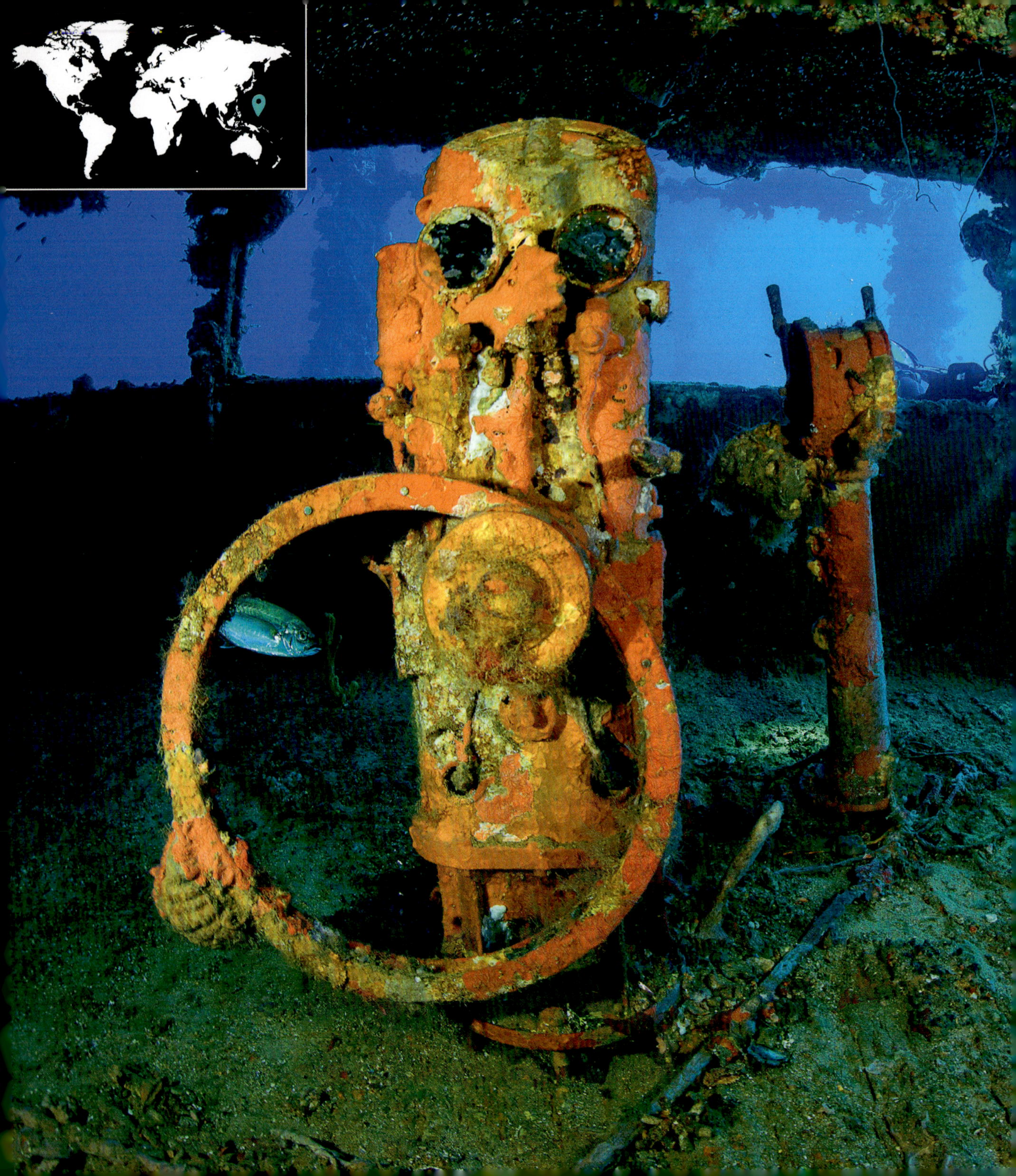

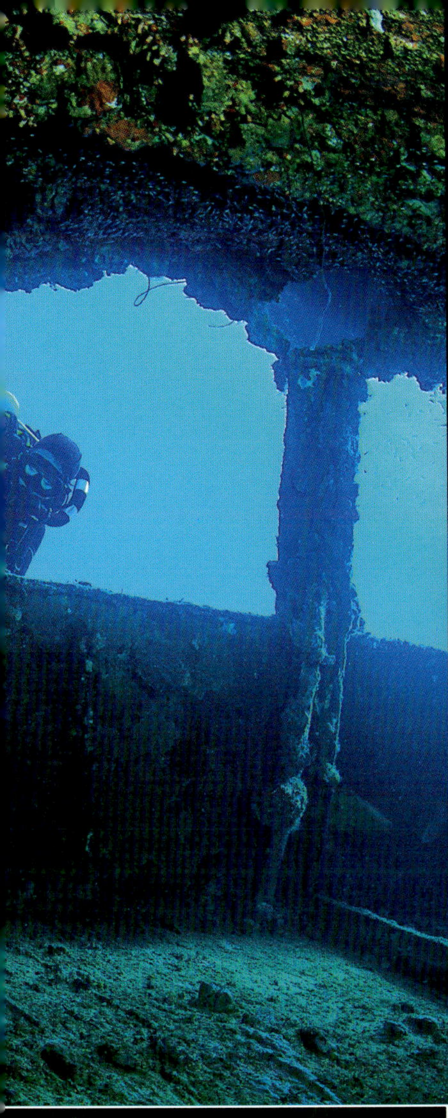

95 Truk Lagoon

Micronesia

The Pacific War raged here during much of World War II, with Japan initially dominant until the latter years when the tide turned in favour of the Americans.

Countless battles resulted in the destruction of numerous military vessels across Asia and Oceania. One of the most remarkable clashes took place on 17–18 February 1944, in the lagoon of the Truk Islands in Micronesia, home to the Japanese fleet's largest fortified base. In just two days, Operation Hailstone sank hundreds of warships, planes and other machinery, creating what became the world's largest underwater graveyard. Polluted by vast amounts of fuel spilled into its waters and abandoned for decades, Truk Lagoon was rediscovered by Commander Cousteau during an expedition in 1969.

Also known as Chuuk Lagoon, it now attracts wreck-diving enthusiasts from around the globe. Its underwater relics include ships, planes, tanks, artillery and artefacts from sailors' daily lives, preserved as a tribute to those who lost their lives there, and strict regulations prohibit any interference with or removal of objects. For divers fortunate enough to explore this underwater memorial, the experience is profoundly moving, offering a chance to connect with a pivotal piece of modern history.

Essential info

While Micronesia's reefs are stunning, most divers visiting Truk are wreck-enthusiasts and history buffs. At least 30 wrecks lie within easy reach at diveable depths.

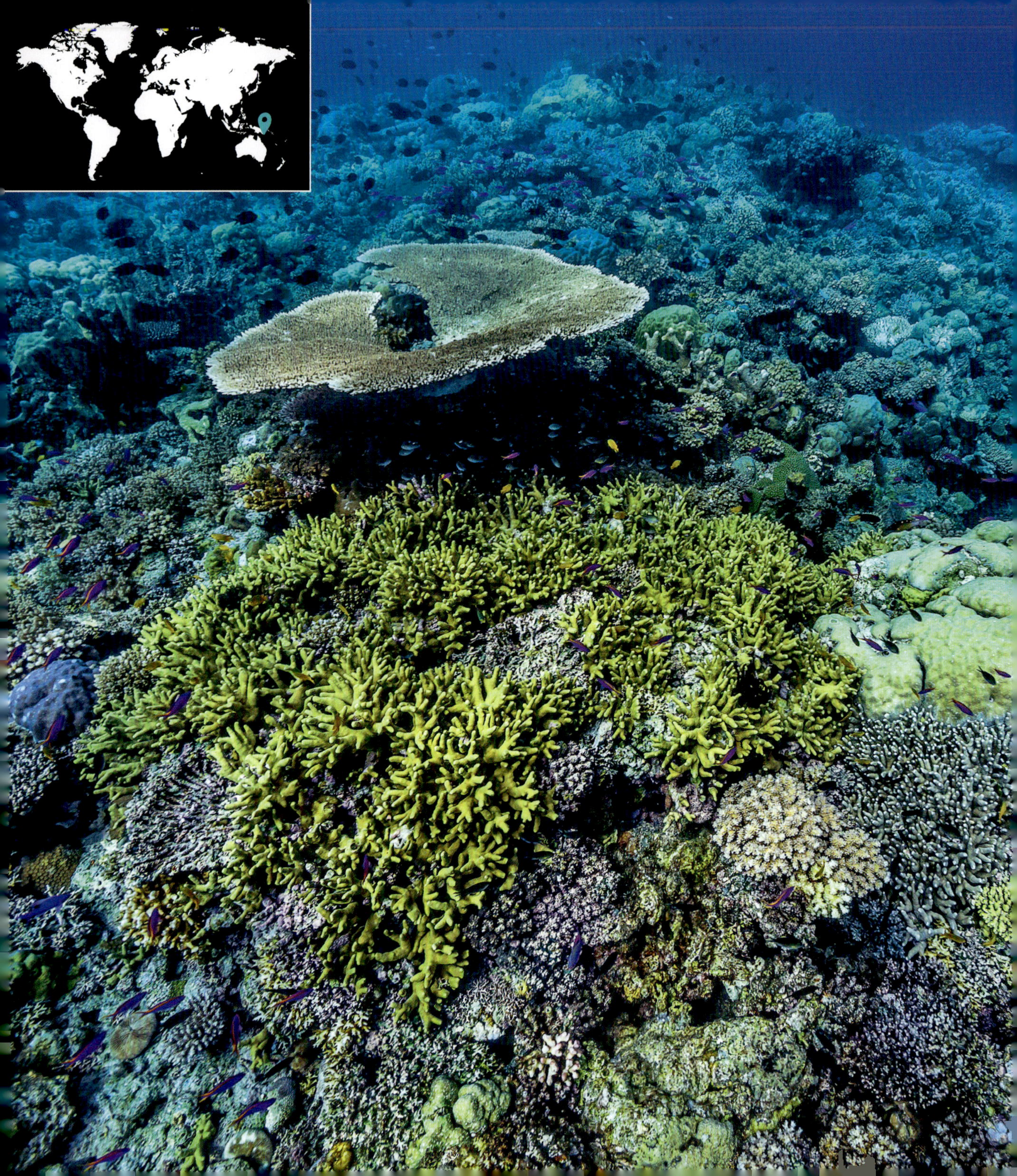

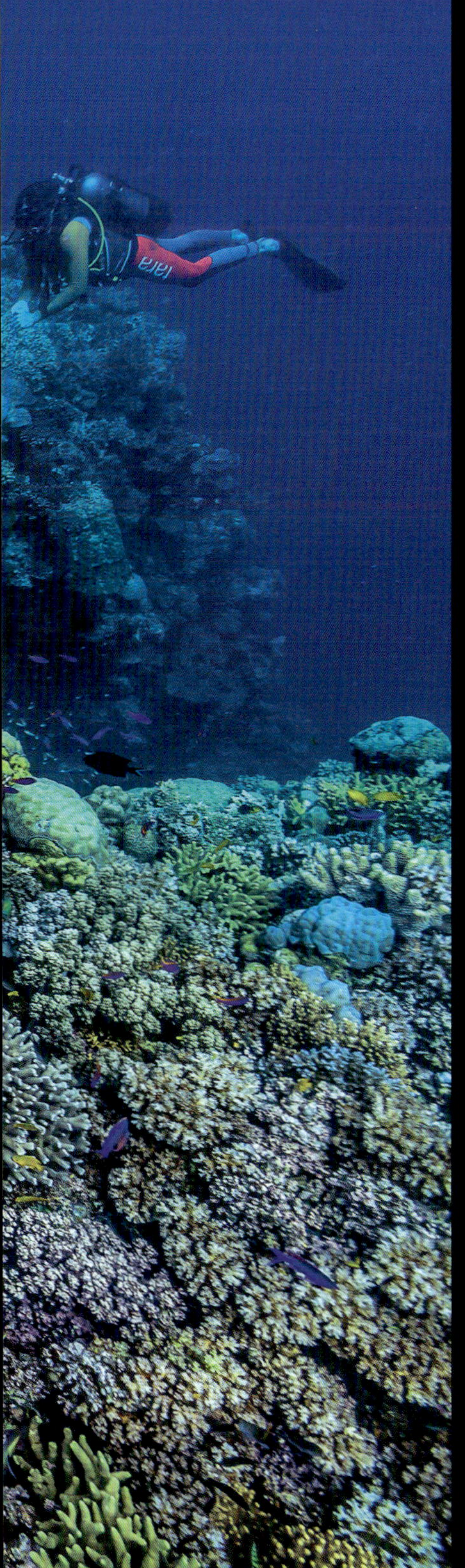

96 Milne Bay

Papua New Guinea

Positioned just north of Australia and extending towards Indonesia, Papua New Guinea lies in the southwestern Pacific Ocean, bordered by the Coral Sea to the south. In the country's eastern Milne Bay province, a strategic Australian defence base was established and became the site of the 1942 Battle of Milne Bay during the Pacific War. With its ideal geographic position, Milne Bay later transformed into one of the region's major scuba diving hubs.

Enriched by nutrient-laden feeder currents, its waters boast coral reefs with incredible biodiversity and abundant marine life. The diversity of dive sites here adds to its unique appeal and offers something for everyone – from beginners to advanced technical divers. The underwater scenes range from pelagic encounters with sharks and graceful manta rays to schools of fish, seahorses, nudibranchs and even historic wrecks, with some dive sites reaching depths close to 100 metres (328 feet).

Essential info

While most dives take place on sandy bottoms, numerous muck dives reveal an astonishing variety of creatures, including nudibranchs, shrimp, crabs and expertly camouflaged species, making this a paradise for underwater photographers.

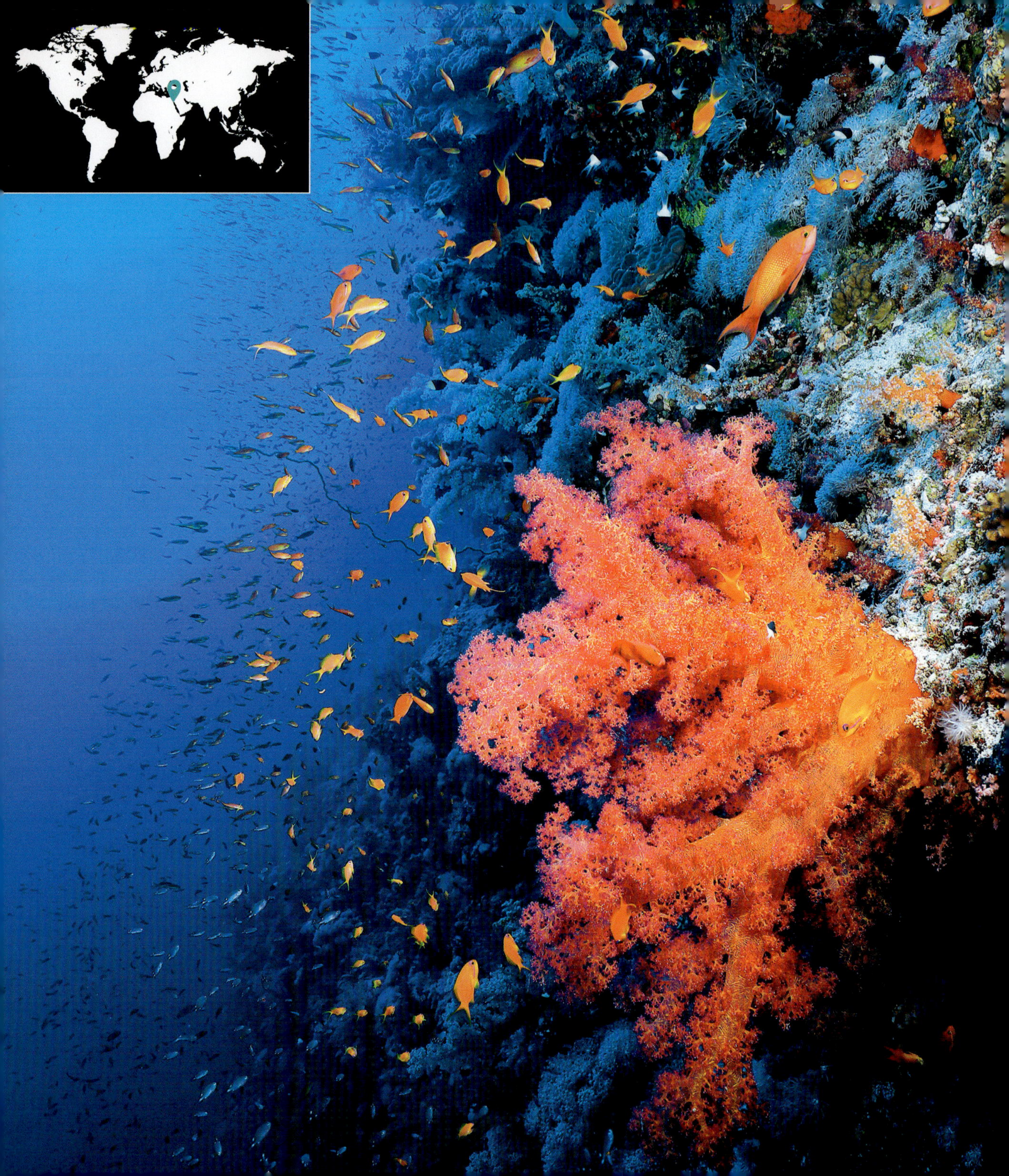

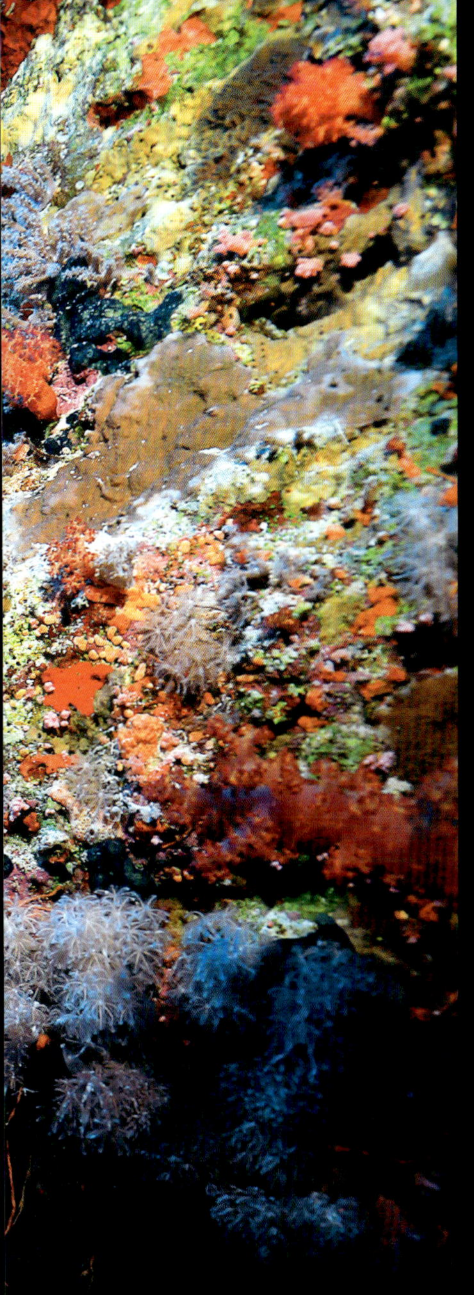

97 Daedalus Reef

Egypt

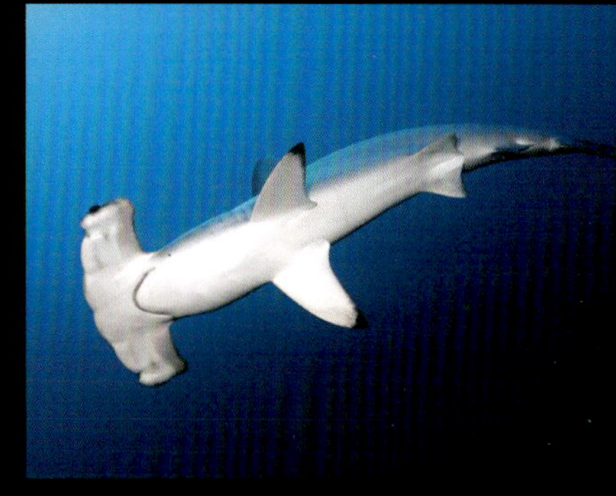

In the heart of the Red Sea, nestled between the Egyptian and Saudi coasts, rises the vast reef of Abu El Kizan, more commonly known as Daedalus. To the south of the reef, a magnificent lighthouse stands proudly at the end of the pontoon, which divers use to access this remarkable site. Views from the top of the lighthouse are breathtaking. However, the real spectacle lies beneath the surface. Down below, vibrant coral reefs burst with life, and the drop-offs, adorned with a dazzling array of colours, plunge steeply into the abyss.

Pelagic wildlife thrives in this environment, attracted to the currents that sweep through the dramatic drop-offs of Daedalus. Hammerhead sharks are frequent visitors to the area (see inset photo), while schools of jacks, tuna, manta rays, yellow butterflyfish, grey sharks, silky sharks and oceanic whitetip sharks can also be spotted. A day of diving in Daedalus guarantees incredible encounters with the wonders of the deep.

Essential info

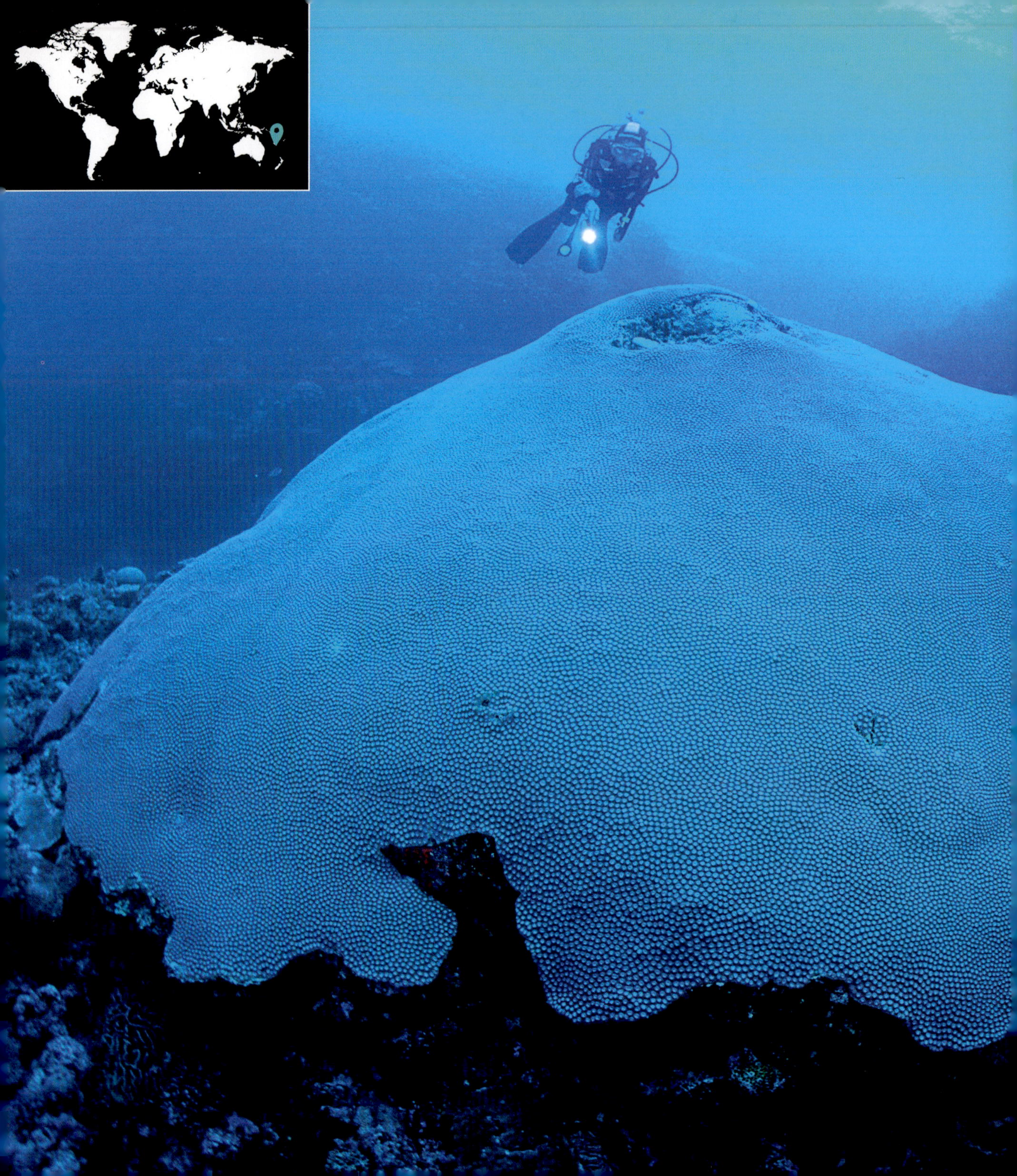

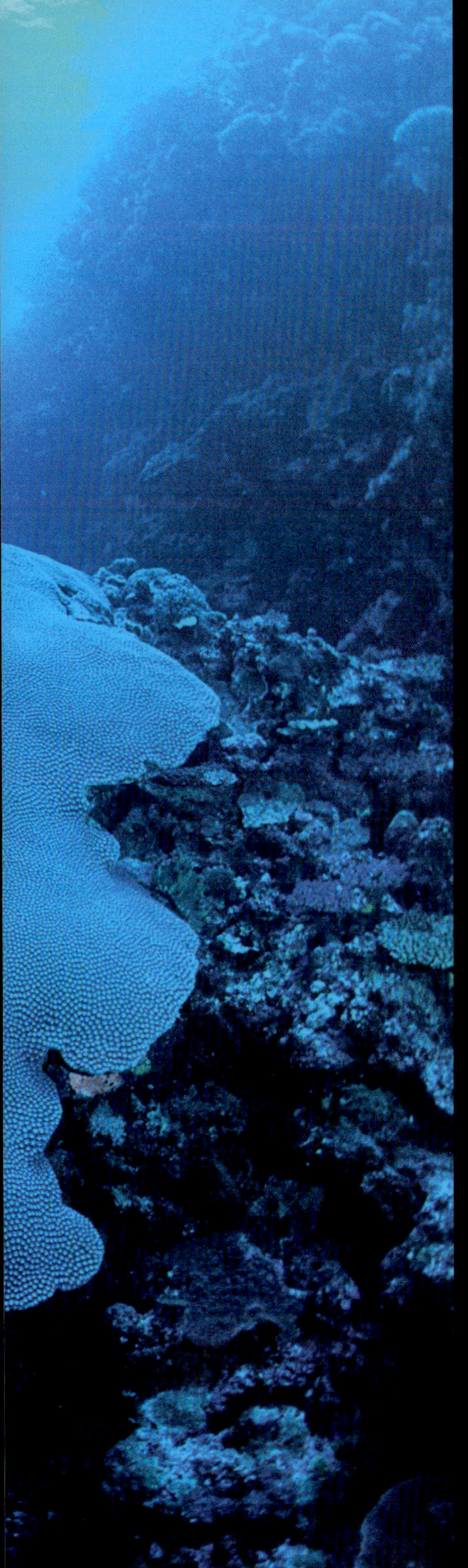

98 Isle of Pines

New Caledonia

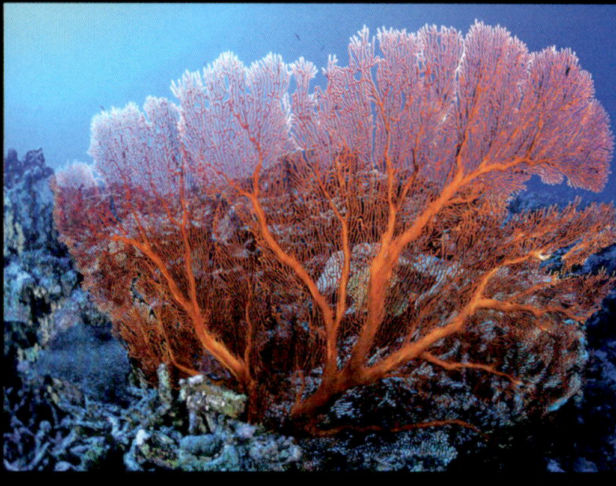

New Caledonia, this French territory overlooking the Coral Sea off Australia's east coast, is an archipelago made up of several dozen islands and islets. It offers pristine white sandy beaches, rows of coconut palms and the world's largest lagoon – spanning 24,000 square kilometres (14,900 square miles) and 1,600 kilometres (995 miles) of coral reefs dotted with passes.

Southeast of Nouméa, the Isle of Pines lives up to its name as it boasts vast pine forests. This Kanak land, home to 2,000 people, features vibrant marine life and rich seascapes. The rugged underwater terrain offers varied dive profiles, from steep drop-offs and coral gardens to numerous caves, perfect for caving enthusiasts. Local marine life abounds with grey and leopard sharks, schools of jacks and barracudas, loggerhead sea turtles and the highly venomous yet non-aggressive banded sea krait.

Essential info

Excellent snorkelling is possible here, especially in Kanumera Bay, in the island's southwest.

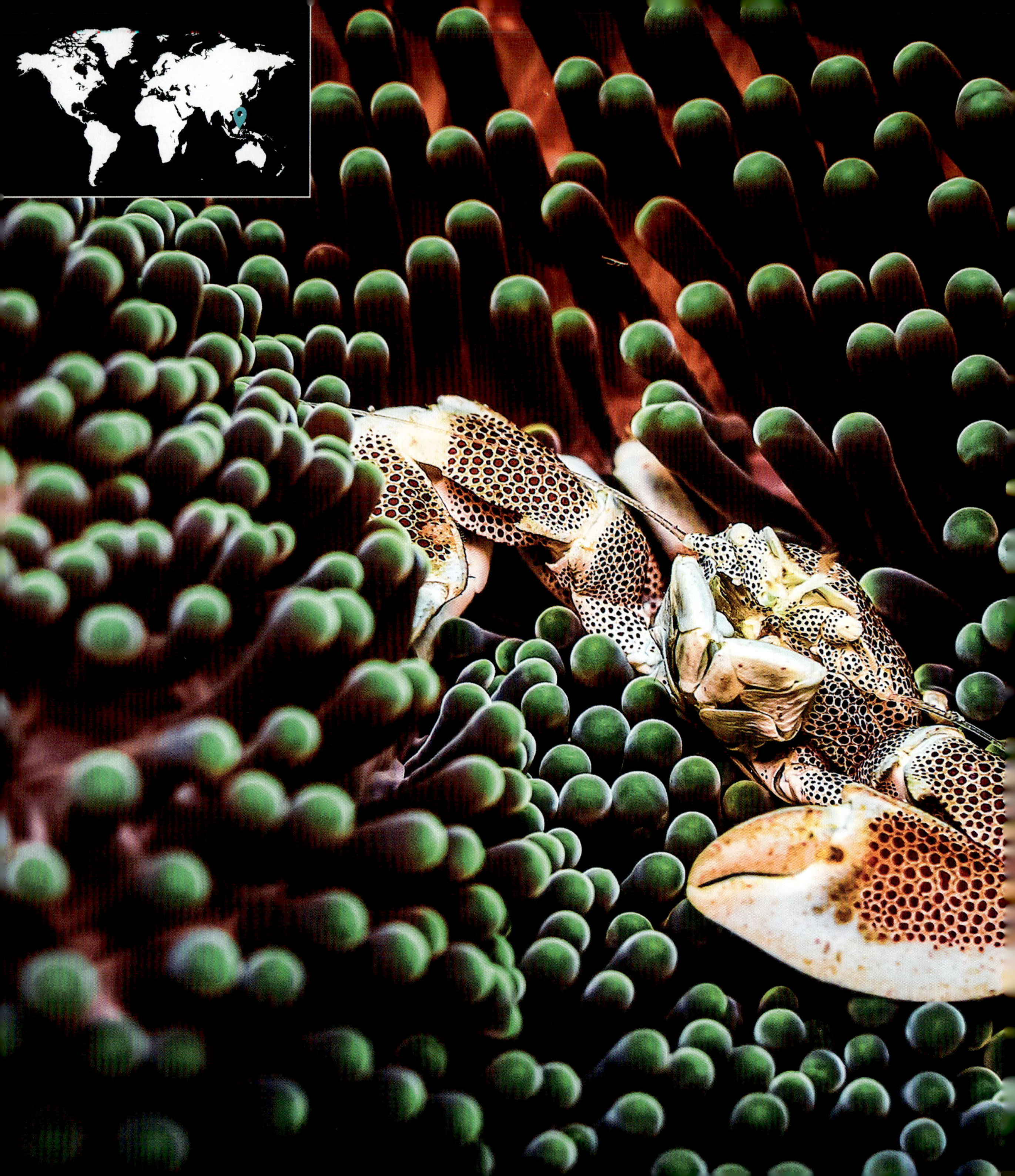

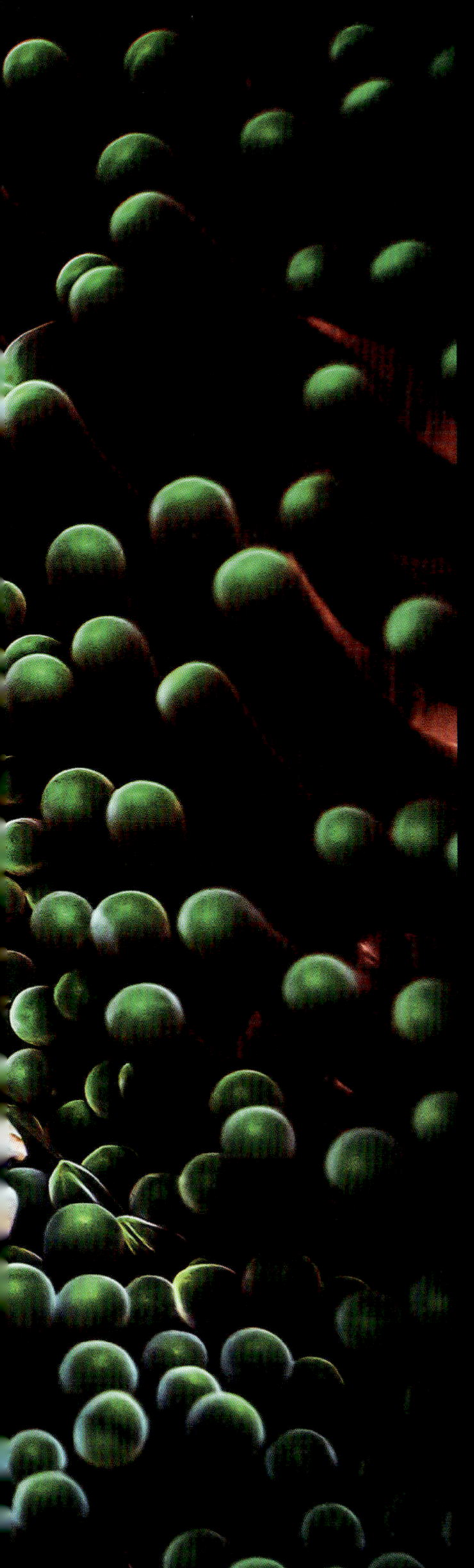

99 Lembeh Strait

Sulawesi, Indonesia

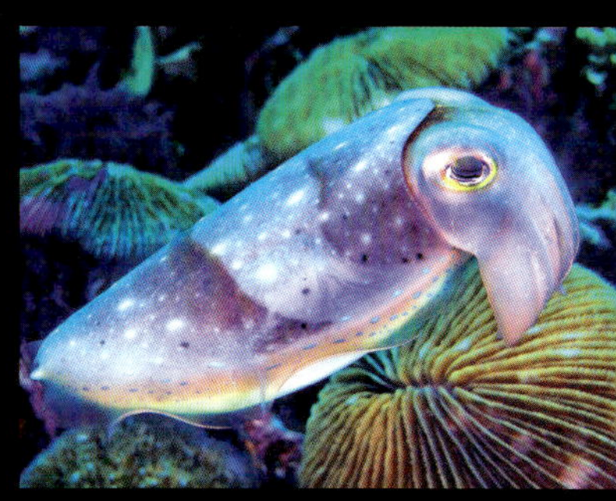

Indonesia is undoubtedly among the world's top scuba diving destinations, offering nearly everything a diver could wish for beneath the surface, from vibrant, healthy coral reefs teeming with life to unique dive spots.

One such location that attracts enthusiasts of smaller underwater creatures is the Lembeh Strait with its global reputation as a muck diving hotspot. At first glance, the seabed of Lembeh may appear unremarkable, with stretches of volcanic black sand, rocks, gravel and debris, yet these seemingly barren landscapes conceal an extraordinary array of life, rich in biodiversity, where countless species use camouflage to survive in this hostile environment.

It's a paradise for macro photographers, who come to capture incredible shots of nudibranchs, cuttlefish (see inset photo), octopuses, pygmy seahorses, shrimp and crabs (see photo), moray eels and a variety of strange fish. Here in Lembeh, divers need to keep both eyes peeled to truly appreciate its treasures.

Essential info

There are many small animals in Lembeh that are not always easy to see. A dive torch is essential to better see the vibrant colours, and prescription masks for those who need them are highly recommended.

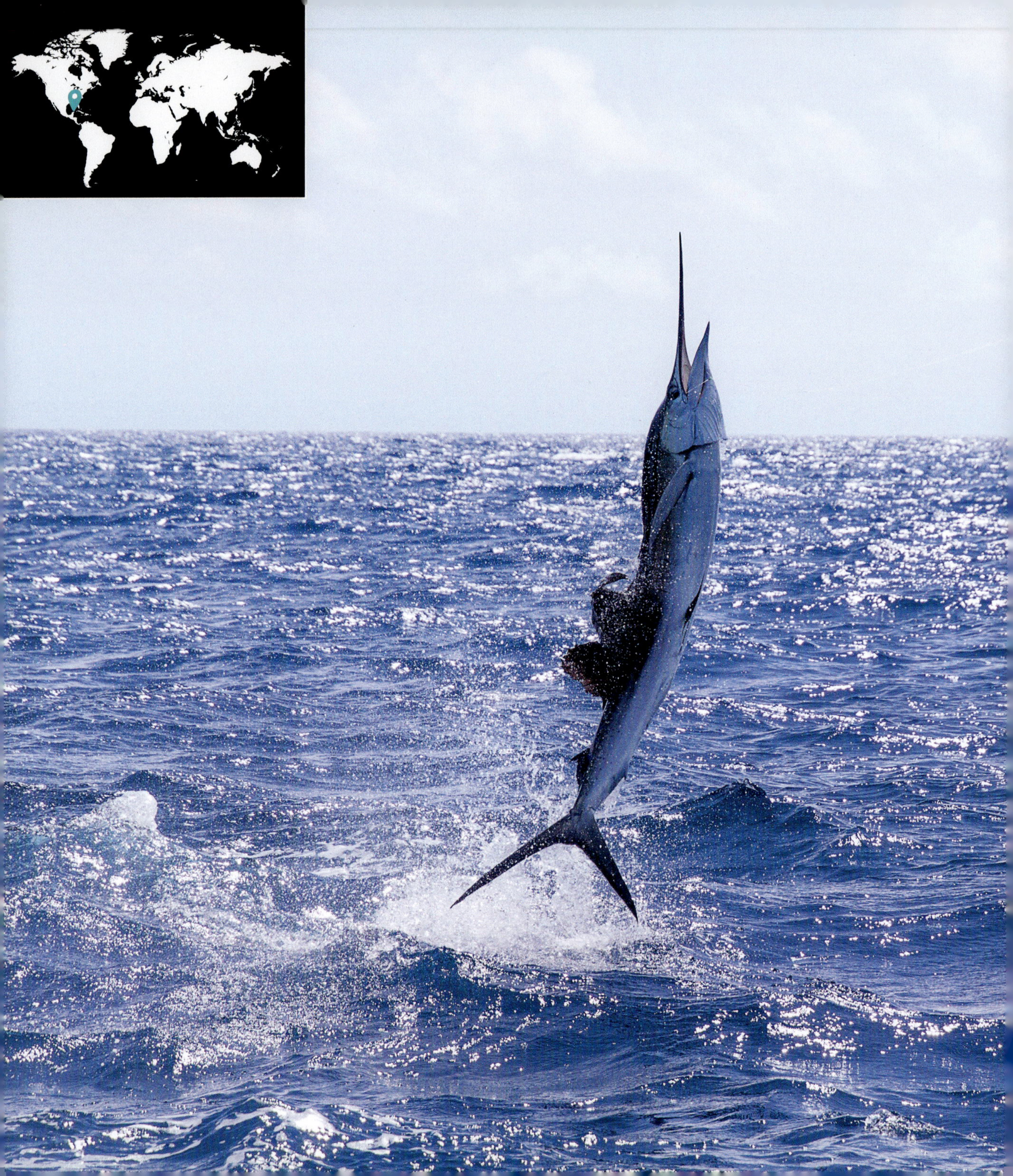

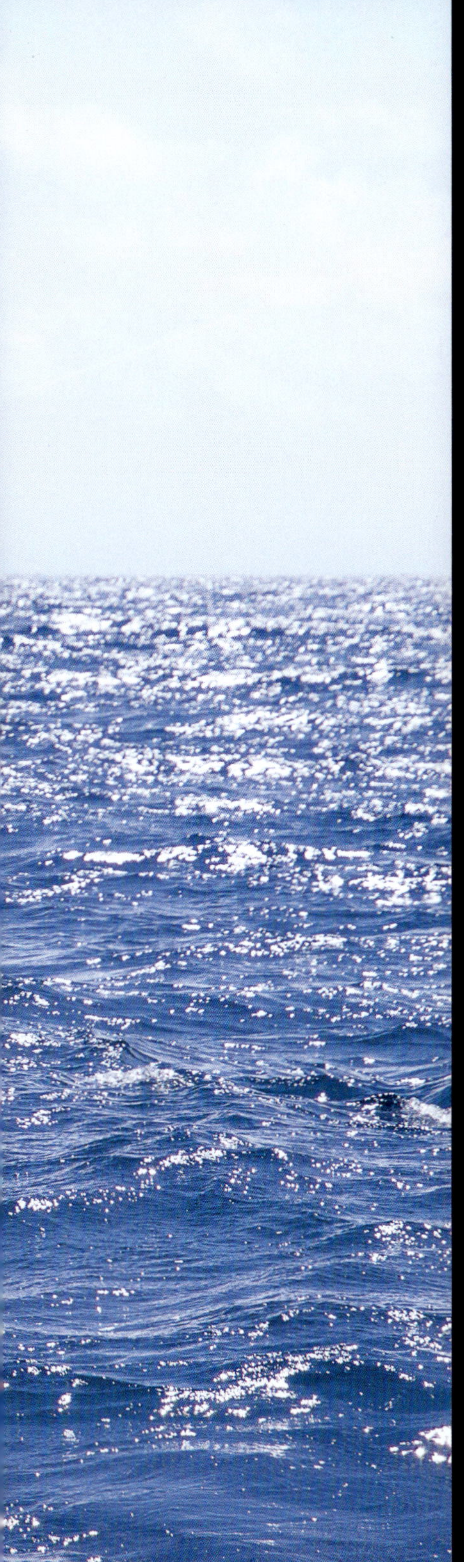

100 Yucatán sailfish

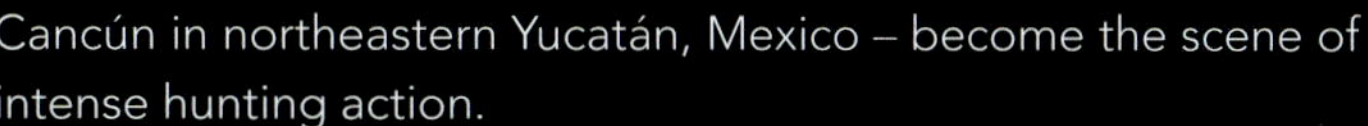

Mexico

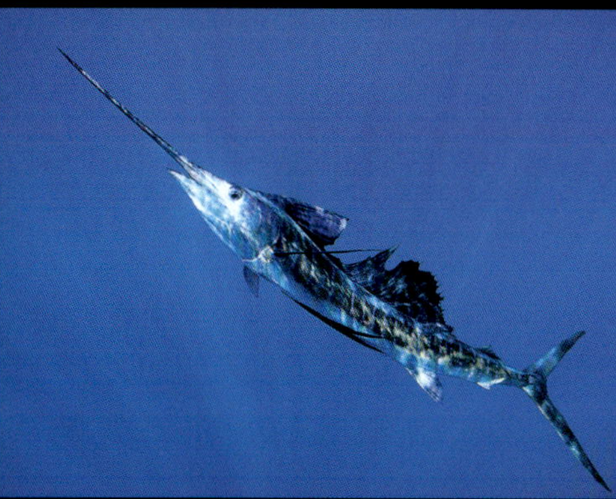

You don't always need heavy diving gear to witness incredible marine spectacles. Sometimes, just a mask, snorkel and fins are enough for a front-row view.

Every February, for only a few weeks, the waters off Isla Mujeres – a small island near Cancún in northeastern Yucatán, Mexico – become the scene of intense hunting action.

Following the schools of sardines that gather in this area, sailfish can sometimes be approached as they race for survival. With their streamlined bodies, sword-like bills and large dorsal fins resembling sails, these stunning fish are the fastest swimmers in the ocean, reaching speeds of up to 110 kilometres (68 miles) per hour. Watching them zip through the water like torpedoes, striking at the sardines that instinctively form swirling, defensive balls in an attempt to disrupt their predators, is a remarkable sight.

Essential info

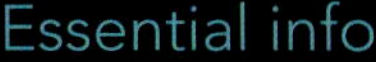

From June to September, these same waters host large gatherings of whale sharks, offering an equally exhilarating, but entirely different spectacle.

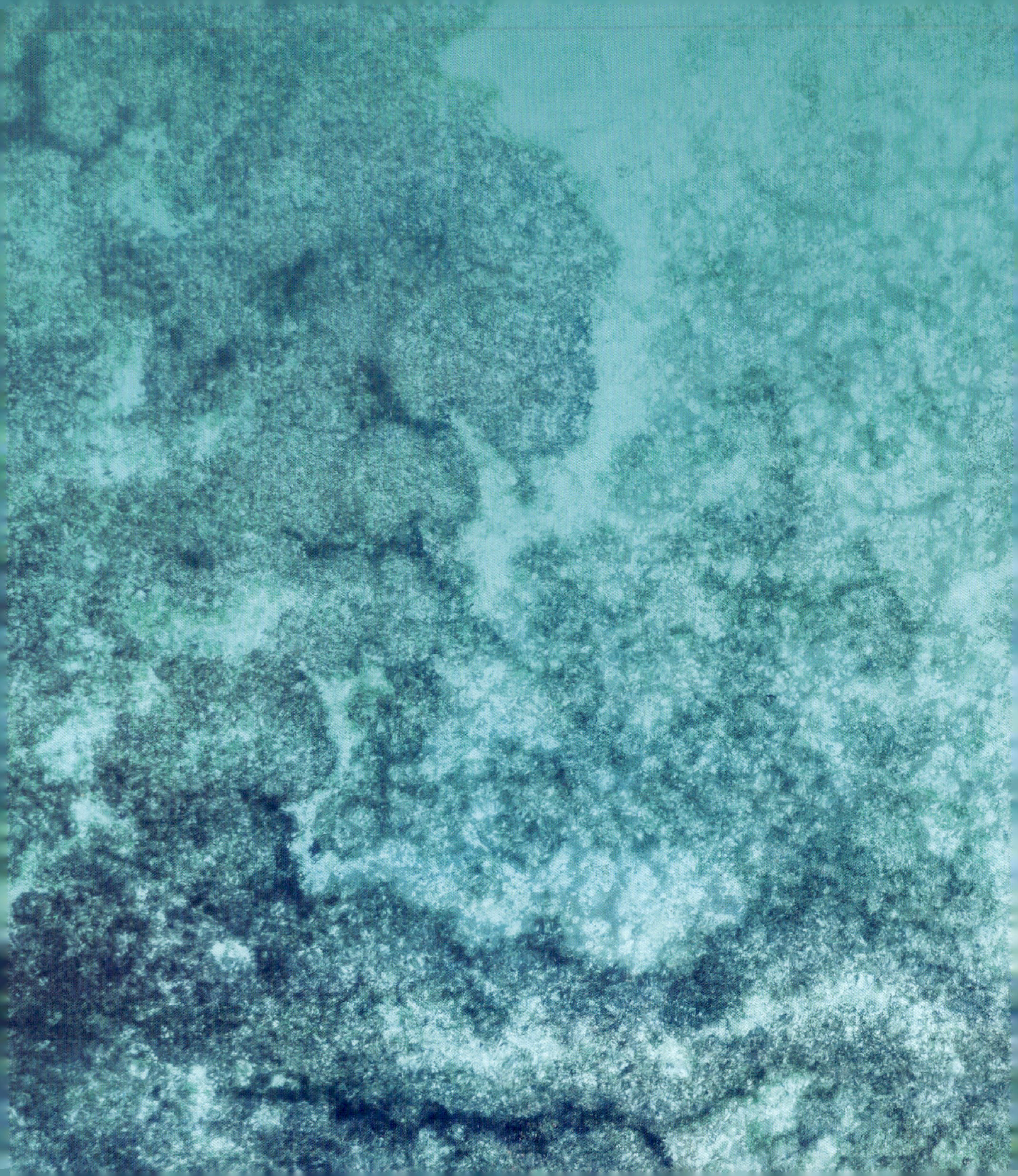

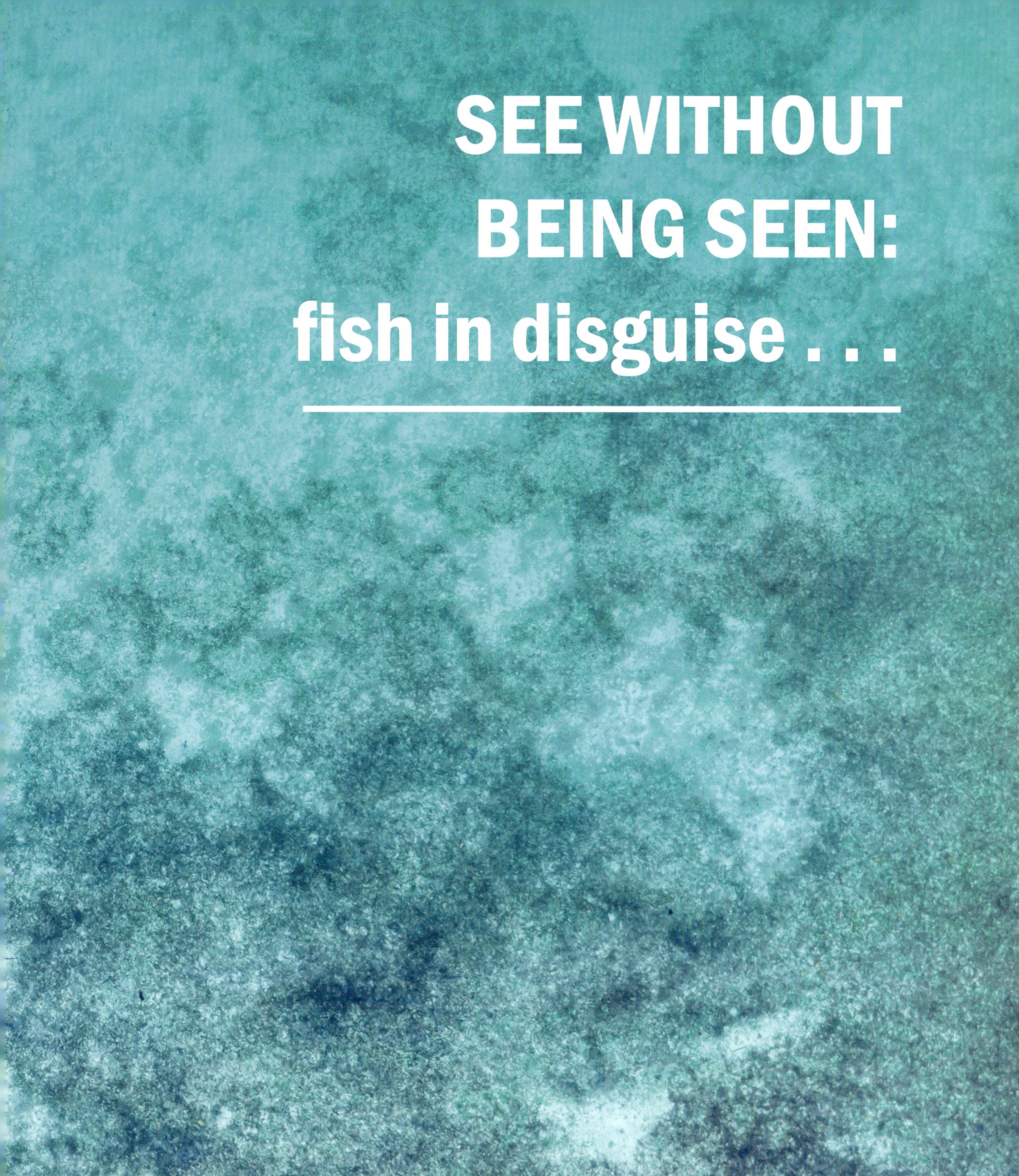
SEE WITHOUT
BEING SEEN:
fish in disguise . . .

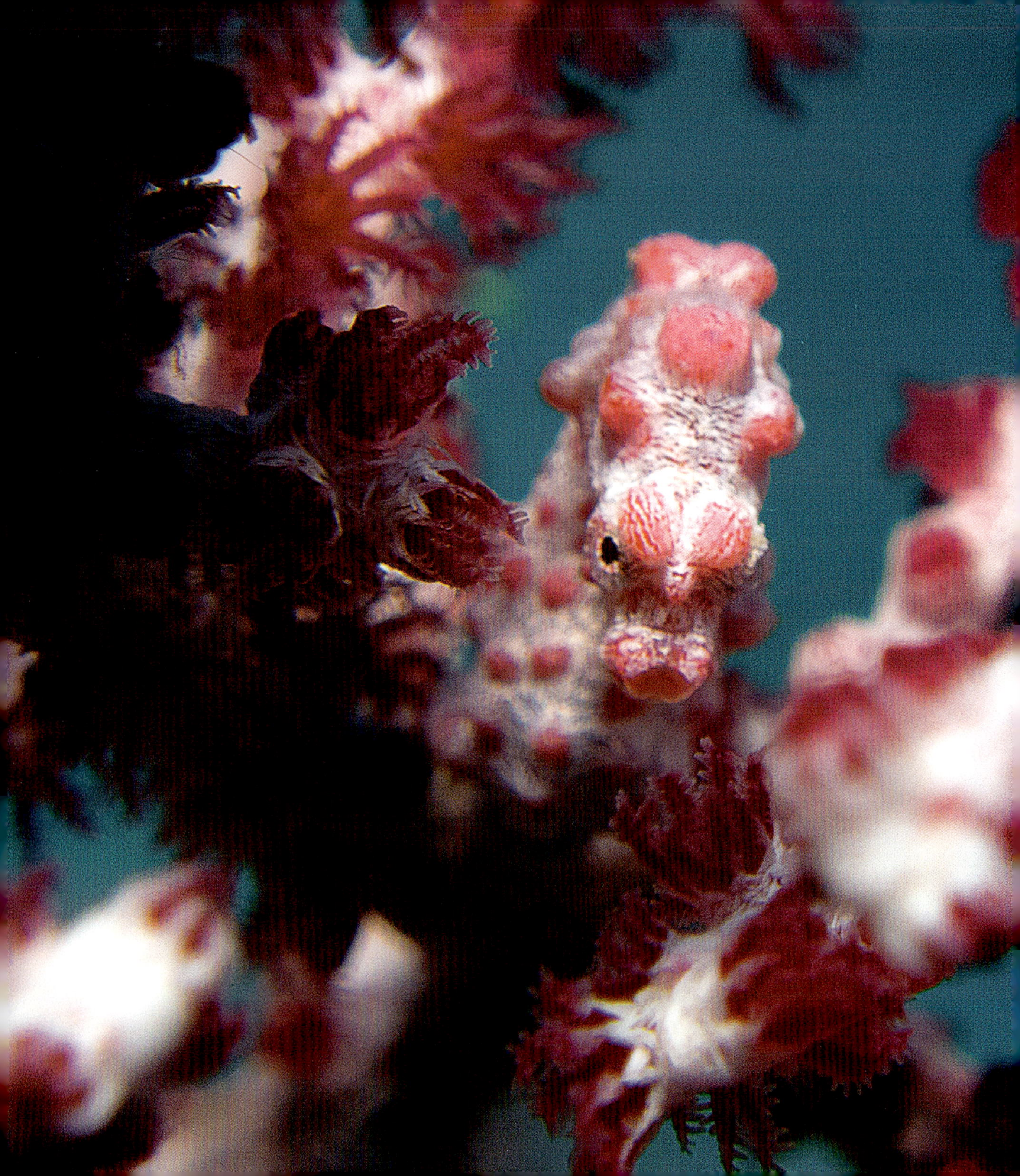

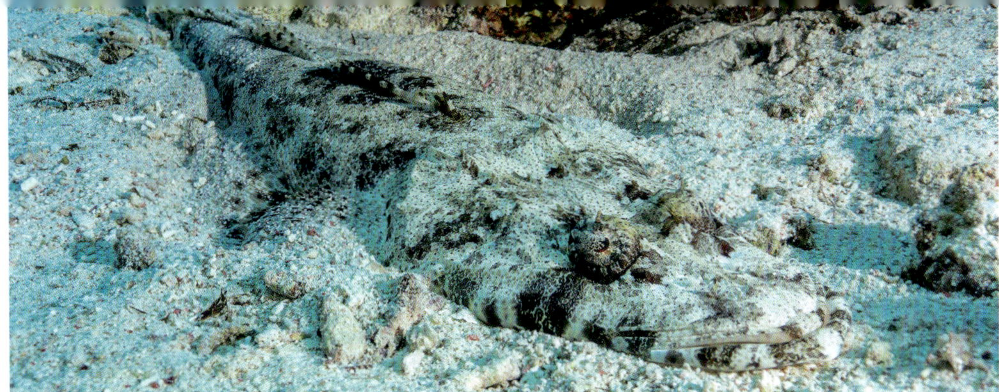

The underwater world, often hostile by nature, shapes the evolution of species in surprising ways. Surviving, feeding and reproducing while avoiding constant danger is no small task. Below is a list of some animals that have mastered the art of making themselves invisible.

• PYGMY SEAHORSE: Measuring no more than two centimetres (one inch) when its tail is uncurled, the pygmy seahorse camouflaged on a 1.5 metre (five foot) gorgonian can be nearly impossible to spot.

• CROCODILE FISH: This harmless fish, reaching up to one metre (three feet) in length, resembles a crocodile. It remains motionless on the sandy bottom, perfectly mimicking its surroundings, and is often found near wrecks.

• STONEFISH: With its rounded, pebble-like appearance, the stonefish blends seamlessly into its environment. It's one of the most venomous fish on the planet, with a sting that causes excruciating pain and muscle paralysis, potentially leading to death.

• TOADFISH: This fish moves by making small leaps and can walk using its pectoral fins. However, it prefers to remain motionless among sponges and colourful organisms, where it camouflages itself.

• PEGASUS FISH: Not resembling a typical fish, the Pegasus fish is a real oddity. Its body is covered with bony plates, featuring a flattened snout and pectoral fins that resemble wings, along with claw-like pelvic fins that help it 'walk' along the sandy bottom and camouflage itself.

• GHOST PIPEFISH: Related to seahorses, this green fish mimics the appearance of *Halimeda* algae, which it likes to inhabit. Its camouflage is enhanced by its tendency to remain motionless.

• LEAFY RHINOPIAS: This scorpionfish excels at camouflage, with numerous extensions and protuberances that make it difficult to detect, despite its ability to display various colours.

• ROMBOU (FLATFISH): This small flatfish possesses exceptional camouflage abilities, allowing it to blend in with sandy bottoms. It can adapt its colour to match its substrate or change according to its mood, using special pigment cells called chromatophores.

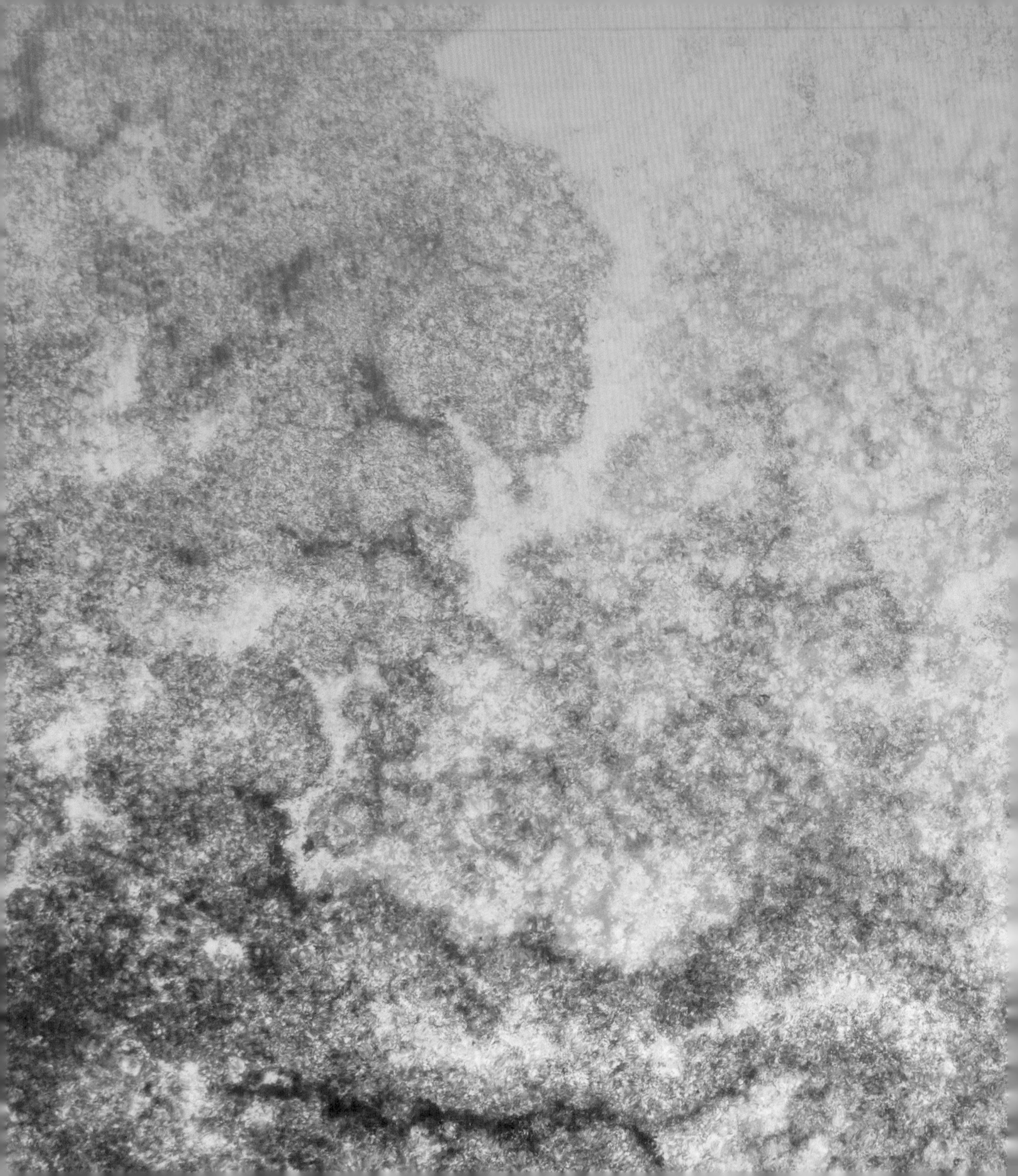

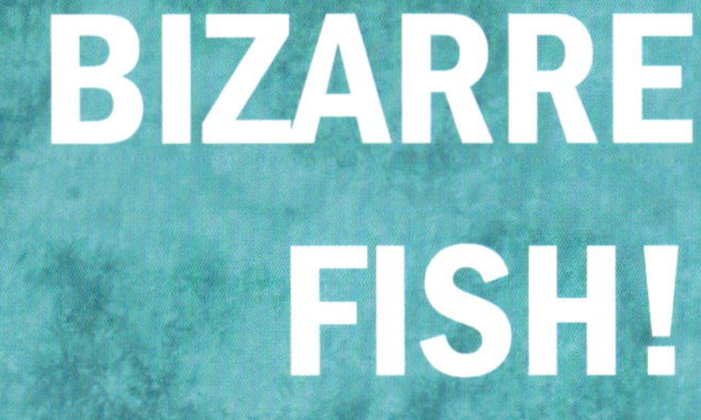
BIZARRE
FISH!

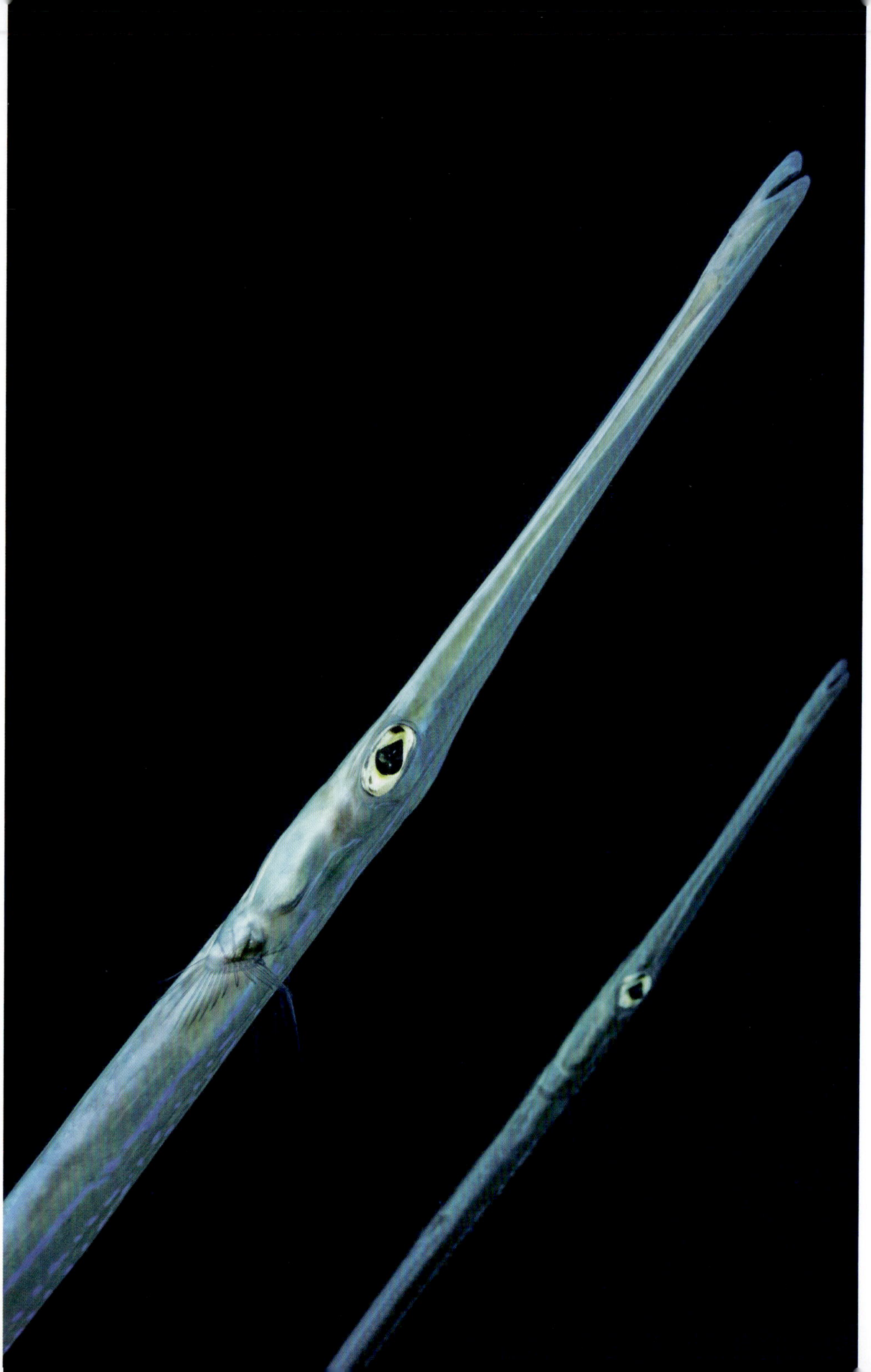

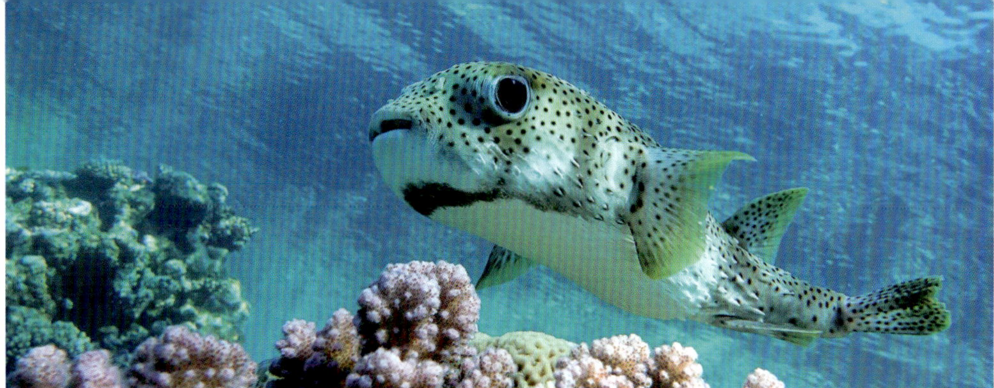

While children may think all fish share the same basic shape, this diverse family is, in fact, quite heterogeneous in morphology. Here are a few examples.

• **OCEAN SUNFISH (*MOLA MOLA*):** With its rounded mouth, large eyes and two fins, the ocean sunfish is one of the most intriguing and heaviest bony fish. A pelagic species, it is rarely encountered while diving. It continues to grow throughout its life, feeding primarily on jellyfish and salps, and reaching lengths of up to three metres (10 feet) and weighing nearly three tons. The more it eats, the bigger it gets.

• **FLUTE FISH:** Known for its thin, elongated body, the flute fish typically measures around one metre (three feet), with some individuals reaching up to 1.6 metres (five feet). Its head accounts for about a third of its body length and ends in a small, extendable mouth that it uses to catch fish, shrimp and squid. It is also one of the few predators of flying scorpion fish. This species, native to the Indo-Pacific, has also colonised the Mediterranean via the Suez Canal as a *Lessepsian* species.

• **TITAN TRIGGERFISH:** This impressive fish can exceed 80 centimetres (2.5 feet) in length and is known for its large head, which makes up half of its oval body. With powerful teeth, it grinds corals and shellfish for food. When nesting or protecting its young, it can be aggressive, often charging at nearby divers.

• **BOXFISH:** In contrast, boxfish glide through coral reefs with their box-shaped bodies, which are covered in bony plates. They can swim backward and turn quickly, with their shiny colours and small round mouths giving them a comical and endearing appearance.

• **GARDEN EEL:** Observing a sandy plain reveals small serpent-like creatures emerging from the substrate, which are in fact fish. Garden eels live in colonies and burrow into the sand, never leaving their homes. They can grow to about 50 centimetres (1.5 feet) in length and have a diameter of 1.5 centimetres (just over half an inch).

• **PORCUPINEFISH (*DIODON*):** This oval fish, resembling a rugby ball, features large round eyes and a beak-like mouth, along with a body covered in spines. Its scales have evolved into a defence mechanism, allowing it to inflate by swallowing water.

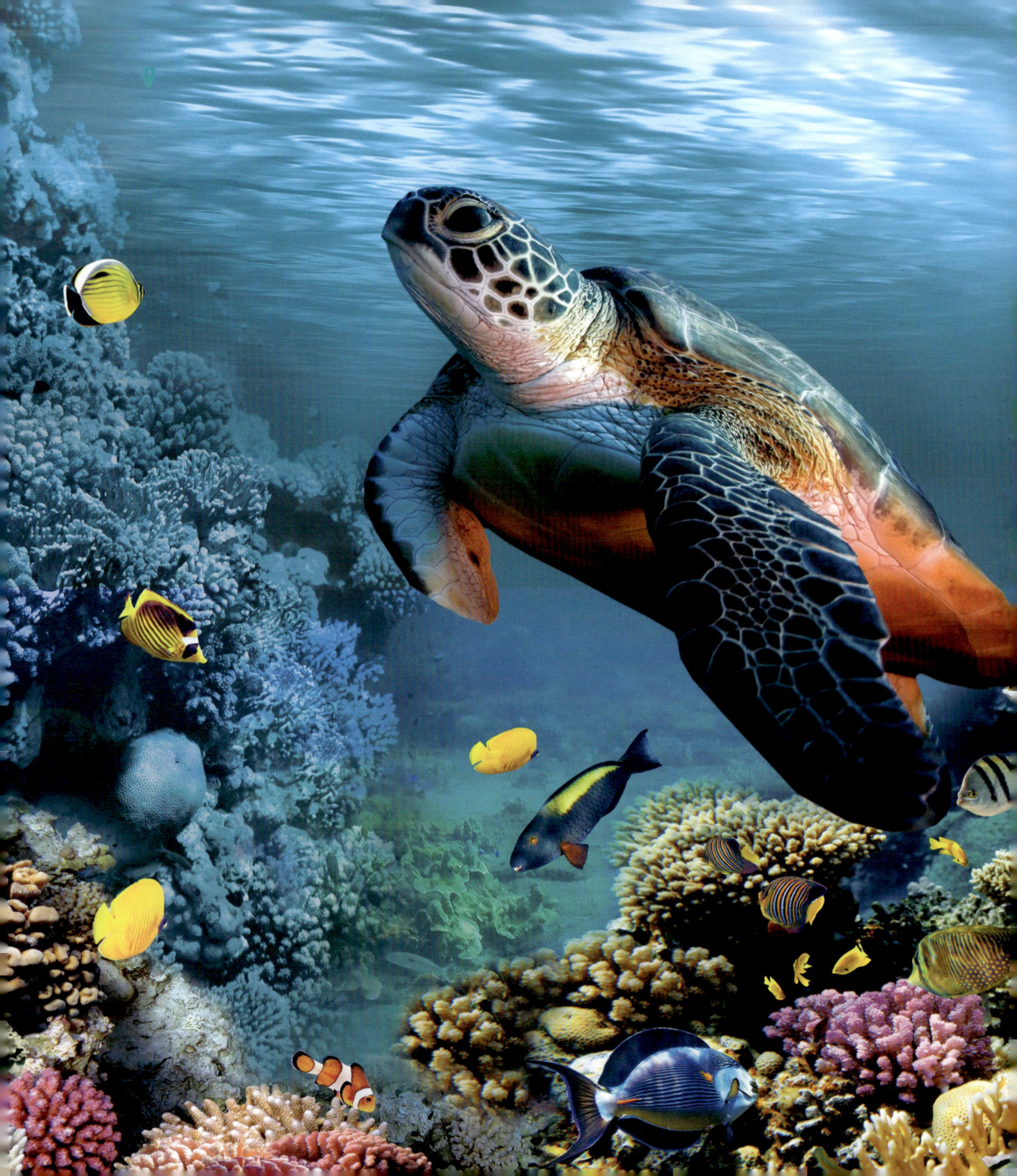

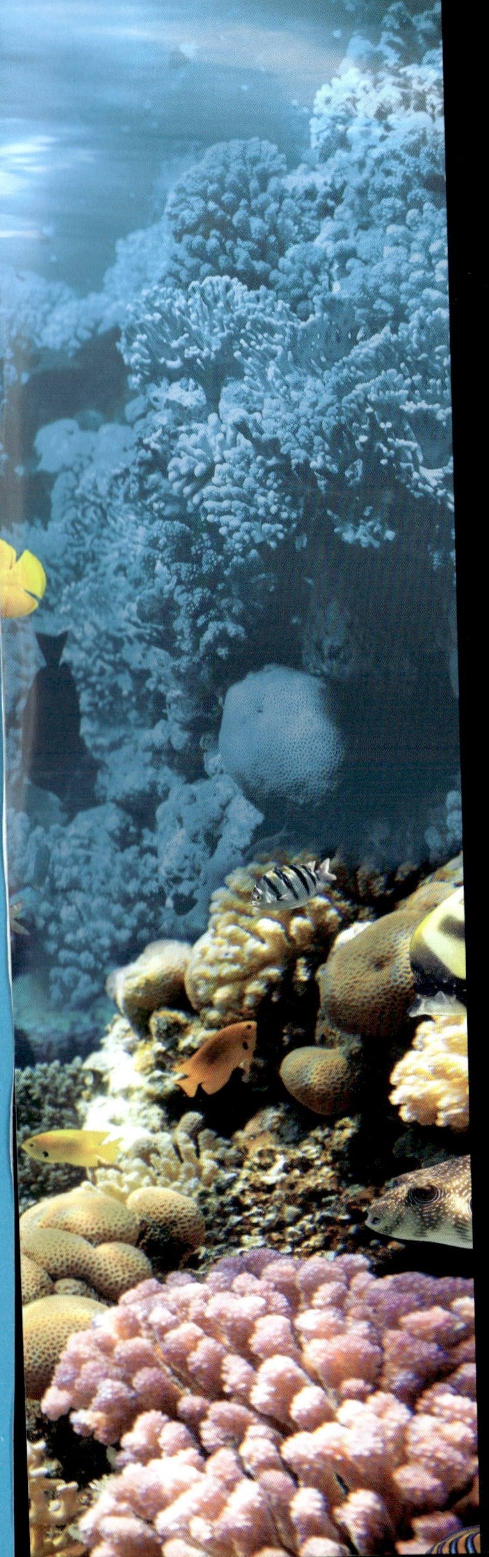

Acknowledgements

I would like to thank my family for their encouragement (my parents, my son and Kara, who was my first support in this incredible journey). Thanks also to everyone who has believed in me over the years, especially Hélène and Serge from Diving Attitude, Hubert Lacour, Elisa Isotta, Olivier clot-Faybesse and Francis Le Guen.

About the author

Anthony Leydet is a well-known French underwater photographer and author whose work has been published in magazines all over the world. Passionate about the diversity of marine ecosystems, Anthony explores the world's oceans to capture images of the most beautiful aquatic species.

anthonyleydet_uw_photography

Image credits

All images are from Shutterstock.com.
Special mentions:
Pages ii–iii, v, 6, 7, 222, 223, 226, 227 and eels, nudibranchs, parrotfish: © Anthony Leydet.
5, 8, 15, 18, 21, 25, 26, 30, 34, 36, 41 (small), 50, 58, 59, 63, 65, 68, 69, 80, 89, 90, 94, 97: © Anthony Leydet.
1. © Reinhard Dirscherl / Biosphoto.
2. © Masa Ushioda / WaterFrame - Agency / Biosphoto.
7. © Brandon Cole / Biosphoto.
20. © Norbert Probst / imageBROKER / Biosphoto.
27. © Reinhard Dirscherl / Biosphoto.
29. © Minden / hemis.fr.
38. © Louis-Marie Preau / hemis.fr
39. © Yves Lefèvre / Biosphoto.
40. © Andre Seale / Robert Harding Picture Library / Biosphoto.
41. © Mathieu Foulquié / Biosphoto.
42. © Mauritius / hemis.fr.
47. © Franco Banfi / Biosphoto.
49. © Reinhard Dirscherl / Biosphoto.
52. © Sergio Hanquet / Biosphoto.
56. © Mathieu Foulquié / Biosphoto.
57. © Photoshot / Biosphoto.
58. © HAUSER Patrice / hemis.fr.
66. © Gabriel Barathieu / Biosphoto.
74. © Alamy / hemis.fr.
82. © Christoph Gerigk / Biosphoto.
85. © Franco Banfi / Biosphoto.
86. Westend 61 / hemis.fr.
92. © Mathieu Meur / Stocktrek images / Biosphoto.
96. © Christoph Gerigk / Biosphoto.
98. © Jean Cassou / Biosphoto.
100. © Brandon Cole / Biosphoto.